Medieval Irish Buildings, 1100–1600

Maynooth Research Guides for Irish Local History

GENERAL EDITOR Mary Ann Lyons

This book is one of the Maynooth Research Guides for Irish Local History series. Written by specialists in the relevant fields, these volumes are designed to provide historians, and especially those interested in local history, with practical advice regarding the consultation of specific collections of historical materials, thereby enabling them to conduct independent research in a competent and thorough manner. Possible avenues for research are suggested and relevant secondary works are also recommended.

IN THIS SERIES

Maynooth Research Guides for Irish Local History: Number 18

Medieval Irish Buildings, 1100–1600

Tadhg O'Keeffe

FOUR COURTS PRESS

Set in 10.5pt on 12.5pt Bembo by
Carrigboy Typesetting Services for
FOUR COURTS PRESS LTD
7 Malpas Street, Dublin 8, Ireland
www.fourcourtspress.ie
and in North America by
FOUR COURTS PRESS
c/o ISBS, 920 N.E. 58th Avenue, Suite 300, Portland, OR 97213

A catalogue record for this title
is available from the British Library.

ISBN 978–1–84682–248–3

Printed in Spain
by Castuera, Pamplona

For Evan

Contents

Illustrations

Abbreviations

AC	*Annála Connacht: the Annals of Connacht, AD1224–1544*, ed. A.M. Freeman (Dublin, 1944)
AFM	*Annals of the Kingdom of Ireland by the Four Masters*, ed. and trans. J. O'Donovan (7 vols, Dublin, 1851)
AH	*Archivium Hibernicum*
AI	*Archaeology Ireland*
AIn.	*The Annals of Inisfallen*, ed. and trans. S. Mac Airt (Dublin, 1951)
AJ	*The Archaeological Journal*
ALC	*The Annals of Lough Cé*, ed. W.M. Hennessy (2 vols, London, 1871)
ASI	Archaeological Survey of Ireland
AT	'The Annals of Tigernach', ed. and trans. W. Stokes, *Revue Celtique*, 16 (1895), 374–419
AU	*Annála Uladh, Annals of Ulster*, ed. W.M. Hennessy and B. MacCarthy (4 vols, Dublin, 1887–1901)
BAACT	*British Archaeological Association Conference Transactions*
CAAR	*Calendar of Archbishop Alen's register, c.1172–1534*, ed. C. McNeill (Dublin, 1950)
Caithr. Thoirdh.	*Caithréim Thoirdhealbhaigh*, ed. S.H. O'Grady (2 vols, London, 1929)
CCM	*Calendar of the Carew manuscripts*, ed. J.S. Brewer and W. Bullen (6 vols, London, 1867–73)
CDI	*Calendar of documents relating to Ireland*, ed. H.S. Sweetman (5 vols, London, 1875–86)
CFR	*Calendar of the fine rolls preserved in the Public Record Office* (22 vols, London, 1911–62)
CG	*Château Gaillard: études de castellologie médiévale* (1962–)
CGR	*Calendar of the Gormanston register*, ed. J. Mills and M.J. McEnery (Dublin, 1916)
Chron. Scot.	*Chronicon Scotorum*, ed. W.M. Hennessy (London, 1866)
CIPM	*Calendar of inquisitions post mortem* (16 vols, London, 1904–74)
Civil Survey	*The Civil Survey, AD1654–56*, ed. R.C. Simington (10 vols, Dublin, 1931–61)
CJRI	*Calendar of the justiciary rolls … of Ireland*, ed. J. Mills (1295–1303; 1305–7), ed. H. Wood and A. Langman (1308–14) (3 vols, Dublin, 1905–56)
CLAHJ	*County Louth Archaeological and Historical Journal*
CNM	*Cathair na Mart*
COD	*Calendar of Ormond deeds*, ed. E. Curtis (6 vols, Dublin, 1932–43)
CPL	*Calendar of entries in the papal registers relating to Great Britain and Ireland: papal letters* (London and Dublin, 1893–)
CPR	*Calendar of the patent rolls* (London, 1906–)
CR, Hen. III	*Close rolls of the reign of Henry III* (London, 1902–38)
CSGJ	*The Castle Studies Group Journal*

CSMD	*Chartularies of St Mary's Abbey, Dublin … and Annals of Ireland, 1162–1370*, ed. J.T. Gilbert (2 vols, Dublin, 1884–6)
CSPI	*Calendar of the state papers relating to Ireland* (24 vols, London, 1869–1911)
DHR	*Dublin Historical Record*
EHR	*English Historical Review*
HMSO	His/Her Majesty's Stationery Office
IG	*Irish Geography*
IHS	*Irish Historical Studies*
Inchiquin MSS	*The Inchiquin manuscripts*, ed. J. Ainsworth (Dublin, 1961)
IPR, 1211–12	'The Irish pipe roll of 14 John, 1211–12', ed. O. Davies and D.B. Quinn, *UJA*, 3rd ser., 4 (supplement, 1941)
JBAA	*Journal of the British Archaeological Association*
JCHAS	*Journal of the Cork Historical and Archaeological Society*
JEH	*Journal of Ecclesiastical History*
JGAHS	*Journal of the Galway Archaeological and Historical Society*
JIA	*Journal of Irish Archaeology*
JKAS	*Journal of the County Kildare Archaeological Society*
JRSAI	*Journal of the Royal Society of Antiquaries of Ireland*
JSAH	*Journal of the Society of Architectural Historians*
JWHS	*Journal of the Wexford Historical Society*
MA	*Medieval Archaeology*
MD	*Medieval Dublin: proceedings of the Friends of Medieval Dublin symposium*
MIA	*Miscellaneous Irish annals, AD1114–1437*, ed. S. Ó hInnse (Dublin, 1947)
NMAJ	*North Munster Antiquarian Journal*
OED	Oxford English dictionary
PRIA	*Proceedings of the Royal Irish Academy*
RA	*Regestum monasterii fratrum praedictorum de Athenry*, ed. A. Coleman, *AH*, 1 (1912), 201–21
RAST	*Register of the abbey of St Thomas, Dublin*, ed. J.T. Gilbert (London, 1889)
RBO	*The red book of Ormond*, ed. N.B. White (Dublin, 1932)
RDKPRI	*Report of the deputy keeper of the Public Records in Ireland* (Dublin, 1869–)
RHASJ	*County Roscommon Historical and Archaeological Society Journal*
RPH	*Rotulorum patentium et clausorum cancellariae Hiberniae calendarium, Henry II–Henry VII*, ed. E. Tresham (London, 1828)
SP, Hen. VIII	*State papers, Henry VIII* (11 vols, London, 1830–52)
SRPI, Ed. IV	*Statute rolls of the parliament of Ireland, 1st to 12th years of the reign of King Edward IV*, ed. H.F. Berry (Dublin, 1914); – *12th & 13th to the 21st & 22nd years of the reign of King Edward IV*, ed. J.F. Morrissey (Dublin, 1939)
SRPI, Hen. VI	*Statute rolls of the parliament of Ireland, reign of King Henry VI*, ed. H.F. Berry (Dublin, 1910)
SRPI, John– Hen. V	*Statutes and ordinances, and acts of the parliament of Ireland, King John– Henry V*, ed. H.F. Berry (Dublin, 1907)
THJ	*Tipperary Historical Journal*
UJA	*Ulster Journal of Archaeology*

Preface and acknowledgments

This book is an attempt to share my knowledge of medieval Irish buildings with those for whom history is a passion, even a profession, but for whom historic buildings remain difficult-to-read testimonies of the medieval past, and with those who are studying medieval archaeology or medieval architectural history at university.

Its first aim is simply to enhance for its readers the experience of visiting medieval buildings, both long-forgotten ruins and manicured National Monuments. What were the functions of the different rooms in a medieval abbey? How were stone vaults constructed? Why do some churches have more than one altar? What is a cusped-ogee window? Where in their castles did medieval lords and ladies eat?

Its second aim is to provide the basic tools needed to identify medieval buildings in the first place, and to assign approximate dates. I must stress, however, that it is not a manual. I subscribe to the simple principle that the more medieval architecture one sees the more one knows about medieval architecture. This book is intended to help the reader 'see', and in so doing provide a foundation for the deep knowledge that a manual cannot give. The non-specialist could be forgiven for thinking that providing tools for identification and dating is superfluous, that every medieval building has already been studied and dated, and that there is little left to say and nothing left to discover. The reality is very different on two counts. First, across Ireland are hundreds of rarely visited medieval buildings, including some very important ones, about which hardly anything has been written. The modern visitor is thus forced to interpret on-site. This need not be a problem; on the contrary, the most enjoyable buildings to visit are often the ones that have generally escaped wider attention. Second, major buildings for which there is a volume of scholarly literature are often insulated against fresh analysis by the perception that they have been 'done', but there is always potential for new interpretations.

The book's third aim is to provide explanations of how medieval buildings 'worked', or, to be a little more precise, how medieval society 'worked' with its buildings. Is this necessary in a book in this series? I think it is. Buildings are sources. Like all sources, they require contextual understanding. There has long been a need for an up-to-date, authoritative and properly referenced account of the cultures of medieval architectural endeavour in Ireland, for the sort of book that might have its time divided between a place on the book-shelf and a place in the glove-compartment. This book is my effort to meet that need. I have been researching and writing about all aspects of medieval architecture in Ireland for thirty years, but the opportunity to write this book was also an opportunity to think afresh about what is known and how it is known, so, while this work offers a comprehensively footnoted synthesis, it is also laced with original content. So much has already been published on ecclesiastical architecture that it has been possible to balance, in the space of a long chapter, summaries of current thinking with some fresh observations and reflections. In the case of castles, one could be forgiven for thinking that the number of new publications over the past twenty years would negate the need for a long discussion here, but I think there is a need for new perspectives on some individual buildings and on most castle types, and especially on castle terminology both medieval and modern, so two chapters carry that burden here.

No agency or institution has done more for medieval studies in Ireland in recent years than Four Courts Press, so I felt very honoured indeed when Martin Fanning invited me to write a book on medieval architecture with this series in mind. I hope that I have repaid his trust. Dr Michael Potterton and Prof. Mary Ann Lyons were very supportive of the project, tolerated the book's length (not to mention its deviation from the series norm) when it eventually reached them, and then eased its passage into print. My thanks to both of them. Michael's editorial skills deserve special acknowledgment. Many of the buildings mentioned here are on private property but landowners normally allow access if asked, and I would like to thank those whom I have had the pleasure of meeting over many years of looking for and at buildings. I long ago stopped counting the number of talks I was giving to local historical societies and heritage groups, but the enjoyment has never abated, and I am grateful to all of those audiences for the warmth of their receptions. Indeed, as I was writing this book, especially Chapter 3, I kept in mind the sorts of questions that such audiences ask. I am similarly grateful to the many students whom I have enjoyed teaching in UCD since 1996, and particularly those whose doctoral research in the field of medieval and early modern architectural history I was privileged to supervise: Hanneke Ronnes, Andrew Tierney, Diarmuid Ó Riain, Sinéad Quirke, Anne-Julie Lafaye and Karen Dempsey. Thanks are due also to Dr David Whelan, one of my non-medievalist PhD graduates, who has sometimes risked life and limb helping me measure medieval buildings. My colleagues in UCD School of Archaeology deserve thanks for providing friendship and support, as well as the intellectual stimulation that one expects in a world-class research environment. I am grateful to Conor McDermott for resolving at the last minute technical issues with some of my drawings. There are colleagues working in the fields of medieval archaeology and architectural history outside Ireland, especially Britain, to whom I owe personal debts, and I am sure they will forgive me if I confine my name-checking here to the late Prof. Mick Aston (of the University of Bristol and *Time Team*), a very dear family friend from the Black Country who died suddenly in 2013.

Closer to home, my debt to Margaret, my wife, is incalculable. It goes way beyond this book of course, and not least to a period when ill health made medieval architecture, and my book about it, seem rather unimportant. My thanks – our thanks – to Anne-Elise for her indomitable spirit. My fascination with old buildings began when my late father, a teacher like myself, brought me as a child to see some ruined castles in Cork (first Cloghleagh, then Castle Cooke – what a start!). It is only fitting that I dedicate this book to my own son, Evan, as a memento of long drives and long chats, and great scrambles through ruins, together.

Note: site-plans; dates; county locations

The site-plans in this book are used to make points rather than provide histories of construction. Lighter shading bounded by solid lines is used in some drawings to signify secondary phases where these are obvious and need to be highlighted. In some cases lighter shading unbounded by solid lines is used to show missing walls. Most plans are oriented with north at the top; the exceptions are those for which such orientations are impractical within single-frame graphics. The purpose of showing orientation is simply to invite the reader to reflect on buildings that might have been turned in relation to prevailing winds or to catch morning or evening sunlight, or, in the case of ecclesiastical buildings, oriented east–west with different degrees of accuracy. In the text itself some quite specific dates and date-ranges are assigned to buildings and parts of the buildings. Although for the sake of brevity I do not spell out the reasons, there is supporting evidence, historical or comparative architectural, in every case. Finally, to avoid tiresome repetition in the text, the counties in which cited buildings are located are only given in the index, except in those rare instances where places/buildings of the same name are found in different counties.

MAP 1 Sites mentioned in the text (Cos Mayo, Sligo, Roscommon, Galway, Clare, Limerick, Kerry and Cork).

MAP 2 Sites mentioned in the text (Cos Donegal, Derry, Tyrone, Fermanagh, Cavan, Monaghan, Leitrim, Longford, Westmeath, Offaly, Laois, Tipperary, Kilkenny and Waterford).

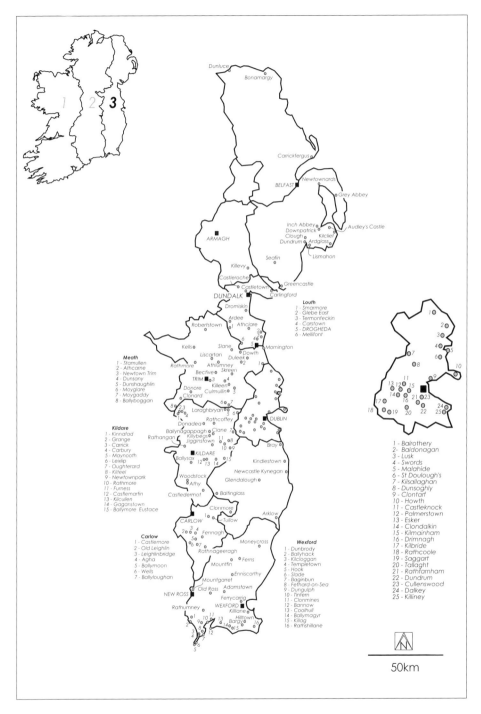

MAP 3 Sites mentioned in the text (Cos Antrim, Down, Armagh, Louth, Meath, Dublin, Kildare, Wicklow, Carlow and Wexford).

CHAPTER I

Medieval architectural styles and their study

INTRODUCTION

Medieval buildings – churches, castles, abbeys – dot the Irish landscape and provide a tangible link with a world far in the past. History is fairly silent about many of them, and such historical information as we possess about any of them rarely casts upon them a bright, and still more rarely a sustained, light. The most comprehensive historical document of a medieval building is always the building itself. It is of course a very particular type of document: there are things that a medieval building can never tell us on its own, such as the names of people involved in its history, but in compensation there is fascinating information about medieval culture and society, about medieval *people*, that a building alone possesses.

The main challenge for non-specialists in medieval architectural history is to know how to 'read' the information locked into medieval buildings; the second challenge is to feel liberated, empowered even, to make a reading in the first place. So, exactly how many works of medieval architecture are available to us in Ireland for 'reading'? Before attempting to answer that question, we might deal briefly with the distinction between a work of architecture and a building. Is there a distinction? Nikolas Pevsner once famously remarked that Lincoln Cathedral is architecture whereas a bicycle shed is a building.[1] I cannot comment on how widely that view is shared, but I certainly do not share it. Underpinning his distinction was cultural elitism, specifically the view that architecture should always be coupled with art, precisely because each is a product of intelligent design, an artefact of 'high' culture.[2] Just as one could contest so narrow a definition of art, one could argue that any built structure in which cultural information is conveyed, no matter how modest the structure or the information, is architecture. If a bicycle shed can, through its design and materiality, reveal something about its builder or about the society in which it functioned, it is architecture. On that basis, I use the words 'architecture' and 'building' somewhat interchangeably in this book. Of

---

1 N. Pevsner, *An outline of European architecture* (London, 1943), p. 15.   **2** Essential reading on the cultural ideologies embedded in historical writing about architecture is David Watkin's marvellous little book, *Morality and architecture* (Chicago, 1977), or its updated version, *Morality and architecture revisited* (Chicago, 2001). Ironically, Pevsner is best known for the *Buildings of England* series, a collection of county surveys not of bicycle sheds but of cathedrals and their ilk. The *Buildings of Ireland* series is an authorized off-shoot, of which four volumes have been published so far: A. Rowan, *North-west Ulster* (New Haven and London, 1979); C. Casey and A. Rowan, *North Leinster* (New Haven and London, 1993); C. Casey, *Dublin* (New Haven and London, 2005); K. Mulligan, *South Ulster* (New Haven and London, 2013).

course, in responding to the question 'how many medieval buildings do we have?', this fairly liberal definition of architecture would have us enumerate alongside the castles and churches all of those structures, particularly those associated with the rural peasantry, which have been revealed in archaeological excavations. My reason for excluding them from the enumeration below, and from the book generally, is simply that this book is concerned with helping the reader make sense of buildings that he or she can actually visit. Were this a cultural history of Irish architecture, or a cultural history of Ireland through the lens of the built environment, there would be no such exclusion.

Archaeological surveys north and south of the border can be mined for very approximate totals of the number of upstanding medieval buildings in Ireland. I estimate that more than two thousand surviving individual buildings (such as stand-alone tower-houses) or integrated architectural complexes (such as big castles with multiple structures, or town walls with mural gates and towers) could be described as 'fortified'. Most of these are castles.[3] Add to this estimate more than 5,500 ecclesiastical works of comparable diversity, ranging from isolated churches to large Anglo-Norman cathedrals, and we have a stock of perhaps eight thousand-odd places with medieval fabric that can be analysed. Every single item, even the most poorly preserved, has the potential to tell us something.

When does 'medieval' start and end?

The period of history that we describe as the Middle Ages is generally regarded in mainland Europe as having lasted about a thousand years. Historians assign its beginning there to the fifth century, specifically to the collapse of the Roman Empire, and its end to the fifteenth century or thereabouts, the period of the Renaissance that originated in Italy. However, the chronology of the medieval period in Ireland has long been a matter of contention, with debates about when we should regard it as having both started *and* ended. In one sense, it is something of a non-issue, since the people of the time in Ireland, no more than their contemporaries across Europe, had no idea that the period in which they lived was in the 'middle' of anything.[4] Nonetheless, it is useful to begin this book with some clarification of the matter, if only because readers are likely to encounter divergent views on what constitutes 'medieval' when they consult scholarly literature.

For many years, probably until the 1980s in fact, the consensus view was that the term 'medieval' was best applied in Ireland to the period that began when the Anglo-Normans arrived in 1169, and that earlier centuries, from about the time of St Patrick

---

3 Con Manning estimates a head-count of 1,200 surviving late medieval tower-houses ('Irish tower houses', *Europa Nostra Scientific Bulletin*, 63 (2009), 19–30 at 19), which is consistent with my estimate. Terry Barry has argued for an original head-count of 7,000 tower-houses alone ('The archaeology of the tower house in late medieval Ireland' in H. Andersson and J. Weinberg (eds), *The study of medieval archaeology* (Stockholm, 1993), pp 211–18).   **4** A 'middle age' was first identified by the Italian scholar Flavio Biondo in the early fifteenth century, and the adjective 'medieval' was coined in the eighteenth century (T. O'Keeffe, 'Medieval' in D.M. Pearsall (ed.), *Encyclopedia of archaeology* (London and New York, 2008), pp 1240–9).

in the fifth century to the turn of the millennium, should be described as the 'Early Christian Period'. It was a view that left all of the eleventh century and most of the twelfth century in something of a terminological limbo. The phrase 'Early Christian Period' is now (thankfully) out of vogue among Irish scholars, although it still enjoys some popularity in non-scholarly circles. It has been dropped because the same term is used by international scholars to describe the period of late Roman Christianity (the first few centuries AD) that immediately *preceded* the Middle Ages on the Continent. The current practice in Ireland is to assign the start of the Irish medieval period to the early fifth century, the period in which Christianity is first documented on the island. Now, this book deals with post-1100 architecture, not as a denial of the designation as medieval of pre-1100 buildings but, rather, to reflect the interplay of two facts. First, the pre-1100 architectural record is now very thoroughly published, as we will see below, and I have little to add to what has already been said. Were I to attempt to cover it, this book would be significantly longer. Second, the year 1100 marks a significant break. It marks the point at which Irish ecclesiastical architecture, already linked conceptually and intellectually (or, perhaps more precisely, eschatologically) to European architecture, adopts *physical* forms that are identifiably part of the main-stream European architectural tradition; from that point on, the trajectory of Irish architectural development, secular as well as ecclesiastical, demands to be looked at with one eye on the trajectories of development of building types and styles on the neighbouring island, and even across north-western Europe.

There is less consensus across Europe on the most appropriate end-date of the Middle Ages. The lack of consensus is not surprising, as not everybody agrees on the criteria, and in any case changes happened at different times in different places. Even in Ireland there is little consensus, although the spread of possible dates is quite narrow. Historians have tended to attach great symbolic importance to individual dated events. For example, the editors of *A new history of Ireland*, published by Oxford University Press over several decades, plumped for 1534, the date of the failed rebellion by Silken Thomas. They might as easily have chosen 1585, marking the failure of the Desmond rebellion in Munster and the start of plantation in that province, or indeed 1607, the date of the flight of the earls from Ireland to the Continent. My own preference among historical dates would be for 1536, the date at which Henry VIII's dissolution of the monasteries started; if the medieval period started with the arrival of (Roman) Christianity, it is perhaps only fitting that we assign its end to the act that began the shutting-down of (Roman) monasteries. But in cultural terms – and this book is about culture, because buildings are cultural artefacts – such political-historical dates are not very useful at all. Cultural change is rarely synchronized with political change, and, in any case, it happens gradually and sometimes diffuses slowly. There is greater continuity than discontinuity in the archaeological and architectural records between the early fifteenth and later sixteenth centuries, and it is only really with the plantations, especially those of Munster (from 1586) and Ulster (from 1609), that one senses that an old order – the medieval order – is dead. My end-date, then, is 1600, with my narrative occasionally nudging into the seventeenth century.

Ethnic identity and architecture in medieval Ireland

We have little need to think about matters of ethnic identity and its terminology when dealing with upstanding buildings of pre-1169 date. The stock of *above-ground* buildings surviving from that period is Irish in the sense that its patrons were Irish; they were born on the island and spoke the native language. At relatively few sites – Cormac's Chapel, Cashel, and Mellifont Abbey are the main ones – is there any evidence of non-Irish hands contributing to the architecture.

The Anglo-Norman invasion took place in 1169, and most of this book is devoted to buildings that were erected after that date. The term 'Anglo-Norman', which connotes somebody of Norman descent but English birth, is not one that the invaders themselves would have recognized. If anything, they would have called themselves English. The last Norman king (Stephen) was fifteen years dead by the time of their invasion, and the first Angevin or Plantagenet king (Henry II) was about halfway through his reign, so the political label appropriate to them is Angevin. Indeed, most of the in-migration of post-1169 settlers probably took place in the thirteenth century, by which stage there were few who had even been alive during Stephen's reign. Still, I am opting to retain the familiar label of 'Anglo-Norman' for all of these people, although I sometimes describe their world as 'Angevin'.

Readers might encounter in the literature another term, 'Anglo-Irish', which is used by many writers to represent those Anglo-Normans who, through intermarriage with the Irish in the fourteenth century, allegedly 'became more Irish than the Irish themselves'. The romantic view is that they had 'gone native' under the influence of Gaelic-Irish culture, and in the process rejected the authority of the English crown. The more prosaic truth is that by the 1300s, many generations after their ancestors had invaded, their *cultural* connection with England was mainly in the historical past, and the 'native' culture to which they were allegedly assimilated had itself been changed, even anglicized, through its contact with them. Moreover, the characterization of so many 'Anglo-Irish' families as physically and metaphorically 'beyond the Pale' – the area around Dublin where English rule was most concentrated in the late Middle Ages – is a misrepresentation of complex and ever-changing political realities. Indeed, of the three great 'Anglo-Irish' earldoms of late medieval Ireland, Kildare, Ormond and Desmond, only the latter was really disconnected from English power and its agents in Dublin.

'Gaelic-Irish' and 'Anglo-Norman' (but not 'Anglo-Irish') will appear occasionally in this book as labels attached to buildings. I must stress, however, that this is not an endorsement of the simplistic view of ethnic identity that these labels tend to suggest. Rather than get ensnared in a thicket of debate about which words we should and should not use, I would advise readers to use those labels only with full cognizance of the assumptions inherent in them. So, while some of the buildings of the early years after the invasion are thoroughly English in style, by the late Middle Ages (the 1400s and 1500s) almost every building on the island could actually be described to some degree as Anglo-Irish. Although I doubt it, if there was such as a thing as a 'national style' in Ireland at any stage of the high Middle Ages – and nobody should use the term 'nation' without first reading Joep Leerssen's commentary on the topic[5] – it is an Anglo-Irish, or Hiberno-English, style.

On a related matter, architecture and architectural sculpture in Britain certainly has comparative analytical relevance, and nobody can claim real expertise in Irish medieval architectural history if ignorant of non-Irish (including continental) material, but one must always steer clear of qualitative judgments of the Irish evidence. Medieval architectural craftsmanship in Ireland, especially between the twelfth and fifteenth centuries, should not be judged second-rate because it deviates from perceived English gold-standard norms, nor should the craftsmen themselves be patronized by modern scholars when their work compares favourably in aesthetic and execution with supposed English exemplars. Unless one can prove that medieval builders in Ireland, both 'English' and 'Irish' alike, looked longingly at the neighbouring island and desired to replicate its admittedly extraordinary architecture, one should resist the temptation to make qualitative comparisons.

A BRIEF INTRODUCTION TO IRELAND'S MEDIEVAL ARCHITECTURAL STYLES

Architectural historians have long identified a series of styles or fashions in the design and execution of buildings. The two main styles identified in medieval European architecture are Romanesque and Gothic, and both are represented in Ireland. Such a simple classification suggests that medieval architecture divides along simple lines, and that each style was itself a well-defined phenomenon, but the truth is quite different. While specialists of historic architecture use style-names, all would be aware of the great variety and complexity of architectural form and concept lurking behind words like Romanesque and Gothic. In this section these two style-labels are accepted uncritically (but see below, pp 98–100), and a simple architectural history is presented around them.

Introducing Romanesque architecture and its study

Romanesque is the dominant style of the eleventh and twelfth centuries, and we first detect it in Ireland in church buildings erected around 1100. Before looking at its constituent buildings, it is useful to note briefly the corpus of many dozens of stone churches surviving in Ireland from the period before the late eleventh century, a corpus that we might describe for convenience as 'pre-Romanesque'. That corpus matters in the context of this book because there is some continuity across the 1100 boundary. Some churches that remained in use into the twelfth century and beyond, as at Killevy, had original features retained, even though they were stylistically out of date. Also, round towers, the first examples of which were built before 950, were still being built to an unchanged template nearly four centuries later.

---

5 J. Leerssen, *Mere Irish and fíor-Ghael: studies of the idea of Irish nationality, its development and literary expression prior to the nineteenth century* (Cork, 1996).

1 Ratass Church, Tralee, from the west. The original pre-Romanesque church is identified by the red sandstone masonry; later repair was executed in grey limestone. The lintelled west doorway is outlined by a broad band of low-relief masonry, a feature which, judging by other sites at which it is found (such as Tuamgraney), suggests an eleventh-century or even later tenth-century date. The *antae* here are of fairly standard width but of markedly bold projection. At the start of the twelfth century this small church was briefly the cathedral church of the newly created diocese of Kerry.

The majority of our pre-Romanesque churches date not from the early centuries of Christianity in Ireland but from the 900s and 1000s. The bulk of the corpus comprises small, single-cell, mortared churches, some of them with short, external end-wall projections, virtually unique to Ireland, called *antae* (fig. 1). The likelihood is that these churches represent, alongside the round towers, a significant expansion of the building industry in a period of rapid transformation: the turbulence of Viking raids had ended, and momentum was building towards ecclesiastical reform. The denominator common to Ireland's stock of pre-Romanesque churches is miniaturism: these are all small buildings by contemporary standards elsewhere, indicating first that more creative energy (in the very narrowest sense) went into stone crosses, illuminated manuscripts and fine metalwork than into architecture, and second that many of the rituals conducted within churches were concealed from the views of pilgrims and penitents.

Ireland's Romanesque history starts immediately before 1100 and ends in the early 1200s. Its earliest phase coincides with the reform of the Irish Church, a process that, over a period of half a century (up to the eve of the Anglo-Norman invasion), drew the Irish Church closer to the contemporary European Church through a standardizing

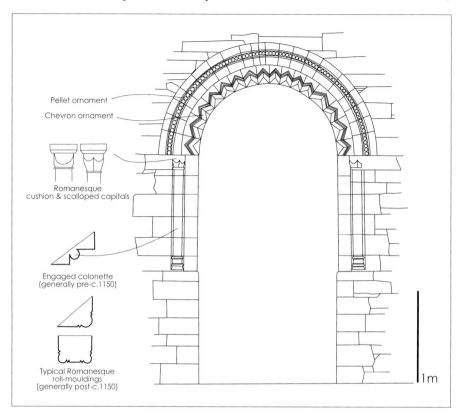

Pellet ornament

Chevron ornament

Romanesque
cushion & scalloped capitals

Engaged colonette
(generally pre-c.1150)

Typical Romanesque
roll-mouldings
(generally post-c.1150)

1m

2 The chancel arch of Kilmalkedar Church, one of Munster's earliest Romanesque churches. Originally this arch framed an altar, which explains why the jambs do not extend to ground level, but it was later converted into an actual chancel arch. It is otherwise fairly typical of the early phases of the Romanesque style in Ireland in that the small columns on each side of the arch are 'engaged colonettes' (which are three-quarter round columns tucked into angles, or 'returns', or the jambs); in the second half of the twelfth century masons used roll-mouldings on the corners of door- and window-jambs to create a similar though shallower affect. The small capitals are in the tradition of European Romanesque cushion and scalloped capitals. The chevron is quite simple: more complex zigzag schemes (with diamonds and interlocking Vs) were used mainly after *c*.1150. Drawing after J. Cuppage (ed.), *Archaeological survey of the Dingle Peninsula* (Ballyferriter, 1986), fig. 188.

of monastic observance, a regularizing of episcopal territorial authority and a stamping out of inappropriate practices. The earliest manifestations of the Romanesque style are probably in a small number of late eleventh-century churches in the hinterland of the Hiberno-Scandinavian town of Dublin, such as Palmerstown and Killiney, and the three Glendalough churches of St Kevin's 'Kitchen', Trinity and Reefert. Their defining characteristic is their combination of an original lintelled west-end doorway, representing continuity with the earlier architectural tradition, with a plain Romanesque chancel arch, representing a technology previously unseen (to our knowledge) in Ireland. St Kevin's in Glendalough has another feature that we would

3 Ardfert Cathedral from the west. This Romanesque façade, repaired in recent years, is preserved in the west wall of the thirteenth-century Gothic cathedral. The wide central doorway was flanked by pairs of blind arches, creating a five-bay façade. Although most of the decoration (such as the chevron) is demonstrably from the Norman-English Romanesque repertoire, the five-bay arrangement is better paralleled in French Romanesque architecture. Is it significant that Ardfert is in a part of Ireland that faces the Atlantic – and France – rather than England?

identify as Romanesque: this is the stone vault, built not with corbelling (such as we see in Gallarus Oratory, not to mention later medieval buildings like Termonfeckin Castle) but with radially set stones that are wedged into each other for stability. The clustering of a number of sites with modest Romanesque forms around Dublin is best explained in terms of influence from now-lost churches in the city itself. There, the Hiberno-Scandinavian population was attuned to international, or at least English, cultural practices, and Romanesque was obviously one such practice.

The flowering of Romanesque as an architectural style in Ireland really began in earnest in the early twelfth century in Munster, the province that hosted the first reforming synods. This was not an evolution from the timid first steps made around Dublin in the previous couple of decades but was a new phenomenon, characterized by a very high proportion of sculptural forms (capitals, roll-mouldings) and ornamental devices and motifs (chevron, most obviously), all of Norman-English origin (fig. 2). The earliest surviving building in this new tradition may be St Flannán's Oratory in Killaloe, a small, stone-vaulted church of the same basic type as St Kevin's in Glendalough but with a round and sculpturally decorated west-end doorway that

4 Dromiskin round tower and Killeshin Church portals. The former is an early twelfth-century example of obvious English derivation if not craftsmanship; the much-worn heads on either side were the work of native stone-carvers. The mid-twelfth-century Killeshin doorway owes less to English style. It is a classic work of Gaelic-Irish Romanesque. The shallow gable over the portal is one of its few relatively atypical features. Such gables are necessary when portals are porched, as at Freshford and Cormac's Chapel (see fig. 50), for example, but here, as in the portals of Clonfert Cathedral and Kildare round tower, the gable is a decorative feature. The sculpture on this portal was almost certainly painted originally, so it is likely that the gable space was also painted. Drawings after H.S. Crawford and H.G. Leask, 'Killeshin church and its Romanesque ornament', *JRSAI*, 55 (1925), 83–94; V.M. Buckley and P.D. Sweetman (eds), *Archaeological survey of County Louth* (Dublin, 1991), pp 225–7.

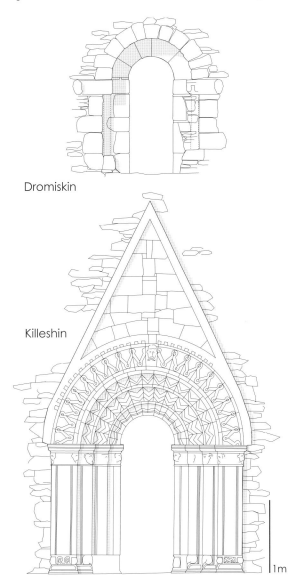

Dromiskin

Killeshin

1m

could almost have come from a Norman-English catalogue of *c.*1100. Slightly later, but probably still before 1120, are the decorated Romanesque façades of St Crónán's Church (originally Cathedral), Roscrea, and Ardfert Cathedral (fig. 3). The masterpiece of Munster's Romanesque, Cormac's Chapel on the Rock of Cashel, was consecrated in 1134. The fact that its consecration was, according to the historical sources, attended by many dignitaries, and the fact that, uniquely, its patron's name was attached to it from the very outset, indicates that it was always regarded as an exceptional building. Evidence for early twelfth-century Romanesque in the other parts of Ireland, including the province of Armagh, is fugitive.

5 A mid-twelfth-century head-capital in the church of Kilteel. Now reconstructed as part of a chancel arch, this and other Romanesque carved stones at the site, retrieved from the nearby castle about eighty years ago, may have originated in another church, probably built under the patronage of Diarmait Mac Murchada.

By 1150 the style, by now a *decorative* style to be applied to arches and their supports rather than an *architectural* style affecting all parts of buildings (as had been the case in Cormac's Chapel in particular), had begun its spread across central and eastern Ireland. As it spread, it lost some of its Englishness, becoming instead what we call Gaelic-Irish Romanesque or Hiberno-Romanesque. Incorporated into its decorative repertoire from the mid-1100s were several elements of Hiberno-Scandinavian decoration, mainly animal-interlace, and these are best seen in the midlands and in Connacht, at sites like Monaincha and Rahan (the latter with a church that sports a remarkable circular Romanesque window). The classic work, if one had to select just one, is the mid-century Killeshin portal, inscribed with the name of its patron, Diarmait Mac Murchada, the Leinster king at whose invitation the Anglo-Normans invaded Ireland. It owes its classic status to its shallow, sculpted rather than constructed, form; earlier Romanesque doorways of direct Norman-English inspiration were more deeply recessed (fig. 4). Also classic is its decoration, which features floral and zoomorphic motifs alongside abstract ornament such as chevron. The 'head-capital', in which a human head is placed at the angle of the capital, was a popular device in Romanesque sculpture, and Irish stone-carvers at Killeshin and elsewhere (fig. 5) enjoyed exploring its potential, often metamorphosing the hair into small snake-like creatures.

6 Later twelfth-century capitals in Monasteranenagh Abbey church. The top image shows a scalloped capital with small plants between the scallops, while the capitals in the bottom image have a design that was influenced by the scalloped form but is formed entirely of small plants; the shallow roll-mouldings on the corners of the pilaster (or wall-pillar) supporting the latter capitals are typical of Gaelic-Irish Romanesque work, and they tell us – it can hardly come as a surprise – that the masons at Monasteranenagh included native Irishmen who were trained in a mid-twelfth-century non-Cistercian context.

7 Drumacoo Church south doorway. The chevron is a classic Romanesque form, and the small snarling animal heads on one of the capitals are a feature of western Irish Romanesque that can be traced to the Romanesque style of western France. But the doorway is pointed rather than round-arched, and all of its other features – the mouldings and the stylized plant decoration on the other capitals, for example – are Gothic. Note how the tubular chevron on the outer order crosses two deeply hollowed channels before resting on a central moulding that is slightly pointed (or keel-shaped). Whether round or keel, roll-mouldings that are deeply undercut like this are called 'bowtell' mouldings and are unknown in Ireland prior to the arrival of Gothic.

The Cistercian order, in Ireland from the mid-1100s, had its own distinctive Romanesque architectural style, reflective of its origins in Burgundy. That style was imported fully formed into the order's first-generation abbeys in Ireland, starting with Mellifont, founded in 1142. There was very little *architectural*-stylistic borrowing between the Gaelic-Irish Romanesque tradition just discussed and the tradition that was newly introduced by the Cistercians. The only major non-Cistercian structure of the later twelfth century in Ireland for which a Gaelic-Irish patron chose a Cistercian model seems to be Limerick Cathedral. However, some sculptural forms and motifs were shared between Gaelic-Irish and Cistercian craftsmen. For example, the Cistercians had a fondness for scalloped capitals, and in some of their early churches, such as Baltinglass and Jerpoint, such capitals were decorated with small beads and plants as well as abstract motifs that are not at all unlike work found in contemporary Gaelic-Irish churches. Monasteranenagh has a particularly rich and revealing selection of decorated capitals (fig. 6). All of the Cistercian Romanesque monasteries would have had native masons in their work-forces, even Mellifont.

The earliest Anglo-Norman settlers in Ireland were themselves users of Romanesque, having arrived in Ireland just before the first great Gothic structure in England – the east end of Canterbury Cathedral – was erected in the mid-1170s. Anglo-Norman ecclesiastical works in the Romanesque idiom in Ireland are relatively few, and include the transeptal arms of Christ Church (formerly Holy Trinity) Cathedral in Dublin, but there are classic Romanesque round-arched windows in some of their castle buildings, such as the donjons ('keeps') of Trim, Maynooth and Carrickfergus (all from the 1170s) and Ballyderown (built before 1200). From *c.*1200, Anglo-Norman buildings in Ireland were Gothic. West of the Shannon, however, where a permanent Anglo-Norman presence was not established until after 1235, the Romanesque style survived into the early thirteenth century in buildings of the so-called 'School of the West'. Examples include the abbeys of Ballintober (Mayo) and Cong (both Augustinian), and Boyle (Cistercian), and the priory of Inishmaine (Augustinian). The sculptural detail of this late Romanesque work indicates that the native craftsmen responsible for it knew something of the new Gothic style then taking root in eastern Ireland. This western Irish style is often called 'Transitional', as if it represents an actual transition from Romanesque to Gothic (fig. 7), but it would be better described as Late Romanesque. Although the 'School of the West' has been studied in some detail, the conduits by which native craftsmen had access to Gothic forms – and a limited repertoire of such forms, at that – remain to be explored.[6]

A review of scholarly literature

The literature on pre-Romanesque and Romanesque buildings is vast. Nineteenth-century publications, first of all, often can be ignored for their scholarly content,

---

6 There might also be value in reconsidering possible connections, first aired by Peter Harbison ('Twelfth- and thirteenth-century Irish stonemasons in Regensburg (Bavaria) and the end of the "school of the west" in Connacht', *Studies*, 64 (1975), 333–46), between this western tradition and continental European architecture: tapering columns, as used in the windows of Cong

although George Petrie's *The ecclesiastical architecture of Ireland anterior to the Anglo-Norman invasion, comprising an essay on the origin and uses of round towers of Ireland* (Dublin, 1845), which covered the twelfth as well as the preceding centuries, must be acknowledged as one of the most important scholarly works produced in Ireland in any field in the 1800s.

The earliest 'modern' work of scholarship is Arthur Champneys' *Irish ecclesiastical architecture* (London, 1910). This laid the main foundation for the following sixty years of study across the entire (pre-Romanesque to late Gothic) spectrum of medieval ecclesiastical architecture in Ireland. It is now outdated, and the relatively poor quality of the illustrations makes it a much less attractive collector's item than Petrie's book, but the quality of its content should not go unacknowledged. Champneys exerted a greater influence on the work of Harold Leask than Leask himself admitted, and this is especially apparent in Leask's treatment of pre- and very early Romanesque architecture in volume 1 of his *Irish churches and monastic buildings* (Dundalk, 1955–60). Leask's *métier* was later, post-1200, architecture, and for many years his work on pre-Norman buildings was far more influential than its quality merited. Françoise Henry's *Irish art in the early Christian period (to AD800)* (London and Ithaca, 1965) and *Irish art during the Viking invasions, AD800–1020* (London and Ithaca, 1967), ground-breaking surveys by an art historian of impeccable pedigree, included relatively brief discussions of pre-Romanesque buildings in the context of a survey of monastic sites, but she added relatively little to what was already known about the actual architecture. Meanwhile, though, the publication of archaeological excavations on Church Island near Valentia Island showed how archaeology could contribute to our knowledge of early medieval ecclesiastical architecture: timber churches were recorded by early medieval writers such as Bede – in the early eighth century he famously described building in timber as the *mos Scottorum*, the manner of the Irish – but none had been found until Michael O'Kelly's excavation on this tiny island.[7] The modern era of research on the stone buildings of the early Church was really ushered in by Peter Harbison's revisiting of the date of Gallarus Oratory in 1970, coincidentally the same year of publication as *Medieval religious houses: Ireland*, Aubrey Gwynn and Neville Hadcock's oft-criticized but generally invaluable catalogue of non-parochial church foundations of all periods.[8] As if liberated by the one-two punch of the O'Kelly-Harbison papers, new syntheses of early church architecture appeared in the late 1970s and early 1980s.[9]

chapter house, are classic features of twelfth-century German Romanesque architecture, especially in the Franco-German border region.   **7** M.J. O'Kelly, 'Church Island, near Valentia, Co. Kerry', *PRIA*, 59C (1959), 57–136.   **8** P. Harbison, 'How old is Gallarus Oratory?', *MA*, 24 (1970), 34–59; A. Gwynn and R.N. Hadcock, *Medieval religious houses: Ireland* (London, 1970). **9** C.A.R. Radford, 'The earliest Irish churches', *UJA*, 40 (1977), 1–11; G. Mettjes, *Frühmittelalterliche Klöster in Irland. Studien zu baugeschichtlichen Problemen am Beispiel der Ruinen von Glendalough* (Frankfurt, 1977); P. Harbison, 'Early Irish churches' in H. Löwe (ed.), *Die Iren und Europe im früheren Mittelalter* (Stuttgart, 1982), pp 618–29; M. Hare with A. Hamlin, 'The study of early church architecture in Ireland: an Anglo-Saxon viewpoint, with an appendix on documentary evidence for round towers' in L.A.S. Butler and R.K. Morris (eds), *The Anglo-Saxon church: papers on history, architecture and archaeology in honour of Dr H.M. Taylor* (London,

Early in the twentieth century monographs on monastic complexes, some of them published as reports of the Commissioners of Public Works and others as proceedings of the Royal Irish Academy, provided valuable raw material for the study of early medieval architecture.[10] The publication of major archaeological surveys, starting with the one-off survey of Co. Down of 1966, the peerless survey of Donegal, published in 1983, and its noble successors, the surveys of the Dingle and Iveragh peninsulas, published in 1986 and 1996 respectively, made additional data on pre-Romanesque architecture widely available from parts of the country especially rich in remains.[11] Michael Herity's surveys of remote island monasteries in the 1980s and early 1990s prefigured more extensive work in the past twenty years on those islands and their buildings.[12] His work on pilgrim rounds and his illumination of the significance of tombs of founder saints were very important contributions to the understanding of early architecture that developed in the 1990s.[13] My own research on pre-Romanesque churches built on Herity's work in arguing the importance of the funerary/memorial chapel in the evolution of early churches, and also developed the thesis that the small scale of Irish churches was an iconographic choice.[14] In recent years Tomás Ó Carragáin has developed these and new ideas in a series of papers on pre-1200 architecture and liturgy, as well as in a sumptuously produced book.[15]

Petrie's book of 1845 was primarily a study of round towers, though he ranged far beyond them in that work. He established their Christian origin. The towers attracted the attention of many subsequent scholars, from Margaret Stokes to Françoise Henry, but it was not until 1979 that another large-scale survey was attempted. George Lennox Barrow's *The round towers of Ireland* (Dublin, 1979) offered a valuable and still unequalled site-by-site survey. Readers should beware his chronology, however: rather like the early eighteenth-century mason who confidently inscribed the legend *This church was*

1986), pp 131–45.   **10** R. Cochrane, 'The ecclesiastical remains at Glendalough, Co. Wicklow', Appendix E, *Eightieth report of the Commissioners of the Public Works in Ireland* (Dublin, 1912); R.A.S. Macalister, 'The history and antiquities of Inis Cealtra', *PRIA*, 33C (1916), 93–174.   **11** M. Jope (ed.), *An archaeological survey of County Down* (Belfast, 1966); B. Lacey (ed.), *Archaeological survey of County Donegal* (Lifford, 1983); Cuppage, *Dingle Peninsula*; A. O'Sullivan and J. Sheehan (eds), *The Iveragh Peninsula: an archaeological survey of south Kerry* (Cork, 1996).   **12** M. Herity, 'The layout of Irish early Christian monasteries' in P. Ní Chatháin and M. Richter (eds), *Irland und Europa: Die Kirche im Frühmittelalter/Ireland and Europe: the early church* (Stuttgart, 1984), pp 105–16; idem, 'Two island hermitages in the Atlantic: Rathlin O'Birne, Donegal, and Caher Island, Mayo', *JRSAI*, 125 (1995), 85–128; see, more recently, J. White Marshall and G.D. Rourke, *High Island: an Irish monastery in the Atlantic* (Dublin, 2000); T. Ó Carragáin and J. O'Sullivan, *Inishmurray: monks and pilgrims in an Atlantic landscape* (Cork, 2008).   **13** M. Herity, 'The antiquity of *an Turas* (the Pilgrimage Round) in Ireland' in A. Lehner and W. Berschin (eds), *Lateinische Kultur im VIII Jahrhundert* (St Ottilien, 1989), pp 95–143; idem, 'The forms of the tomb-shrine of the founder saint in Ireland' in R.M. Spearman and J. Higgitt (eds), *The age of migrating ideas* (Stroud, 1993), pp 188–95.   **14** T. O'Keeffe, 'Architectural traditions of the early medieval church in Munster' in M.A. Monk and J. Sheehan (eds), *Early medieval Munster* (Cork, 1998), pp 112–24; idem, 'Form and content in pre-Romanesque architecture in Ireland', *European Symposium for Teachers of Medieval Archaeology*, 4 (2001), 65–83; idem, *Romanesque Ireland: architecture and ideology in the twelfth century* (Dublin, 2003), pp 61–95.   **15** T. Ó Carragáin, *Churches in early medieval Ireland: architecture, ritual and memory* (New Haven and London, 2011). For an independently alternative reading of the fabric of the early churches, see J.F. Potter, *Patterns in*

built in ye year of God 474 on the church in Banagher, Barrow thought incorrectly that the towers dated back to Patrician times. Brian Lalor's book, *The Irish round tower* (Cork, 1999), corrected Barrow's errors and offered some new insights, to which a later Roger Stalley paper added further insights, as well as the suggestion that the bells inside the towers were hung.[16] My own book, *Ireland's round towers: buildings, rituals and landscapes of the early Irish church* (Stroud, 2004), offered another new reading of the towers (see below, pp 174–5).

Turning now to the twelfth-century architecture, Champneys' book of 1910 is, again, the first work of long-lived value and influence. He pointed correctly to England as the source of much of the architectural sculpture of the 1100s. Leask's 1955 volume on church architecture devotes much space to the Romanesque material, but his analysis was fatally weakened – surprisingly for a scholar of his training – by a lack of knowledge of contemporary architecture outside Ireland and by a concomitant assumption that the style developed independently in Ireland. Henry, in the second volume of her trilogy, was rather stronger on the Romanesque architecture than on the architecture that preceded it, but she over-emphasized twelfth-century French parallels at the expense of English parallels. By the time her work was published in an English-language version in 1970, Liam de Paor's paper on Cormac's Chapel in Cashel was three years in the public domain and well on its way to being regarded as one of the key studies in the entire historiography of Irish medieval architecture.[17]

De Paor's argument, that the building of the famous Cashel church kick-started the Irish Romanesque architectural sequence, was not particularly original – Champneys had the same view of the chapel's primacy – but his name is popularly attached to the theory. Cormac's Chapel has been the subject of much comment since then, the key works being Stalley's 1978 conference paper (published in 1981) in which its western English pedigree, already known to scholars, was spelled out, and my own 1994 paper in which I argued that it is the best preserved of an early Munster tradition, of which Ardfert and Roscrea are actually earlier; Richard Gem has more recently made a convincing claim for the chronological primacy in Munster of St Flannán's Oratory in Killaloe.[18]

There has been a steady stream of other publications on Irish Romanesque architecture over the past three or four decades, with the focus spread between individual buildings, patronage, the relationship between Romanesque and ecclesiastical reform,

stonework: the early church in Britain and Ireland (Oxford, 2009). **16** R. Stalley, 'Sex, symbol and myth: some observations on the Irish round towers' in C. Hourihane (ed.), *From Ireland coming: Irish art from the early Christian to the late Gothic period and its European context* (Princeton, 2001), pp 27–47. **17** L. de Paor, 'Cormac's Chapel: the beginnings of Irish Romanesque' in E. Rynne (ed.), *North Munster studies* (Limerick, 1967), pp 133–45. **18** R.A. Stalley, 'Three Irish buildings with West Country origins', *BAACT*, 4 (1981), 62–80; T. O'Keeffe, 'Lismore and Cashel: reflections on the beginnings of Romanesque architecture in Munster', *JRSAI*, 124 (1994), 118–52; R. Stalley, 'Design and function: the construction and decoration of Cormac's Chapel at Cashel' in D. Bracken and D. Ó Riain-Raedel (eds), *Ireland and Europe in the twelfth century* (Dublin, 2006), pp 162–75; T. O'Keeffe, 'Wheels of words, networks of knowledge: Romanesque scholarship and Cormac's Chapel' in ibid., pp 257–70; R. Gem, 'St Flannán's Oratory at Killaloe: a Romanesque building of *c.*1100 and the patronage of King Muirchertach

and various specific aspects of the architecture.[19] The key work on Cistercian Romanesque is Stalley's *The Cistercian monasteries of Ireland* (London and New Haven, 1987). The late Romanesque tradition of western Ireland, a subject of some interest to Harbison in the 1970s,[20] was the subject of Britta Kalkreuter's *Boyle Abbey and the School of the West* (Bray, 2001). The only book-length study of Romanesque architecture is my own *Romanesque Ireland* (Dublin, 2003), one major theme of which, picked up by other writers since then, is the symbolic purpose of the adoption of Romanesque forms by Irish polities of the twelfth century.

Introducing Gothic architecture and its study

All the major ecclesiastical buildings in all parts of Europe between the 'end' of the Romanesque, which was generally in the second half of the twelfth century, and the 'start' of the Renaissance, which was generally no later than the sixteenth century, are described by scholars as Gothic, the style characterized simplistically (though not inaccurately) as the 'pointed-arch' style. A good number of high-status non-ecclesiastical buildings are similarly described. In Ireland, the chronology of the style spans the period between the last decade of the twelfth century and the middle of the 1500s, but with a long tail that stretches into the 1600s and contains one late and deliberately anachronistic work, St Columb's Cathedral, Derry (*c.*1630).

The Gothic architectural style appeared in England in the 1170s. It was executed from a very early stage with a distinctive aesthetic that made it quite unlike the famous Gothic of north-eastern France. That fact is captured in the name given two centuries

---

Ua Briain' in ibid., pp 74–105.   **19** The list includes T. Garton, 'A Romanesque doorway at Killaloe', *JBAA*, 134 (1981), 31–57; R. Stalley, 'The Romanesque sculpture of Tuam' in A. Borg and A. Martindale (eds), *The vanishing past* (Oxford, 1981), pp 179–95; S. McNab, 'The Romanesque figure sculpture at Maghera, Co. Derry, and Raphoe, Co. Donegal' in J. Fenlon, N. Figgis and C. Marshall (eds), *New perspectives: studies in art history in honour of Anne Crookshank* (Dublin, 1987), pp 19–33; T. O'Keeffe, 'La façade romane en Irlande', *Cahiers de Civilisation Médiévale*, 34 (1991), 357–65; idem, 'Romanesque architecture and sculpture at Ardmore' in W. Nolan (ed.), *Waterford: history and society* (Dublin, 1992), pp 73–104; idem, 'The Romanesque portal at Clonfert Cathedral and its iconography' in C. Bourke (ed.), *From the isles of the north* (Belfast, 1995), pp 261–9; idem, 'Diarmait Mac Murchada and Romanesque Leinster: four twelfth-century churches in context', *JRSAI*, 127 (1997), 52–79; idem, 'Romanesque as metaphor: architecture and reform in twelfth-century Ireland' in A.P. Smyth (ed.), *Seanchas: studies in early and medieval Irish archaeology, history and literature in honour of Francis J. Byrne* (Dublin, 2000), pp 313–22; idem, 'Angevin lordship and colonial Romanesque in Ireland' in M. Costen (ed.), *People and places: essays in honour of Michael Aston* (Oxford, 2007), pp 117–29; J. Ní Ghrádaigh, '"But what exactly did she give?": Derbforgaill and the Nuns' Church at Clonmacnoise' in H.A. King (ed.), *Clonmacnoise studies*, 2 (Dublin, 2003), pp 175–208; idem, 'Style over substance: architectural fashion and identity building in medieval Ireland' in J. Ní Ghrádaigh and E. O'Byrne (eds), *The march in the islands of the medieval west* (Leiden and Boston, 2012), pp 97–138; R. Gem, 'The Irish cathedral in the 12th century: the diocese of Limerick and Killaloe', *BAACT*, 34 (2010), 63–88. See also the online Corpus of Romanesque Sculpture in Britain and Ireland (www.crsbi.ac.uk/index.html).   **20** Harbison, 'Twelfth- and thirteenth-century Irish stonemasons'; idem, 'The "Ballintober Master" and a date for the Clonfert Cathedral chancel', *JGAHS*, 35 (1976), 96–9.

8 The nave of Christ Church Cathedral, Dublin. The elevations of the walls have the classic tripartite arrangement of large-scale Romanesque and earlier Gothic architecture that is encountered widely in Europe but very rarely in Ireland: (1) an arcade at ground level, (2) a narrow gallery called a triforium above it, and (3) clerestory windows at the top to bring in additional light (taken from G.E. Street and E. Seymour, *The cathedral of the Holy Trinity, commonly called Christ Church Cathedral, Dublin: an account of the restoration of the fabric* (London, 1882)).

ago to its earliest (1174–*c.*1240) phase: *Early English*.[21] We use this terminology in Ireland too, though for a period that only started *c.*1190 and continued to *c.*1300.

One of the characteristics of Early English Gothic in England is the use of rib-vaults, carried on thick walls. This type of vaulting was used in Romanesque architecture as well, and Cormac's Chapel has a unique Irish example, but in Gothic architecture the vaults are pointed. Gothic rib-vaults are actually quite rare in Ireland. The Cistercians, despite their reputation for architectural austerity, had a liking for them, and parts of two of their abbeys founded in the immediate aftermath of the Anglo-Norman invasion, Inch in Co. Down (*c.*1200) and Duiske in Graiguenamanagh (post-1204), were rib-vaulted. Ribs were used more extensively in some of the early

21 T. Rickman, *An attempt to discriminate the styles of English architecture from the conquest to the*

Anglo-Norman cathedral churches: they were installed in the 1210s in Newtown Trim, and slightly later in St Patrick's and Christ Church in Dublin (fig. 8). There are some interesting examples of Gothic rib-vaulting over circular-plan spaces in Wexford: an eight-part vault was used in the chapel in Ferns Castle in the third quarter of the thirteenth century, while square-sectioned rib-vaults were used in the remarkable early thirteenth-century lighthouse on the Hook Peninsula and again (in imitation of the Hook example?) in the later medieval corner tower of Fethard-on-Sea Castle. Rib-vaulting enjoyed a revival in the late Middle Ages, especially in the southern half of Ireland: it was mainly used for the spaces under belfry or crossing towers, usually in mendicant churches, but occasionally it was used to roof quite extensive areas, as in the eastern parts of early fifteenth-century church of Holycross Cistercian abbey (fig. 9).[22]

Another characteristic feature of Early English Gothic is the use of tall and pointed arches for nave arcades, chancel arches and windows (lancets). The east-end lancets in St Mary's parish church, New Ross (fig. 10), are fairly typical for the early and mid-1200s in Ireland: there is a row of openings, odd in number, with each opening separated on the outside by a narrow band of walling, and with the heights of the openings graded in size from the centre outwards. Tall lancets were also used to illuminate the interiors of large (mainly monastic) churches from the side; the east ends (choirs and presbyteries) of

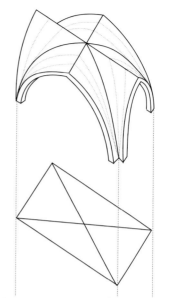

Romanesque and early Gothic rib-vault plan
used for vaulting large spaces
[eg Cormac's Chapel chancel;
Duiske Abbey choir; St Patrick's Cathedral nave]

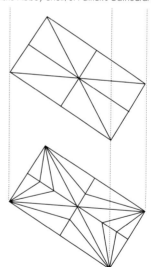

Late medieval rib-vault plan, with many variations
used for vaulting main spaces [eg Kilcooly Abbey transept],
under belfries/crossing towers [eg Kilkenny & Leighlin cathedrals],
and for font & tomb decoration [eg Kilcooly; Grangefertagh]

9 The basic structure and plan of a rib-vault.

Reformation (London, 1817). **22** The best summary of medieval vaulting, especially late medieval, is Stalley, *Cistercian monasteries of Ireland*, ch. 6.

10 The east end of St Mary's Church, New Ross. Associated with William Marshal, who succeeded Strongbow as lord of Leinster in 1207, this was one of the biggest and most elaborately decorated parish churches of medieval Ireland. Note how two of the lancets are very slightly pointed while the third (on the left) is round-headed.

11 The south wall of the choir of Ardfert Friary church, founded *c.*1253 by Thomas FitzMaurice, lord of Kerry.

12 This pair of trefoil-arched clerestory windows in Dunbrody is pointed externally but has round trefoil arches internally. Drawing adopted from R. Cochrane, *Seventy-eighth report of the Commissioners of the Public Works in Ireland* (1909–10), p. 29.

Exterior

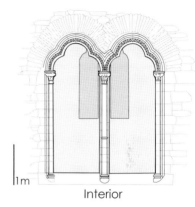

1m

Interior

such churches were lit by rows of such windows, usually on their south sides to avail of natural light. At Ardfert Friary (Franciscan) there is a very typical example of that arrangement, although the rear-arches of its lancets are not pointed themselves, as was normal, but are of another shape that one encounters in the Early English repertoire in both England and Ireland: they are trefoil-headed (fig. 11; see also fig. 27). The trefoil-arch, whether round or pointed, was first used around the second quarter of the thirteenth century – Dunbrody Abbey (Cistercian) has examples of this date (fig. 12) – but only became popular with masons in Ireland after 1250 and it was used for windows in castles as well as churches, as well as for the arches of wall-tombs and different features of the liturgical 'furnishing' in churches.

Also indicative of Early English Gothic is a particular repertoire of ornamental forms and motifs. Door and window jambs are often embellished with roll-mouldings, cut more deeply into the stone than was the case with Romanesque roll-mouldings (fig. 13 top; see also fig. 7). Arches were sometimes sprung from piers or jambs without capitals in-between, as we often observe in Cistercian Gothic, but capitals, when used, are basically round in 'plan' (whereas Romanesque capitals were squared-off) and are normally elongated tubes of inverted-bell shape, embellished with small moulded rings (fig. 13, bottom left). These 'bell' capitals remained popular in Ireland right through the 1200s but went out of vogue in the later Middle Ages when masons either adopted Perpendicular-style forms (see below, pp 49–50) or stopped using capitals altogether. A very popular ornamental device for capitals from *c*.1200 until the third quarter of the thirteenth century was so-called 'stiff-leaf', basically carved foliage in which the

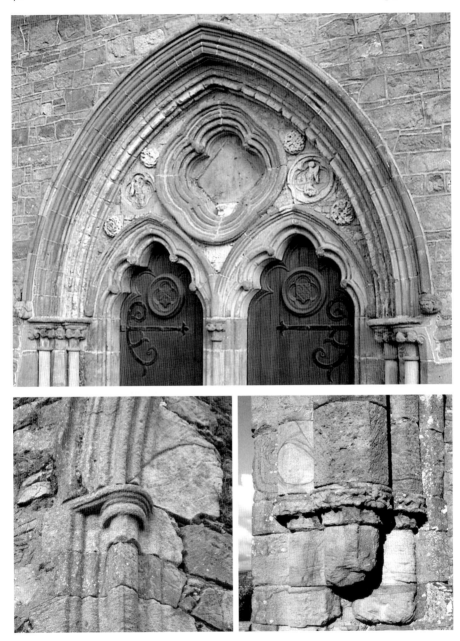

13 The mid-thirteenth-century west doorway of St Canice's Cathedral, Kilkenny (top); late thirteenth-century capitals from Youghal Friary (Dominican), one of which has 'stiff-leaf' ornament. Note how the two Youghal capitals have narrow and shallow square-sectioned projections facing outwards and continuing down the shafts; these are called 'fillets' and are a feature of Gothic craftsmanship (see also fig. 7).

14 The doorway through the choir screen of Athassel Priory church (Augustinian), founded shortly after 1200 by William de Burgo. Note that the capitals that support the arches are of 'stiff-leaf' type. The doorway probably dates from the 1210s.

sprouts and flowers spring outwards at the top of the capital (fig. 13, bottom right; fig. 14); in a small number of cases in south-east Ireland there are human heads protruding from the foliage. The bases equivalent to the Early English capitals often have multiple rings too, but also feature concave (or 'hollow') mouldings that allow them be described as 'waterholding' bases. It is not uncommon to find that the roll-mouldings on jambs (and on window jambs in particular) are interrupted halfway along, or at one-third intervals, by rings or bands. One mainly finds these on interior or rear-arches rather than on exterior arches. 'Banded shafts', as they are often called, are a recurring feature of Early English in its homeland and seem to have come to Ireland in the first wave of Gothic: the processional doorway in Duiske Abbey had them (they have since been chiselled-off), and they can also be seen on the nave piers in Christ Church Cathedral (see fig. 8). Finally, the arches carried by the capitals are often moulded as well, their smooth curves uninterrupted by any radial ornament like chevron. One ornamental device that was used very occasionally in Early English work in Ireland on both arches and capitals is so-called 'dog-tooth' ornament. In its classic form (fig. 14) the ornament is actually composed of four small leaves or petals meeting at one point. The canine allusion in the terminology, in use since the early 1800s, makes no sense.

The Early English Gothic style lasted seventy-odd years in England until, starting with the building of Westminster Abbey in the 1240s, Gothic builders turned in a new direction. The loading of more and more decorative devices onto architectural elements such as arches and windows, and indeed the treatment of the architecture

15 The south transept window in Kilkenny Friary, which was founded in the early thirteenth century but was substantially refurbished at the start of the fourteenth century.

itself as an ornamental field, gives this next English Gothic style its popular name: the *Decorated Style*.[23] This only infiltrated Ireland at the end of the thirteenth century or the start of the fourteenth, overlapping with the last Early English works. It is represented primarily in Ireland by tracery, in both windows and tomb-canopies. The earliest examples are difficult to date, and one cannot be sure if any predate 1300, but one early fourteenth-century work that can at least be paralleled in England and Wales during the last quarter of the thirteenth century is the south transept window in the Dominican friary in Kilkenny (fig. 15). A cluster of other works demonstrably of the early fourteenth century, such as two of the choir windows in Fethard Friary (Augustinian), the north transept window in Athenry Friary (Dominican), the windows of the choir of Tuam Cathedral, and probably the east window of Fenagh 'Abbey', suggest a lively industry at a time when the historical record of economic decline and increasing social-political unrest might have us imagine a downturn, at least in eastern Ireland.

23 See J. Bony, *The English Decorated Style* (Oxford, 1979); N. Coldstream, *The Decorated Style: architecture and ornament, 1240–1360* (Toronto and Buffalo, NY, 1994).

16 Late medieval canopied tombs with tracery: (a) Sligo Friary (Dominican); (b) Strade Friary (Dominican); (c, d) Kilconnell Friary (Franciscan). See also fig. 20.

Some migrant masons must have carried the designs of the Decorated Style to Ireland, such is the confidence of execution of some of these early works, but dissemination thereafter probably involved pattern books. Irish masons in the 1400s

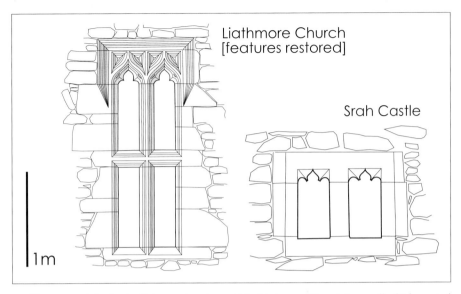

17 The accomplished twin-light window (*c.*1500?) in Liathmore Church is actually fairly typical of what parish communities aspired to and managed to achieve. Drawing adopted from H.G. Leask and R.A.S. Macalister, 'Liathmore-Mochoemóg (Leigh), County Tipperary', *PRIA*, 51 (1948–51), 1–14 at 11. The scope for invention with ogees and cusped ogees was limited, but this did not stop masons playing with forms, as at Srah Castle from the 1580s.

and 1500s experimented freely with the aesthetic spirit of the Decorated Style when designing tracery, and they sometimes created designs that would be ascribed to the so-called 'Rayonnant' and 'Flamboyant' styles of Gothic architecture were they in France.[24] The simplest form of tracery that they used is called 'switch-line', and is characterized by simple criss-crossing or intersecting lines, rather like railway tracks. Indeed, the tracery of the Kilkenny Friary window just discussed is essentially switch-line, but with embellishments. The earliest examples of plain or unembellished switch-line tracery may be in Castledermot Friary (Franciscan), dating from the early fourteenth century, but there are many fifteenth- and early sixteenth-century windows of comparable simplicity. At the other extreme, the most accomplished tracery designs may be those associated with the canopied tombs that are found mainly in the western half of Ireland (fig. 16).[25]

The designs of tracery in Ireland can be dated very approximately by the dates of the buildings in which they are found, but the chronology that emerges suggests no obvious pattern; we cannot say, in other words, that certain shapes are indicative of one decade rather than another. Tracery without cusps is probably later in the chronology, given that cusping was common in English Decorated tracery of the fourteenth century, but even that suggestion cannot be sustained through hard evidence.

24 W.W. Clark, 'Gothic architecture' in W.W. Kibler (ed.), *Medieval France: an encyclopedia* (New York, 1995), pp 765–72 at pp 767–72.   **25** D. O'Donovan, 'Holycross and the language of Irish late Gothic', *BAACT*, 34 (2010), 132–57 at 141–8.

18 Two pairs of highly elaborated cusped-ogee windows from Lynch's Castle in Galway, built *c.*1500. The lower pair has standard cusped-ogee forms, with two cusps (or spurs) to each ogee-arch, but the upper pair is a little more unusual – though certainly not unique – in having four cusps to each arch. In common with many twin-light cusped-ogee windows, this example has a hood-mould, which is a squared-off projecting bracket above it that kept away dripping water (and is therefore sometimes called a 'drip-mould'). Note how the horizontal top of the hood-mould is decorated with stylized leaves from the vine plant, and how the terminals of the hood-mould break out into actual vine plants, complete with bunches of grapes. Vine-leaf ornament, often highly stylized, was commonly used in late medieval Ireland. Its Christian symbolism is self-evident.

19 The earliest known example of an ogee in Ireland is the archway of the doorway into the *c.*1310 chapter house of the Augustinian friary in Fethard. Ogee-form (or ogival) doorways are not common; there is a very fine fifteenth-century example in Holycross Abbey.

Commissioning and installing tracery was expensive, and the larger the traceried window the more glass was needed, which was another considerable expense. No painted window glass in medieval Ireland was more admired than that installed in 1354 in the east window of St Canice's Cathedral, Kilkenny, by Bishop Richard de Ledrede; in 1648 the papal nuncio to Ireland, Giovanni Battista Rinuccini, offered £700 to buy the glass so that it could be installed in Rome, and it is unfortunate that he was turned down because in 1650 it was destroyed by Cromwell's army.[26] Devoted patrons could sometimes be relied upon to meet the expense of glass (as well as other materials), and the mendicants, sporting vows of poverty, benefitted especially from such largesse.[27] Less expensive than a traceried window was a simple single-light or twin-light ogee-headed window, sometimes with small spurs or cusps (to give us the 'cusped ogee'). An ogee is itself a type of arch that is flame-like in character; it differs from the trefoil

26 J. Graves, *The history, architecture and antiquities of the cathedral church of St Canice, Kilkenny* (Kilkenny, 1857), pp 35, 42.   **27** K. Smith, 'An investigation of the material culture of Donegal Franciscan friaries in the late 16th and 17th centuries', *Donegal Annual*, 63 (2011), 96–104.

20 Decorated tracery at Dungiven (tomb) and Kilcooly (window) compared with Perpendicular-styled tracery in windows in the parish churches of Malahide and Callan. Not to scale.

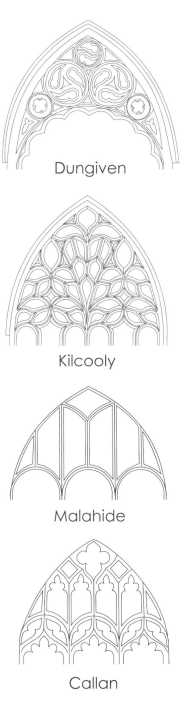

Dungiven

Kilcooly

Malahide

Callan

arch in having concave as well as convex curves, but is made to look superficially like a trefoil when it has cusps (see fig. 27). Part of the English Decorated repertoire originally, both ogees and cusped ogees were used for minor windows in major churches and for major windows in minor churches, and were also used in castles (figs 17, 18). The date range is from the early fourteenth century (fig. 19) to the end of the sixteenth.

The style that succeeded the Decorated in England in the second quarter of the fourteenth century, the *Perpendicular Style* (again, named by Thomas Rickman),[28] had an unusual impact in Ireland. In its homeland, it was characterized by many things but the most obvious was that which inspired its name: the strong verticality of its architectural sculpture. In window tracery, this meant the breaking-up of the flowing patterns of the English Decorated style by mullions (fig. 20). The first appearance in Ireland of its very distinctive tracery may have been in the original later fourteenth century west window of St Patrick's Cathedral, Dublin. Perpendicular-style tracery was not very common in Ireland, remaining largely confined in the fifteenth century to the Dublin region (as in the major Meath churches of Dunsany, Killeen and Rathmore), although there are examples beyond the Pale (as at Callan and, now in fragments, Drumlane). However, other features of Perpendicular were distributed widely in contemporary Ireland. The octagonal and semi-octagonal shapes of capitals and corbels, the moulding profiles of capitals and bases, and the cross-section profiles of cloister-arcade piers, all owe something to Perpendicular work (fig. 21). The adoption in Ireland of some Perpendicular features and eschewing of others is wholly puzzling. More research is needed to

28 See also J. Harvey, *The Perpendicular Style* (London, 1978).

21 The fifteenth-century reconstructed cloister arcade at Holycross Abbey is overtly Perpendicular. The extensive later medieval remodelling of this abbey was not just a vanity project by its patrons, the earls of Ormond. It must have been necessitated by, and part-funded by, pilgrim traffic to the abbey's relic of the True Cross.

build on Danielle O'Donovan's work on Holycross and other Ormond sites where there are manifestations of the style.[29]

Finally, Gothic forms appear so infrequently in castle architecture in Ireland before *c.*1400 that one hesitates to use the term at all in that context. The finely sculpted capitals of 1235–40 in Athenry Castle, the post-1250 vaulted chapel in Ferns Castle, and the distinctively Gothic base of the newel of the stairs in late thirteenth-century Tullowmacjames Castle are among the few explicit nods that castle builders made to the style that was everywhere in ecclesiastical buildings. There is a bigger head-count of Gothic forms in the castles of the later Middle Ages, but it mainly comprises pointed-arched windows and doors, the former including many ogees and cusped ogees. By the later 1500s these Gothic features were on the way out in castle architecture: the widespread adoption in castles after *c.*1600 of rectangular windows with mullions and transoms is linked not to the late Gothic Perpendicular style but to the Renaissance, and it really marks the end of the Gothic experience in Ireland. The choosing of box-like windows in preference to arched windows was more than just an aesthetic shift; it was actually a shift in worldview, quite literally: box windows allowed far more light into building interiors, and allowed more of the insides of those buildings to be seen from the outside.

29 O'Donovan, 'Holycross and the language of Irish late Gothic'.

A review of scholarly literature

In 2003 Colum Hourihane described Gothic art in Ireland as 'an art forgotten'.[30] It is less forgotten now,[31] but the same could not have been said of the architecture back then, even though its historiography was fairly thin up to middle of the last century. Although surveys and reports of many key Gothic buildings were published under the auspices of the Commissioners of Public Works,[32] Champneys' brilliant *Irish ecclesiastical architecture* was the most significant scholarly work until the 1950s, when Canice Mooney's valuable four-part study of Franciscan architecture was published.[33] Harold Leask's two volumes on Gothic architecture in his *Irish churches and monastic buildings* trilogy were published in 1960, and even though they contain little more than parades of descriptions of buildings, arranged chronologically, they do at least map out the general development of the Gothic style in Ireland from the late 1100s to the late 1500s. They remain essential book-shelf items.[34] Stalley's *Architecture and sculpture in Ireland, 1150–1350*, published in 1971, marked the arrival of the most influential voice in the field. Although best known for his work on Cistercian buildings, both Romanesque and Gothic, there is no aspect of Gothic architecture in Ireland about which he has not written. A prolific scholar, his published work is never less than elegant in style and is always insightful in content. His 1971 book, the first scholarly work to put Ireland's ecclesiastical and military architecture side-by-side (and, in doing so, refute implicitly Martyn Jope's denial that fortification is de facto architecture),[35] is a small classic.

No single book-length study of Gothic architecture in Ireland has been published. Hourihane's *Gothic art in Ireland, 1169–1550* from 2003 contains discussions of architecture, but only two of his chapters – on Cashel Cathedral and Gothic portals – have architectural themes. Cashel Cathedral is now one of the most studied Gothic buildings in Ireland, and is certainly the best-studied of the cathedrals outside the big urban centres.[36] By contrast, some of the rural cathedrals, like Kilfenora, have received little attention. Christ Church and St Patrick's in Dublin are by some distance the best-studied of all Irish Gothic buildings.[37] Michael O'Neill is now the leading authority

---

30 C. Hourihane, *Gothic art in Ireland, 1169–1550* (New Haven and London, 2003). **31** See, for example, the papers in R. Moss, C. Ó Clabaigh and S. Ryan (eds), *Art and devotion in late medieval Ireland* (Dublin, 2006). **32** See, for example, the surveys of four Cork friaries (Sherkin, Timoleague, Kilcrea and Buttevant) in the *Seventy-seventh report of the Commissioners of the Public Works in Ireland*, 1908–9. **33** C. Mooney, 'Franciscan architecture in pre-Reformation Ireland', *JRSAI*, 85 (1955), 133–73; 86 (1956), 125–69; 87 (1957), 1–39, 103–24. **34** Useful book-shelf companions to Leask are Mike Salter's two small guides, covering Romanesque and, mainly, Gothic: *Medieval churches of Ireland* and *Abbeys and friaries of Ireland* (Malvern, 2009). **35** E.M. Jope, 'Moyry, Charlemont, Castleraw and Richhill: fortification to architecture in the north of Ireland, 1570–1700', *UJA*, 23 (1960), 97–123. **36** R. Stalley, 'The construction of Cashel Cathedral' in R. Stalley (ed.), *Irish Gothic architecture: construction, decay and reinvention* (Dublin, 2012), pp 55–98; R. Moss, 'Reconstructing Cashel' in ibid., pp 99–114. See also C. Hourihane, *The mason and his mark: masons' marks in the medieval Irish archbishoprics of Cashel and Dublin* (Oxford, 2000). For St Canice's Cathedral, Kilkenny, see S. Barry, 'The architecture of the cathedral' in A. Empey (ed.), *A worthy foundation: the cathedral church of St Canice, Kilkenny* (Kilkenny, 1985), pp 25–48. For other cathedrals, see A.W. Clapham, 'Some minor Irish cathedrals' in *Papers by Sir Alfred Clapham*, supplement to *Archaeological Journal*, 106 (1949), 16–39. For a general survey of Irish cathedrals, see P. Galloway, *The cathedrals of Ireland* (Belfast, 1992). **37** R. Stalley, 'The

on these two buildings, and his study of the architectural relationships between St Patrick's Cathedral and its prebendal churches shows the need for more research into the architectural connections (or indeed non-connections) between cathedrals and the churches within their jurisdictions.[38] Moulding profiles provide a means by which networks between such churches and the various types of monastic church can be reconstructed, and O'Donovan's collection of such profiles is an important resource.[39]

Non-monastic churches below the level of the cathedrals remain under-studied. The great collegiate churches in Ireland, which are a real mixed architectural bag, have escaped analysis as a group, with St Nicholas' in Galway being the only one that has been studied comprehensively.[40] Parish churches have also been somewhat neglected, although the contexts in and for which they were built have recently been established with greater confidence than hitherto.[41] By contrast, much has been written about the Gothic architecture of the monastic orders, and accounts of individual foundations have been published. Benedictine communities were few in Ireland, although such a community might have served Cashel Cathedral for 170-odd years until its recorded expulsion in 1272.[42] The limited patronage Benedictines enjoyed under the Anglo-Normans has left just one significant monument, Fore Priory, for which Leask's modest account remains the most accessible publication.[43] For the Cistercians, Stalley's work, already mentioned, is fairly definitive.[44] I have published accounts of the architecture of the Augustinian canons regular, and Miriam Clyne has written about

medieval sculpture of Christ Church Cathedral, Dublin', *Archaeologia*, 106 (1979), 107–22; idem, 'Three Irish buildings' (for Christ Church); idem, 'The construction of the medieval cathedral, *c.*1030–1250' in K. Milne (ed.), *Christ Church Cathedral, Dublin: a history* (Dublin, 2000), pp 53–74; E.C. Rae, 'The medieval fabric of the cathedral church of St Patrick in Dublin', *JRSAI*, 109 (1979), 29–73; M. O'Neill, 'Design sources for St Patrick's Cathedral, Dublin, and its relationship to Christ Church Cathedral', *PRIA*, 100C (2000), 207–56; idem, 'The architectural history of the medieval cathedral' in J. Crawford and R. Gillespie (eds), *St Patrick's Cathedral: a history* (Dublin, 2009), pp 96–119. For Waterford Cathedral, the other major early thirteenth-century urban cathedral, see Stalley, 'Three Irish buildings', pp 66–71, and idem, 'Cathedral-building in thirteenth-century Ireland' in Stalley, *Irish Gothic architecture*, pp 15–54 at pp 24–9. **38** M. O'Neill, 'St Patrick's Cathedral, Dublin, and its prebendal churches: Gothic architectural relationships', *MD*, 5 (2004), 243–76. **39** *Gothic past: moulding profiles* (www.tara.tcd.ie/handle/2262/21904). See also R.K. Morris, 'The development of later Gothic mouldings in England, *c.*1250–1400', *Architectural History*, 21 (1978), 18–57; 22 (1979), 1–48; idem, 'An English glossary of medieval mouldings: with an introduction to mouldings, *c.*1040–1240', ibid., 35 (1992), 1–17. **40** H.G. Leask, 'The collegiate church of St Nicholas, Galway', *JGAHS*, 17, 1/2 (1936), 2–23; J. McKeon, 'St Nicholas's parish church, Galway: structural and architectural evidence for the high medieval period', *JIA*, 18 (2009), 95–113; see also J. Higgins and S. Heringklee, *Monuments of St Nicholas' collegiate church, Galway: a historical, genealogical and archaeological record* (Galway, 1992). **41** E. FitzPatrick and R. Gillespie (eds), *The parish in medieval and early modern Ireland* (Dublin, 2006). Studies of parish churches include M. MacMahon, *Medieval church sites of north Dublin* (Dublin, 1991); M. Ní Mharcaigh, 'The medieval parish churches of south-west Dublin', *PRIA*, 96C (1997), 245–96; E. FitzPatrick and C. O'Brien, *The medieval churches of County Offaly* (Dublin, 1998), pp 111–48; M. O'Neill, 'The medieval parish churches in County Meath', *JRSAI*, 132 (2002), 1–56. **42** D. Ó Riain-Raedel, 'Cashel and Germany: the documentary evidence' in Bracken and Ó Riain-Raedel, *Ireland and Europe in the twelfth century*, pp 176–217 at p. 215. **43** H.G. Leask, *Fore, County Westmeath* (Dublin, no date). **44** Stalley, *Cistercian monasteries of Ireland*; see also B. Lynch, *A monastic landscape: the Cistercians in medieval Ireland*

the Premonstratensian canons regular.[45] After many years of relatively little scholarly movement around them, the medieval mendicant orders have received much attention of late, and the key work is Colmán Ó Clabaigh's wonderful survey, *The friars in Ireland, 1224–1540* (Dublin, 2012).[46] Of the four main mendicant orders in medieval Ireland, the Franciscans and Dominicans have fared rather better in the recent historiography than the Augustinian friars and Carmelites.[47]

One of the most significant lacunae in research on Gothic Ireland is the regional study that uses political lordship to define spatial boundaries for analysis. Exceptions are O'Donovan's study of the great lordship of Ormond, Anne-Julie Lafaye's study of Desmond to the west, and my own forthcoming study of the lordship of Meath (modern Cos Meath, Westmeath and Longford).[48]

Stone castles of post-1200 date – fewer than a dozen have pre-1200 fabric – are generally not described as Gothic in the Irish literature even though they have features

(Bloomington, 2010).   **45** T. O'Keeffe, *An Anglo-Norman monastery: Bridgetown Priory and the architecture of the Augustinian canons regular in Ireland* (Kinsale, 1999); idem, 'Augustinian regular canons in twelfth- and thirteenth-century Ireland: history, architecture and identity' in J. Burton and K. Stober (eds), *The regular canons in the medieval British Isles* (Turnhout, 2011), pp 469–84; see also M. Clyne, *Kells Priory, Co. Kilkenny: archaeological excavations by T. Fanning and M. Clyne* (Dublin, 2007); idem, 'The founders and patrons of the Premonstratensian houses in Ireland' in Burton and Stober, *The regular canons in the medieval British Isles*, pp 145–72; idem, 'Archaeological excavations at Holy Trinity Abbey, Lough Key, Co. Roscommon', *PRIA*, 105C (2005), 23–98.   **46** Publications of greater thematic specificity that this compliments and/or updates include F.X. Martin, 'The Augustinian friaries in pre-Reformation Ireland, 1280–1500', *Augustiniana*, 6 (1956), 346–84; P. O'Dwyer, *The Irish Carmelites* (Dublin, 1988); C. Ó Clabaigh, *The Franciscans in Ireland, 1400–1534* (Dublin, 2002); H. Fenning (ed.), *Medieval Irish Dominican studies by B. O'Sullivan* (Dublin, 2009). Recent European scholarship is reviewed by C. Bruzelius, 'The architecture of the mendicant orders in the Middle Ages: an overview of recent literature', *Perspective*, 2 (2012), 365–86.   **47** D. Maher, *Kilcrea Friary: Franciscan heritage in County Cork* (Cork, 1999); M. O'Neill, 'Irish Franciscan friary architecture: late medieval and early modern' in E. Bhreathnach, J. MacMahon OFM and J. McCafferty (eds), *The Irish Franciscans, 1534–1990* (Dublin, 2009), pp 305–27; A. O'Donoghue, 'Mendicant cloisters in Munster', *BAACT*, 34 (2010), 111–31; A.-J. Lafaye, 'Medieval mendicant communities in east Munster: history, archaeology, landscapes' (PhD, UCD, 2012); idem, 'Reconstructing the landscape of the mendicants in east Munster: the Franciscans' in E. Cotter (ed.), *Buttevant: a medieval Anglo-French town in Ireland* (Rathcormac, 2013), pp 67–82; idem, *Mendicant landscapes in medieval Ireland* (Turnhout, forthcoming 2016); A. Hogan, *Kilmallock Dominican priory: an architectural perspective, 1291–1991* (Kilmallock, 1991); A. Halpin and L.A. Buckley, 'Archaeological excavations at the Dominican priory, Drogheda, Co. Louth', *PRIA*, 95C (1995), 175–253; M.F. Hurley and C.M. Sheehan, *Excavations at the Dominican priory, St Mary's of the Isle, Crosse's Green, Cork* (Cork, 1995); J. McKeon, 'The Dominican priory of Saints Peter and Paul, Athenry', *JGAHS*, 61 (2009), 24–56; Y. McDermott, 'Strade Friary: patronage and development at a medieval mendicant friary', *CNM*, 27 (2009), 92–108; idem, 'The priory of the Holy Cross, Cloonshanville: a fourteenth-century Dominican foundation', *RHASJ*, 10 (2009), 22–5; idem, 'Murrisk Friary: a late medieval house of the Austin Friars', *CNM*, 26 (2008), 22–32; K. O'Conor and B. Shanahan, *Roscommon Abbey: a visitor's guide* (Boyle, 2013).   **48** D. O'Donovan, 'Building the Butler lordship' (PhD, TCD, 2010); idem, 'Holycross and the language of Irish late Gothic'; idem, 'Callan and Ormond: architecture of the "middle nation"?' in Ní Ghrádaigh and O'Byrne (eds), *The march in the islands of the medieval west*, pp 171–94; Lafaye, 'Medieval mendicant communities in east Munster'. My Meath study will appear in my forthcoming *The archaeology and architecture of*

that can be so described,[49] but a brief comment on their historiography is in order here. The body of literature on castles is huge, with popular and scholarly works competing for shelf-space in most bookshops, and with many dozens of articles in scholarly journals. Identifying trends in the literature would take up too much space – Terry Barry's bibliographic essay of 2008 should suffice for most readers[50] – but a few books deserve to be mentioned here. The best-known is Leask's *Irish castles and castellated houses*, first published in 1941 and frequently reissued thereafter, sometimes with revisions. It is out of date in matters of interpretation and is far from comprehensive anyway but it remains a much-loved book: Leask's affection for and fascination with castles shines through, and his very distinctive line drawings garland his clear prose. Nobody interested in Irish castles should pass up a chance to own a copy, especially an early edition.[51] Two other books of much more recent vintage cover similar ground: Tom McNeill's *Castles in Ireland* (1997) and David Sweetman's *Medieval castles of Ireland* (1999). The latter, anecdotally the more widely read of the two, updates very substantially the content of Leask's book, making use of data from the Archaeological Survey of Ireland, which its author directed successfully for many years. McNeill's book is the more scholarly work: attention is paid to social-political historical context and to castles outside Ireland, and care is taken with respect to the classification and chronology of castles. Other works to be noted here, finally, are Paul Kerrigan's 1995 study of military architecture from the late Middle Ages on, Hanneke Ronnes' study of 'polite' castle architecture in north-western Europe, including Ireland, the set of five gazetteer-style books published privately by Mike Salter (a dedicated and highly observant amateur whose contribution to castle studies has often been ignored unfairly by many professionals), the small but rising number of monographs on individual castles, and the recent monograph on castles of Co. Wexford – a county well-served by earlier scholars – by the late Billy Colfer.[52] Finally, there has been no book-length study of Irish castles from an exclusively historical perspective. Charles Coulson's *Castles in medieval society: fortresses in England, France and Ireland in the central Middle Ages* (Oxford, 2003) has a very enticing title but Ireland actually features relatively little. Coulson's knowledge of source materials is phenomenal, making this book essential reading for specialists in both castellology and medieval history, but his writing style (especially in the footnotes) is nearly impenetrable, at times even to professional scholars. *Caveat emptor.*

monastic Ireland, 1100–1600. Studies in the Archaeology of Medieval Europe (London, 2016). **49** A laudable exception is J. Lyttleton, 'Gaelic classicism in the Irish midland plantations: an archaeological perspective' in T. Herron and M. Potterton (eds), *Ireland in the Renaissance, c.1540–1660* (Dublin, 2007), pp 231–54. **50** T. Barry, 'The study of medieval Irish castles: a bibliographic survey', *PRIA*, 108C (2008), 115–36. **51** For Leask and his contribution to scholarship, see A. Carey, 'Harold G. Leask: aspects of his work as inspector of National Monuments', *JRSAI*, 134 (2003), 24–35; and T. O'Keeffe, 'Historiography, heritage, inheritance: Irish castellology and Leask's *Irish castles*' in M. Fanning and R. Gillespie (eds), *Print culture and intellectual life in Ireland, 1660–1941* (Dublin, 2003), pp 143–63. **52** T.E. McNeill, *Carrickfergus Castle* (Belfast, 1981); P.M. Kerrigan, *Castles and fortifications in Ireland, 1485–1945* (Cork, 1995); H. Ronnes, *Architecture and elite culture in the United Provinces, England and Ireland, 1500–1700* (Amsterdam, 2006); C. Manning (ed.), *Excavations at Roscrea Castle* (Dublin, 2003); M. Salter, *The*

NEITHER CHURCHES NOT CASTLES

The corpus of upstanding medieval architecture in Ireland is composed mainly of castles, churches and church-related structures, so these are the focus of attention in this book, but other types of above-ground built structures need to be acknowledged here.

Towns founded in the Middle Ages are often rich in medieval fabric. The study of towns is a specialized area in itself, so the topic can be bypassed somewhat here in the knowledge that the principal buildings that one finds in medieval towns are covered elsewhere in this book. The general literature on such towns and on the circumstances of their creation is substantial. Contrary to the common perception that they grew organically, medieval towns were planned, and the late John Bradley's study of such planning endures after three decades as the best introduction to the phenomenon in Ireland.[53] Avril Thomas' two-volume *The walled towns of Ireland* (Dublin, 1992) is an indispensable guide to those towns that were ringed by walls; since any settlement worthy of being called a town in the Middle Ages was walled, it is effectively a study of medieval towns in general. Michael Potterton's monograph on medieval Trim is a model of its type,[54] and one hopes that more towns are given comparable treatment. The Irish Historic Towns Atlas, a project of the Royal Irish Academy, produces large-format fascicles on important Irish towns, and most of the towns that have featured already have medieval phases, some more substantial and significant than others.[55] Unfortunately, two important works on medieval urbanism are generally inaccessible for different reasons: Gearóid Mac Niocaill's valuable compilation of town charters of the Middle Ages, an important companion to archaeological and architectural-historical enquiry, was published with an Irish-language commentary,[56] while the Urban Archaeological Survey, a multi-volume report commissioned three decades ago by the Office of Public Works, has not been circulated widely.

Among the features of towns that are not covered later in this book are town walls. These were built using money that was generated under licence for restricted periods within the towns themselves. The money usually issued from the diversion into

castles of Connacht; *The castles of Leinster*; *The castles of North Munster*; *The castles of South Munster*; *The castles of Ulster* (all Malvern, 2004); C. Manning, *The history and archaeology of Glanworth Castle, Co. Cork: excavations, 1982–4* (Dublin, 2009); A.R. Hayden, *Trim Castle, Co. Meath: excavations, 1995–8* (Dublin, 2011); J. Lyttleton, *Blarney Castle: an Irish tower house* (Dublin, 2011); C. Breen, *Dunluce Castle: history and archaeology* (Dublin, 2012); C. Foley and C. Donnelly, *Parke's Castle, Co. Leitrim: archaeology, history and architecture* (Dublin, 2012); C. Manning, *Clough Oughter Castle, Co. Cavan: archaeology, history and architecture* (Dublin, 2013); B. Colfer, *Wexford castles: landscape, context and settlement* (Cork, 2013); see also J. O'Callaghan, 'Fortified houses of the sixteenth century in south Wexford', *Journal of the Old Wexford Society*, 8 (1980–1), 1–51; A.J. Jordan, 'Date, chronology and evolution of the County Wexford tower house', ibid., 13 (1990–1), 30–81. **53** J. Bradley, 'Planned Anglo-Norman towns in Ireland' in H.B. Clarke and A. Simms (eds), *The comparative history of urban origins in non-Roman Europe* (Oxford, 1985), pp 411–87. **54** M. Potterton, *Medieval Trim: history and archaeology* (Dublin, 2005). **55** Towns published to date are: Armagh, Athlone, Bandon, Belfast, Bray, Carlingford, Carrickfergus, Derry/Londonderry, Downpatrick, Dublin (to 1756), Dundalk, Ennis, Fethard, Kells, Kildare, Kilkenny, Limerick, Longford, Maynooth, Mullingar, Sligo, Trim, Tuam and Youghal. **56** G. Mac Niocaill, *Na*

specific coffers of levies on various goods bought and sold in the towns' markets. Although the Hiberno-Scandinavian towns were walled from early dates, the great era of town wall construction started in the late 1200s when the Anglo-Norman lordship was under pressure from the Gaelic resurgence and there was a particular need to enclose urban settlements for their own protection. Given that construction was funded locally, and that walling projects continued into late medieval times when the security threat was reduced, the walls were surely as expressive of community identity as they were of community fear. Also, by enclosing their towns, urban communities were able to funnel outsider traders through the town gates, thus claiming greater control of their own market spaces.[57] More than fifty Irish towns were walled in the Middle Ages, and some of these, notably Athenry, Fethard (pl. I) and Youghal, have considerable stretches of their walling still surviving. The town founded beside the royal castle on the peninsula of Rindown did not survive the Middle Ages but its wall – a straight wall running from one side of the peninsula to the other – is still standing. Medieval town walls (unlike the early post-medieval town walls of places like Bandon and Derry) were not built in single episodes but were raised in fits and starts, each stage of work corresponding to a murage grant, which was essentially the licence to raise money for the purpose of walling. Unfortunately, it is rarely possible to relate surviving stone fabric to any single grant, and there is no simple rule of thumb to help the non-specialist determine the date, and therefore the associated murage grant, of a section of town wall. In some cases, possibly many, the first walls to have been built under murage grant were earthen ramparts, and they were only replaced in stone once additional grants permitted the collecting of money. One town where earthen ramparts were built and never replaced is Fore; at either end of the tiny town, however, the gates were in stone towers.

Few of the original gateways survive in any of our medieval walled towns, so the matter of their architectural diversity need not detain us. Twin-towered gateways, akin to those found in thirteenth-century castles (see below, pp 250–2), were certainly a feature of big towns like Dublin and Waterford, and the former existence of one at Drogheda is indicated by the survival of St Lawrence's Gate, which was actually not a gateway but a barbican, a protective structure that was *outside* the town but was connected by a bridge with a gateway on the town wall.[58] Most town gates were probably contained within rectangular towers, such as we see today in Carlingford, Athenry and Kilmallock, or were arched entrances flanked by rectangular towers, as in the case of Fethard. Gate towers provided more than mere physical protection. They often had municipal functions, commonly of a judicial nature. This reflected the fact that, in physically occupying and commanding points of entry and egress, they symbolically represented the boundaries between legality and illegality, between right and wrong. Thus, a now-demolished gate house in Carrickfergus' town wall was a

---

buirgéisí, *xx–xv aois* (2 vols, Dublin, 1964).   **57** T. O'Keeffe, 'Townscape as text: the topography of social interaction in Fethard, County Tipperary, AD1300–1700', *IG*, 32:1 (1999), 9–25. **58** Drogheda had a murage grant in 1234 and the design of this structure resembles sufficiently that of the twin-towered entrance to Castleroche, built *c.*1235, that a date in the 1230s is likely

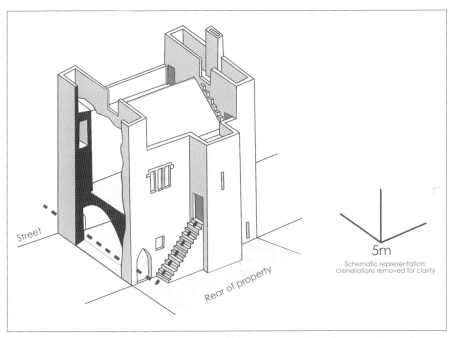

Street

Rear of property

5m

Schematic representation;
crenellations removed for clarity

22 Court Castle, Fethard. The lower storey of this tower was directly accessible without an intervening lobby from the street, suggesting that it had a commercial function. The residential upper storey was accessible only from the back of the property via partly closed-in stairs (O'Keeffe, 'Townscape as text').

prison in the late Middle Ages before becoming a court-house and then a tholsel (literally a room, *sale*, for paying tolls).[59]

Urban castles and churches feature in the chapters that follow. Big towns had big parish churches, but the urban settings are otherwise somewhat incidental to their architecture, so they are accounted for in Chapter 3 below (pp 127–39). Big towns also had monastic communities, especially suburban mendicant communities, but the monastic houses in question are better attended to later in this book. Regarding castles, Anglo-Norman fortresses are found in association with some towns (Dublin, Limerick, Waterford, Carlingford, Kilkenny, Carlow, Roscrea and so on), but their urban settings generally did not impact hugely on their architectural designs, so there is, again, no reason to separate a commentary on them from the discussion below of other Anglo-Norman castles. The situation is slightly different, however, for later medieval castles of tower-house form, so a short comment is necessary here.

(T. O'Keeffe, 'Roesia de Verdun and the building of Castleroche, Co. Louth', *CSGJ*, 28 (2014/15), 122–33).   **59** P. Robinson, *Carrickfergus*, Irish Historic Towns Atlas, 2 (Dublin, 1986), p. 11. Urban tholsels and courts often shared the same buildings, or at least the same sites, either sequentially or contemporaneously. For example, the original tholsel in Kilkenny, demolished *c.*1795, was built in 1507 on the site of an earlier (late fourteenth-century) 'hundred' (or district) court. Already regarded as old in 1614, in 1628 its lower part was colonized by four shops (J. Bradley, *Kilkenny*, Irish Historic Towns Atlas, 10 (Dublin, 2010), p. 15).

5m

23 Kirwan's Lane houses, Galway. This row of houses (with conjectural features shaded) seems typical of the late sixteenth- and early seventeenth-century streetscape of central Galway. Other big Irish towns may have had similar streetscapes near their cores but smaller towns must have had greater numbers of lower-elevation timber and half-timber buildings. Although the door openings on Kirwan Lane are of different sizes (reflecting the different functions of the buildings?), the fact that the walls are continuous from one house to another, and that windows are all at more or less the same level, indicates that these were designed and built as a unit. Urban terraces built in this manner and with this regularity were probably not common until the 1500s at the earliest, and the conventional wisdom – unproven – is that they, like the 'fortified town-houses', were built by merchants (see E. FitzPatrick, M. O'Brien and P. Walsh (eds), *Archaeological investigations in Galway city, 1987–1998* (Bray, 2004)). The drawing is adapted from G. Walsh, 'Kirwan's Lane (92E82): survey' and N. O'Flanagan, 'Kirwan's Lane (93E60): excavation' in idem, pp 180–92, 193–5 respectively. Note: the exact spatial relationship between the two sets of houses is not clear from the published sources of this drawing. For Lynch's Castle, another important property in the city, see D.N. Johnson, 'Lynch's Castle, Galway city: a re-assessment' in C. Manning (ed.), *Dublin and beyond the Pale* (Bray, 1998), pp 211–51.

Tower-houses in urban settings are generally described today as 'fortified town-houses', following Ben Murtagh's guidance in particular.[60] Outwardly similar to rural tower-houses, their location along streets, where they were hemmed in by structures on adjacent property plots, often restricted their size and always prevented their builders from replicating exactly those rural designs that we will see in Chapter 5. Moreover, those towers that contained commercial premises, such as 'Court Castle' in Fethard (fig. 22), required a design that allowed more open access to the lower storey than was sensible in a rural environment.[61]

Murtagh's thesis that 'fortified town houses' were the possessions of merchants is now quite firmly established, and it makes sense to posit that such people had access to the capital needed to build such structures. But there are probably cases to be made for assigning at least some later medieval 'fortified town houses' to members of the urban elite whose money was 'old'; in other words, their capital originated in their

60 More than three dozen examples have been identified by him: see his 'The Bridge Castle, Thomastown, Co. Kilkenny' in G. Mac Niocaill and P.F. Wallace (eds), *Keimelia: studies in medieval archaeology and history in memory of Tom Delaney* (Galway, 1988), pp 536–56 at p. 536. **61** Medieval services-buildings inside and outside towns – shops and warehouses, for example – are little studied as categories, and the low number of examples identified might not be because of a low survival rate but, rather, because archaeologists have not thought deeply enough about how they might be identified in the first instance. An exception is T. McNeill, 'Three medieval buildings in the port of Ardglass, Co. Down', *PRIA*, 105C (2005), 1–21.

possession for several centuries of rural estates, and they used this capital to purchase and develop urban properties whenever opportunity knocked. Such an explanation probably applies to those 'castles' in Fethard that were owned by members of the Everard family around the end of the Middle Ages.[62] Capital was similarly invested in medieval urban stone-built houses for which the prefix 'fortified' is not merited. Some later sixteenth- and early seventeenth-century examples survive. The best survival is Rothe House in Kilkenny, actually a complex of houses from 1594 to 1610 that occupies a burgage plot of the medieval town.[63] The quality of the evidence in Galway is particularly striking (fig. 23).

There are hardly any above-ground remains of medieval rural houses. Those that have been revealed in archaeological excavation were quite modest structures. Although we must be mindful of the danger of circular thinking, the smallest ones were probably the possessions of the servile tenantry while the larger and better-built examples, especially those inside moated sites,[64] probably belonged to free tenants – tenants who had freeholds and therefore rights to pass properties to next-of-kin – and therefore merit the adjective 'manorial'. The two later medieval stone houses in Kilmalkedar, the so-called 'Chancellor's House' and 'St Brendan's House', are such rare survivals that we cannot ascertain the typicality of either (fig. 24).[65] Although the analysis of the excavated houses falls outside the scope of this book, it is useful just to note that most of these houses must have been single storey, with no more than a loft to create some extra space. How long could they have lasted before they needed rebuilding? Houses with stone foundations could have had their superstructures rebuilt regularly, leaving no strong archaeological trace, but houses that were entirely of organic material could hardly have survived more than a generation. Such houses were

62 O'Keeffe, *Fethard*, Irish Historic Towns Atlas, 13 (Dublin, 2003). **63** K.M. Lanigan, *Rothe House, Kilkenny* (Kilkenny, 1967). For other houses in the town, see Bradley, *Kilkenny* and G. Keane, 'The early modern townhouses of Kilkenny city, 1550–1650' (MA, UCD, 2010). Other inland towns with rich evidence include Kilmallock and Fethard: see respectively H.G. Leask, 'Sarsfield's House, Kilmallock', *JCHAS*, 46 (1941), 73–5; and O'Keeffe, *Fethard*. **64** Moated sites are ramparted enclosures of square or rectangular plan that are surrounded by moats (some still water-filled), and are mainly later thirteenth century; see T.B. Barry, *Medieval moated sites of south-east Ireland* (Oxford, 1977). There is an argument that their construction, and therefore also of the houses within them, should be attributed to English settlers who were farming previously uncultivated land in order to provide food for export to Edward I's warring armies in France and elsewhere; see T. O'Keeffe, 'Aristocrats, immigrants and entrepreneurs: settlers and settlement initiatives in late 13th-century Ireland', *Ruralia*, 2 (1998), 87–96. **65** See S.P. Ó Ríordáin and J. Hunt, 'Medieval dwellings at Caheraguillamore, County Limerick', *JRSAI*, 72 (1942), 37–63; P.D. Sweetman, 'Excavations of a medieval moated site at Rigsdale, County Cork', *PRIA*, 81C (1981), 103–205; R. Cleary, 'Excavations at Lough Gur, Co. Limerick: pt II', *JCHAS*, 87 (1982), 77–106; C. Foley, 'Excavation at a medieval settlement site in Jerpointchurch townland, Co. Kilkenny', *PRIA*, 89C (1989), 5–12; Cuppage, *Dingle Peninsula*, pp 317–21; K.D. O'Conor, *The archaeology of medieval rural settlement in Ireland* (Dublin, 1998), pp 48–57; H. Schweitzer, 'A medieval farmstead at Moneycross Upper, Co. Wexford' in C. Corlett and M. Potterton (eds), *Rural settlement in medieval Ireland in the light of recent archaeological excavations* (Dublin, 2009), pp 175–88; A. Quinn, 'Mondaniel 3 – undefended rural farmstead' in K. Hanley and M.F. Hurley (eds), *Generations: the archaeology of five national road schemes* (Dublin, 2013), pp 252–7; E. Cotter, 'Ballinvinny South AR16: moated settlement' in ibid., pp 258–64.

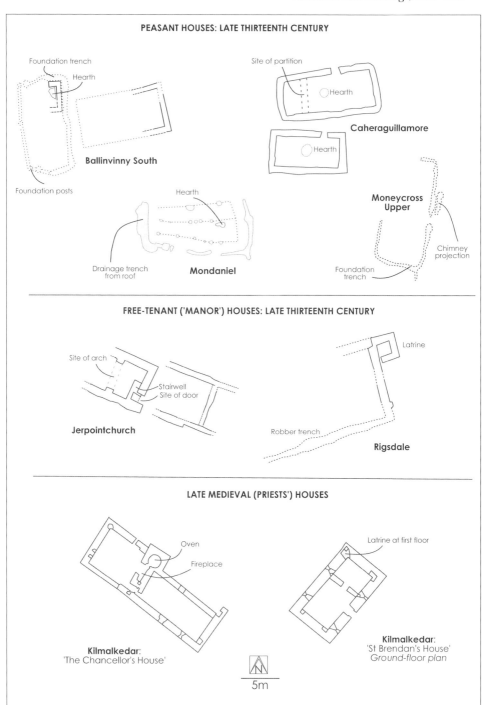

24 Rural (non-fortified) medieval houses, from the thirteenth to the sixteenth century. It is worth noting that the houses reveal no preferred orientation, although doorways tend to be sheltered from Ireland's prevailing westerly winds.

certainly in the majority: houses on posts covered with straw are recorded at the start of the fourteenth century at Palmerstown and Rosbercon, for example.[66] There is little evidence in the excavation reports to suggest lengthy settlement on the rural sites, so houses may have been abandoned after their natural decay started. The relatively low quality of many of the houses becomes even more noteworthy when one considers how few are known to us: archaeological excavations during the Celtic Tiger boom produced far fewer hitherto-unknown houses than one might have expected, leaving us less familiar with the rural houses of the high Middle Ages than we are with houses of either the Neolithic or the Bronze Age. What does this say about the population density of medieval rural Ireland?

Medieval bridges are the only substantial features to survive of the medieval inland transportation infrastructure, and their architecture has been discussed by Peter O'Keeffe and Tom Simington.[67] Movement along the coast was aided by lighthouses, and the one on Hook Head, documented in the thirteenth century, is a remarkable survival.[68] Less spectacular but almost as remarkable are two monuments almost 100m apart at Mornington. A narrow sixteenth-century battlemented turret called the Maiden's Tower and an undated but probably contemporary obelisk called the Lady's Finger aided vessels heading into the Boyne Estuary: when the latter was lined up against the former, a ship knew it was on target for the central channel of the river.[69]

The survival rate of medieval agricultural buildings in Ireland, very numerous originally,[70] is extremely poor and the scholarly literature on their morphology is matchingly thin. Non-descript fragments in or against the walls of the bawns of some tower-houses are probably the remains of such buildings, but the stables, barns and pens of the countryside have either disappeared or have been gobbled up by (and therefore remain undetected in) later structures. And, of course, many were of timber anyway: for example, at the start of the fourteenth century there was 'a sheep-cot on logs covered with straw' at Newtown Jerpoint, and it was already in bad condition.[71] Timber could be recycled – in 1306–7 at Forth (Castlemore) 'a grange ... of 10 weak forks [crucks]' was almost fully demolished and was of no value apart from the crucks, which could be reused[72] – but there would have been a limit to how often timbers could be reused before ending up as firewood. Archaeological excavation might eventually fill out the picture for such structures, but the omens are not good if the paltry remains of the medieval granary excavated near St Michan's Church in Dublin are any indication.[73] The loss of substantial above-ground remains of medieval mills from the thirteenth century is especially to be regretted. Almost every manor had a mill, and in areas of good arable, where the volume of grain processed for export as well as local consumption would have been enormous during the economic boom of

66 *CDI, 1302–7*, nos 189, 194. 67 P. O'Keeffe and T. Simington, *Irish stone bridges: history and heritage* (Dublin, 1991). 68 B. Colfer, 'The tower of Hook', *JWHS*, 10 (1984–5), 69–78. 69 N. Brady and E. Pollard, 'Archaeology and development in a maritime context, highlighting Drogheda and the Boyne Estuary as a case study' in H.J. Jamieson and J. Eogan (eds), *Training and practice for modern day archaeologists* (New York, 2012), pp 237–70 at p. 259. 70 There is a very good documentary record of agricultural structures attached to monastic farms (granges): see especially the information contained in charters that have been edited with an excellent analysis by Arlene Hogan, *The priory of Llanthony Prima and Secunda in Ireland, 1172–1541* (Dublin, 2008), passim. 71 *CDI, 1302–7*, no. 188. 72 Ibid., no. 617. 73 G. Dawkes, 'Medieval building

the later 1200s, the mills must have been substantial structures, with stone foundations if not also superstructures. Fragments of monastic mills do survive, some quite complete (like at Moyne). They were not particularly sophisticated structurally but they presumably sufficed for processing grain for monastic consumption. Given that medieval millers must have had a good eye for the best river meanders from which to cut mill-races, the likelihood is that many of the water-powered corn mills of the late 1700s and 1800s occupy medieval mill sites, their races being re-cuts of the originals. Windmills were presumably quite common also, and were probably of post form, with each mill supported by and rotated on an earthfast timber post. Being of organic material, none survives. The low, circular-plan mound of earth that was banked up against the post of a mill of *c.*1270 survives beneath a seventeenth-century stone tower-mill at Rindown.[74] It is likely that many other tower-mills of post-medieval date occupy earlier sites, the tell-tale signs being the low – sometimes imperceptibly low – mounds on which some of those later mills stand (as at the appropriately named Windmillhill near Rathcoole).

We have many documentary references to 'curtileges'/'curtilages'. Although not strictly architectural, they seem to have been a common feature of the built environment, and some may survive and simply await identification. A late sixteenth-century definition probably captures the essence of a curtilage: 'A curtylage is a lytell croft or court, or place of easment to put in catell for a tyme, or to ley in woode, cole or tymbre, or suche other thynges necessary for housholde'.[75] The term was used from the thirteenth century but examples of its use in Ireland seem mainly to be fourteenth century, although that may be a consequence of the differential survival of written sources. Some of the surviving historical references make clear the association of a curtilage with a house, while others give the impression of a haggard or a walled garden separate from a house.[76] From 1309 we have a record of flax and hemp in one curtilage.[77] From 1311 we have Symon le Deyer of Leyghlyn's assertion in a law case that

> he bought a curtilage contiguous to the highway, and at the time of the purchase the highway against the curtilage was three perches broad, and afterwards he let the curtilage lie waste, and people crossing made a way through the said curtilage, and so of his curtilage they made as it were a highway for about half a year; [and] that he built a mound around the curtilage as he had full right.[78]

In 1341 it is recorded that the castle of Aherlow had 'a curtilege and a garden adjoining, [and] a dove-cote in the same curtilege'.[79]

Dovecotes

The Aherlow reference brings us to a type of agricultural building that does survive: the dovecote or *columbarium*, literally a pigeon-house.[80] The number of extant

survival', *AI*, 21:4 (2007), 24–5.   **74** J.A. Claffey, 'Rindoon windmill tower' in H. Murtagh (ed.), *Irish midland studies* (Athlone, 1980), pp 84–8.   **75** 'Curtilage, n.', OED.   **76** *RBO*, pp 24, 25–6, 56–7, 61, 62, 64.   **77** *CJRI, 1308–14*, p. 122.   **78** Ibid., pp 172–3.   **79** *CGR*, p. 115. **80** Doves and pigeons are effectively the same, with the latter simply larger.

25 The dovecote of Ballybeg Priory (Augustinian). Built into the fabric of this large cylindrical tower, 5m high and 4.6m in internal diameter, were eleven rows of roosting boxes, with thirty-two boxes per row. Above the boxes was a dome vault with a central aperture at the top through which the birds flew in and out, safe from predators. The tower was entered at ground level through a low and narrow doorway, and this would have been kept secure, again to keep out natural predators; dovecote doorways were always very small, possibly to minimize sudden light-blasts on the roosting birds when opened. Pigeons which were boxed close to the ground in dovecots could be easily grabbed by monks or manorial servants, but those higher up in towers of Ballybeg's size were accessible by ladders attached to revolving poles or potences set into plinths. One cannot see Ballybeg's great dome vault from the outside because the vertical walls of the tower rise over it. This is unusual, and one explanation is that the high walls sheltered the roof-top opening from driving rain (thus helping to keep the roosting boxes dry) while also providing a place for the birds to perch safely. Ballybeg had a doorway at roof level, presumably accessible via an external wooden ladder, and this might have allowed a member of the monastic community access to the manure left by the perching birds.

26 The plinth of the potence in the dovecote of Fore Priory (Benedictine). As at Ballybeg, this dovecote was very close to the east end – the main liturgical end – of the church, and one can easily imagine the birds sitting on (and soiling) the outside sills of the windows that illuminated the altar.

examples is still low: many dozens of old dovecotes survive in Ireland today but it is actually difficult to find more than a dozen of *certain* (rather than presumed) medieval date. Although not particularly valuable in a monetary sense,[81] pigeons were prized for their meat and eggs, both of which were consumed in monasteries and high-status secular residences, for their manure, which fertilized small monastic and manorial gardens, for their blood, which had potential medicinal uses, and for their down and feathers, both of which were ideal bed-fillers.[82] Value was not restricted to the birds themselves: the dovecote of Kilmaclenine, for example, a small settlement owned by the diocese of Cloyne, returned a rent of 12*d*. in the thirteenth century.[83] The extant free-standing medieval examples in Ireland are almost all associated with monastic houses, as in Adare, Ballybeg (fig. 25), Fore (fig. 26), Kilcooly and Monasternagalliagh-duff; incidentally, the latter two dovecots have traditions of having been penitential prisons. There is a rare survival of a non-monastic dovecote of medieval date at Kiltinan, but the documentary record suggests that such 'secular' dovecotes were actually very common: there are records, for example, of criminal cases taken against

81 The forty-five 'doves' stolen from a dovecot in Lismore in 1314 were valued at 22*d*. (*CJRI, 1308–14*, p. 314).   **82** J. Hansell and P. Hansell, *Doves and dovecotes* (Princes Risborough, 1988). **83** P. MacCotter and K. Nicholls, *The pipe roll of Cloyne* (Cloyne, 1996), p. 249.

people who broke into privately owned dovecotes.[84] Ownership of such dovecotes could sometimes be shared among several people: for example, three parties shared a dovecote in a Kilkenny croft (garden) in 1328.[85] One occasionally finds clusters of roosting spaces for pigeons in the walls of medieval buildings. Although there are apparent medieval examples, as in Trim, in most cases these are likely to be installations of the post-medieval period (probably the eighteenth century) rather than original medieval features. In Kildare, for example, parts of the castles of Carrick and Oughterard were clearly altered to provide such roosting spaces, while in Carlinstown a circular bawn-tower of *c*.1600 was fully converted into a dovecote more than a century after it was built.

PRIMARY SOURCES FOR THE STUDY OF BUILDINGS

This is a book about 'reading' buildings, which are primary sources in themselves, not about reading medieval documentary sources in which buildings feature. Our consideration of written sources must therefore be brief. Philomena Connolly's *Medieval record sources* (2002) and Katherine Simms' *Medieval Gaelic sources* (2009), both in the same series as this book, are essential surveys of such sources and invaluable guides to their use.[86]

Briefly, although a huge number of records was lost in the destruction of the Public Records Office in the Four Courts in 1922, a substantial volume of medieval source material survives. Many of the English sources are of an 'official' nature, generated by and for government, which explains how they ended up in a public records office in the first instance. Medieval wills, deeds and receipts – documents generated by and for individuals and familial or religious groups – survive but are in short supply relative to what must once have existed; many must have perished when medieval households and religious communities were broken up in the turmoil of the later sixteenth and seventeenth centuries. Transcripts or summaries of those medieval documents that survived the Middle Ages have been published over the past century and more, including a good number of those lost forever in 1922. The reader can find many of the more useful ones in the list of abbreviations above (pp 13–14). Many are now available online: Internet Archive is always a useful place to look, especially for copies of nineteenth-century calendars, but the main on-line repositories are curated by the Irish Manuscripts Commission and by University College Cork's CELT (Corpus of Electronic Texts) project.[87] The serious student of medieval architecture needs to be familiar with these published sources, not because they contain architectural information – they very rarely do – but because they often contain relevant contextual information. Thus, for example, if one seeks to make the fullest sense possible of a

84 *CJRI, 1295–1303*, pp 19, 187; *1305–7*, p. 489; *1308–14*, pp 183, 277.　**85** *COD, 1172–1350*, p. 258. **86** A.J. Fletcher, 'The annals and chronicles of Dublin: an overview', *MD*, 8 (2008), 194–212, is a valuable overview of primary sources for the capital.　**87** archive.org/index.php; www. irishmanuscripts.ie/servlet/Controller?action=digitisation_backlist; celt.ucc.ie/index.html, accessed 6 Dec. 2012.

ruined castle in one's neighbourhood, a trawl through the indexes of the published medieval sources for references to it (or, rather, its townland name) is essential. One should never expect too much success from such a trawl – undocumented places and buildings far outnumber documented ones – but it might be possible to determine, for example, who owned land in the vicinity of the castle at different times in the Middle Ages.

Needless to say, finding a reference is only the start. Making use of a reference is more difficult. A record of a castle at a certain place in, say, 1250, only means that a castle had been built by that date. It might not be the castle that is still there. Equally, it might be, but it might not have been built by the person whose name features alongside it in 1250. Similarly, a scatter of references to a castle at the one place over a period of several decades might not refer to the same castle; it may have been rebuilt during those years and no record made. And what does one conclude when a place is mentioned in an historical source at a certain date but no mention is made of a castle or a church and yet there is one present in the landscape? Had it not been built yet, or had its presence simply not been relevant to the matter noted in the historical reference? These are common difficulties one faces when moving between buildings and documents, and resolving them really requires the capacity to 'read' the architecture. As a rule of thumb, the more important a building or building complex in the political or ecclesiastical life of medieval Ireland, or the more important its builder or patron, the more likely there is to be at very least a passing reference to it in the published sources. And, of course, the more likely it is that earlier scholars have already written about it. As a second rule of thumb, the later the date of construction the *less* likely there is to be a reference to a building: most castles, monastic foundations and, to a lesser degree, parish churches of the twelfth and thirteenth centuries are recorded, albeit with little elaboration in many cases, but the great majority of new buildings of the fifteenth and sixteenth centuries, except monastic ones, are not mentioned at all in surviving contemporary sources. Relatively few tower-houses, for example, are documented until after the Middle Ages.

The ease with which published medieval sources can be accessed and read contrasts with the difficulty of dealing with unpublished or manuscript-only sources. One normally needs palaeographical skills to transcribe original medieval manuscript material, and, for most documents up to the seventeenth century, some competence with Latin. Until such time as transcripts and translations of all medieval source materials are published, architectural historians specializing in the Middle Ages will remain unsure that they have accounted for every single surviving record of a building or pertaining to a building's immediate historical context. Like many scholars working in this field, I have learned to live with that uncertainty, presuming that any historical information of which I am unaware will not contradict what can be said about a building based on the sources that are more freely available. In an ideal world, scholars from different disciplines with different skill-bases – archaeologists, art and architectural historians, economic historians, historians of medieval administration – would always work together, marrying their particular skills to understand medieval culture across a range of contexts. But it is not an ideal world.

What about post-medieval sources? Only a brief comment is possible here. Late sixteenth- and seventeenth-century sources, particularly those associated with the survey and redistribution of land in the middle of the 1600s, are most useful for alerting us to lost buildings.[88] Another late seventeenth-century source of great value is Thomas Dineley's record of his tour of Ireland in 1680–1.[89] A good number of the buildings that Dineley took the trouble to draw are ones that have since disappeared, and we are fortunate that he had both a good eye for buildings and a reasonable (if rather scratchy) drawing style. The eighteenth century was the great century of antiquarianism, and many medieval buildings – again, many of them missing or more ruined today – were depicted by such luminaries as Austin Cooper, Daniel Grose, Francis Grose, Gabriel Beranger and Francis Place. Many of the drawings have been (re-)published in recent years, with Peter Harbison the most assiduous modern compiler and commentator.[90] The nineteenth century is, of course, the century of the Ordnance Survey. The Ordnance Survey letters – the correspondence of John O'Donovan and others 'from the field' as they encountered antiquities – contain a huge amount of information on buildings.[91] Finally, the nineteenth century is also the era of the earliest photography of buildings, and old photographs are a useful source of information for buildings since destroyed or at least heavily altered.[92]

88 Some depictions of buildings in the late sixteenth century in Sir Thomas Stafford's *Pacata Hibernia; or, A history of the wars in Ireland during the reign of Queen Elizabeth*, published in 1633 and republished in a new edition by Standish O'Grady (London, 1896), are convincing, others are not; the drawing made of Enniskillen Castle in 1594 is certainly convincing (see E. Halpin, 'Excavations at Enniskillen Castle, Co. Fermanagh', *UJA*, 57 (1994), 119–44 at 124). The main seventeenth-century sources, the Civil Survey of 1654–6 and the Books of Survey and Distribution of 1636–1703 (for Clare, Galway, Mayo and Roscommon), are available online (www.irishmanuscripts.ie); Books of Survey and Distribution for another twenty-five counties are in the NLI. The Down Survey maps of 1656–8 include small drawings of buildings, some of them stylized and others quite realistic, and are available online at downsurvey.tcd.ie/index.html.   **89** Extracts were published in *The Journal of the Kilkenny and South-East of Ireland Archaeological Society*, 1:1 (1856), 143–6, 170–88; ibid., 4:2 (1862), 38–52, 103–9; ibid., 6:1 (1867), pp 73–91, 176–204; *JRSAI*, 43 (1913), 275–309.   **90** The literature is substantial and requires a far more comprehensive listing than is possible here. Here is a sample: L. Price (ed.), *An eighteenth-century antiquary: the sketches, notes and diaries of Austin Cooper (1759–1830)* (Dublin, 1942); R. Stalley (ed.), *Daniel Grose, c.1766–1838/The antiquities of Ireland: a supplement to Francis Grose* (Dublin, 1991); P. Harbison (ed.), *Beranger's views of Ireland* (Dublin, 1991); C. Manning, 'Some unpublished Austin Cooper illustrations', *JIA*, 9 (1998), 127–34; P. Harbison (ed.), *'Our treasure of antiquities': Beranger and Bigari's antiquarian sketching tour of Connacht in 1779* (Dublin, 2002); idem, 'Barralet and Beranger's antiquarian sketching tour through Wicklow and Wexford in the autumn of 1780', *PRIA*, 104C (2004), 131–90; D. Ó Riain-Raedel, '"Rambles through the South of Ireland": an antiquarian's journey', *JCHAS*, 113 (2008), 40–52.   **91** For fifteen years Michael Herity has assiduously been editing and publishing county-by-county transcriptions of these, with commentaries, through Four Masters Press.   **92** For a general guide, see L. Kelly, *Photographs and photography in Irish local history* (Dublin, 2008). Students of Clare's historic architecture are especially well served by an extensive corpus of old images published online by the county library (www.clarelibrary.ie).

VISITING BUILDINGS

Primary historical research is normally carried out in places where one can sit comfortably, tap on a laptop, and break for coffee. In many repositories the simple filling-in of a docket will ensure the archival material is even delivered straight to one's desk. The business of conducting research 'in the field', literally, is usually more arduous. Buildings that are in state care, or still in use (churches and cathedrals), or privately owned but open to the public, can be visited with some comfort, although there are caveats, as we will see. But most of our medieval buildings are to some degree in an active state of ruination and are therefore potentially dangerous, so visiting them and then making sense of them requires physical effort.

It is generally the case that the more ruined or neglected a medieval building the less has been written about it already, and the more dependent the researcher will be on his or her resources. Finding the means of access to such buildings is often a challenge in itself, even when the researcher sees the walls from his/her car. It is sometimes necessary to knock on doors for guidance. It is always good manners to contact a landowner when a building is on private land, although there are many privately owned sites to which there are well-worn pathways, suggesting that the sites are regularly visited and that the landowners concerned are quite sanguine about it. It is a judgment call, case by case. If necessary, finding a landowner's name and place of residence is usually relatively easy once one has arrived in the vicinity of a site. If the researcher knows that there is a 'no trespassing' sign that clearly relates to a site or to the land around a site, or is travelling some distance to a site and is alert to the possibility of a wasted trip, it is prudent to contact a landowner a few days in advance. It is possible to get the name with a little forward planning: a phone call to a local post office or to a named person on the website of a local history or heritage group will usually yield a name; even if no contact can be made before a visit, it is good to be able to report the effort to the landowner should he or she suddenly appear. Landowners fear liability, so researchers should be ready with assurances that they will take no risks and take full responsibility for their own safety; such assurances carry no legal weight, as landowners will know, but they put minds at ease. It probably goes without saying, but gates found closed should be closed again, fields with standing crops should be walked around, not through, and animals should not be disturbed. Bulls are rarely encountered but nobody should ever cross a field, even an empty one, without knowing what one looks like from a distance!

Leaving aside those that are signposted, the easiest medieval buildings to find and gain access to are the ruined parish churches in churchyards that are still in use (even if only occasionally). One often finds these churches very decayed, ivy-strangled and generally unrewarding, although some sense can be made of even the most fragmentary remains. Searching in the grass around such churches will often turn up architectural fragments (window and door jambs, window sills and so on) that have been used as grave-markers. Many churchyards in which burial activity ceased in the nineteenth century or earlier still have pathways to them, but they are more likely to be isolated and/or neglected sites today. They are so rarely visited that the difficulties of getting to them and of moving around them is offset by the fun of searching for fragments that nobody else has spotted. The better preserved examples of monastic foundations – abbeys, friaries, priories, convents and so on – are generally in state care and are therefore accessible (to a point). Of those that are not in such care, the foundations with churches that served parochial functions in the Middle Ages are the ones most likely to have still-used graveyards around them, and these are generally accessible. Such churchyards will invariably yield reused architectural fragments when searched: the churches themselves were usually larger and therefore architecturally richer than parish churches, and have often shed a larger selection of carved stones. Also, there were buildings other than churches in these architectural complexes, and some of these would have had carved stone as well: cloister arcade fragments, for example, can sometimes be found in such churchyards of former monastic houses.

Finally, National Monuments in state care are often the most interesting examples of their type and are usually fairly easy to find. Many are open to the public and one is allowed explore them without a guide; a small number have guides and unless one can argue one's expertise one has to stick to the guided tour. The downside of medieval buildings in state care is the general inaccessibility of the interiors or parts of the interiors of a significant number of them. Tower-houses are normally under lock and key, but so too are some churches, as are spaces (small rooms and stairwells, and even whole courtyards) in larger buildings and building complexes. Few of these have keys that one can obtain without considerable advance planning. This curatorial policy is obviously driven by public liability concerns and even fears of vandalism (or theft, in cases where rooms are used for storage of loose fragments of carved stone), but it is at very least ironic – I prefer to think of it as scandalous – that buildings 'saved' for the nation are often the ones that the nation can least enjoy. There should be selected days in the year when every national monument is open.

CHAPTER 2

Approaches to the study of medieval buildings

The pleasure, even thrill, of exploring a medieval building has a limit: there is a point at which there is no physical space left to explore, and it might take only a few minutes to reach that point. The capacity to make sense of a building brings a longer-lasting pleasure, precisely because it gives a greater purpose to exploration: after all, what exactly, if not knowledge and understanding, are we really looking for when we explore? Architectural historians have a range of analytical techniques by which they can generate knowledge about buildings, and they are reviewed here.

STYLISTIC ANALYSIS

Style is a complex, multi-layered and multi-scalar concept, and it appears in many guises throughout this book. It is perhaps sufficient in the context of this section to restrict the comment on style to a brief review of the stylistic features to which the architectural historian's eye always drifts when first encountering a medieval building: the arch types that are associated with doors and windows. Knowing the basic arch shapes and their chronology is the bread-and-butter of architectural history (fig. 27), although there is, of course, much more to dating a building or part of a building than simply looking at the arches and deciding on their originality or otherwise. Plain round arches and pointed arches have the longest chronologies. Context is critical to fine-dating arches of these two particular types, but there are other indicators, as demonstrated here using two late medieval examples (figs 28, 29).

FABRIC ANALYSIS

Even without a specialist knowledge of architectural styles, it is often possible to work out from observation of stonework, from patterns and states of decay, and even from the variety of stone types, if a building is single-phase or multi-phase. It is not always an easy task, however, and evidence can be ambiguous or misleading. The mid-sixteenth-century Castlerea Castle, for example, is a single-phase structure but has no fewer than three different stone types – sandstone, limestone and quartz – in its walls. Medieval Irish builders were usually faced with hard stones like limestone and granite so they generally favoured roughly coursed rubble-centred construction for both initial phases and repair-work. Their structural and aesthetic achievements with such stones were considerable – locally sourced flat stones were used to notably exquisite affect at

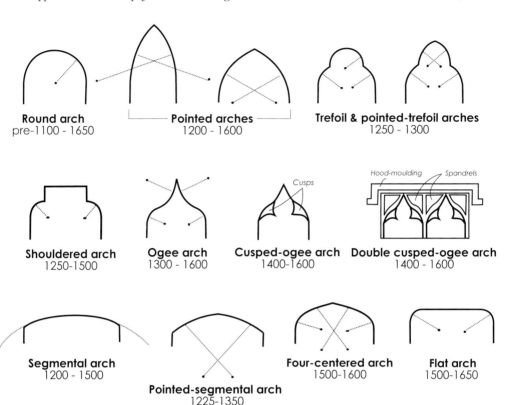

27 Medieval arch-types. All arches are formed of arcs, and the radii of the informing circles for each arch-type are shown here. The date-ranges given here are based on the *majority* of examples.

Carrigafoyle and some other coastal tower-houses in Kerry and Clare – but it does mean that repairs are not always apparent.

Ashlar, in which blocks of equal size with 90° corner-angles have very precise horizontal coursing, appeared for the first time in Ireland around 1100, and was especially popular for round towers, as witness the examples in Cashel and Ardmore (fig. 30). Some pre-Romanesque churches such as Agha, which was built with small granite boulders laid in regular courses, reveal an ashlar sensibility. Stone that was cut and laid so precisely was probably not rendered; on the contrary, it seems likely that such stone was left exposed so that spectators could appreciate the masons' craftsmanship as much as they appreciated the metalworkers'. Ashlar-walled and stone-roofed, Cormac's Chapel in Cashel, although modelled on one or more substantial Romanesque buildings outside Ireland, might even have appeared like an enlarged reliquary casket to spectators on its consecration in 1134. Ashlar construction was generally eschewed by Gothic builders in Ireland, but the sharp limestone fabric of many buildings, especially of the later Middle Ages, would qualify with a less dogmatically enforced definition.

28 The façade of late medieval Desmond Castle (a.k.a. 'French Prison'), Kinsale, with its pointed-arched entrance doorway. Typical of late medieval architecture is the manner in which the entire doorway was composed of a small number of large stones, with the arch made of only two stones meeting at the apex.

29 (*opposite*) The fifteenth-century west door of Lorrha Priory church (Augustinian). The actual doorway has a pointed arch but its hood-moulding is ogee-form. It is decorated with crockets – small leaves that are curled downwards – and it has classic late Gothic crocketed pinnacles at either side. Such pinnacles, not always crocketed, are found on a good number of late medieval

church doorways and canopied tombs in Ireland. This doorway has two other interesting features. One is the small carving of a woman's head at the apex of the arch. She wears a headdress: medieval women customarily covered their heads, and a headdress was obligatory in churches and in the company of clergy in medieval culture. This particular carving is thought locally to be a representation of the wife of Walter de Burgh, the earl of Ulster who founded the nearby Dominican priory in the late thirteenth century, but that is highly unlikely; perhaps the carving alludes to the fact that church doorways were settings for two rites of passage in medieval women's lives, churching and marriage (see below, p. 96). The other feature, which is more unusual, is the pair of deep recesses on either side of the central pinnacle. Lorrha had relics, including the hand of the local saint, Ruadhán, which was preserved in a silver case. It is hard to think that these recesses were not for the display of relics, perhaps on feastdays (as well as churching and wedding days?).

30 The ashlar masonry of the base of the later twelfth-century round tower at Ardmore, one of the latest and by far the most elegant example of its type in Ireland.

Distinctively coloured or textured stones were often chosen for architectural features between the late twelfth and the fourteenth century. One commonly finds that the original doorways, windows and other 'sculpted' features (capitals, for example, and even quoin-stones at the corners of buildings) of Anglo-Norman buildings are made using lighter-coloured stone than is found in the surrounding masonry. Close inspection will normally show these are soft, finely grained stones, capable of being carved without flaking or shattering. In east Ulster, local Cultra limestone, a soft, pale-yellow limestone, was commonly used in buildings and even in tomb sculpture up to the fourteenth century.[1] Tufa, another soft stone, was used in the Ulster castles of Dundrum and Greencastle (Down), and in a small cluster of sites in Kildare (Maynooth Castle, and Furness and Oughterard churches).[2] The builders of Ballyderown Castle chose a local arkosic limestone, also soft and warm-coloured, for their windows and quoins.[3] Many patrons chose to import soft stone. Fine-grained, creamy-coloured oolitic limestone was transported from southern England for use in sites in south-east Ireland, especially in coastal and river-valley places. Such stone was quarried almost entirely from Dundry Hill in Somerset (pl. II), but some Doulting, Bath and Painswick stone, also from the English West Country, and even some Caen stone from northern France, have also been identified.[4] The date at which the importation of stone ended is not clear, but the practice was most common in the 1200s.

In the late Middle Ages cut-stone architectural features like doorways and windows were often highlighted visually by the application of lime-and-sand harling (the coarsely made top-coat of a render) to the surfaces *around* them, leaving their own surfaces fully visible (fig. 31).[5] Render itself provided water-proofing to the walls to which it was applied.[6] Its colour depended on its chemical content, but that colour was presumably white or near-white in most cases.[7] It might also have improved the brightness of interiors by reflecting light. Restored medieval buildings that have been re-rendered or re-harled with proper materials look distinctly odd to modern eyes because we are so accustomed to seeing exposed stonework, but close examination of all bare-stoned medieval buildings will actually reveal some traces of original render.

The way in which stone is dressed can also be used for dating purposes. Extremely closely set striations in relatively soft stones, the result of saw action and honing down, is often described as 'diagonal dressing' or 'diagonal tooling' and is generally characteristic of the thirteenth century (fig. 32). By contrast, small pock-marks made with chisels are distinctively later medieval (fig. 33), with some examples dating to the early

1 T.E. McNeill, *Anglo-Norman Ulster* (Edinburgh, 1980), p. 45.　**2** J. Knight, 'Medieval imported building stone and utilised stone in Wales and Ireland' in C. Manning (ed.), *From ringforts to fortified houses: studies on castles and other monuments in honour of David Sweetman* (Bray 2007), pp 143–54 at p. 151.　**3** T. O'Keeffe, 'An early Anglo-Norman castle at Ballyderown, County Cork', *JRSAI*, 114 (1984), 48–56 at 49.　**4** D.M. Waterman, 'Somersetshire and other foreign building stone in medieval Ireland, *c.*1175–1400', *UJA*, 33 (1970), 63–75. Some stone from Purbeck in Devon, much desired in England from Roman times, has been identified in Ireland (M. McMahon, 'Archaeological excavation at the site of the Four Courts, Inns Quay, Dublin', *PRIA*, 88C (1988), 271–319 at 317).　**5** Jean Farrelly has usefully collected examples of late decorative plasterwork on the exteriors of buildings: 'Decorative render in the late sixteenth/early seventeenth century' in Manning, *From ringforts to fortified houses*, pp 237–48.　**6** The positive effect of rendering on the 'internal climate' of Ballyportry Castle, one such re-harled castle, has been noted (K. Morton, 'Irish medieval wall paintings' in J. Ludlow and N. Jameson (eds), *Medieval Ireland: Barryscourt lectures I–X* (Kinsale, 2004), pp 311–49 at p. 326).　**7** A late medieval Irish poem refers to 'white-gleaming castles' (Leerssen, *Mere Irish and fior-Ghael*, p. 181).

31 Remains of a late sixteenth-century window in Roscommon Castle outlined in plaster. This belongs to the phase of extensive repair and modernization overseen by Sir Nicholas Malby, governor of Connacht, when he was granted the (originally thirteenth-century) castle in 1578.

32 The top surface of an *ex situ* stiff-leaf capital from Bridgetown Priory (Augustinian), maximum length (left–right) 40cm. Though not intended to be seen, this surface is carefully dressed in the characteristic thirteenth-century manner (see also fig. 6, top). Note the two straight lines incised by the mason at 90° to each other: this was to align the top of the stone with the first stone of the arch that sprang from it originally.

33 Dressed-stone window-jambs from St Nicholas' Church, Galway, with characteristic late medieval decorative chisel marks comprised of rows of closely set dots. The rather cruder hammer-dressed stones on the right-hand-side of the image were prepared for rendering – the plaster remained attached to the small surface holes – and are certainly late medieval, although this technique of hammer-dressing survived into the post-medieval period. This image shows the dreadful curse that is modern cement re-pointing: apart from being an inappropriate and indeed harmful medium in what were originally mortar-bonded walls, the straight lines make it impossible for the architectural historian to spot evidence of medieval fabric alteration.

34 A detail of the only remaining external doorway from the early seventeenth-century phase of Loughmoe Castle (see pls XII, XIII, fig. 134). This is a late example of such decorative dressing.

years of the seventeenth century (fig. 34). Masons' marks, which are small, generally incised, motifs (of cross-, interlace- or letter-form), are found on the visible surfaces of dressed stone from the 1200s but mainly from the 1400s and 1500s. Their actual function is not known but, presuming them to be the identification marks of individual masons, the likelihood is that the work of a mason could be calculated for payment purposes from the stones marked with his logo. Similarly, a mason failing to reach the required standard of work could be detected if he dared to mark a stone in order to be paid for it. Colum Hourihane has produced the only comprehensive study of such marks in Gothic contexts in Ireland, and has demonstrated how the marks can be used to reconstruct connections between building projects.[8] The earliest known use of marks on stones is probably in eleventh-century Killeenemer Church, where, unlike in the later examples, they all have the exact same motif (a small, dolmen-like shape) and are found on almost all the wall-facing stones.[9]

Brick was virtually unknown in medieval Ireland. Its earliest use may have been in cannon-ports inserted into Carrickfergus Castle in the 1560s, and it was used sporadically for houses in the early seventeenth century, but it was not in widespread circulation until after the Restoration.[10] Timber was used as a building material, as we will see in chapters 3 and 4, but timber buildings do not survive. There are some medieval timber roofs – Dunsoghly Castle has the latest and (somewhat inexplicably) most famous example in a group that includes St Mary's Church in Youghal and the two Dublin cathedrals – but Ireland has nothing like the richness that one encounters in England.[11] Generally, the only traces we have of timber are ghosts. First, missing timber buildings attached to stone buildings can be detected from marks in external rendering and from joist sockets. Few are as interesting as the now-lost timber fore-building and chapel at Coonagh Castle (fig. 35).[12] Second, timber floors inside buildings are represented by joist sockets in walls, sometimes in conjunction with corbels.[13] Third, putlog holes (fig. 36) show where the timber scaffolding poles were embedded in walls as those walls were being constructed; the poles were either pulled out when building work finished, and the holes were filled in (and then plastered over), or they

8 Hourihane, *The mason and his mark.* 9 T. O'Keeffe, 'Killeenemer Church and its archaeological importance', *Ogham*, 4 (1998), 23–5. 10 McNeill, *Carrickfergus Castle*, pp 47–8. Its use in Jigginstown House (1635–7) is discussed in G. Lynch (ed.), *The history of gauged brickwork* (London, 2010). For its use in plantation Ulster see, for example, E.M. Jope, 'Mongavlin Castle, Co. Donegal', *UJA*, 17 (1954), 169–72. 11 For surviving medieval church roofs, see M. Geaney, '"Raising the roof" in the Middle Ages: a survey of two medieval structures in Ireland' in G. Cunningham (ed.), *The Roscrea conference* (Roscrea, 2007), pp 29–47; idem, 'Christ Church Cathedral, Dublin: a survey of the nave and south transept roofs', *MD*, 7 (2006), 233–49; C. Lyons, 'Dublin's oldest roof? The choir of St Patrick's Cathedral', ibid., 177–213. Geaney's dating of Youghal's remarkable scissor-braced roof to the mid-fourteenth century is too late; very close parallels with mid-thirteenth-century roofs in the Dominican house in Gloucester (see O. Rackham, W.J. Blair and J.T. Munby, 'The thirteenth-century roofs and floor of the Blackfriars Priory at Gloucester', *MA*, 22 (1978), 105–22) not only draw St Mary's date back into the previous century but raise the possibility that it and the town's Dominican friary, founded within sight of the parish church in 1268, were roofed around the same time, probably in the 1270s or 1280s. I am grateful to my colleague on the Royal Irish Academy's Youghal Town Atlas project, David Kelly, for first suggesting a late thirteenth-century date. The roof in Holy Trinity (parish) Church, Fethard, has recently been dated by dendrochronology to the end of the fifteenth century (*Irish Examiner*, 25 Aug. 2011). Incidentally, the exteriors of medieval roofs were both thatched (see, for example, T. Crofton Croker (ed.), *The tour of ... M. de la Boullaye le Gouz in Ireland, AD1644* (Oxford, 1837), p. 41) and slated (see, for example, *COD, 1547–1584*, pp 22–3). Small fragments of such slate, sometimes with nail holes, can often be found in rubble at medieval sites; slate was sometimes imported from Wales (see McNeill, 'Ardglass', pp 14–15). 12 T. O'Keeffe, 'Building lordship in thirteenth-century Ireland: the donjon of Coonagh Castle, Co. Limerick', *JRSAI*, 111 (2011), 91–127. 13 See, for example, M.E. McKenna, 'Evidence for the use of timber in mediaeval Irish tower-houses: a regional study in Lacale and Tipperary', *UJA*, 47 (1984), 171–4.

35 Coonagh Castle, built *c.*1225. Originally enclosed in a timber fore-building at second-floor level, the arched opening on the left gave access to the interior of this great tower while the arched recess on the right contained a privileged seat – for an officiating chaplain? – in what would have been a small, east-facing chapel beside the entrance. The scar of the pitched roof of the timber fore-building is visible in the render.

were sawn off, leaving the butts to decay in the walls.[14] Fourth, timber was used in the building of vaults and arches. In the twelfth and thirteenth centuries (and rarely thereafter) stone arches and vaults were built on short planks set on timber frames, and, once the mortar was set, the impressions of the planks remained after they and the supporting frames were removed (fig. 37). The later medieval preference was to put wicker mats (of hazel)[15] rather than planks on the supporting frames. The mats were left *in situ* after the mortar dried; in 1644 it was observed that 'many' castle-owners 'ornament the ceilings [of their castles] with branches'.[16] In most cases the mats decayed *in situ* to leave distinctive impressions (fig. 38). Canvas or skin seems to have been used instead of wicker in at least one late castle, Ballymagyr.[17]

14 Sawn-off timbers in Trim donjon allowed that structure to be dated by dendrochronology (T. Condit, 'Rings of truth at Trim Castle, Co. Meath', *AI*, 10:3 (1996), 30–3; see below, p. 218). **15** R. Sherlock, 'Using new techniques to date old castles', *AI*, 27:2 (2013), 19–23. **16** Crofton Croker, *M. de la Boullaye le Gouz in Ireland*, p. 41. **17** O'Callaghan, 'Fortified houses, south Wexford', p. 5.

36 The putlog-holed west wall of Armagh Friary church (Franciscan), founded in the 1260s. Putlogs are not confined to thirteenth-century buildings but they are certainly less prevalent in later medieval contexts.

SPATIAL ANALYSIS

Architecture can be imagined as series of spaces rather than as sets of walls. Thus, instead of concentrating solely on the physical structures of buildings, architectural historians can look at ways in which spaces were organized, largely with a view to understanding function through the inter-accessibility.

Let us think, for example, of the difference between spiral and straight stairs, both of which we commonly find in the same buildings. Straight stairs hold no element of surprise; the steps literally bring individuals from one level to the next, with full visibility (fig. 39). In spiral stairs, by contrast, there is little visibility of what is ahead, as each step has its own half-turn ahead of it. Each half-turn allows a moment of privacy (as captured in Frederic William Burton's famous watercolour, *Hellelil and Hildebrand: the Meeting on the Turret Stairs*, in the National Gallery of Ireland); each half-turn has an element of the unknown, either for a person on the stairs or for a person in a room off the stairs. It is surely not insignificant, then, that spiral stairs tend to be

37 Plank impressions on the underside of a mid-thirteenth-century window recess at Buttevant Friary church (Franciscan). Planks of this size were normal, regardless of the size of the space to be vaulted. The actual twin-light window is a late medieval insertion.

38 Late medieval wicker-mat impressions (exposed under later plaster) from the tower-house that is the earliest phase of the multi-period castle of Donadea.

39 The main stairs at Barryscourt Castle. Note that the windows are at foot level on the ascent, lighting the steps, and that the window at the top of the stairs on the left-hand side is at eye-level, perhaps to encourage visitors to look out onto the estate before entering the room to the right. Some steps rise a little higher than others, a common phenomenon that is often interpreted as a device to trick attackers as they gather momentum when ascending, but it is more likely that the builders were fumbling to match the number of steps to the gradient.

higher than straight stairs in castle buildings, serving spaces of greater private than public purpose. There is no evidence, incidentally, to support the popular view that spiral stairs were built to aid defence, and that their clockwise ascent was specifically

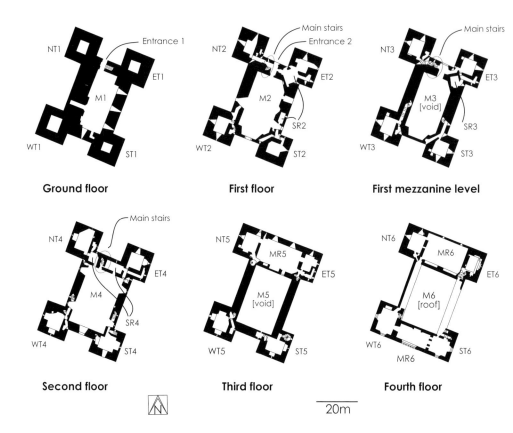

40 The floor plans of Bunratty Castle (the plans are derived from R. Sherlock, 'An introduction to Bunratty Castle', *BAACT*, 34 (2010), 202–18; the access analysis graphic is my own).

to give an advantage to right-handed swordsmen: these clockwise stairs are common across medieval Europe, and in churches as well as castles. Their right-hand rotation reflects the traditional clockwise pattern of procession.

A technique used effectively to represent the spaces of buildings and the routes between them is so-called 'access analysis', which involves the representation of 'rooms' with shapes or symbols and the representation of access-routes with lines.[18] There are many ways in which such an analysis can be done,[19] and one method, employed on the tower of Bunratty Castle, is demonstrated here.

18 The original key work is W. Hillier and J. Hanson, *The social logic of space* (Cambridge, 1984).
19 S.M. Foster, 'Analysis of spatial patterns in buildings (access analysis) as an insight into social structure: examples from the Scottish Atlantic Iron Age', *Antiquity*, 63 (1989), 40–50; G. Fairclough, 'Meaningful constructions: spatial and functional analysis of medieval buildings', *Antiquity*, 66 (1992), 348–66. For other applications of this method in medieval Irish buildings, see T. O'Keeffe, 'Ballyloughan, Ballymoon and Clonmore: three castles of *c*.1300 in County Carlow', *Anglo-Norman Studies*, 23 (2001), 167–97; idem, 'Barryscourt Castle and the Irish tower-

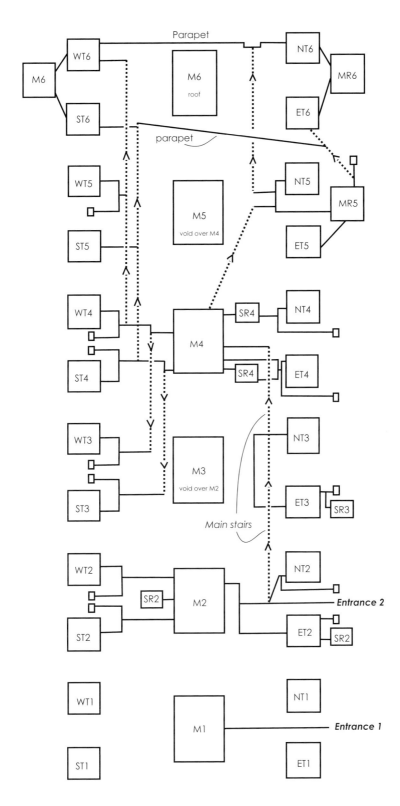

41 An access analysis diagram of Bunratty Castle.

There are three stages in making an access diagram. First, the rooms are given codes: in this case M indicates a main floor, mezzanine or roof space, NT, ET, ST and WT indicate the rooms in the towers at the north, east, south and west points respectively, and MR and SR indicate 'middle' and small subsidiary rooms respectively. Numbers are assigned according to floor level (fig. 40). Second, the main line of vertical access through the building is identified – in the case of Bunratty it is the spiral stairs in the north wall of the main block – and represented on the diagram by a vertical line, outwards from which the graphic is then constructed. Third, the rooms are represented by square and rectangular shapes on either side of that vertical line, with horizontal and angled lines used to represent connections between spaces at each floor level, and dotted lines used to show stairs (fig. 41). The diagram that results captures more effectively than floor plans could ever do the complex connections between the building's internal spaces, and helps us make sense of the building. The diagram also explains why modern visitors struggle so hard to orient themselves in Bunratty's interior: there is too much spatial information to process.

The real value of the diagram is that it reveals the building's plan principles. First, the main stairs ascends directly from the outside (at entrance 2) to the large room marked M4, effectively isolating the lower parts of the building. This is a variation on what one finds regularly in tower-houses, the classic late medieval castles that are discussed in Chapter 5. Second, M4 is the hub from which the entire upper part of the building (including WT3 and ST3, which are in the storey below) is accessible. M4 was obviously a place of gathering, and might therefore be identified as a very rare example of hall inside a tower-house; in 1629 in Bunratty rent was paid 'in the hall of the mansion house',[20] which is presumably this very room. Third, in a repeat of the arrangement with the main stairs, smaller stairs lead from M4 to the rooms at the top of the towers on the west and south, bypassing rooms in between. Here, M4 acted as an atrium to blocks of rooms that were arranged like the rooms in tower-houses. So, rather like a Russian doll, conceptually Bunratty is a very big tower-house containing a pair of smaller tower-houses on the south side. One wonders if this scheme reflects differential ownership of space within the castle, following the pattern that we know from other Clare castles (see below, pp 270–1). Finally, the rooms at the top of Bunratty on the north and east sides involve a circuitous route that does *not* imitate what one finds in tower-houses, and it is here that we find the so-called 'lady's chapel'.

On that latter observation, evidence from various parts of Europe suggests that the spaces exclusive to women were usually somewhat secluded, either hidden behind high walls in the case of gardens and orchards (both of which symbolized fertility) or deep within castle complexes, where there was symbolic link between the female body and 'the interior, protected spaces of the castle'.[21] Thus, it is no coincidence that, for example, the Bunratty chapel was at the top of the building (ET6), as remote as possible within that castle's complex architecture (see fig. 40). Interestingly, as Roberta

house' in Ludlow and Jameson, *Medieval Ireland: Barryscourt lectures*, pp 1–32; G. Eadie, 'Detecting privacy and private space in the Irish tower house', *CG*, 24 (2010), 69–73.   **20** *Inchiquin MSS*, no. 1046.   **21** R. Gilchrist, *Gender and archaeology: contesting the past* (London, 1999), p. 139; see also T. O'Keeffe, 'Concepts of "castle" and the construction of identity in medieval and post-

Gilchrist has shown,[22] the bedchamber of a domestic residence in the Middle Ages was a space associated strongly with women as it was also the birth-chamber, and it was therefore a space of intrinsic religiosity and intense devotional activity; indeed, the medieval practice of bringing mothers into church chancels as part of the ritual of churching forged a symbolic link between the domestic bedchamber (and its relationship with the domestic hall) and the church sanctuary (and its relationship with the church nave). The 'lady's chapel' in Bunratty can be understood, then, as more than simply a venue for private prayer. This is not to suggest that the lord's wife in Bunratty (or her counterpart elsewhere) was passive, content to sit in the garden or pray in the chapel surrounded by her ladies-in-waiting. Her rather extreme seclusion in her private spaces may have been a deliberate or conscious contrast with her heightened visibility when present in a more public space lower down: the archbishop of Lincoln famously entreated the local countess to 'sit you ever in the middle of the high board that your visage and cheer be showed to all men … So much as you may without peril of sickness and weariness eat you in the hall afore your many, for that shall be to your profit and worship'.[23]

So, access analysis helps us to evaluate the relative importance of spaces: 'public' spaces in buildings are shown to be (relatively) freely accessible whereas 'private' spaces are shown to have had more circuitous access routes. One drawback with the technique is the presumption that spaces were used as designed – physical structures are fixed but the uses to which spaces are put can change – but the benefits outweigh the problems.

FUNCTIONAL ANALYSIS

Analysing the functions of buildings demands that we look for complexity beyond the traditional understandings of how certain types of building operated. So, in seeing churches primarily as places of worship we should not forget the importance of these buildings as places where local elites had their wealth and power displayed in acts of benefaction. Similarly, in seeing castles primarily as places of defence we should not forget that they were also places of peaceful habitation and estate management. These matters are addressed in the chapters that follow. One aspect of architecture to which the visitor to a medieval building must always be mindful is the capacity of medieval (and post-medieval) people to change the functions of buildings, or even just the functions of rooms within buildings. Medieval monasteries re-founded as residences after the Reformation – Tintern is the most obvious example[24] – are a special case in point. Even when the functions of rooms in structures did not change, the ways in which those functions were prosecuted sometimes did. Here is one example.

Hearths in side-wall fireplaces were better than hearths in central braziers because chimney flues retained heat and reduced draught. The multiplication of such fireplaces

medieval Ireland', *IG*, 34:1 (2001), 69–88 at 77–9. **22** R. Gilchrist, *Medieval life: archaeology and the life course* (Woodbridge, 2012), pp 139–40, 143, 156. **23** M. Girouard, *Life in the English country house: a social and architectural history* (London, 1978), p. 30. **24** A. Lynch, *Tintern Abbey, Co. Wexford: Cistercians and Colcloughs, excavations, 1982–2007* (Dublin, 2010).

in many castles built between the last quarter of the sixteenth century (fig. 42) and the second quarter of the seventeenth cannot be unconnected to the severe drop in temperature – the so-called Little Ice Age – that started in the 1560s.[25] It is not uncommon to find *inserted* side-wall fireplaces of late sixteenth- or early seventeenth-century date in the upper rooms of older tower-houses, the insertions sometimes involving the blocking of windows (pl. III). The presence of a side-wall fireplace, especially one that blocked a window, did more than simply change the heat regime of a room. The geography of social interaction changed with the opening up of the central floor space and the 'booking' of positions close to a fire that only radiated heat in a half-circle. The function of a room did not change, then, but the manner in which it functioned did.

METROLOGICAL ANALYSIS

Measurements and proportions used in the designs of buildings are intrinsically interesting because they allow us to reconstruct in our minds how builders went about the practical tasks of laying out plans on the ground and designing stable and structurally satisfying superstructures above. Different units of measurement were used in the Middle Ages, but the basic unit, in Ireland as elsewhere, was the foot. Rare documentary expressions of the medieval use of the foot in Ireland come from 1456 and 1459 when the measurements of castles to be built in Kilcullen and Bray respectively are given in 'Paul's feet'.[26] This is clearly a reference to the template for a foot that was carved into the base of a column in St Paul's Cathedral, London, and was first recorded in the 1180s.[27] One unit other than the foot might also have been used in medieval Ireland: the *canna*. This unit, with a given length of 2.2m, has been identified in thirteenth-century Trim and Roscrea castles.[28] Notwithstanding the fact that it was mentioned in papal instructions of 1265 and 1268 issued to mendicants everywhere in Europe in respect of locations of friaries relative to each other,[29] I am not convinced that this (mainly southern European) unit was knowingly used in Ireland, and in any case its length was not consistent.[30]

---

25 J.M. Grove, *The Little Ice Age* (London, 2003).   **26** *SRPI*, *Hen. VI*, pp 457, 663.   **27** P. Grierson, *English linear measurements: an essay in origins* (Reading, 1972), pp 18–19.   **28** Manning, *Roscrea Castle*, p. 136.   **29** The minimum distance in 1265 was 300 *cannae* but this was reduced to 140 in 1268 (J. Röhrkasten, *The medieval mendicant houses of London, 1221–1539* (New Brunswick and London, 2004), pp 38, 58). For knowledge of this rule in Ireland, see Ó Clabaigh, *The friars in Ireland*, p. 204.   **30** It is given as 2–2.15m in N. Masini, C.D. Fonseca, E. Geraldi and G. Sabino, 'An algorithm for computing the original units of measure of medieval architecture', *Journal of Cultural Heritage*, 5 (2004), 7–15, and as 2m in C.M. Richardson, *Reclaiming Rome: cardinals in the fifteenth century* (Leiden, 2009), p. 441.

---

42 (*opposite*) The tower-house of Kilduff Castle, the thin walls, tall gables and box-like windows of which indicate a date in the late 1500s. Each of the floors above the basement (or ground-floor) level would have had a fireplace, including the attic, and each of the four gables would have carried chimneys (as can still be seen with the two that survive).

The length of the medieval foot was certainly not standardized,[31] which creates considerable problems when we attempt to work out the metrology of buildings or parts of buildings. If the dimensions in imperial (twelve-inch) feet of a medieval building are not divisible by twelve it is easy to assume that the imperial foot was not used, but can we be sure that no other foot measurement was used instead? If we presume that masons did actually use scaled rulers to measure stones before cutting them, we can aspire to determine the exact length of foot used in medieval buildings by taking very *exact* measurements of cut-stone surfaces with sharp edges (the jambs, mullions and tracery-lines of windows in particular) and by observing the frequency with which the widths of those surfaces are consistent fractions – ¼, ⅓, ½, ⅔, ¾ – of particular lengths. Thus, for example, the use of the standard English medieval foot of 30.48cm would be attested to by finding surfaces 7.62cm, 15.24cm and 22.86cm in width (reflecting a division of the foot into quarters), or 10.16cm and 20.32cm (reflecting a division into thirds). The so-called Anglo-Saxon foot of 28cm would be attested to by widths of 7cm, 14cm and 21cm (in quarters) and 9.33cm and 18.66cm (in thirds). Another medieval English foot-length, 31.67cm, would be attested to by widths of 7.92cm, 15.83cm and 23.75cm (in quarters) and 10.55cm and 21.11cm (in thirds).

Why do we use measurements from cut-stone surfaces to establish units of measurement? Would it not be wiser to measure the lengths and widths of buildings instead, especially as so many of our buildings lack cut-stone features today? There is a very simple answer. With barely any exceptions, our buildings were built not with ashlar but with crudely shaped stones. So, no two people measuring the length or width of the same building, especially internally, will produce the *exact* same measurements (unless by an extraordinary coincidence they take their measurements from the exact same spots on the same stones). Our measurements need to be as *exact* as possible to work out units of measure. Only cut-stone features yield exact measurements.

It has been suggested on the basis of careful measurements of cut-stone features that all three foot-lengths were used in medieval Ireland.[32] That may well have been the case, but the 30.48cm foot must have been the most common: units of about 5m can often be identified in the plans of buildings and even towns, and, using the 30.48 foot specifically, these can equated with the medieval perch of 16½ feet (fig. 43).[33]

Consistency in measurement had a practical purpose. Parts of windows could be cut separately in masons' yards with confidence that the parts would later fit together properly on building sites. Consistency in the proportional systems used for the laying out of buildings and of features in buildings (such as windows) was valued even more highly. By using a limited number of proportional formulae – mainly based on the

31 E. Fernie, 'Historical metrology and architectural history', *Art History*, 1 (1978), 388–99. **32** A. Behan and R. Moss, 'Metrology and proportion in the ecclesiastical architecture of medieval Ireland', *Nexus VII: architecture and mathematics* (Turin, 2008), pp 171–84.   **33** For the perch, see P. Kidson, 'A metrological investigation', *Journal of the Warburg and Courtauld Institutes*, 53 (1990), 71–97 at 74–80. For demonstrations of its use in Ireland, see M. O'Neill, 'Design sources for St Patrick's Cathedral', p. 221; ibid., 'Medieval parish churches in County Meath', p. 41; O'Keeffe, *Fethard*, p. 2. A perch based on the Anglo-Saxon foot would be 4.62m long, which is too short to approximate to 5m, and one based on the 31.67cm foot would be 5.22m

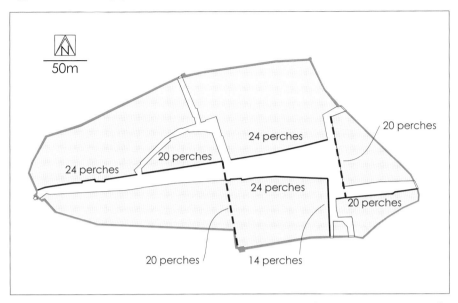

43 The metrological regularity of Fethard, founded in the early 1200s, is testimony to the precision with which urban settlements were sometimes planned.

ratios of 1:2, 1:3 and so on, or on the more complex arithmetical ratios of 1:1.414 (1:√2), and 1:1.618 – masons created spaces of consistent relative shape. This had aesthetic value, in that it gave a satisfying consistency to lengths (and heights) of spaces relative to their widths. It also had a symbolic value in that some of these proportions were used in Antiquity, as we will see momentarily. We should not underestimate the subtle effect of consistent length–breadth ratios: the buildings designed with rigid proportional systems were generally in the ownership of (as in the case of castles), or at least under the control of (as in the case of churches), medieval elites, so the *metrological* order possessed by the architecture stood in a metaphorical relationship to the *social* order imposed by those elites.

Simple ratios like 1:2 and 1:3 involved making squares and repeating them. Plans could be marked out on the ground very easily. Masons knew that the ratios were also achievable through simple multiplication. They had no more difficulty with the more complex ratios, and seem even to have preferred them. The 1:1.414 (or 1:√2)[34] ratio, approved of by Marcus Vitruvius Pollio, the first-century BC Roman architect, was especially common in the Middle Ages.[35] A shape of this proportion could be laid out on the ground by simply making a square and taking the length of the diagonal of that square as the length of a rectangle formed from that square. Another ratio, 1:1.618, the Golden Ratio, which was also used in Antiquity,[36] was laid out using a very similar

long, which is slightly too long.   **34** In other words, 1.414 multiplied by itself is 2.   **35** K.J. Conant, 'The after-life of Vitruvius in the Middle Ages', *JSAH*, 27:1 (1968), 33–8.   **36** R. Padovan, *Proportion: science, philosophy, architecture* (London, 1999).

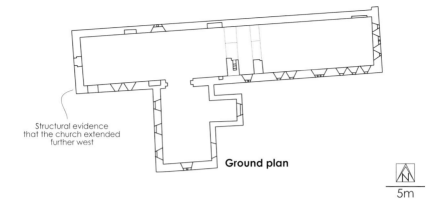

Structural evidence
that the church extended
further west

Ground plan

5m

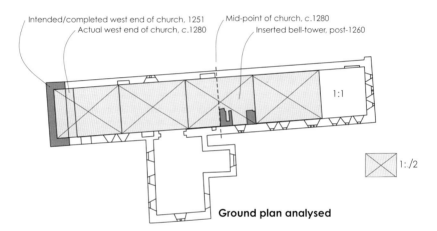

Intended/completed west end of church, 1251   Mid-point of church, *c.*1280
Actual west end of church, *c.*1280   Inserted bell-tower, post-1260

1:1

1:√2

Ground plan analysed

44 The friary church at Buttevant has several thirteenth-century phases. An early twentieth-century survey found evidence that the church was longer, or was intended to be longer, at its west end. Reconstructing the metrology of the entire building allows us posit that the present west wall of *c.*1280 is a few metres to the east of the original of *c.*1250. It also indicates that the inserted bell-tower, one of the earliest mendicant bell-towers in Ireland, was placed with considerable care exactly between the east end of one of the 1:√2 boxes of the original (*c.*1250) church and the halfway point of the *c.*1280 church.

technique: the length of the diagonal of half of the square was used to determine the length of the rectangle. Alternatively, masons knew that they could achieve the same ratios by simple multiplication: once the width of a space (a room or a building) was decided, that width was simply multiplied by either 1.414 or 1.618. Buildings and parts of buildings laid out using these ratios are easily identified today, and there are many demonstrations in print of their use.[37] The value of working out proportional systems

37 See, for example, N. Walsh, 'Pre-Romanesque churches in County Dublin and its hinterland: the Golden Ratio', *MD*, 8 (2008), 21–35; O'Neill, 'Medieval parish churches in

is that they can sometimes help us reconstruct sequences of building. Thus, for example, the original design of Buttevant Friary church (Franciscan) can be retrieved from the building's metrology (fig. 44).[38]

SCIENTIFIC AND RELATED ANALYSIS

Various scientific techniques can be used to date structures. These can only be deployed under licence and involve the hiring of specialists, so are best used in structures of demonstrable interest or importance but for which there is some doubt about date. Briefly, radiocarbon dating of charcoal in building-mortar has been used effectively for dating some early medieval buildings, the architecture of which does not always by itself permit accurate dating. Rory Sherlock has recently been obtaining radiocarbon dates from the wicker mats used to hold vault-mortar in place in tower-houses.[39] Dendrochronology, the dating of tree-rings in pieces of timber, also has potential, as witness the accurate dating of the donjon (or keep) of Trim Castle through analysis of the stubs of timber beams preserved in its walls.[40] Other modes of analysis that require the use of specialized equipment include geophysical survey, or access to (and the ability to process) spatial and photographic data, such as GIS (Geographic Information System).[41] LiDAR (Light Detection and Ranging), a remote sensing technology that illuminates a target from an airborne or satellite laser and then uses the reflected light to map the micro-contours of a surface, is invaluable for detecting landscape features associated with buildings that cannot be discerned at ground level (figs 45, 89).

THE ANALYSIS OF MEANING

The analysis of 'meaning' is simultaneously the most interesting and trickiest of the analytical challenges. 'Meaning' is a far more subtle concept than 'function' or 'symbolism', though it includes both. In one perspective it equates most closely with symbolism. Thus, for example, we can hold that castles symbolized power. Of course, symbolism does not just 'happen'; it needs an agent. We can speculate that the symbolism of power that was possessed by a castle was at least partly effected through the knowledge that its spectators had of the resources commanded and consumed by

County Meath', pp 35–42.   **38** T. O'Keeffe, 'The sequence of construction of Buttevant friary church in the thirteenth century' in Cotter, *Buttevant*, pp 83–102.   **39** R. Berger, 'Radiocarbon dating of early medieval Irish monuments', *PRIA*, 95C (1995), 159–74; Sherlock, 'New techniques to date old castles'.   **40** Condit, 'Rings of truth at Trim Castle'. The same technique has pointed to a date of after 1410 for Tyrellspass Castle (Casey and Rowan, *North Leinster*, pp 528–9) and *c.*1540 for Clara Castle (Manning, 'Irish tower houses', p. 27). See also D. Brown, 'Dendrochronologically dated buildings from Ireland', *Vernacular Architecture*, 33 (2002), 71–3. **41** For the use of geophysics, see T. O'Rourke and P.J. Gibson, 'Geophysical investigation of the environs of Rattin Castle tower house, County Westmeath, Ireland', *Archaeological Prospection*, 16 (2009), 65–75; K. McManama-Kearin, *The use of GIS in determining the role of visibility in the siting of early Anglo-Norman stone castles in Ireland* (Oxford, 2013).

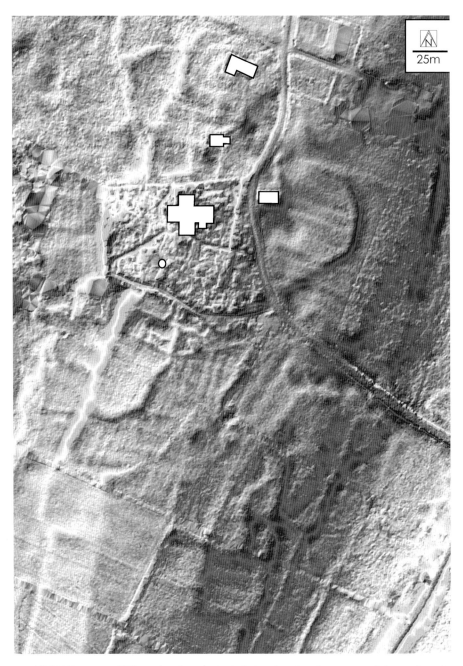

45 A LiDAR image of Kilmacduagh ecclesiastical site, showing the pattern of the earthworks that one can see but not interpret easily at ground level (image courtesy of Steve Davis, UCD School of Archaeology; data courtesy of the National Roads Authority). The large highlighted building is Kilmacduagh Cathedral. To its south is the round tower, and to its north are, in succession, a church dedicated to St John the Baptist and a secular building identified as the episcopal residence. To the east of the cathedral is the church known as Templemurray. Another church, O'Heyne's Church, to the north-west, is not in the image. The curvilinear enclosure around the cathedral is apparent on its south and east sides. Small enclosures run in a linear pattern north and south of the cathedral, and St John's Church and the episcopal residence occupy two of these. The likelihood is that some of these small enclosures are crofts that contained houses, even though house-sites themselves cannot be identified.

its builders in its construction: hundreds of tons of soil moved, stone quarried, and lime and sand mixed for mortar, not to mention dozens of trees felled for wood for gangway planks and scaffolding poles. The *act* of building might have been as important symbolically as the finished product: to witness a castle being built was to witness nature, the soil and rocks that God had put in place, being reconfigured by people whose power must have seemed to carry God's own imprimatur.[42]

There were presumably many subtle and some not-so subtle signifiers or symbols of power in the castles once they were finished and occupied. For example, such is the size and visibility of the toilet outlets in many thirteenth-century castles (see below, pp 205–7) that we might consider the possibility that castle-owners were quite happy to have their rendered walls streaked with foul-smelling excrement because it connoted a rich diet. Far-fetched though this may seem, we should note that animal manure had symbolic significance as well as functional value in medieval society, and we can deduce that, just as 'peasant manure … looked different from seigneurial manure',[43] so too did their own body waste. Similarly, from the other end of our period, chimneys visible from afar in castles of the Little Ice Age informed distant spectators of residences that were warm on the inside, and by extension of castle-owners whose power gave them access to plentiful fuel. That is presumably why the chimneys in many late castles rose higher than was needed for the smoke to clear their roofs, and why some castles, like Grange (Kildare) and Ballycowan, were given dummy chimneys.

From another perspective, 'meaning' equates with the allegorical purpose to which architecture is sometimes put. Thus, we have the mid-twelfth-century commentary of an English abbot that in a castle the ditch represents humility, the wall represents chastity and 'the great tower (*magna turris*) … is charity', and that 'just as the *turris* should be higher than all other structures in the castle, so charity is higher than all other virtues'.[44] It is unlikely that castle builders were privileging such allegorical meanings when they were thinking about designs, but that is certainly not to say that there was no medieval consciousness of how physical structures conveyed virtuous ideas to contemporary populations.

From another perspective again, we might think not of the buildings but of the builders, and ask 'what did *they* mean?' when they built something. What, in other words, are they telling us through the choices they made? To elaborate, let us consider one of the biggest research questions in the study of medieval architecture in Ireland. It concerns the retention in Ireland of the Decorated Style long after it had gone out of date in England, and its occasional modification with selected forms borrowed from English Perpendicular architecture. We noted this above (pp 49–50). What did the builders – the patrons and/or masons – of the 1300s in Ireland *mean* when they bypassed English Perpendicular? Did they knowingly reject it, and, if so, was it an act of political resistance? Or was it an aesthetic rejection? Was there something in the Irish psyche, in other words, that found the straight lines of Perpendicular tracery

42 T.O'Keeffe, 'Were there designed landscapes in medieval Ireland?', *Landscapes*, 5 (2004), 52–68.   **43** R. Jones, 'Understanding medieval manure' in R. Jones (ed.), *Manure matters: historical, archaeological and ethnographic perspectives* (Farnham, 2013), pp 145–58 at p. 155.   **44** M.W. Thompson, *The rise of the castle* (Cambridge, 2008), p. 181. See also C. Whitehead, *Castles of the mind: a study of medieval architectural allegory* (Cardiff, 2003); and A. Wheatley, *The idea of the castle in medieval England* (Woodbridge, 2004).

simply unappealing? And was it even a rejection in the first place? Did they know that the English architects of the 1300s had created a new style? Did it register in their consciousness as a new style they could choose to accept or reject?

And from yet another perspective, 'meaning' connotes the capacity of architecture, its structures, its spaces and its carved surfaces, to stimulate in its spectators thoughts about matters extrinsic to the architecture itself, and in so doing to shape society itself. This is not the place for a discussion of such a concept. Suffice it to say here that readers who find architecture intrinsically fascinating will instinctively know that buildings are not passive backdrops to human culture but active agents in shaping the human experience.[45] I want to offer here some simple reflections on how such meanings 'work', or, put more accurately, how buildings 'work' in this active way. These reflections might liberate the reader to think about medieval buildings in more imaginative (though no less truthful) ways.

Thinking first about the meanings that medieval buildings possessed for medieval people themselves, there can be no disputing that these buildings had multiple sets of spectators, each with its own relationship of comfort or discomfort with those buildings, its own way of reading or decoding architectural structure and space, its own motivation for so engaging with architecture, or its own reasons for being indifferent to architecture. There was a clear cognizance among church-builders, for example, of how complex meanings could be expressed through the organization of internal spaces and through the rules governing access to those spaces, as well as through the provision of (and indeed the prohibition of) lines of sight between the pew and the altar. In an age in which everybody believed genuinely that prayers after death would ensure salvation for the souls of departed relatives, we can imagine that regular parishioners of the Middle Ages viewed with envy and resentment the capacity of the wealthy to fast-track their way past Purgatory by gathering up indulgences through financial gifts to churches and by endowing priests to celebrate post-mortem masses in perpetuity in specially designed chapels. Here, then, is an example of architecture actively shaping human experience and emotion.

The main doorway of a medieval building is a place where the modern visitor can reflect very profitably on the meaning of architecture and architectural space in the Middle Ages. Given that church interiors were consecrated, the liminal qualities of the church doorway – liminality refers to the state of being in-between, of being on a threshold between different states of being – are self-evident. It is no coincidence that the rite of baptism was located inside the doorway, as we will see (pp 114–15). Also, the churching of women after childbirth, which was a process of purification in the medieval Roman tradition but became a celebration of safe delivery in the Protestant tradition, involved a rendezvous with a priest at the church doorway.[46] And marriage was celebrated publically at the doorway.[47] We might add the observation that a parish

45 There is a vast literature on agency in art and architecture; especially influential is A. Gell, *Art and agency: an anthropological theory* (Oxford, 1998).   **46** D. Cressy, *Birth, marriage and death: ritual, religion and the life-cycle in Tudor and Stuart England* (Oxford, 1997), esp. pp 197–229; see also Gilchrist, *Medieval life*, pp 182–3.   **47** It is not clear from the sources if marriage celebrations were outside or inside the doorway; one would expect the former, as it was public, but in France church was the only roofed-over space in the Middle Ages where people of different tenurial grade and ethnic background came into contact with each other, so passage through the doorway symbolically united God's family.

The importance that we attach today to the main doorway in castle architecture has much to do with our preoccupation with the military functions of castles, but here too we might recognize some contemporary consciousness of what we today describe as liminality. Cross-slabs from early church sites acquired votive significance when recycled as doorway lintels, as attested to in, for example, Clonmore Castle from the late thirteenth century and Archbold's Castle, Dalkey, from the fifteenth.[48] Deaths in doorways are often recorded,[49] as if dying in that space was more noteworthy than dying elsewhere. Moreover, inside the main door of a tower-house there is normally a lobby where, thanks to locked doors, even a legitimate visitor could be made to wait, feeling himself or herself neither inside nor outside the tower, and aware of being watched through the murder-hole above. The physical object of the door itself may have had a value beyond merely its material worth: three different annalists describe the capture in 1536 of the door (variously described as 'variegated', 'speckled' and 'ornamented'[50]) of the castle of Turrock and its removal for use in Sligo Castle, suggesting the loss of a front door as a physical object was especially embarrassing.[51]

Medieval buildings did not stop being meaningful when the Middle Ages ended. On the contrary, one could argue that changes in the meanings of those buildings actually define the end of the Middle Ages. For example, of the many castles that were abandoned as residences in the seventeenth century, a process attested to in the mid-century land surveys, some must have been abandoned on grounds that we might vaguely describe as ideological: they were buildings with historical associations, and their abandonment did not render them meaningless but was an acknowledgment of their old meanings and an assignment to them of new meanings. Ivy-covered castle ruins on landlord estates in the eighteenth century were not meaningless; they acquired new meanings in the context of the picturesque. And for those castles that were retained in use into the period of landlordism, their very antiquity was put at the service of a new spectrum of meanings.[52] Post-medieval, or at least post-Reformation, changes of meaning in ecclesiastical architecture are almost self-evident,[53] but that does not mean that they do not need, or cannot sustain, deep analysis.[54]

it was sometimes the latter: see C. Sparks, *Heresy, inquisition and life cycle in medieval Languedoc* (Woodbridge, 2014), p. 102.   **48** O'Keeffe, 'Ballyloughan, Ballymoon and Clonmore'; A. Mason, 'Cross-inscribed slab in Archbold's Castle, Dalkey, County Dublin', *JRSAI*, 113 (1983), 143–4.   **49** *AU*, 1214.3; 1266.6; 1339.12; 1422.2; 1478.17; 1486.29; 1500.12, are examples from one annalistic source alone.   **50** *AFM*, 1536.14, *ALC*, 1536.20 and *AC*, 1536.23 respectively. Turrock is identified in the latter as in the parish of Taghboy, about 95km from Sligo.   **51** The gate of Ballylahan was taken in a raid a century and a half earlier and brought to Ballymote (*AFM*, 1381.9).   **52** A case in point is Lohort Castle: see T. Barnard, *Improving Ireland? Projectors, prophets and profiteers, 1641–1786* (Dublin, 2008), pp 120–42; T. O'Keeffe, 'Lohort Castle: medieval architecture, medievalist imagination', *JCHAS*, 118 (2013), 60–70. See also C. Corlett, 'Kiltimon Castle: medieval castle or modern folly?', *JRSAI*, 138 (2008), 47–70.   **53** See, for example, the interesting account of the post-medieval reuse of a medieval church in plantation Ulster in N.F. Brannon and B.S. Blades, 'Dungiven Bawn re-edified', *UJA*, 43 (1980), 91–6.   **54** For such

THE SMALL MATTER OF THEORY: A WORD IN THE STUDENT EAR

Mention of Theory – the upper-case T is deliberate here – usually draws one of two responses: an affirmation of its importance or a condemnation of it as irrelevant. There is an ever-increasing number of building-specialist archaeologists outside Ireland who belong in the former camp.[55] In Ireland, however, as any informed perusal of even the most recent literature will reveal, the field of medieval architectural history is, like that of medieval archaeology, fairly conservative in its research agenda and in its supporting menu of interpretative strategies. There is at best little appetite for, and at worst actual hostility towards, interpretations that draw explicitly on structuralism, post-structuralism, phenomenology and so on. This is a pity. These are frameworks that attempt to explain the structures and operations of the human world. Many scholars already embrace unconsciously some of these ways of thinking, especially structuralism, so there should be no hostility to exploring systematically what they have to offer. In any case, even the most ostensibly atheoretical (or 'common sense') work in the field of architectural-historical analysis – simple typology – has a deep theoretical foundation: the principles by which we typologize or classify buildings and parts of buildings do not come to us naturally but are theoretical propositions that we have simply naturalized through use.

The study of medieval architecture actually has at its core two theoretical propositions: Romanesque and Gothic. These are not real historical phenomena, even if many scholars treat them as if they are, but nineteenth-century conceptual inventions. I hope that student readers of this book might adopt, or at least think about the value of adopting, a critical perspective on those two concepts. This book is certainly not the place for an extended discussion, but here I want to offer some thoughts that might persuade some readers to explore the possibilities of radical revisionism.

Critical interrogation within the cohort of disciplines – archaeology, art history, architectural history – that engage with the material and visual cultures of the historic past rarely extends to the structures or frameworks within which facts have residence and are validated. On the contrary, those structures, although fundamentally interpretative and mutable (and therefore better described as models), are often maintained as fixed and immutable, as factual in and of themselves; they are the categories that the disciplines themselves invented, but their immutability comes from their reimagining over time as the categories for which those disciplines were created. Romanesque and Gothic are two such structures. They are so firmly cemented into the study of European (including Irish) medieval architecture that they have passed

analysis, see R. Moss, 'Reduce, reuse, recycle: Irish monastic architecture, *c.*1540–1640' in Stalley, *Irish Gothic architecture*, pp 115–60; N. Nic Ghabhann, 'Irish architects and the restoration of medieval buildings, 1835–1904', ibid., pp 201–20.   **55** M. Johnson, *Archaeological theory: an introduction* (2nd ed. Oxford, 2010), for example, is a useful general introduction to how theory 'works' in archaeology in general; his case study of Bodiam Castle shows how it helps us make sense of medieval architecture more specifically. For a historiographic perspective on theory's place within ecclesiastical architectural-historical research, see R. Gilchrist, 'Monastic and church archaeology', *Annual Review of Anthropology*, 43 (2014), 235–50. Theory appears more explicity in O'Keeffe, *Archaeology and the pan-European Romanesque*.

into immutability. We are chained to them. It is now 'fact' that certain buildings belong in one or the other category.

The capacity for radical rethinking in fields of research in which one instinctively feels that there is a need for it, or even the capacity to explore what radicalism might entail and what it might produce, is impeded by the fact that one cannot stand far enough back within the boundaries of one's discipline, *as it has evolved historically*, to view with complete detachment its structures, its established models. Of course, if one believes that there is nothing beyond the point of furthest reach there is no issue: in such a view the chain does not restrict movement but, rather, its length tells us how far we can go before we reach the boundaries of meaningful interpretation. There is little evidence in the international scholarly literature on so-called (though it seems superfluous here to offer that qualification) Romanesque and Gothic architectures that a space comprising anything other than theoretical fantasy is perceived beyond that boundary; there is no space in our intellectual culture, in other words, wherein the things that constitute Romanesque and Gothic can be imagined differently.

For all the acknowledgment in that literature that Romanesque and Gothic are creations of scholarship and are therefore genuinely mutable constructs, their value is still asserted.[56] The underlying message, if one might divine one, is that, alongside any debate that some scholars might desire to provoke about terminology, we can still get on with the business of making sense of Romanesque and Gothic buildings *as* Romanesque and Gothic buildings because we basically know what we are talking about: we 'know' that *romanitas* so underpins the earlier style that 'Romanesque' is not particularly objectionable, and we 'know' that nineteenth-century antiquarians were fundamentally correct in giving a single style-name to post-Romanesque pre-Renaissance architecture, absurd though their reasoning may have been in choosing 'Gothic' for that name. Even those few scholars – and I include myself here – who cannot shake off misgivings about epistemologies that leave these terms in place after more than two centuries, as if they have proved their value and as if they are at worst neutral and innocuous, are usually complicit in two linked ways in maintaining the status quo. The first is the tendency to focus critical thoughts on those terms and on the historiography that buttresses them, rather than attempt to develop an alternative discourse around the buildings that are described by those terms. The second is the tendency, in the absence of alternative discourses, to use the terms when it is too much trouble, or the context renders it inappropriate (as in this book), to debate them.

My own concern with the Romanesque and Gothic constructs is not that they demonstrably fail us but that we do not allow the possibility that they might be failing us. Buildings fit within them, so they appear unproblematic, but that cannot be taken as proof that they are the constructs that best capture both the formal variety and complex intellectual fabric of the constituent architectures. And some importance

---

56 The most recent example might be Eric Fernie's defence of the Romanesque construct (E. Fernie, 'The concept of the Romanesque' in J. McNeill and R. Plant (eds), *Romanesque and the past: retrospection in the art and architecture of Romanesque Europe* (London, 2013), pp 283–90). His defence is partly in response to my own critique of Romanesque: see most recently O'Keeffe, *Archaeology and the pan-European Romanesque*. Others might have a different view, but to my mind

should be attached to the fact that we instinctively shift the boundaries of their definitions to make sure that they do not fail us. Marvin Trachtenburg has shown how senior scholars in the field of architectural history have found inherently contradictory solutions within the Gothic paradigm to explain the apparent problem of the 'Classical-looking' columns in the Gothic nave of Notre-Dame in Paris;[57] of course, the problem was never one of Notre-Dame's creation but one entirely created by the paradigm itself. It is surely self-evident that many of the key questions that we ask of medieval architecture in Ireland – When did Romanesque first appear? Is the 'School of the West' Romanesque or Gothic? What is the relationship between ethnic identity and the adoption of Gothic in the 1200s? Why did Ireland generally eschew Perpendicular Gothic in favour of old-fashioned Decorated Gothic in the fifteenth century? – presuppose that the problems are embedded in the architecture. In reality, they are problems created by the categories. This is not to say that they are non-questions but, rather, to point out that they are to some degree problematic questions because their answers are automatically imprisoned by the very paradigms within which they have their sole validity as questions.

It is probable that Romanesque and Gothic, both as constructs and terms, are here to stay, regardless of any attempt to dismantle them, and that all debate will remain where it has always been, which is within those two conceptual spaces. But that is not to deny the value of a very radical critique of their conceptual foundations, if only as an intellectual exercise that reminds us to remain cognizant of how scholarly tradition possesses hegemonic power. I hope that we will see such a questioning literature, sooner rather than later.

his defence *still* misses the point.   **57** M. Trachtenberg, 'Desedimenting time: Gothic column/ paradigm shifter', *RES: Anthropology and Aesthetics*, 40 (2001), 5–28.

CHAPTER 3

Ecclesiastical architecture: from reform to reformation

The past may indeed be a foreign country, but the rituals of medieval Christianity are neither remote nor alien, and many of the practices familiar to modern Christians, especially in the Roman Catholic tradition, the direct successor of the medieval Roman tradition, were established in the Middle Ages. In the twelfth century, for example, priests started the practice of holding the host aloft after its consecration, while the practice of receiving the bread but not the wine at Communion (presumably to avoid the danger of spillage of the precious transubstantiated blood)[1] was established in the thirteenth century. In one major respect, though, the medieval Church is truly distant from us now, in the twenty-first century. Christian collectives – monks, canons, nuns, priests – were in every corner of Ireland in the Middle Ages, and while their monasteries, convents and colleges were fewer in number than parish churches and lesser chapels, their impact on the medieval landscape and on the spiritual consciousness of the Middle Ages was significantly greater. The Reformation changed many things, and that was one of the most profound changes that it effected.[2]

The Reformation also explains in large measure the loss from the overwhelming majority of our medieval churches of furnishings, non-sculptural decoration, and liturgical and devotional objects and accoutrements. Timber structures and fittings, such as the screens that were in front of presbyteries and the panels that were usually behind altars, were especially vulnerable in the turmoil of the later 1500s and 1600s. The most significant church furniture to survive is the set of twenty-one misericords in the north transept of St Mary's Cathedral, Limerick: these late fifteenth-century oak seats, presumed to have been imported from an English workshop, folded up (rather like modern cinema seats) to reveal playful carvings on their undersides.[3] We have tantalizing glimpses of how common wall paintings featuring both abstract and figurative/iconographic devices must have been, and that heritage has been ably documented by Karena Morton, but the loss of church roofs helps explain the high

---

1 If wine did spill on the altar it was to be 'sucked up at once' according to an English manual of *c.*1400 for parish priests (see B.A. Barr, *Pastoral care of women* (Woodbridge, 2008), p. 29). 2 For an account of the pace and effectiveness of the Reformation in the heart of 'English Ireland' in the sixteenth century, see J. Murray, *Enforcing the English Reformation in Ireland: clerical resistance and political conflict in the diocese of Dublin, 1534–1590* (Cambridge, 2009). 3 C. Grössinger, 'At the uttermost ends of the Earth', *BAACT*, 34 (2010), 243–52; J. Cherry, 'The misericords in St Mary's Cathedral, Limerick: an additional note', ibid., 253–8. The use of classic Irish vine-leaf ornament on many of the misericords does make one question the suggestion that they were

rate of decay of internal painted stone and plaster.[4] The portable objects that were inside churches and were used liturgically or devotionally fall well outside the scope of this book,[5] but, as a sole concession, mention can be made here of the wooden sculptures from churches, including a magnificent set of three near-life-size statues from Fethard, which happily survived the search by Henry VIII's Commissioners for 'notable images or reliques to which the simple people of the said lord the king were wont to assemble superstitiously and as vagrants to walk and roam in pilgrimage, or else to lick, kiss or honour, contrary to God's honour'.[6]

CLERGY

Two prerequisites to understanding the physical remains of medieval ecclesiastical buildings are a basic knowledge of the types of clergy and a basic knowledge of liturgy. The former, first of all, fell into two categories: monastic and secular. Monastic clerics lived under vow in communities according to regulations (Rules).[7] The earliest Christian monastics were hermits who lived on their own or in small communities in the deserts of northern Africa and western Asia in the early centuries AD. From the fifth and sixth centuries, when Christianity was established across all of Europe (apart from the northern lands), there were increasingly systematic guidelines or Rules for those who desired to live in religious communities. The most influential of these Rules was associated with St Benedict of Nursia (*c.*480–*c.*550), and it was followed by many

imported from England.   **4** Morton, 'Irish medieval wall painting'; idem, 'Aspects of image and meaning in Irish medieval wall paintings' in Moss et al. (eds), *Art and devotion in late medieval Ireland*, pp 51–71; C. Manning and K. Morton, *Clare Island, Co. Mayo: the abbey and its paintings*. Archaeology Ireland Heritage Guide, 46 (Dublin, 2009). For the late twelfth-century paintings in Cashel, see R. Stalley, 'Solving a mystery at Cashel: the Romanesque painting in Cormac's Chapel', *Irish Arts Review*, 28 (2001), 25–9. For consecration crosses painted onto the plaster of churches, see C. Manning, 'Consecration crosses at Castlemartyr', *AI*, 27:1 (2013), 40–2. Depictions of ships incised into plaster are discussed in K. Brady and C. Corlett, 'Holy ships: ships on plaster at medieval ecclesiastical sites in Ireland', *AI*, 18:2 (2004), 28–31. For church glass, see J. Moran, 'The shattered image: archaeological evidence for painted and stained glass in medieval Ireland' in Moss et al. (eds), *Art and devotion in late medieval Ireland*, pp 121–41.   **5** The relevant literature is huge, especially for the early medieval and Romanesque periods. P. Harbison, *The golden age of Irish art: the medieval achievement, 600–1200* (London, 1999), is as good a place to start as any. There are no comparable syntheses covering the period 1200–1600, but papers of particular interest include C. Hourihane, 'Holye crossys: a catalogue of processional, altar, pendant and crucifix figures for late medieval Ireland', *PRIA*, 100C (2000), 1–85; E. McEneaney, 'Politics and the art of devotion in late fifteenth-century Waterford' in Moss et al. (eds), *Art and devotion in late medieval Ireland*, pp 33–50; R. Ó Floinn, 'Irish Franciscan church furnishings in the pre-Reformation period' in idem (ed.), *Franciscan faith: sacred art in Ireland, AD1600–1750* (Dublin, 2011), pp 7–20; and Smith, 'The material culture of Donegal Franciscan friaries'. The material culture of the medieval church was not just 'high art' but included such disposables as bread, wine and wax (as mentioned inter alia, for example, in *RA*).   **6** C. MacLeod, 'Some late mediaeval wood sculptures in Ireland', *JRSAI*, 77 (1947), 53–62.   **7** The literature on medieval monasticism is vast. A useful introduction is C.H. Lawrence, *Medieval monasticism: forms of religious life in western Europe in the Middle Ages* (London, 2001).

of the religious communities that emerged during the church reforms of the tenth and eleventh centuries in Europe, including the Cistercian monks.[8] Rivalling the Rule of St Benedict in popularity across Europe from the eleventh century was the Rule of St Augustine of Hippo (354–430), a more flexible set of regulations assembled from the saint's various writings long after his death. Its many adherents included the Augustinian canons regular.[9] The church reforms under which these and other monastic congregations had emerged in pre-1000 Europe only spread to Ireland around the start of the twelfth century.[10] Augustinians (after 1140)[11] and Cistercians (starting in 1142)[12] soaked up most of the patronage that secular lordship had to offer up to *c.*1230, leaving little room for any expansion of the longer-established Benedictine presence, or for groups like the Carthusians and Cluniacs.[13]

The canons regular

The first couple of generations of Augustinians in Ireland was composed of native clerics for whom the adoption of the Rule of St Augustine was a gesture of their embrace of the new reform ideals.[14] The particular recension of the Rule that these canons followed was that observed in the northern French monastery of Arrouaise: St Malachy of Armagh, one of the drivers of the reform movement in Ireland, had been there in 1139 and on his return to Ireland introduced Irish clerics to its austere and contemplative observances.[15] The number of monasteries of Augustinian canons regular in pre-1169 Ireland is difficult to estimate. Several dozen are listed as certain or possible examples by Gwynn and Hadcock,[16] but the evidence is thin for many of them. In any case, in the absence of a comprehensive knowledge of the regulations followed in pre-reform Irish monasticism, we cannot easily distinguish between those monasteries where the Rule was adopted as a package, thereby effecting a radical transformation of identity, and those where improvements were made to existing regulations using the Rule of St Augustine for guidance.

---

8 M. Dunn, 'Mastering Benedict: monastic rules and their authors in the early medieval west', *EHR*, 105:416 (1990), 567–94.   9 'Canons regular' refers to priests (canons) following a rule (or living a 'regular' life).   10 M.T. Flanagan, *The transformation of the Irish church in the twelfth century* (Woodbridge, 2010); Bracken and Ó Riain-Raedel, *Ireland and Europe in the twelfth century*; O'Keeffe, *Romanesque Ireland*.   11 There is no evidence of Augustinians in Ireland prior to this (Flanagan, *The transformation of the Irish church*, p. 137).   12 Stalley, *Cistercian monasteries of Ireland*, pp 11–16; Flanagan, *The transformation of the Irish church*, pp 123–35.   13 See E. Bhreathnach, 'Benedictine influence in Ireland in the late eleventh and early twelfth centuries: a reflection', *Journal of Medieval Monastic Studies*, 1 (2012), 63–91. The only Carthusian house in Ireland became Franciscan and the surviving church is of that order. See A. Gray, 'Kinaleghin: a forgotten Irish charterhouse of the thirteenth century', *JRSAI*, 89 (1959), 35–58. For the Cluniacs, whose house is now lost, see P. Conlon, 'The medieval priory of SS Peter and Paul in Athlone' in Murtagh (ed.), *Irish midland studies*, pp 73–83.   14 The best introduction remains S. Preston, 'The canons regular of St Augustine: the twelfth-century reform in action' in S. Kinsella (ed.), *Augustinians at Christ Church: the canons regular of the cathedral priory of Holy Trinity, Dublin* (Dublin, 2000), pp 23–40.   15 G. Dunning, 'The Arroasian order in medieval Ireland', *IHS* 4:16 (1945), 297–315. For the origins of the Arrouaisian observance in Ireland, see Flanagan, *The transformation of the Irish church*, pp 136–9.   16 Gwynn and Hadcock, *Medieval religious houses*, pp 153–6.

The Anglo-Normans added many new foundations to the Augustinian portfolio, including some houses of Premonstratensians, canons who also followed the Rule of St Augustine but had observances borrowed from the Cistercians. Most of the new Augustinian foundations from the late twelfth century were priories rather than abbeys, so they were houses of slightly lesser rank in the spectrum of monastery types in the high Middle Ages, but this might not have made much difference to how they operated: for example, Athassel remained a priory through the Middle Ages and yet was one of the largest monasteries ever built in Ireland. It is not clear if the Anglo-Norman houses followed the Arrouaisian observance.[17] The one specific observance that we know some of them followed was that associated with the abbey of St Victor in Paris, a famed centre of scholasticism. The Victorine observance was introduced into Ireland in the late 1100s via the priory (later abbey) of St Thomas the Martyr in Dublin; Henry II, for whom the priory was founded, had been a benefactor of the leading English Victorine house, St Augustine's Abbey in Bristol.[18] The distribution of Victorine sites is markedly east coast, with the one exception of Bridgetown Priory.[19]

It is appropriate to mention here also the communities of nuns and canonesses – distinctions are not easily made[20] – that were also present in medieval Ireland and that generally, from the twelfth century on, followed the Rule of St Augustine as well.[21] Though small, their monastic houses were, with the major exception of Monaster-nagalliaghduff, not dissimilar in their physical make-up to those of male communities. Their churches required priests to officiate at Mass and Holy Week ceremonies, but they looked after other liturgical duties themselves.

Cistercian monks

Actual Augustinian canons of non-Irish birth were scarce (if they were present at all) before the Anglo-Normans arrived in 1169. By contrast, the first Cistercians in Ireland included French brethren. They quickly abandoned to the Irish brethren the first monastery of that affiliation, Mellifont Abbey (founded 1142). The ethnic discord that persuaded French monks to leave Ireland echoed into the Anglo-Norman period when, in the early thirteenth century, violence erupted between Gaelic-Irish and Anglo-Norman Cistercian brethren.[22] The expansion of Cistercianism in Ireland from its first roots at Mellifont was rapid: seven new monasteries were founded as its daughter-houses – they were colonized from it, in other words – within a decade of its foundation, and some of them in turn had their own daughter-houses. However, a

17 Anglo-Norman Rathkeale has been identified as Arrouaisian (Gwynn and Hadcock, *Medieval religious houses*, pp 190–1), but the source is unreliable.   18 V. Davis, 'Relations between the abbey of St Thomas the Martyr and the municipality of Dublin, *c*.1176–1527', *DHR*, 40:2 (1987), 57–65.   19 O'Keeffe, *An Anglo-Norman monastery*, pp 20–3.   20 E. Makowski, *A pernicious sort of woman: quasi-religious women and canon lawyers in the later Middle Ages* (Washington, DC, 1998), esp. pp 5–6.   21 The major study, which includes an account of nunnery architecture alongside discussions of different aspects of female piety, is D. Hall, *Women and the church in medieval Ireland, c.1140–1540* (Dublin, 2003).   22 Historical context is provided by Stalley, *Cistercian monasteries of Ireland*. For ethnic violence, see B.W. O'Dwyer, *The conspiracy of Mellifont, 1216–1231: an episode in the history of the Cistercian order in medieval Ireland* (Dublin, 1970).

number of the order's Irish monasteries were not new foundations in the affiliation but had started life as houses of other monastic communities. St Mary's Abbey, Dublin, for example, was founded in 1139 as a house of the Congregation of Savigny, a less well-known monastic collective of French origin. In 1147 all Savigniac houses shifted affiliation to the Cistercian order, and St Mary's became Cistercian in that context.[23] An earlier Savigniac house in Ireland, *Erynagh*, founded in Co. Down in 1127 (and affiliated to the Cistercians after 1147), was destroyed by John de Courcy shortly after his invasion of Ulster in 1177, and in its place he founded the Cistercian monastery of Inch on an early monastic site; indeed, contrary to what is widely understood to have been the situation with the Cistercians, Inch's native pre-Cistercian community might have adopted the order's customs (and its observance of the Rule of St Benedict) in the way that many pre-reform communities in Ireland adopted the Rule of St Augustine.[24]

Cistercian monasteries founded under Anglo-Norman patronage were frequently colonized directly from houses in England or from older Irish houses where the congregations were English. By shortly after 1200 the great phase of Cistercian foundation was over, with Hore Abbey, Cashel, an isolated late foundation of 1272. No new abbeys were added in the late Middle Ages, and many existing houses were relatively impoverished by then, but generous local patronage allowed some, notably Holycross and Kilcooly, to enjoy new building programmes.

Mendicants

The various communities of mendicant ('begging' or alms-collecting) friars that were formed in thirteenth-century Europe also followed the major monastic rules. They had no choice: the Fourth Lateran Council of 1215 had decreed that all new religious orders were to adhere to existing Church-approved regulations.[25] The friars came to Ireland some decades after the establishment of Anglo-Norman lordship, and they not only replaced monks and canons as the recipients of whatever patronage was still available but stirred many patrons to reach again into their pockets to fund whole new projects. The significance of mendicantism in the political and economic growth of Anglo-Norman lordship in Ireland is hugely underappreciated. The chronology of the first wave of mendicant foundations coincides with the upward turn of the curve of economic prosperity in the middle decades of the thirteenth century. Given that the two major congregations, the Dominicans (also known as 'black friars', on account of their habit) and Franciscans (or 'grey friars'), were not long formed on the Continent, the early appearance of mendicantism in a land where political overlordship had been hotly and often violently contested over the previous half century is a clear indication that economic growth had started.

The popularity of mendicants among lordly patrons of the thirteenth century was certainly a consequence of the special venerability that they had come to possess very

---

23 Flanagan, *The transformation of the Irish church*, pp 156–8. **24** Ibid., p. 160. **25** 'Mendicant' is derived from the Latin *mendicare*, to beg (for alms). For enunciation of the theories that the mendicant friars were, in their early stages anyway, more concerned with preaching than with begging, and that later they were more focused on defending the poor than on actually being

quickly across contemporary western Christendom. They also had a more intimate interaction with laypeople than either Augustinian canons or (especially) Cistercian monks, and that naturally reflected well on the patrons responsible for their intro-duction. Moreover, their modest needs made them attractively inexpensive to potential sponsors: they needed no land other than that on which their friaries stood, and they needed little additional investment from patrons once they were set up. One thing they did need, at least initially, was access to urban populations, as neither their dependence on alms nor their need to preach could be satisfied easily in rural venues. Thus, their first foundations were attached to substantial, trade-rich towns.

The friary-sites themselves were usually outside rather than inside the gates of those towns. Although it often asserted that only extra-mural sites were available by the time friars arrived, it is unlikely that towns were so full in the mid-thirteenth century that no space could be made available. In any case, none of the towns, apart from the old Hiberno-Scandinavian ones, was so enclosed that additional urban space could not have been created, and the friars were sufficiently well regarded among town founders and burgesses in medieval society that space would have been created if needed. So, many of the fraternal communities must have chosen extra-mural sites, provided they were accessible. The extra-mural preference underscored mendicant 'otherness', without 'othering' it too radically. It allowed friars to collect alms from suburban dwellers who had limited access to town spaces, as well as from the non-resident traders who regularly headed home with bulging pockets from urban fairs and markets. And, of course, the support of people living inside the towns was assured anyway, thanks in no small part to the sermons that friars were allowed to deliver in the parish churches (at least until tensions over such matters as burial fees soured relations between friars and curates), as well as to their use of market crosses in town-squares as venues for preaching.[26] Today, almost all of the mendicant sites in question are outside town walls (or, rather, the sites of town walls) that were built after the friars had first settled. It is conceivable that some urban communities, much as they cherished the presence of friars, found mendicant sites to be quite inconvenient when they started to build stone walls under murage grants: in Cashel, for example, the town wall had to be zigzagged around the precincts of Dominican and Franciscan houses that had been founded quite close to the market place. By the later thirteenth century the preference for suburban sites had abated somewhat, and small settlements like Lorrha, and even some very rural locations like Rathfran, were host to new mendicant houses.

All the mendicant communities experienced a difficult late fourteenth century, thanks in part to the Great Schism (from 1378) that split the Latin Church between supporters of Rome and supporters of Avignon. However, from the start of the fifteenth century their fortunes turned and new friaries sprung up almost everywhere, especially in Gaelic-Irish lands west of the Shannon.

poor themselves, see D. Prudio (ed.), *The origin, development and refinement of medieval religious mendicancies* (Turnhout, 2011).   **26** M. Robson, 'The greyfriars of Lincoln, *c.*1230–1330' in M.J.P. Robson and J. Röhrkasten (eds), *Franciscan organisation in the mendicant context* (Berlin, 2010), pp 119–46 at pp 120–2. Some medieval Irish market crosses may actually have been erected as preaching crosses by mendicants. For English examples of this, see D. O'Sullivan, *In the company*

The arrival and spread of mendicantism in Ireland is fully documented by Colmán Ó Clabaigh.[27] What follows below is inevitably drawn largely from his work. One note of caution specifically for the architectural historian concerns foundation dates: we must assume some gap between the founding of a community's house – the legal act by which a new establishment was sanctioned – and the start of actual construction. That caution is noted here because such gaps are documented with Franciscan friaries,[28] but it applies in general to all monastic foundations.

The Dominicans – the Order of Preachers – constituted the earliest custom-built mendicant movement, having been founded by St Dominic Guzman who died in 1221. They adopted the Rule of St Augustine, which was a natural choice given that their founder was originally an Augustinian canon. Successive generations of Dominicans moulded the Rule to their own needs. Dominicans first appeared in Ireland in 1224, founding a house in Dublin on the north side of the Liffey with permission from the adjacent St Mary's Abbey (Cistercian), as well as a house on the north side of Drogheda, dedicated to St Mary Magdalene. There followed in quick succession houses in Kilkenny (1225), Limerick (1227), Cork (1229), Waterford (1235), Mullingar (1237), Cashel (1243) and Newtownards (1244). For the foundation of the Waterford house we have documentation of the king's approval of the proposal of the citizens of the city 'to construct an edifice for the use of the Dominicans in a vacant space under the walls of their city in which anciently existed a small field',[29] but those citizens would have had little say in the process post-approval: Dominican guidelines on church construction from the 1230s specified that three friars were to be chosen from every congregation to oversee and make rulings on that congregation's architecture, and that, whatever else those friars did, the churches had to be thirty feet high, and stone vaults were permissible only in the choirs and sacristies.[30]

The 'conquest' of Connacht after 1235 brought the order west of the Shannon where, with the foundations in Athenry (1241), Sligo and Strade (both 1252), Roscommon (1253), and Rathfran (1274), it enjoyed both Anglo-Norman and Gaelic-Irish patronage. The Connacht foundations brought the Dominicans away from the edges of large towns where the first-generation friaries had been located and into rural environs. Meanwhile, the process of founding new houses continued east of the Shannon, at Youghal (1268), Lorrha (1269) and Kilmallock (1291). In the late Middle Ages, starting at the end of the fourteenth century, the Friars Preachers embraced the Observant reform. Observants were friars who returned to what they regarded as a more appropriately rigorous regime of regular discipline, and their houses are described as 'Observant' in contradistinction to 'Conventual', the term that describes the houses of non-reformed mendicants. The Observant movement among

of the preachers: the archaeology of medieval friaries in England and Wales (Leicester, 2013), p. 4. **27** Ó Clabaigh, *The friars in Ireland*. There are also many general accounts, including Y. McDermott, 'Returning to core principles', *History Ireland*, 15:1 (2007), 12–17. **28** N. Gallagher, 'The Irish Franciscan province: from foundation to the aftermath of the Bruce invasion' in Robson and Röhrkasten (eds), *Franciscan organisation in the mendicant context*, pp 19–42 at pp 28–9. **29** *CDI, 1171–1251*, no. 2249. **30** R.A. Sundt, '*Mediocres domus et humiles habeant fratres nostri*. Dominican legislation on architecture and architectural decoration in the 13th century', *JSAH*, 46 (1987),

Dominicans took root in Connacht first, with major new building work at Athenry and Portumna in the 1420s heralding its arrival. New, predominantly rural, foundations followed, including at Urlar (1434), Tulsk (1448), Burrishoole (1486) and Ballindoon (1507).

The Franciscans – the Friars Minor – were founded by St Francis of Assisi (who died in 1226) and possessed a rule in which the vow of poverty was emphasized at the cost of guidelines on other aspects of community life and devotion; they even described themselves as Friars Minors (*fraters minores*) to distinguish themselves from higher ranks of clergy. There is some uncertainty as to the date of their arrival in Ireland, but it was probably around 1230, with Dublin (rather than Youghal, the other contender) having the first house.[31] Within two decades there were friaries on the outskirts of at least eleven towns: Athlone, Carrickfergus, Castledermot, Cork, Downpatrick, Drogheda, Dublin, Dundalk, Kilkenny, Waterford and Youghal, if not also Ennis, Nenagh and New Ross. In subsequent decades there were further new houses at Claregalway (*c.*1250), Buttevant (1251), Ardfert (by 1253), Kildare (between 1254 and 1260), Clane (1258), Armagh (1264), Cashel (*c.*1265), Multyfarnham (1268), Clonmel (1269), Trim (by 1282) and Galway (1296).[32] The Friars Minor enjoyed an extraordinary fifteenth-century renaissance, starting with the foundation of Askeaton Friary shortly before 1400. As with their Dominican contemporaries, the later Franciscans divided into Conventuals and Observants. The heartland of the renaissance was west of the Shannon. Kilconnell (by 1414), Quin (*c.*1433), Meelick and Muckross (1440s), Clonkeenkerrill (1453) and Galbally (1471) were Conventual, although the Quin and Muckross communities attended to their mission with a rigidity that anticipated the Observant reforms. The main expansion of Observant Franciscan houses, both new foundations and reformed older ones, was after 1460, starting with Adare (1464). The foundation dates of the other friaries of the movement are less certain, but Kilcrea, Moyne, Ross and Sherkin are of the 1460s, and Lislaughtin and Donegal were certainly founded in the mid-1470s, the latter colonizing a new Observant friary at Creevelea in 1508.

Dominicans and Franciscans tracked each other's new foundations carefully, because whenever a town of any magnitude attracted the attention of one fraternal congregation the other one generally turned up shortly afterwards. This was not a uniquely Irish pattern, and the two papal instructions of the 1260s concerning the recommended distances in *cannae* between mendicant communities (see above, p. 89) reflect the fact that friaries arrived in convoy. A benign view identifies unhealthy inter-community competition for alms as the sole rationale for these instructions, but the rise of anti-fraternal sentiment a decade earlier suggests that the papal edicts were also intended to regulate the urban mendicants for their own good.[33] The Dominicans were usually first to arrive in towns in Ireland, with Franciscans turning up within a

---

394–407.   **31** The case against Youghal is made convincingly by Gallagher, 'The Irish Franciscan province'.   **32** See ibid. for detailed studies of the friaries of Cork, Ardfert, Dundalk, Multyfarnham and Armagh.   **33** The rise of anti-fraternalism is documented by C.H. Lawrence, *The friars: the impact of the early mendicant movement on Western society* (London, 1994), pp 127–65. See also Ó Clabaigh, *The friars in Ireland*, ch. 6.

generation, but Youghal is an interesting exception.[34] Arriving in the second quarter of the thirteenth century, the Franciscans were given a site a short distance outside the town (the area of which was not walled until *c*.1275) on the side that would have seen heavy traffic from the city of Cork and from the small market settlements that were springing up on the rich farmland of Imokilly. The Dominicans settled at the opposite end of the town just before 1270. Passing traffic was much lighter here, but their monastery, known today as North Abbey, was very close to the town's parish church and fairly close to its original market area, so they probably benefited more than their competitors from the benevolence of the town community.

So-called Tertiary (or Third Order [Regular]) Dominicans and Franciscans were lay penitents who were attracted to the rules of the orders and adopted the appropriate lifestyles. Their emergence on the Continent in the thirteenth century reflects the inspirational qualities of the mendicant concept, especially to townspeople, inevitably the very people who had most direct experience of it. Ireland's encounter with the tertiary movement was late, with Franciscan tertiaries first recorded in 1425 and Dominican tertiaries first recorded in 1426–7. In both cases, their emergence was linked to the Observant reform. Franciscan Rosserk (*c*.1440) has the finest tertiary architecture in Ireland.

The Carmelites – the Order of Friars of Our Lady of Mount Carmel, also known as 'white friars' – originated as an order of hermits in the Holy Land in the first decade of the thirteenth century, but it was only when they migrated to Europe in the mid-1200s that they became mendicants in the mould of the Dominicans and Franciscans. The first Carmelites in Ireland are recorded in the 1260s, with their earliest foundation being Leighlinbridge. There were relatively few foundations thereafter, and only four of pre-Black Death vintage are of particular archaeological interest: Burriscarra (1298), Loughrea (*c*.1300), Castlelyons (1307/9), and Ardfinnan (1314). Reform came to the Carmelites in the late Middle Ages, with five new houses established between 1396 and 1516. Rathmullan was the last of the five, and was the initiative of a noblewoman, Máire Ní Mhaille.

The Augustinian (or Austin) friars – the Friars Hermits of St Augustine – adopted the Rule of St Augustine when they were founded in 1256, and they were able, like the Dominicans, to adjust its requirements as needed. Of the four principal mendicant groups, they were apparently the last to arrive in Ireland. Their Dublin house, Holy Trinity, was probably not founded until the reign of Edward I. There followed a series of foundations in quick succession: Dungarvan (*c*.1290), Fethard (by 1305), Cork's 'Red Abbey' (by 1306), Ballinrobe (possibly *c*.1312), Adare (by 1316) and Clonmines (1317). The late medieval revival saw Augustinian friars occupy a new house at Ardnaree (*c*.1400) and the former Carmelite house at Burriscarra (from before 1413). The Augustinian friars' Observant movement is first manifest at Banada in 1423, followed by Dunmore in Co. Galway (by 1425), Ballyhaunis (by *c*.1430), Murrisk (1457) and Callan (1461). Just as the last Carmelite friary in medieval Ireland was founded by a Gaelic noblewoman, so too was the last house of Augustinian friars: the priory of St Augustine in Galway was founded by Margaret Athy in 1506.

34 D. Kelly and T. O'Keeffe, *Youghal*, Irish Historic Towns Atlas, 27 (Dublin, 2015).

The military orders

The two great medieval military orders, the Knights Templar (the Poor Fellow-Soldiers of Christ and of the Temple of Solomon) and the Knights Hospitaller (of St John of Jerusalem), had quite extensive possessions in Ireland.[35] A third order, the Knights of St Thomas the Martyr of Acre, had just two houses in Ireland, in Carrick-on-Suir and Kilkenny, both gone, while the not-unrelated Trinitarians – the Order of the Most Holy Trinity for the Redemption of the Captives, originally formed to raise ransoms to secure the release of Christians from Muslim captivity – had a single house in Adare, which does survive.[36] All three military orders began life in the crusades, providing pastoral care and military protection to pilgrims before they eventually transformed into armed forces in their own right, albeit without losing their mission as monastics. Templars followed a rule closely modelled on that of the Cistercians while Hospitallers (as well as the Knights of St Thomas) followed the Rule of St Augustine. Templars and Hospitallers were hostile to each other from the outset, and attempts to unite them always failed. Following their persecution for alleged heresies, the Order of Knights Templar was disbanded in 1312 by Pope Clement V.[37] By contrast, the Knights Hospitaller survived through the Middle Ages, even acquiring former Templar property. The Order of St John of Jerusalem, also known as the *fratres cruciferi* (friars of the cross, or the 'crutched'/'crouched' friars), was also a hospitaller order, and is therefore easily confused with the Knights Hospitaller, but it was not of military character; to add to the confusion, its friars were not mendicants but were canons regular who followed the Rule of St Augustine.[38]

---

35 C.L. Falkiner, 'The Hospital of St John of Jerusalem in Ireland', *PRIA*, 26C (1906), 275–317; H. Wood, 'The Templars in Ireland', *PRIA*, 26C (1907), 327–77; H. Nicholson, 'Serving king and crusade: the military orders in royal service in Ireland, 1220–1400' in N. Housely and M. Bull (eds), *The experience of crusading, 1: western approaches* (Cambridge, 2003), pp 233–52. For general surveys, see H. Nicholson, *The Knights Hospitaller* (Woodbridge, 2001); idem, *The Knights Templar: a new history* (Stroud, 2001); M. Browne and C. Ó Clabaigh (eds), *Soldiers of Christ: the Knights Hospitaller and the Knights Templar in medieval Ireland* (Dublin, 2015). **36** E. St J. Brooks, 'Irish possessions of St Thomas of Acre', *PRIA*, 58C (1956/7), 21–44. The proximity of Carrick-on-Suir (St Thomas of Acre) to the cluster of military order sites around Waterford harbour is worth noting. For Trinitarian Adare – a building that has never been studied properly – see Gwynn and Hadcock, *Medieval religious houses*, p. 217. **37** The trials and executions of Templars, and the afterlife of their order, have long fascinated people, and conspiracy theories centred on them have featured prominently in pseudo-historical writings and in popular fiction. Clement had actually absolved Templars in 1308 but violently disbanded the order under political pressure. The innocence of the Knights Templar was officially acknowledged by the Vatican exactly seven centuries after their persecution. **38** R.N. Hadcock, 'The order of the Holy Cross in Ireland' in J.A. Watt, J.B. Morall and F.X. Martin (eds), *Medieval studies presented to Aubrey Gwynn* (Dublin, 1961), pp 44–53. The friars' hospital of St John the Baptist at Newgate in Dublin, on a site now occupied by John's Lane Church, is especially well documented: E. St John Brooks (ed.), *Register of the hospital of St John the Baptist, without the Newgate, Dublin* (Dublin, 1936); M. Hennessy, 'The priory and hospital of the Newgate: the evolution and decline of a medieval monastic estate' in W.J. Smyth and K. Whelan (eds), *Common ground: essays on the historical geography of Ireland* (Cork, 1988), pp 41–54; G. O'Keeffe, 'The hospital of St John the Baptist in medieval Dublin: functions and maintenance', *MD*, 9 (2009), 166–82.

Secular clergy

Secular clerics were not bound by monastic regulations. They mainly worked as individuals in local churches, providing sacramental services to local communities.[39] We often describe these medieval clerics as 'parish priests'. It is not an inappropriate designation, although we should be careful about using the word 'parish' before the late twelfth century, as we will see below (pp 128–9). The priests themselves were called *curates* in the Middle Ages. In modern Roman Catholicism a curate is an assisting priest, below the rank of a parish priest, but in the Middle Ages the term simply connoted the fact that, under canon law, his ecclesiastical office (or *benefice*) obligated the priest to *care for* souls; the modern word 'curator' (as in museum curator) comes for the same Latin root, *curatus*. Engagement with the local community provided a curate with a portion of his income. There were customary offerings from that community at key junctures in the Christian calendar, such as Easter (the one time of the year that parishioners received the host)[40] and Christmas. Fees were also received for officiating at marriages and funerals (although income from burial fees was threatened whenever the mendicants arrived and offered burial in their friary precincts[41]). Small gifts of money might come a curate's way any time he said a Mass. From the twelfth century on, a substantial portion of a curate's wage derived from tithing, which was basically a taxation on the earnings – from agriculture, for example, or from the profits of mining, manufacturing or trade – of those to whom pastoral care was given. A curate who received the whole of the tithes as his income (not counting other sources of income) was called a *rector*. Under canon law, an ecclesiastical office to which a tithe is paid is called a *rectory*; in the Middle Ages that term also came to mean the residence of the rector, and it is still used in that sense today in the Protestant Church.

By the time of the Anglo-Norman invasion of Ireland it had become standard practice in western Christendom for rectories (in the sense of the ecclesiastical office) to be granted by local landowners to monastic houses. The monasteries became, in other words, the rectors, and they collected the tithes. They were enriched by this practice during the economic boom of the thirteenth century. The relatively low architectural quality of many Irish parish churches connected to monasteries through this system might well be explained by the siphoning of locally generated money away from the local building project to the main monastic house.

Monasteries were also granted advowson by many local lords. This was the right to appoint a parish's priest. The practice of transferring advowson to a monastic house was promoted because it reduced lay influence in the provision of pastoral care to local communities, thus preventing local lords from reserving church-offices for family

---

39 Useful sources for an explanation of the context include C. Platt, *The parish churches of medieval England* (London, 1981), and FitzPatrick and Gillespie (eds), *The parish in medieval and early modern Ireland*.   **40** A. Empey, 'The layperson in the parish: the medieval inheritance, 1169–1536' in R. Gillespie and W.G. Neely (eds), *The laity and the church of Ireland, 1000–2000* (Dublin, 2002), pp 7–48 at p. 8.   **41** Mendicants were authorized in 1250 to bury laypeople (M. Mersch, 'Programme, pragmatism and symbolism in mendicant architecture' in A. Müller and K. Stöber (eds), *Self-representation of medieval religious communities: the British Isles in context* (New Brunswick and London, 2009), pp 143–66 at pp 151–3).

members and from appropriating for private use any tithes or moneys brought in by parishioners.[42] But not all lords granted advowson; there are parish churches of the thirteenth century in Ireland for which there is no evidence of any monastic 'ownership', while significant numbers of churches in the late Middle Ages certainly had the advowson retained by their patrons.[43] Those curates who were appointed by the monasteries in the 1200s were paid a portion (usually a third) of the tithe as their salary. Curates so appointed were called *vicars*, and their residences were called *vicarages*.[44] Many of the 'parish priests' of Anglo-Norman Ireland were technically vicars.[45] These men were never wealthy, and when the economy went into decline in the fourteenth century, bringing with it a fall in tithe revenue, many of them must have been quite impoverished. A career in the secular priesthood could hardly have been very appealing in the 1300s. It is very likely that the retention of advowson by landed families in the late Middle Ages in Ireland reflects the same general dissatisfaction that contemporary English patrons felt with monastic control of appointments. By retaining advowson, a local lord could at least ensure that there *was* a priest; the English evidence makes clear that if a rectory was unprofitable, a monastery might leave a vicarage vacant – and a community without appropriate pastoral care – sooner than lose money on a salaried appointment.

Medieval curates generally lived alone. They did not always work alone, however. If a parish could afford it (or, more precisely, if a monastery holding a rectory wanted to provide it), aid for a priest might come in the form of a deacon (a fellow-celibate who was not allowed to celebrate the Eucharist or to absolve sins but who was authorized to baptize) or a clerk (a clerical assistant who, unlike the curate, was not required to be celibate). Ireland's medieval population was relatively low and overwhelmingly rural, so most parishioners' pastoral care was probably provided by a single priest working unaccompanied (and probably dependent on some form of manual to keep him informed about how to do his job[46]).

Occasionally secular priests lived in small communities of priests, often of less than half-a-dozen, and one of them would have served as dean, or head of community. Also

---

42 For a useful summary, see M. Hennessy, 'Parochial organisation in medieval Tipperary' in W. Nolan (ed.), *Tipperary: history and society* (Dublin, 1985), pp 60–70. See also C.H. Lawrence, 'The English parish and its clergy in the thirteenth century' in P. Linehan and J. Nelson (eds), *The medieval world* (London, 2013), pp 648–70 at pp 648–51. **43** It is recorded in 1282 in Youghal, for example, that 'the advowson of the church pertains to the lord' (*CIPM*, 2, p. 430). For the retention of advowson-rights by the fitzGeralds of Kildare in dioceses across Leinster and parts of Munster, and the context of that retention, see M.A. Lyons, 'Sidelights on the Kildare ascendancy: a survey of Geraldine involvement in the Church, *c.*1470–*c.*1520', *AH*, 48 (1994), 73–87. **44** R.A.R. Hartridge, *A history of vicarages in the Middle Ages* (Cambridge, 1930) is still a valuable summary. **45** A vicars choral was a community of clerics of lesser rank than the canons attached to cathedrals. Its purpose was to provide such services in the cathedrals as the canons did not, or would not, provide. The vicars fulfilled such functions by living close to the cathedrals: see R. Hall and D. Stocker (eds), *Vicars choral at English cathedrals:* Cantate Domino: *history, architecture and archaeology* (London, 2005). The residence at the entrance to the Rock of Cashel is known as the Vicars Choral, reflecting its apparent former occupancy by such a community. **46** For such literature in England, see Barr, *Pastoral care of women*, pp 28–30. I am not aware of work on this subject in Ireland.

living in these communities could be various ranks of assistant, as well as young boys starting out on the road to priesthood. These communities were called colleges (as were their residential building complexes). They appear most frequently to have been perpetual-chantry foundations; in other words, they were communities of priests endowed by wealthy landowners for the celebration in perpetuity of memorial masses for their benefactors. Although they generally served local pastoral as well as other needs,[47] colleges were liturgy focused communities. And just as parish priests had financial support, so too had collegiate priests: for example, the four priests, four lay brothers and four choristers housed in the college in Slane, founded in 1512 by Sir Christopher Fleming and his wife, Elizabeth Stuckley, were supported by the rentals of twenty houses as well as assorted lands.[48] College life was governed by statute rather than regulated by monastic rule, so these colleges should not be considered monastic places, despite superficial similarities.

Anchorites and hermits

Finally, mention must be made of those virtuous individuals of the Middle Ages who desired to pursue their religious vocation in physical isolation. Many who chose such eremitical life were unattached to religious orders and operated as sole-agents, often living in small cells attached to churches and dependent on alms for survival. A small cell incorporated in the west end of Kilbride Church is probably an example, while a small beehive-like cell attached to the east end of Okyle Church was certainly one. Some recluses were tertiaries: St Erc's Hermitage, Slane, probably founded originally in the thirteenth century, was 'restored' in 1512 by Fleming and Stuckley, whom we just met, for two recluses of the Third Order of St Francis who were replacing at least one earlier Franciscan tertiary recluse.[49] Other recluses were clerics who had already signed up to monastic collectives and needed distraction-free accommodation within monasteries that were naturally busy. Anchorholds at such sites as Athassel Priory (Augustinian), Adare Friary (Augustinian), Kilmallock Friary (Dominican) and Moyne Friary (Franciscan) testify to their presence.[50]

---

47 In Ireland, as elsewhere, colleges may well have provided both physical (hospital) care and educational training: see respectively P. Cullum, 'Medieval colleges and charity' and J. Willoughby, 'The provision of books in the English secular college' in C. Burgess and M. Heale (eds), *The late medieval English college* (Woodbridge, 2008), pp 140–53, 154–79 respectively. It may be relevant, as Colm Lennon has noted ('The parish fraternities of County Meath in the late Middle Ages', *Ríocht na Midhe*, 19 (2008), 85–101 at 95), that 'works of charity' are specified in the foundation charters of some chantries, and that the chaplain of Trim Castle – chantry priests are commonly referred to as chaplains – was also warden of the hospital of St Mary Magdalen. **48** M. Griffiths (ed.), *Calendar of inquisitions formerly in the office of the Chief Remembrancer of the Exchequer* (Dublin, 1991), p. 243. **49** T.J. Westropp, '"Slane in Bregia", County Meath: its friary and hermitage', *JRSAI*, 31 (1901), 404–30 at 424–30. **50** See C. Ó Clabaigh, 'Anchorites in late medieval Ireland' in L.H. McAvoy (ed.), *Anchoritic traditions of medieval Europe* (Woodbridge, 2010), pp 153–77; idem, 'The hermits and anchorites of medieval Dublin', *MD*, 10 (2010), 267–86. See also L.H. McAvoy, *Medieval anchoritisms: gender, space and the solitary life* (Woodbridge, 2011).

LITURGY

Liturgy is a topic of specialist research in itself, but a basic knowledge of the rites of Christian worship and their required furnishings is useful if one is to make sense of a medieval church.[51] By the start of the period covered in this book, liturgical practices had largely stabilized after several centuries of considerable regional variation across Europe. The new common rite was the Roman Rite, and there was plenty of variation in ceremonial and organizational practices within it. Any one such practice is known as a 'use'. The Use of Sarum (Salisbury), the set of rituals and ceremonies that was used in Salisbury Cathedral in southern England, was universally popular in these islands in the Middle Ages.[52] The Use of Sarum penetrated parish liturgy, which is hardly surprising given that curates would have received whatever training they got in cathedral schools. The universally accepted principles governing the structure and content of the Mass, the Divine Office and other sacramental rituals, overrode any variation in 'uses'.[53]

Baptism was, as now, the ritual by which the Christian community was entered; some parish communities might have had visual reminders of the life-stage immediately preceding baptism, if one accepts Barbara Freitag's thesis that sheela-na-gigs represent women in childbirth.[54] From the twelfth century at the very latest, baptism was a ritual for infants and young children; adult baptisms, common in the early centuries of Christianity, were rare.[55] Baptismal fonts reflect the changing age-profile of new entrants to the Christian family: early medieval fonts, of which Tallaght has the most impressive example, were large, floor-sited basins, hollowed out to accommodate the immersion of adults, but from at least the 1100s the font-bowls, by

---

51 Liturgy in pre-Anglo-Norman Ireland is well-served by N.X. O'Donoghue, *The Eucharist in pre-Norman Ireland* (Notre Dame, IN, 2010) and Y. Hen, 'The nature and character of the early Irish liturgy', *Settimane di Studi del Centro Italiano di Studi sull'Alto Medioevo*, 57 (Spoleto, 2010), 353–80; for the architecture, see T. Ó Carragáin, 'The architectural setting of the mass in early medieval Ireland', *MA*, 53 (2009), 119–54. Relatively little appears to have been published on post-1169 liturgy and architecture Ireland: coverage of liturgy in S. Duffy (ed.), *Medieval Ireland: an encyclopedia* (London, 2004), for example, is focused on the early medieval period. Until such time as it is properly addressed, we can turn for guidance to commentaries on English medieval liturgy and its architectural settings (see, for example, P. Draper, *The formation of English Gothic* (New Haven and London, 2006), pp 197–215).   **52** J. Harper, *The forms and orders of western liturgy from the tenth to the eighteenth century* (Oxford, 1991); F. Lawrence, 'What did they sing at Cashel in 1172? Winchester, Sarum and Romano-Frankish chant in Ireland', *Journal of the Society for Musicology in Ireland*, 3 (2007–8), 111–25; A. Fletcher, 'Liturgy and music in the medieval cathedral' in Crawford and R. Gillespie, *St Patrick's Cathedral*, pp 120–48.   **53** Shorter and more compact liturgies of the Roman Rite were designed for busy clergy in the thirteenth century. These became the universal liturgical practices – together they constitute the so-called Tridentine Rite – in the Roman (Catholic) Church after the Council of Trent in the mid-sixteenth century. They remained in use in Roman Catholicism until the Second Vatican Council exactly four centuries later.   **54** B. Freitag, *Sheela-na-gigs: unravelling an enigma* (London, 2004); see also Gilchrist, *Medieval life*, pp 183–4. The fact that sheela-na-gigs are also found on castles does not undermine this interpretation, given the heightened religiosity of the domestic bedchamber at childbirth (see above, p. 87).   **55** P. Cramer, *Baptism and change in the early Middle Ages, c.200–c.1150* (Cambridge, 1993); N. Orme, 'Children and the Church in

now mounted on pedestals, were only large enough for the immersion of infants. Many of our fonts are quite plain and so must be dated (unreliably) according to the dates of their host churches, but fonts decorated with sculpture can generally be dated quite accurately, with most examples being late medieval.[56] Some exceptionally fine fonts of Dundry stone survive in eastern Ireland, from St Audoen's in Dublin, Kells (Kilkenny),[57] Bannow and Fethard-on-Sea, and are likely to date stylistically (at least in the case of the latter two) to the 1180s or 1190s. One wonders if they were imported and installed in response to the decree of the synod held in Dublin in 1186 that

> an immoveable font be placed in the middle of every baptismal church, or in such other part of it as the paschal procession may conveniently pass round. That it be made of stone, or of wood lined with lead for cleanness, wide and large above, bored through to the bottom, and so contrived, that, after the ceremony of baptism be ended, the holy water may by a secret pipe be conveyed down to mother earth.[58]

The synodal decree specified baptismal churches, not to connote a particularly specialized type of church but, rather, a church in which baptism was permitted. In the twelfth century and certainly from the thirteenth, a baptismal church was a parish church, or, more accurately considering the presence of fonts in monastic churches, a church of parochial function. The place of baptism was normally inside the main entrance where it symbolized the entry of the individual into the Christian community. Unlike today, mothers did not witness the incorporation of their children but were at home preparing for their churching (see above, p. 96). Evidence that children could be baptized in rural chapels comes from Castlemartin, where 2*d.* of the 3*d.* baptismal fee went to the parish church to which the chapel was attached, while the other penny went to the chapel itself.[59]

At the other end of the cycle of life was death. The rites and monuments of burial constitute a major area of study in their own right,[60] so they fall outside the scope of this book. Burial-places inside churches were much desired by founders and benefactors. Under-floor burial was the most modest option on the menu of privileged burials; in the late Middle Ages such burials were marked by large, often rim-inscribed, floor-slabs.[61] The least modest option was the tomb marked with near-life-size effigial sculpture; most of our surviving examples are late medieval, but there is a small though important corpus of mid-thirteenth-century effigial tomb sculpture that includes the misidentified 'tomb of Strongbow' in Christ Church Cathedral, and the

medieval England', *JEH*, 45 (1994), 563–87. **56** Some of the heavily decorated later medieval fonts in the Pale are described and analysed in H.M. Roe, *The medieval fonts of Meath* (1968). A useful survey of the corpus of fonts is J. Pike, *Medieval fonts of Ireland* (Greystones, 1989). **57** This is now kept in St Mary's Church, Inistioge. **58** J. d'Alton, *The memoirs of the archbishops of Dublin* (Dublin, 1838), p. 73. **59** J. Murray, 'The sources of clerical income in the Tudor diocese of Dublin, *c.*1530–1600', *AH*, 46 (1991/2), 139–60 at 154–5. **60** For an historical perspective, see S. Fry, *Burial in medieval Ireland, 900–1500* (Dublin, 1999). **61** See the survey of Kilkenny Cathedral slabs by John Bradley, 'The medieval tombs of St Canice's' in Empey (ed.), *A worthy foundation*, pp 49–103. The corpus of slabs in Fethard is discussed in G. Crotty, *Heraldic*

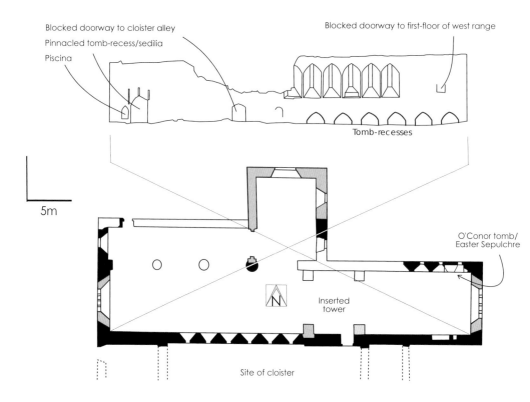

Blocked doorway to cloister alley

Pinnacled tomb-recess/sedilia

Piscina

Blocked doorway to first-floor of west range

Tomb-recesses

5m

O'Conor tomb/
Easter Sepulchre

Inserted
tower

Site of cloister

46 The interior south wall of Roscommon Friary (Dominican), founded 1253, showing the six tomb recesses in the nave.

Cantwell effigy in Kilfane Church.[62] For most benefactors, the most privileged place in which they could have some hope of burial was an arched recess in the actual architecture itself (fig. 46). Such recesses are especially common in monastic churches: secular lords with good resources were avid supporters of monasteries, and there was considerably more spiritual kudos being buried in a monastic church, even if it meant sharing the church with other deceased donors, than in a parish church. Occasionally tomb-recesses were installed in parish churches: a fine example is Killag, where recesses line the chancel. It is not possible to identify the 'owners' of most recessed tombs.

memorials in Fethard (Fethard, 2012).   **62** Tomb-sculpture features prominently in J. Hunt, *Irish medieval figure sculpture, 1200–1600* (Dublin, 1974). See also R. Stalley, 'A misunderstood Gothic masterpiece; the Cantwell effigy at Kilfane, Co. Kilkenny' in E. Rynne (ed.), *Figures from the past: studies on figurative art in Christian Ireland in honour of Helen Roe* (Dublin, 1987), pp 209–22. The popularity (lower in Ireland than in England, admittedly) of representations of individuals on tombs in the thirteenth century may be linked to contemporary thinking on purgatory (see S. Badham, 'Evidence for the minor funerary monument industry, 1100–1500' in K. Giles and C. Dyer (eds), *Town and country in the Middle Ages* (Leeds, 2005), pp 165–95).

47 The restored Gothic *sedilia* in Ardfert Cathedral is typical in having three seats, with a double *piscina* to its west. A *piscina* (or *sacrarium*) was a small, round or marigold-shaped holed basin set into the wall and arched-over, and always on the east side of the priest's seat. It was intended for the pouring away of the water after the washing of the vessels. In a double *piscina*, as here at Ardfert, the second holed basin was provided for the water with which the priest washed his hands. The wall-set *piscina* is not known in pre-Anglo-Norman Ireland (the earliest reference to a *piscina* in Ireland appears to date to 1186 (D'Alton, *The memoirs of the archbishops of Dublin*, pp 73–4)).

Burial in the chancel or choir was generally reserved for founders and their families. Priests could also be buried there.[63] The south wall of that space was usually set aside for the use of clergy: that was the place where the *sedilia*, the set of seats (*sedile* is Latin for seat) for officiating clerics, was always placed (fig. 47). So if recesses were required, they were generally put in the north wall. Having said that, south-wall tombs are certainly not unknown: for example, there is a very fine canopied tomb with an effigy in the south wall of the chancel of Dungiven Augustinian priory (fig. 20), and there is a pair of recesses in the same position relative to an altar in the south aisle at Gowran. Moreover, it was not unusual for privileged burials to be contained in *sedilia*: for example, the tombs of Johanna O'Phelan and of the O'Brien barons of Inchiquin were so presented in the friary churches of Adare and Ennis respectively.[64] Even when there is no monument to indicate a sepulchral function, the designs of *sedilia* can sometimes tell us that they doubled-up as tomb recesses (fig. 48).

Although the cachet value of clerical backsides parked on one's grave during Mass was doubtless considerable, burial in a recess in the north wall of a chancel or

63 Gilchrist, *Medieval life*, p. 206.   **64** Ó Clabaigh, *The friars in Ireland*, p. 109.

48 The *sedilia* of *c.*1300 in Burriscarra Friary church (Carmelite) was probably also a tomb. The window in its back wall is an insertion of the fifteenth century by the Augustinian friars who had recently taken over the site. The *piscina* also dates from *c.*1300.

presbytery could have a greater benefit in one's quest for salvation. Tombs located there were often used as Easter Sepulchres. Easter was at the centre of the medieval Christian calendar, and was the one time of the year when thirteenth-century and later Christians would certainly fulfil their obligation, according to one of the many decrees of the Fourth Lateran Council (1215), to receive the Eucharist; this is not to say, of course, that it was the only time of the year they attended Mass. One of the rituals of the Easter Triduum was the keeping of the consecrated host in a box – the Easter Sepulchre – between Maundy Thursday and its 'raising' on Easter Sunday.[65] As we know to have been the case in England, the Sepulchre would have been a simple wooden box or chest. It was kept customarily on the north side of the altar, reflecting the fact that Christ was buried on the north side of the Holy Sepulchre. It may have been placed on a table in lesser churches but in larger churches the mensa or top surface of a tomb in a recess was its preferred position.[66] The iconography of the sculpture on such spectacular later medieval north-side tombs as those in Ennis, Quin and Strade (fig. 16b) leaves one in little doubt about their uses during the Easter ceremonies. Even in the absence of figurative sculpture, an elaborate tomb in the north-side position of

65 Harper, *Forms and orders of western liturgy*, pp 137–8.   **66** S. Roffey, *The medieval chantry chapel: an archaeology* (Woodbridge, 2007), pp 62–3.

49 The tomb recess/Easter Sepulchre in the north wall of the choir of Timoleague Friary church (Franciscan). This is an insertion of the fifteenth century and is associated with the blocking of one of the friary's thirteenth-century 'giant order' arches (see pp 157–8). Many north-wall tombs, even recessed ones, are demonstrably secondary features, although the interval between the construction of a chancel and the insertion of a tomb was not always as long as at Timoleague.

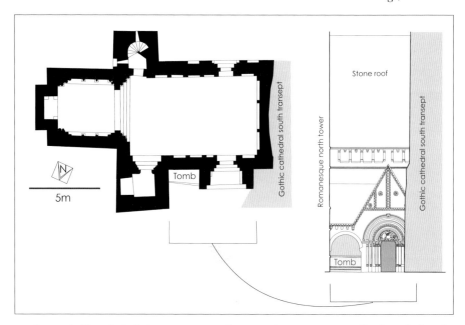

50 Cormac's Chapel, Cashel, was consecrated in 1134. Its main entrance faced north, but the new Gothic cathedral of the thirteenth century blocked it off.

a major church can be identified confidently as a Sepulchre. One such example is at Timoleague (fig. 49).

Only one premier-league medieval tomb in Ireland is on the *outside* of the church with which it is associated: the recessed tomb on the north wall of Cormac's Chapel (fig. 50). It is commonly presumed to be the resting place of Cormac Mac Carthaig, the king who had the chapel built, and to be the place from which an early thirteenth-century Limousin crozier was extracted around 1730.[67] There are many questions to be asked of it. First, is it Cormac's? He was still alive when it was made, so are we happy to imagine that he was content to see his own empty tomb any time he was in Cashel? Second, might it have contained instead the bones of a saint, translated to Cashel when the chapel was consecrated in 1134? Third, did the tomb's mensa act as an altar for ceremonies that took place in front of the chapel? Given that north-side tombs had Easter connotations, might it have had particular functions then? Is it purely coincidental that it is the same length – seven imperial feet – as Christ's tomb in the Holy Sepulchre?

Mass was, of course, the main liturgical activity, and all churches were primarily the architectural settings of its celebration. Most churches had just one altar: in single-

---

67 R. Ó Floinn, 'Bishops, liturgy and reform: some archaeological evidence' in Bracken and Ó Riain-Raedel (eds), *Ireland and Europe in the twelfth century*, pp 218–38 at p. 229; of the bishops whom Ó Floinn regards as possible depositors of the crozier in the tomb, David Mac Cerbaill, the bishop who removed the Benedictines from Cashel and replaced them with Cistercians, is the most likely candidate. Might the depositing of the crozier be interpreted as a gesture of

51 One of the earliest belfries in any mendicant church in Ireland was in Lorrha. Unfortunately it no longer survives. One of its stumps has an arched recess for an altar facing the nave, beside which is a *piscina* and a trefoil-arched tomb recess/*sedilia* similar to that in Burriscarra (fig. 48).

cell churches it was at the east end, under the same roof as the congregation, while in churches of nave-and-chancel design it was in the chancel (or presbytery). In cathedral, monastic and collegiate churches, normally quite large buildings, there were often several altars, although one – the high altar – had special status over the others. A common location for ancillary altars in those large churches was at the east end of the nave, either in front of or to the side of the screen or tower separating the nave from the choir, as in the Dominican friary church in Lorrha (fig. 51), or at the east ends of the aisles, as at Gowran. The provision of L-shaped aisle-transept units to Franciscan churches (pl. IV, figs 52, 53) was normally to service additional altars (and also, in all probability, to provide additional floor space for burials).[68]

There are many reasons why big churches had multiple altars. One is that it was customary in the Middle Ages for an altar to have only one Mass celebrated at it per day, so multiple altars would have provided 'Mass space' in major churches where there were many priests. Another is the segregation of the laity from the ecclesiastics and the patrons: altars in naves allowed Mass to be celebrated separately for the laity, thus

reconciliation with his predecessors at the moment that he banished the monks of the order that served those predecessors?   **68** Mersch, 'Programme, pragmatism and symbolism', p. 152.

52 The floor of the south transept of Ross Franciscan friary, viewed here from the nave, is carpeted with tombs-slabs. Note how patches of original plaster have survived on the walls.

53 The aisle and transept on the south side of the nave of Kilconnell Friary church (Franciscan).

enhancing their sense that the chancel behind or beyond *their* altar was a very privileged place indeed. Yet another is private donation: altars in screened-off parts of the aisles and transepts of the larger medieval churches were often chantries. These were small, privately endowed chapels with their own priests who celebrated daily Eucharist and Divine Office for the souls of the patrons.

The altars themselves were always rectangular tables, adorned (if at all) with five incised crosses – four at the corners and one in the centre – marking the places where the altar was anointed with chrism at the moment of first consecration. Altar bases in Ireland were commonly simple rectangular blocks of masonry, built up in irregular courses, but columnar bases are also known; most altars are missing whatever frontal and side panels they had originally, but some very fine decorated examples survive.[69] The adoption of the doctrine of transubstantiation – the changing of the bread and wine into the body and blood of Christ – as an article of faith by the Fourth Lateran Council in 1215 precipitated an enrichment of the rituals surrounding the holding and displaying of the host, but the altar-tops themselves remained generally empty of the paraphernalia of liturgy. The tabernacle for the consecrated host, which was essentially a small locked box, seems to have been kept off the altar until quite late in medieval western Europe and was instead either attached to the retable (an ornamental panel rising at the back of the altar) or suspended from the roof.[70] Retables must have been common but traces are fragmentary in Ireland. Wooden retables are suggested by sockets in rear-walls behind altars, as in Adare Friary church (Franciscan). An alabaster retable is known from Holy Cross Priory in Limerick. A stone retable with a *pieta* survives at Strade.[71] Aumbries are small wall-recesses or niches close to altars, and we know from examples surviving intact elsewhere in Europe that they had small lockable doors, indicating that altar plate and service books were probably kept in them. Canopies (civories/ciboriums or baldachinos) were common above medieval altars, and one often sees them today high above altars in modern churches, but, again, none survives in Ireland. However, roof-vaults, specifically rib-vaults and groin-vaults, were perhaps de facto vast canopies; the vaulted east ends of Duiske Abbey, Newtown Trim Cathedral and Clonmacnoise Cathedral, are examples.

A church's main or high altar was always positioned at the back (the east side) rather than in the centre of its liturgical host-space, and was oriented north–south. Normally a narrow space was left between the altar and the wall behind it, although in smaller churches where space was at a premium the altars sometimes physically abutted the back walls. The gap between the altar and the back wall allowed it to be regarded as a structurally free-standing unit, thus recalling the altars of the early Church, but it was rarely wide enough for a priest to walk fully around the back of it, reminding us that in the Middle Ages (from the tenth century, at least) Mass was celebrated with the priest's back to the congregation (or, expressed better, with his face to the east).

69 G. Murray, 'Altars in Ireland, 1050–1200: a survey', *JIA*, 19 (2011), 101–12. **70** G.J.C. Snoek, *Medieval piety from relics to the Eucharist: a process of mutual interaction* (Leiden, 1995), pp 205–6. **71** C. Ó Clabaigh, 'Patronage, prestige and politics: the Observant Franciscans at Adare' in J. Burton and K. Stöber (eds), *Monasteries and society in the British Isles in the later Middle Ages* (Woodbridge, 2008), pp 71–82 at p. 79.

The space in front of the high altar in a large church was systematically subdivided. The east end of the presbytery, accessible only to the celebrant and his deacons, was often square in plan (fig. 44) and was demarcated by a stepped rise in floor level and possibly a low rail. Three steps were normal, the top step – the *predella*[72] – being level with the base of the altar. Evidence that the top step was sometimes onto a wooden platform can be seen in an early thirteenth-century context at New Ross, where the *piscina* in St Mary's Church is much higher than hand-level, indicating the one-time presence of a raised timber floor, and in a fifteenth-century context in Quin Friary church (Franciscan) where the stone altar was recessed at the base to accommodate a timber floor. The use of the steps for burials is attested to in the historical record at Dominican Athenry, when the archbishop of Tuam was buried on 'the deacon's step',[73] and in Castlelyons, where a collection of very worn (mainly fourteenth-century?) grave-slabs lines a series of broad steps. The east window, behind the altar, was invariably the most elaborate window in the entire church, and the side-wall windows flanking the altar often surpassed other side-wall windows in quality. Beyond the steps to the west was the choir, where the wooden stalls were arranged along the side-walls in rows. The higher stalls at the back were for senior-ranked members of the community, the lower ones at the front for trainees.

Unlike in modern churches, screens generally prevented unimpeded views between parts of medieval churches. Whether they were made of timber, wrought-iron or even stone, they seem (from extant medieval examples outside Ireland) not to have blocked fully the spaces into which they were set but to have stopped well short of roof- or arch-level, thus allowing some light and sound travel over them; parclose screens, with 'blind' lower sections and 'open' (fenestrated or traceried) upper sections at eye-level, were probably the norm. Whatever the arrangement in a modest parish church, in a cathedral, monastic or collegiate church the vista from the west end (the entrance end) to the east end (the main liturgical end) was never unimpeded. At very least there was one screen between the nave and choir – the choir screen – and it was permeated by a single central doorway or by three doorways. The Dominicans, who were fond of building regulations from the outset, made choir screens obligatory in their churches in a general decree of 1249. They instructed that the screen doors were kept closed while the friars prayed but were open at other times to allow laymen (but not laywomen) access to the spaces beyond.[74]

The medieval choir screen was also known as the *pulpitum*. It was here that the gospel was read, sometimes from a loft or platform that was on top of the screen and was accessible by steps. The normal position of the choir screen was under the chancel arch or, in churches with transepts, under the eastern arch of the group of four crossing arches. At Athassel the choir screen is an actual wall on the *west* side of the crossing. It is permeated by a much-decorated doorway flanked by windows (see fig. 14), and the loft opening above it survives, albeit filled in with later masonry.[75] There is an almost identical scheme in the parish church of Aghaviller (fig. 54). There was sometimes a

72 'Predella, n.' OED online. Ó Clabaigh describes the three steps collectively as the predella (*The friars in Ireland*, p. 243).   **73** *RA*, p. 205.   **74** Mersch, 'Programme, pragmaticism and symbolism', p. 155.   **75** It has been suggested that the very fine Romanesque doorway

54 The chancel of Aghaviller parish church with its surmounting late medieval tower, viewed from the south side of the foundations-only nave. There is a narrow doorway (with Romanesque detailing on the inside) where one normally finds a chancel arch, and it is flanked by two small windows. The arched recess of the *pulpitum* above the doorway was blocked when the upper parts of the chancel were altered in the late Middle Ages.

second or outer screen further to the west of the choir screen. This was *usually* a rood screen, so-named because positioned directly above it, normally carried on a transverse beam (or suspended by a chain from above) and not supported at all by the screen below, was a rood, a representation of the crucifixion. Such screens are found in churches in many parts of the Continent and in Scandinavia, but their frequency in Ireland is uncertain. The missing screens attested to in Irish parish churches, as in a small number of important central-Pale churches such as Killeen, Dunsany and Rathmore,[76] are often described as rood screens on the presumption that they had roods associated with them. The outer screen was more a feature of monastic architecture than parish-church architecture, and by its position within a monastic church it effectively commandeered for use by the monastic community the east end

re-erected in Killaloe Cathedral originally came from a choir screen too: J. Ellis and R. Moss, 'The conservation of the Romanesque portal at Killaloe: exposing the history of one of Clare's finest carved doorways', *JRSAI*, 129 (1999), 67–89 at 83.   **76** O'Neill, 'Medieval parish churches in County Meath', pp 18–26.

55 The screen in Ross Friary church (Franciscan) viewed from the nave. Two original altars stand on either side of the opening, and there is a wall tomb in the north wall of the nave (to the left).

of the physical structure of the nave: in Ireland we see this most clearly in the architecture of Cistercian churches, where these outer screens separated the lay brethren from the monks. Examples of choir and rood screens joined by a single common loft are not unknown outside Ireland, and the type best describes perhaps the well-preserved vaulted screens at Ballindoon Priory (Dominican), the Franciscan friaries of Kilconnell and Ross (fig. 55), Clontuskert Priory (Augustinian), and the rather poorly preserved screen at Abbeyshrule monastery (Cistercian). Chantry chapels in parish and cathedral churches, discussed below, were also screened-off, usually with parclose screens.

The rules surrounding Mass and its celebration in the late Middle Ages were outlined at a synod of the province of Cashel held in Limerick in 1453, and two of the clauses are worth quoting in full because they provide us with a fascinating portrait of the responsibilities placed on medieval Christians:

> That ministers of churches should say the canonical hours in their churches on all Sundays and holidays, and week-days as often as possible. The bell ought to be rung three times before commencing Mass and the other divine offices on Sundays and holidays, and also thrice on weekdays, the excommunicated and interdicted are to be excluded, under pain of a fine of 40 pence, payable by the

exorcists and curates to the bishop at the time of his visitation or to his official. All the faithful are to cease from all civil works on Sundays and holidays, and come together in the churches to hear the divine offices under the pain of excommunication.

The parishioners of every parish should have in their parochial churches, at their own expense, for the proper celebration of the divine offices and the administration of the sacraments, a Missal, silver or gilt chalice, an amice, alb, cincture, maniple, stole, chasuble, surplice, a baptismal font of stone neatly constructed and well covered, and a suitable vessel for keeping the chrism for the use of the sick. The church, in nave and chancel, in roof and walls, inside and outside, should be well constructed, and kept clean according to the means of the people, corn and animals and such things belonging to the laity should be excluded, and that men and women of whatever description, whether married or single, should not cohabit therein under pain of mortal sin and excommunication.[77]

Although Archdeacon John Begley, who published this translation, understood 'church' in the second of these passages to refer to the precinct as well as the building, the housing of 'corn and animals' inside an actual church was a common-enough practice in medieval Ireland: in 1295, for example, one Nicholas Strange was imprisoned for stealing cloth and wheat from the mendicant church in Tralee.[78] Such 'secular' use of churches in the Middle Ages even extended to the educational realm, as is known from the discovery in Smarmore Church of a large collection of roof slates that had been inscribed with medical recipes, musical notation, and assorted ecclesiastical material by a supposed schoolmaster-priest in the early fifteenth century.[79] The importance attached to the ringing of the bell may help explain the proliferation of bellcotes in later medieval churches (fig. 56). The protection afforded by a machicolation to the bellcote at the delightful late medieval church of Killeen Cowpark was symbolic of the bell's importance.

PARISH CHURCHES

A medieval parish church was a local or neighbourhood church, with the allegiance of the community fastened by its payment of tithes. The parish was thus the geographical area around the church from which its tithes were assigned.[80] The civil parishes marked on the first-edition Ordnance Survey maps of *c.*1840 – not to be confused with modern Roman Catholic parishes – are the best indicators of the geography of the medieval

77 J. Begley, *The diocese of Limerick* (Dublin, 1906), pp 289–94 at p. 289. Amice, alb, cincture, maniple, stole and surplice are all parts of the priest's attire. **78** *CJRI, 1295–1303*, p. 19. **79** A.J. Bliss, 'The inscribed slates at Smarmore', *PRIA*, 64C (1965/6), 33–60; D. Briton and A.J. Fletcher, 'Medieval Hiberno-English inscriptions on the inscribed slates of Smarmore: some reconsiderations and additions', *Irish University Review*, 20:1 (1990), 55–72. **80** For deeper historical analysis, see C. Doherty, 'The idea of the parish' in FitzPatrick and Gillespie (eds),

56 The double bellcote at fifteenth-century Killybegs Church. In a bellcote the bell hung on a horizontal bar just underneath the arch. Double-cotes like this one are far more common than single-cotes. Assuming that each cote carried a bell (a not-inexpensive item for a small rural parish like Killybegs), one bell might have been used for Mass and the other for all other occasions.

parish system. And, given that the ecclesiastical parish was naturally coterminous spatially with a political territory or estate, the same civil parishes generally provide us also with a geography of medieval secular power.[81]

The start-date of the parish system in Ireland is uncertain. With a new diocesan structure in place, the establishment of a fit-for-purpose territorial framework for local Christian communities was a natural next step for the early twelfth-century reformers. Gillebertus, the early twelfth-century bishop of Limerick, in a discussion document he prepared for fellow reformers, even identified the *parochia ecclesialis* as one of the pillars of the Irish reformed church.[82] A decree of the Synod in Cashel in 1170–1 that tithes should be paid by every man to his parish church, combined with Gerald of Wales' testimony of 1185 that the Irish 'do not yet pay tithes', strongly suggests that

The parish in medieval and early modern Ireland, pp 21–32.   **81** P.J. Duffy, *Exploring the history and heritage of Irish landscapes* (Dublin, 2007), pp 59–63; ibid., 'The shape of the parish' in FitzPatrick and Gillespie (eds), *The parish in medieval and early modern Ireland*, pp 33–61. One should not assume, though, that in every case the boundary of a civil parish follows exactly that of a medieval estate, as some parishes contracted, others expanded and some were largely created after the Middle Ages. But the model holds fairly well, especially in Anglo-Norman parts of Ireland. The essential guide to the macro-geography of medieval Ireland – the cantreds in which the parishes were located – is Paul MacCotter, *Medieval Ireland: territorial, political and economic divisions* (Dublin, 2008).   **82** Flanagan, *The transformation of the Irish church*, p. 55.

there had been no system of tithing on the island, and therefore no parish system – and therefore no churches that we can describe properly as parochial – before the Anglo-Normans arrived.[83] In support of this interpretation, Adrian Empey has pointed out that had there been tithing before *c.*1170 it is probable that somewhere in Ireland a row would have erupted over the ownership of tithes after the Anglo-Norman takeover, and yet none is recorded.[84] Marie Therese Flanagan has suggested that the process of parish formation was actually in train in the pre-invasion twelfth century – a process for which the small number of new, apparently non-monastic, Romanesque churches in the 1100s might be corroborating evidence – and that the real issue that the Anglo-Normans had to address was not that tithes were not being paid but that they might not have been paid punctually, or were not going to the appropriate churches, or were not being distributed in ways that allowed bishops receive their allocations.[85] Either way, the lack of firm evidence for parishes in Gaelic Ireland before the late 1100s (in the case of Clare) or even the mid-1200s (in the case of Connacht)[86] would seem to add weight to the suggestion that, whatever progress had been made by *c.*1170, the process of parochial organization in Ireland benefitted hugely from the intervention of the Anglo-Normans.[87]

The post-invasion development of parishes must have moved fast in eastern Ireland because there are records of tithes being granted to monastic houses in the late 1100s and early 1200s, especially to the abbey of St Thomas in Dublin.[88] It is interesting, though, that these same records seem not to sit particularly comfortably with the archaeological evidence from the parish churches. Late twelfth-century and early thirteenth-century parish churches of Anglo-Norman construction are not common (fig. 57), whereas there are many churches in the lordship that seem to date from the second and third quarters of the thirteenth century (fig. 58).[89] The probability is that older churches were kept in use until such time as new churches could be built.[90] It is even possible that chapels in the precincts of castles sometimes served wider communities until new churches were built: this seems to have been the case in Skreen, where Adam de Feypo's castle chapel of the 1170s was the seed out of which an actual parish grew.[91]

83 A.J. Otway-Ruthven, 'Parochial development in the rural deanery of Skreen', *JRSAI*, 94:2 (1964), 111–22. 84 'Layperson in the parish', pp 13–14. 85 Flanagan, *The transformation of the Irish church*, pp 88–9. 86 For Clare, see S. Ní Ghabhláin, 'Late twelfth-century church construction: evidence of parish formation?' in FitzPatrick and Gillespie (eds), *The parish in medieval and early modern Ireland*, pp 147–67; P. Nugent, 'The dynamics of parish formation in high medieval and late medieval Clare', ibid., pp 186–210; Luke McInerney, *Clerical and learned lineages of medieval Clare: a survey of the fifteenth-century papal registers* (Dublin, 2014) is a major contribution to that county's ecclesiastical history. For Connacht, see K.W. Nicholls, 'Rectory, vicarage and parish in the western Irish dioceses', *JRSAI*, 101 (1971), 53–84. 87 The possibility of an incipient parish system in the eleventh century in the Hiberno-Scandinavian towns and their hinterlands is discussed in T. O'Keeffe, 'The built environment of local community worship' in FitzPatrick and Gillespie (eds), *The parish in medieval and early modern Ireland*, pp 124–46 at pp 128–30. 88 *RAST*, passim. 89 O'Keeffe, 'The built environment of local community worship'. 90 A 1216 synodal direction that churches were to be checked for their condition and repaired if needed suggests that, in Meath at least, a stock of pre-Anglo-Norman churches was still in use nearly half a century after the invasion. See J. Healy, *History of the diocese of Meath, 1* (Dublin, 1908), p. 75. 91 Otway-Ruthven, 'Parochial development in the rural

57 The east end of Laraghbryan parish church: the round-arched windows of the chancel are consistent with a date around 1200. Another important early Anglo-Norman parish church in Kildare is Furness.

I hesitate to draw too firm a conclusion in the absence of the sort of systematic and comprehensive survey of the architecture of parish churches that might produce a better chronology for the twelfth and thirteenth centuries, but, if church-building is a measure of political stability and economic well-being, I think the evidence points to the middle decades of the thirteenth century as the period in which Anglo-Norman lordship was sufficiently secure for massive economic growth (aided perhaps by new settlers) to start.[92] So, while the acquisition of tithes by early Anglo-Norman monasteries followed a conventional strategy in western Christendom, it must therefore have had an overt colonial purpose in the context of the embryonic Irish lordship. That might explain the almost militaristic character of some of those monasteries, especially the Augustinian priories (see below, p. 159).

deanery of Skreen'. It might be significant that in England, and possibly in Ireland too, castle chaplains served outside of their castles as parish priests to local communities (S. Speight, 'Religion in the bailey: charters, chapels and the clergy', *CG*, 21 (2004), 271–80). By their nature, of course, castle-chapels (see below, pp 175–8) were not parochial, and were not equipped to provide in the long term any of the essential functions of parish churches (such as baptism and burial, most obviously).   **92** O'Keeffe, 'Aristocrats, immigrants and entrepreneurs'.

58 The interior east end of Monsea parish church, mid-thirteenth-century judging by its original windows. Note how the central window was filled, possibly in the late Middle Ages though possibly later again, with a smaller window of fifteenth-century type; similar alterations were made in many other ecclesiastical buildings, such as the thirteenth-century chapter house of Monasteranenagh.

The medieval parish community and its local church

The medieval parish community always gathered in the nave, or western part, of its local church, whether that church was monastic, mendicant or collegiate, or was a conventional parish church with its own curate. Entry through a central doorway in the west wall was a long-standing tradition, possibly not breached until the very end of the eleventh century. Even then, the preference through the 1100s was for western doors; original south-wall twelfth-century Romanesque doorways are few. Entry through a west-wall doorway was somewhat theatrical, allowing a parish community its own sense of procession into the consecrated interior space. This spatial pattern was sometimes retained post-1200, but it was really only retained consistently in cathedral, monastic and collegiate churches, and only then in tandem with (if not originally then at least by the fifteenth century) a major side-wall entrance. Thus, for example, St Canice's Cathedral in Kilkenny and the collegiate church of St Nicholas in Galway had both elaborate west doors *and* south doors. There are many other examples. In monastic houses with attached cloisters the west door was needed for lay people as there was no other means of entry, but whenever a big church had the two doorways it was probably the side-wall doorway that was used by parishioners as the normal point of entry. One imagines that the west doors were opened only on those occasions when it was necessary for a clerical procession through the nave.

South-wall and north-wall doorways became increasingly common in churches in the 1200s, and it was not unusual for a parish church to have both, one facing the other across the width of the nave and leaving space for a gallery to the west. Insofar as one can rank them, the more important doorway was in the south wall. Dual entrances might be telling us something about local social hierarchies, with different entrances reserved to different parts of the population. Of the many people whom we describe as parishioners and envisage jostling for space in the church naves, some were landowners of insufficient influence to gain access to the chancels, and some were merchants, but most were tenants of the land. In the thirteenth century in particular the tenantry was itself very stratified, with some tenants enjoying considerable autonomy as freeholders and others pinned down by more onerous burdens. Given this, it is difficult to believe that space in naves was *not* allocated to individuals and groups according to social rank, even though there is no architectural evidence of corresponding partitions in the naves of most of our churches. We can presume, for example, that proximity to the altar, as well as lines of sight to the altar, came with rank, and that benches were provided for those whose rank allowed them a station near to the chancel.[93] One wonders if dual entrances were not also connected to gender. A famous seventh-century description of the double-monastery at Kildare tells us that the abbess and nuns entered the church from the north, or left, and the abbot and the monks entered from the south, or right.[94] Until recent decades it was not uncommon for men and women to part from each other on entering Roman Catholic churches in rural Ireland, the women taking seats to the left (the north side) and the men to the right (the south side). In the Sarum Rite male babies were on the baptizing priest's right-hand side and female babies on his left.[95]

The size of a parish church generally reflected the size of a parish's population, either as observed at the time of its construction or as it was anticipated to grow. Rural communities were small and never expected to grow significantly, so their churches were rarely very big, but medieval towns were founded with optimal population sizes in mind and urban parish churches were accordingly laid-out at larger scales.[96] Once built, parish churches rarely expanded or contracted in significant rhythm with the ebb and flow of medieval population size: alterations brought architecture up to date but rarely increased or decreased capacity. When there was enlargement, it was usually in the form of a chantry chapel (see below, pp 169–73). Alteration was almost always a

---

93 The relationship of lines of sight to social ranking requires investigation in Ireland: see C.P. Graves, 'Social space in the English medieval parish church', *Economy and Society*, 18:3 (1989), 297–322.   94 S. Connolly and J.-M. Picard, 'Cogitosus: life of Saint Brigit', *JRSAI*, 117 (1987), 5–27 at 25–6.   95 K. French, *The good women of the parish: gender and religion after the Black Death* (Philadelphia, PA, 2008), p. 54.   96 Numbers of townspeople needed were calculated in advance if only to allow the founders of towns to set aside appropriate acreages of land for them: see O'Keeffe, 'Aristocrats, immigrants and entrepreneurs'.

59 Thomas fitzGerald, eighth earl of Desmond, founded Our Lady's College of Youghal in 1464 and attached it to St Mary's Church, which was re-designated a collegiate church but continued to serve as the town's parish church. Reflecting its change in status, its chancel, seen here from the south, was substantially rebuilt on its original thirteenth-century footprint. The college community had its own door into this most sacred part of the church.

pious gift of a local patron (who was not necessarily an individual of great wealth), sometimes made during his or her lifetime, but sometimes also after his or her death (the provision having been made in a will).[97] One context in which alteration to a parish church was normal was the foundation of a college (fig. 59).

97 H.F. Berry (ed.), *Register of the wills and inventories of the diocese of Dublin in the time of archbishops Tregury and Walton, 1457–1483* (Dublin, 1898); for examples from a specific parish, see J.L. Robinson, 'On the ancient deeds of the parish of St John, Dublin, preserved in the library of Trinity College', *PRIA*, 33C (1916–17), 175–224. Gifts to parish churches were not confined to structural changes: chalices, candles and robes were often gifted as well, and making inventories of these were among the many roles of the churchwardens whom the parishioners elected: see Empey, 'Layperson in the parish', pp 25–31. See also R. Moss, 'Continuity and change: the material setting of public worship in the sixteenth-century Pale' in M. Potterton and T. Herron (eds), *Dublin and the Pale in the Renaissance, c.1540–1660* (Dublin, 2011), pp 182–206. The gifts given to churches were gender-differentiated and often included household goods and clothes, and evidence outside Ireland suggests that men allowed the churchwardens dispose of bequests as they felt best whereas women had very strong views on how gifts were to be used and were not slow to communicate them (French, *The good women of the parish*, esp. p. 42).

60 A typical late medieval parish church at Garryvoe. Note the base of a bellcote above the west gable.

An interesting phenomenon worth mentioning at this point is the building programme of the late Middle Ages. Running parallel to the great fifteenth-century mushrooming of new mendicant friaries was an utterly remarkable programme of building and/or rebuilding parish churches, funded by secular benefactors. Henry Jeffries quite correctly uses this evidence to counter assertions that the medieval Church was in decline in the lead-up to the Reformation.[98] From the architectural historian's point of view, not the least remarkable feature of this phenomenon is that the new churches of the 1400s were not big (fig. 60). Indeed, they were almost invariably shorter than the churches of the thirteenth century. The implication is that this 'great rebuilding' of parish churches, if that is the appropriate phrase, was driven not by a desire to accommodate parishioners for whom older churches were too small but by a desire among secular patrons to be seen to be replenishing church buildings and, by extension, the institution of the Church itself.

From the fifteenth century, and possibly much earlier to judge by comparative English evidence, parishioners were responsible for the upkeep of the church naves, and priests for the upkeep of the chancels.[99] It might be significant to note that in 1304 the archbishop of Dublin ordered a visitation by canons of St Patrick's Cathedral to

98 H.A. Jeffries, 'A church "in decline"? The pre-Reformation Irish Church', *History Ireland*, 14:6 (2006), 13–18; idem, *The Irish church and the Tudor reformations* (Dublin, 2010). 99 Begley, *The*

the chancels – there was no mention of naves – of its prebendal churches, the parish churches to which the secular canons of the cathedral provided ministry and from which they drew tithe-incomes.[100] Similarly, in 1347 the prior and convent of Christ Church agreed that Sir Philip Walsh, chaplain of the church of Rathothull (Rathcoole?), was 'to repair the gable of the chancel, and to roof it with double boards, and to clean the lower part of the chancel and the altar etc.'[101] Again, there is no mention of the nave. The fact that naves and chancels often have slightly different architectural details, and sometimes even differential states of preservation, may reflect this division of responsibility. Seventeenth-century diocesan visitations record many chancels in poor condition, suggesting that successive priests in those churches had experienced difficulty in maintaining fabric.[102] One strategy by which penitents in the Middle Ages could be induced to fund blanket repairs to existing churches (or indeed whole additions to them) was through the granting of indulgences. We will encounter presently the use of indulgences in the Franciscan friary of Claregalway (see p. 154), but suffice it to mention here the case of St Doulagh's Church, a small sub-parochial chapel. In 1406 an indulgence was on offer to those who confessed their sins to its resident anchorite, Eustace Roche, and gave alms for his support and for the upkeep of the church.[103] The fifteenth-century bell-tower and residence attached to the tiny church may well have been funded in this way.

Plan types

The plans of medieval Irish parish churches conform to a very simple scheme. The most basic plan is single cell (fig. 61). The interiors of the great majority of pre-1169 (Romanesque and pre-Romanesque) single-cell churches were very small indeed, and while that did not preclude them accommodating a congregation, as Tomás Ó Carragáin has noted,[104] it must have impacted on how clearly demarcated was the

---

diocese of Limerick, p. 289. For England, see E. Mason, 'The role of the English parishioner, 1100–1500', *JEH*, 27 (1976), 17–29.   **100** W. Monck Mason, *The history and antiquities of the collegiate and cathedral church of St Patrick near Dublin* (Dublin, 1820), p. 116. This book also documents how the post-Dissolution inquest into the cathedral's possessions, actually held on the very day in January 1547 that Henry VIII died, noted the provisions for the care of the prebendary chancels.   **101** H.J. Lawlor, 'A calendar of the *Liber Niger* and *Liber Albus* of Christ Church, Dublin', *PRIA*, 27C (1908/9), 1–93 at 17–18.   **102** The patterns varied from one diocese to another. The majority were in repair in Dublin and Ardfert (M.V. Ronan, 'Royal visitation of Dublin, 1615', *AH*, 8 (1941), 1–55; M.A. Murphy, 'The royal visitation, 1615: dioceses of Ardfert [and Aghadoe]', ibid., 4 (1915), 178–98), equal numbers were in repair/disrepair in Killaloe (M.A. Murphy and W. Ormond, 'The royal visitation, 1615: diocese of Killaloe', idem, 3 (1914), 210–26), and the majority were in disrepair in Cashel and Emly, and in the diocese of Cork (M.A. Murphy, 'Royal visitation of Cashel and Emly, 1615', ibid., 1 (1912), 277–311; idem, 'The royal visitation of Cork, Cloyne, Ross and the college of Youghal', ibid., 2 (1913), 173–215). This pattern should hardly surprise us: the population at large remained Catholic after the Reformation, especially outside the Pale, and as the numbers comprising Protestant populations dwindled, so too did the condition of the stock of parish churches (see Jeffries, *Irish church and the Tudor reformations*).   **103** W. Reeves, 'Memoir of the church of St Duilech', *PRIA*, 7 (1857–61), 141–7 at 145–6; P. Harbison, 'St Doulagh's Church', *Studies*, 71:281 (1982), 27–42.   **104** T. Ó Carragáin, 'Church buildings and pastoral care in early medieval Ireland' in FitzPatrick and Gillespie (eds), *The parish in medieval and early*

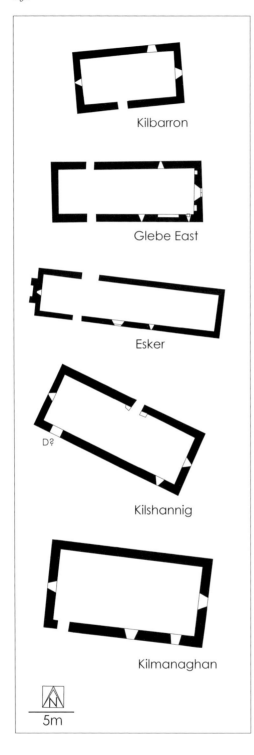

Kilbarron

Glebe East

Esker

D?

Kilshannig

Kilmanaghan

5m

61 Some single-cell parish church plans.

division between the sanctuary with its altar and the more 'public' space on its west side. The new single-cell churches built under Anglo-Norman patronage for tithe-paying congregations were wider and considerably longer, allowing greater demarcation of the division between naves and chancels. We describe such churches as 'undifferentiated nave-and-chancel churches' to reflect the fact that, while they were long enough to have had clearly demarcated spaces within them, the separation of 'public' and sanctuary spaces was not marked externally. Their elongation might be explained by liturgical practices shaped by the proclamation by the Fourth Lateran Council (1215) of the exclusive right of priests to affect the sacrament of transubstantiation. Undifferentiated nave-and-chancel churches never went out of vogue, but they generally shortened in the late Middle Ages.

Churches with physically distinctive naves and chancels are not uncommon throughout the Middle Ages (fig. 62). The format first appeared at the end of the 1000s in Ireland, and specifically in the Dublin region. While the parochial status of these early examples is open to debate, there can be little doubt that their designs reflect influence from eleventh-century English parish churches, funnelled through the major urban centres – Winchester, for example – with which Dublin had connections.[105]

modern Ireland, pp 91–123. **105** O'Keeffe, *Romanesque Ireland*, pp 83–7.

62 A typical Anglo-Norman parish church of nave-and-chancel plan at Wells. Historical evidence suggests a date in the second quarter of the thirteenth century. The small east window seems to be a careful insertion of the later years of the century. The bellcote is late medieval.

Nave-and-chancel plans must have been normal within the Hiberno-Scandinavian towns of the later 1000s and early 1100s, and some may have had building histories as complex as that of St Peter's in Waterford: here an apse with thick walls and slightly elongated sides was built to the east of the (late eleventh- or early twelfth-century) chancel, a stone-built nave with opposed west-end entrances was constructed to the west of the chancel, and a stone-built structure, probably a sacristy, was added to the south side of the apse and chancel.[106] Contact with England, strengthened by the role of senior English clerics in the early twelfth-century reform of the Irish Church, also explains the rising popularity of nave-and-chancel churches in Romanesque building projects in parts of Ireland distant from the Hiberno-Scandinavian towns. In some cases the naves and chancels were contemporary, while in others a single-cell church was converted through an extension to the east or west. New nave-and-chancel churches also appeared alongside the undifferentiated types in the Anglo-Norman landscape, and elongation is their most striking characteristic. Fewer examples were built in the fifteenth century.

Parish churches with aisled naves, ancillary chapels and transepts, or some combination of them, are relatively few and are found mainly in towns. Being populous and spatially concentrated parochial communities, townspeople needed big

106 M.F. Hurley and S.W.J. McCutcheon, 'St Peter's church and graveyard' in M.F. Hurley and O.M.B. Scully (with S.W.J. McCutcheon), *Late Viking and medieval Waterford: excavations, 1986–1992* (Waterford, 1997), pp 198–205; B. Murtagh, 'The architecture of St Peter's Church', ibid., pp 228–43; O'Keeffe, *Romanesque Ireland*, pp 102–4.

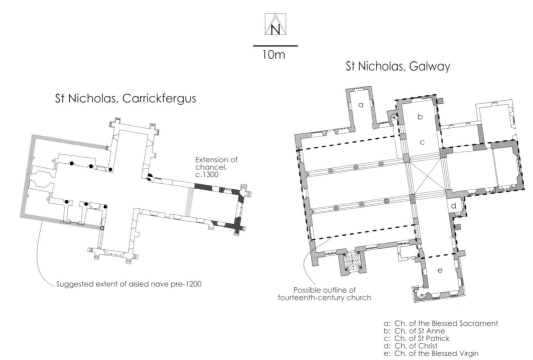

63 Plans of the urban parish churches dedicated to St Nicholas in Carrickfergus and Galway.

churches and could generate through their parish duties the sort of finance needed for upkeep. No less important was the central-place value of an urban setting for a lord wishing to display as widely as possible his piety and wealth through the patronage of the community's church. The major port-town churches dedicated to St Nicholas (the patron saint of sailors) in Carrickfergus and Galway illustrate very well how complex-plan urban churches changed shape over time, their major phases being expressions of the identities and architectural preferences of successive generations of patrons (fig. 63). Founded in the 1180s and therefore one of the earliest Anglo-Norman churches in Ireland, the former had an aisled nave from the outset, and probably transepts as well. The original chancel was then elongated around 1300, to better accommodate liturgies of increasing elaboration, while the south transept was (?re-)built at the same time or possibly a little later, almost certainly to accommodate a new chapel or chapels of chantry. Extensions to its nave aisles in the late Middle Ages, some of which must have been for chantries, enlarged the church's floor area considerably. Much of this work was undone during the Ulster Plantation when the entire church was given a makeover deemed appropriate to the ideology of a new elite.[107] The church in Galway is commonly given a foundation date of 1320, but it has recently been suggested by Jim

107 R. Ó Baoill, *St Nicholas' Church, Carrickfergus, Co. Antrim.* Archaeology Ireland Heritage Guide 43 (Dublin, 2009).

McKeon that it began life as a thirteenth-century unaisled cruciform church. Much of what we see today is fifteenth and sixteenth century in date. Its complex plan accommodated a number of chapels, the most elaborate of which was the chapel of chantry in the south transept.[108]

Inland towns were smaller than port towns, and their churches, while often still of elaborate plan, were generally commensurably smaller, though they still exceeded their rural counterparts. The biggest examples, which rival those of the ports, include St Mary's parish church in Kilkenny, which was cruciform and aisled, and St Mary's in Callan, aisled with a west tower, as well as the great collegiate parish churches of Kilmallock, aisled with a south transept, and Gowran, aisled with a tower marking the entry to a long chancel. Fethard, a small town, had an aisled church courtesy of the archbishop of Cashel in the early thirteenth century; the town's secular elite then added a huge western tower in the fifteenth century (see pl. I).

CATHEDRALS

Whereas the bishops of early medieval Ireland, of which there were very many indeed, had sacramental powers but inexactly defined territorial jurisdictions, the reform movement of the late eleventh and early twelfth centuries created for the Irish episcopate a proper territorial diocesan system. The key events were the Synod of Cashel in 1101, at which principles of reform were established, the Synod of Ráith Bressail in 1111, at which the new dioceses were created under the authority of Armagh as primatial see and with Cashel as the second-ranked see, and the Synod of Kells-Mellifont in 1152, at which the diocesan structure was altered (with a view to disconnecting the dioceses from the tribal units); Dublin and Tuam were also added to the roster of archiepiscopal sees in 1152. When the Anglo-Normans came to Ireland less than two decades after the Kells-Mellifont synod, the diocesan system that they encountered was familiar: thanks to the involvement in the Irish reform movement of two great Norman archbishops of Canterbury, Lanfranc and Anselm, the Irish structure was closely modelled on the English, with the archbishops of Armagh and Cashel standing in relation to their fellow bishops as did the archbishops of Canterbury and York to fellow English bishops.[109] That is not to say, however, that diocesan organization needed no further work. For one thing, the number of suffragan dioceses – ten in the province of Armagh, twelve in Cashel, seven in Tuam and five in Dublin – was overkill in a small country with a relatively low and largely rural population,[110] and had less to do with need than with local and regional political bargaining. For another, the lack of a fully functioning parish system meant that episcopal authority was compromised.

---

108 Leask, 'Collegiate church of St Nicholas, Galway'; McKeon, 'St Nicholas's parish church, Galway'.   109 Flanagan, *The transformation of the Irish church*.   110 J. Watt, *The church in medieval Ireland* (Dublin, 1972), pp 30–1.

Eleventh-century Hiberno-Scandinavian cathedrals

The first cathedrals of reform-era Ireland were those of the later eleventh-century Hiberno-Scandinavian communities in Dublin, Limerick and Waterford. These communities appointed as their bishops clerics who had trained outside Ireland, mainly in Norman England. By the time the synodians convened at Cashel in 1101 to kick-start ecclesiastical reform across Gaelic-Ireland, these bishoprics were well established, and each urban centre had a purpose-built cathedral several decades old. The eleventh-century structures in Limerick and Waterford did not survive long: the former was rebuilt under Gaelic-Irish patronage between 1160 and 1180, and the latter was rebuilt under the Anglo-Normans.[111] The situation is slightly different in the case of Dublin's Christ Church Cathedral (formerly Holy Trinity).

The crypt is one of the distinguishing features of this cathedral church. Crypts developed in the early Middle Ages as places within churches where high-status burials (the tombs of saints and others of exceptional sanctity) and/or relics were on display to penitents and pilgrims. Original crypts are rare in Ireland.[112] Christ Church's crypt, uniquely, runs for almost the full length of the corresponding church above, stopping short of the westernmost bay of the nave. It was built in two phases, the western section (which is below the nave) being the later. The dates of both parts are unknown. The most recent commentator, Michael O'Neill, opts for an original foundation date no earlier than the late twelfth century.[113] Roger Stalley wondered about a date around the 1080s, citing the crypt of Winchester.[114] But there is a case for pushing the date of its eastern end further back, into the episcopacy of Dúnán (or Donatus, his Latin name). Consecrated Dublin's first archbishop between 1028 and 1036, and in the see until his death in 1074, his place of consecration was long assumed to have been Canterbury, but the presence of German-origin relics and of a German recension of an early medieval martyrology (a list of saints' feastdays) points, as Raghnall Ó Floinn has suggested, to Cologne as the more likely place.[115] This fits very well with the evidence of possible German, indeed Rhenish, influence in the design of the crypt (fig. 64).[116]

---

111 Gem, 'The Irish cathedral in the 12th century'; Stalley, 'Three Irish buildings', pp 66–71 (for Waterford).   112 For Killone, a late twelfth-century nunnery church with a later-vaulted crypt, see T. Collins, *The other monasticism*, Archaeology Ireland Heritage Guide, 38 (Dublin, 2007). For the crypt at Buttevant Friary church (Franciscan) see T. O'Keeffe, 'Buttevant Friary and its crypt', *AI*, 26:3 (2012), 23–5 and p. 157 below. The crypt at Mellifont Abbey church is under the west end, propping up the church as it hangs over a river bluff; it had no clear liturgical function.   113 M. O'Neill, 'Christ Church Cathedral as a blueprint for other Augustinian buildings in Ireland' in J. Bradley, A. Simms and J. Fletcher (eds), *Dublin in the medieval world: studies in honour of Howard B. Clarke* (Dublin, 2009), pp 168–87 at pp 182–3. 114 'Construction of the medieval cathedral', pp 65–7.   115 H.B. Clarke, 'Conversion, church and cathedral: the diocese of Dublin to 1152' in J. Kelly and D. Keogh (eds), *History of the Catholic diocese of Dublin* (Dublin, 2000), pp 19–50 at p. 35; P. Ó Riain, 'Dublin's oldest book? A list of saints "made in Germany"', *MD*, 5 (2004), 52–72; R. Ó Floinn, 'The foundation relics of Christ Church Cathedral and the origins of the diocese of Dublin', *MD*, 7 (2006), 89–102; M. Kelly, 'Twelfth-century ways of learning: from Worcester or Glendalough to Cologne', *JRSAI*, 141 (2011), 47–65.   116 O'Keeffe, *Romanesque Ireland*, pp 97–102.

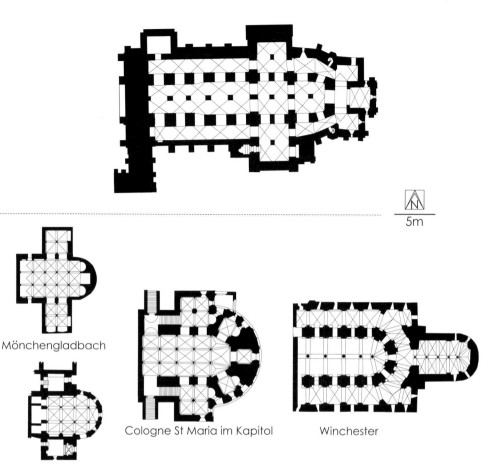

64 The plan of the crypt of Christ Church Cathedral and some non-Irish parallels.

Gaelic-Irish cathedrals of the twelfth century

New cathedrals were necessitated by church reform, especially after the 1111 synod, but the reformers were satisfied for pre-existing churches to be re-designated cathedrals, sometimes enlarged a little, and normally embellished with architectural sculpture of classic twelfth-century form. Important early churches so transformed include the cathedrals of Clonfert and Clonmacnoise. Interestingly, even oddly, the alterations were made to them several decades after their status was changed, almost as if some of the reformers had not considered the symbolic traction that new architecture offered the reform process. At the first of these, the original entrance doorway was replaced late in the twelfth century with a magnificent gabled portal, executed as a two-dimensional form but imitative of an actual building, intended perhaps to signify the Heavenly Jerusalem.[117] At the second, Clonmacnoise, a new west doorway was also provided, but was far more modest than that at Clonfert.[118]

What of the provincial cathedrals? That at Armagh was presumably another refurbishment of an existing church, but nothing of it survived Gothic and post-medieval re-buildings.[119] One possible echo of its early twelfth-century architecture, however, is the doorway – an English type, rarely found in Ireland – of the round tower at Dromiskin (fig. 4), in the same diocese. The cathedral at Tuam was, by contrast, a new building, replacing in 1184 an older cathedral church that had fallen down; its 1180s sculpture is very elaborate indeed,[120] but the new church that it adorned was small and could hardly have been much of an improvement on the old one. The original cathedral at Cashel is also gone, having been replaced by the choir of the Gothic cathedral. To compensate somewhat for its loss, parts of two early cathedrals in the Cashel province do survive: Ardfert was by 1117 the diocesan centre for Kerry, and remains of its Romanesque church are incorporated in a thirteenth-century rebuild (fig. 3), while St Crónán's Church in Roscrea, of which one wall survives, was built around 1120 to sustain an ultimately unsuccessful diocesan claim.[121]

The physical modesty of these bishops' seats surely tells us that the spirit of the concept of cathedral as it was understood across contemporary Europe had not quite been embraced by the reformers. These buildings should have been equipped to accommodate the complex rituals expected universally of the mother churches of dioceses. It is difficult to see how they were. If we did not know it from the historical record, we would not guess from the architectural record of the cathedrals that there had been diocesan reform. Moreover, many of these early twelfth-century cathedrals are at places of relatively low settlement density today. Those that seem most isolated, like Kilmacduagh, would have had settlement associated with them (fig. 45), but not on the scale that one finds with cathedrals in other medieval jurisdictions.

Gothic cathedrals

The earliest cathedral in Ireland in the new Gothic style was an entirely new foundation. Newtown Trim – now very ruined – was built after 1202 when Bishop Simon de Rochfort moved the diocesan centre for Meath from Clonard to a site within view of the de Lacy castle of Trim.[122] It was, like Christ Church in Dublin, a cathedral-priory, a peculiarly English institution in which a cathedral had a monastic chapter. In this case it was a chapter of Victorine canons regular, members of the extended family of Augustinian canons. In one regard the church was absolutely up-to-date: it had elegant rib-vaults, as fine as those installed by the Cistercians in Duiske Abbey around the same time. In another regard it was old-fashioned: plain, shallow and closely set,

---

117 Idem, 'The Romanesque portal at Clonfert Cathedral'.   **118** C. Manning, 'Clonmacnoise Cathedral' in H.A. King (ed.), *Clonmacnoise studies*, 1 (Dublin, 1998), pp 57–86.   **119** Ó Carragáin, *Churches in early medieval Ireland*, p. 63.   **120** Stalley, 'The Romanesque sculpture of Tuam'.   **121** For the propagandist agenda at Cormac's Chapel, see O'Keeffe, 'Wheels of words, networks of knowledge'. Ardfert and Roscrea are discussed in idem, *Romanesque Ireland*, pp 173–81.   **122** Ibid., pp 97–8.

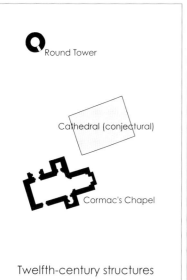
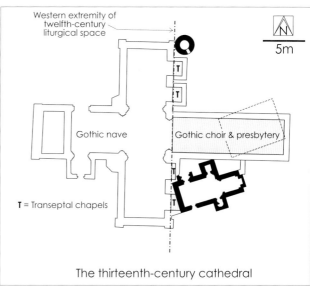

65 The ecclesiastical buildings on the Rock of Cashel.

the external buttresses that supported the now-collapsed vaults are more Romanesque than Gothic.

But it did not kick-start a serious campaign of Gothic cathedral-building. Its influence is hard to gauge: the early Anglo-Norman Augustinian priory of Ballyboggan, located in the same lordship, was probably a cousin, but even that is hard to prove. Bequeathing eventually to the Irish landscape a most heterogeneous collection of buildings, the nature of which is understudied (thanks in no small measure to the substantial post-medieval alterations made to some of them, such as Downpatrick and Raphoe), the programme of replacing twelfth-century cathedrals with new Gothic cathedrals was neither systematic nor brisk. Kilkenny, for example, the de facto political capital of the lordship of Leinster under William Marshal, did not have its Romanesque cathedral (the seat of the diocese of Ossory) replaced until perhaps the second quarter of the thirteenth century. The cathedrals of Kildare and Ferns, scarcely unimportant Leinster dioceses, were not replaced until after 1223 when each had appointed to it an Anglo-Norman bishop.[123]

123 The east part – the earlier part – of Kilkenny Cathedral is normally attributed to the Anglo-Norman Hugo de Rous, bishop from *c.*1202 to 1218 (Stalley, *Architecture and sculpture in Ireland*, p. 73; Barry, 'The architecture of the cathedral', p. 26), but a date before the 1220s is unlikely from its architecture; the nave dates from the third quarter of the century, so one hesitates to posit too long a gap between the two parts of the church. For Kildare, see J. Bradley, 'Archaeology, topography and building fabric: the cathedral and town of medieval Kildare', *JKAS*, 19 (2000), 27–47. For Ferns, see T. O'Keeffe and R. Carey Bates, 'The abbey and cathedral of Ferns, 1111–1253' in B. Browne and I.W. Doyle (eds), *Medieval Wexford: essays in memory of Billy Colfer* (Dublin, forthcoming 2016).

Although the cathedral of Tuam was not upgraded until an Anglo-Norman archbishop was appointed at the end of the thirteenth century,[124] the ethnic identity of bishops was not a factor in the timing of the Gothic replacements of older cathedrals. In the case of Ferns, for example, the last Gaelic-Irish bishop, Ailbe Ua Máel Muaid, was actually appointed under Anglo-Norman hegemony and was as highly regarded in royal and metropolitan circles as any English bishop in Ireland, so the delay in replacing its Romanesque cathedral cannot be attributed to cultural backwardness or to any hostility that Anglo-Normans had to him. The province of Cashel retained Gaelic-Irish bishops long after the lowlands below the Rock of Cashel had been divided up into Anglo-Norman manors, and its Gothic cathedral was actually built under native episcopal authority.[125] Indeed, the ethnic identities of the Cashel bishops is surely reflected in the fact that they deliberately located the liturgical spaces of the new Gothic cathedral to the east of the line that had demarcated the cognitive boundary between secular and sacred spaces prior to the Anglo-Norman invasion (fig. 65). Killaloe, a cathedral of quite different design, can possibly also be attributed to a period in which the see had a native bishop.[126] Similarly, Armagh's Romanesque cathedral was apparently first rebuilt in the Gothic style not by its sole Anglo-Norman archbishop (1217–27) but by a Gaelic-Irish prelate in the late 1260s.[127]

So, given that the Cistercians were building in Gothic from *c.*1200, often under the noses of their local bishops, how do we explain the delay? The problem actually has nothing to do with the architectural style itself; after all, neither of the two Cistercians who held the bishopric of Leighlin between 1197 and 1217 attempted to replace its cathedral in the Gothic style.[128] It is clearly the case that in the late 1100s and early 1200s diocesan organization was prioritized over cathedral architecture. It was evidently deemed more important to appoint deans and chapters where none existed – there is no evidence that *any* existed in any of the Gaelic-Irish dioceses before *c.*1170 – than to rebuild diocesan seats. The chapters were needed because they had responsibility for the election of bishops. And there might have been an economic need for such prioritization: cash-flow for new buildings may have been dependent on the organization of parishes and especially of prebends (the benefices assigned to the clergy serving a cathedral).

---

124 Stalley, 'Cathedral-building in thirteenth-century Ireland', pp 33–4. The same might also be true of Ardfert Cathedral. Its architecture would better fit a date between the 1230s and 1250s, but archaeological evidence (F. Moore, *Ardfert Cathedral: summary of excavation results* (Dublin, 2007), p. 28), combined with the first record of a bishop, an Anglo-Norman, being buried in the cathedral in 1285 (*The whole works of Sir James Ware concerning Ireland*, 1 (Dublin, 1739), p. 521), raises the possibility of a very late date.   **125** Current thinking is that it was started by David Mac Cellaig Ó Gilla Patraic, archbishop from 1238 to 1253, and largely completed by David Mac Cerbaill, archbishop from 1253 to 1289 (Stalley, 'The construction of Cashel Cathedral').   **126** Although stylistically Killaloe's east end would attract a postulated date of around the 1220s, the most likely period of construction, given the see's history (A. Gwynn and D.F. Gleeson, *A history of the diocese of Killaloe*, 1 (Dublin, 1961), pp 223–33), is after the appointment of Domnall Ua Cennétig as bishop in 1231.   **127** *AU*, 1266.5; *AFM*, 1268.2. See also S. Mac Airt and T. Ó Fiaich (eds), 'A thirteenth century poem on Armagh Cathedral, by Giolla Brighde Mac Con Midhe', *Seanchas Ardmhacha*, 2:1 (1956), 145–62.   **128** Gwynn and Hadcock, *Medieval religious houses*, p. 89.

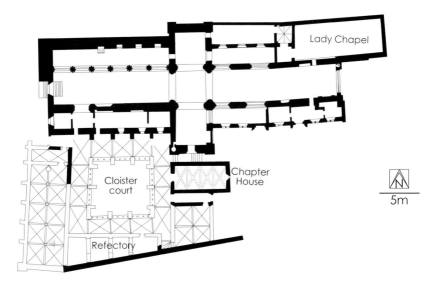

The pre-restoration cathedral, 1761 (after Thomas Reading)
The claustral ranges, 1882 (after Sir Thomas Drew)

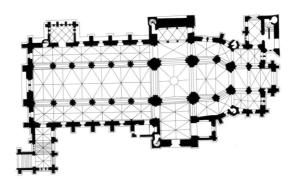

The cathedral restored, 1878 (after George Street & Edward Seymour)

66 The eighteenth-century record tells us that substantial parts of Christ Church Cathedral's Anglo-Norman fabric, though not the transept arms and the north arcade of the nave, had been lost before the restoration project of the late 1800s.

It is probably significant, then, that the first cathedral church to have been *re*built under Anglo-Norman patronage was one that already had a dean and chapter (of Augustinian canons regular, like the Victorine cathedral of Newtown Trim), as well as control over a parish system: Christ Church in Dublin (fig. 66).[129] It is ironic that

129 For a history of investigations, early plans and depictions, and restorations, see Milne, *Christ Church Cathedral*; R. Stalley, *George Edmund Street and the restoration of Christ Church* (Dublin,

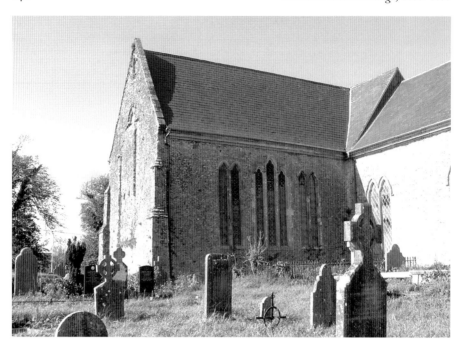

67 The south transept of the mid-thirteenth-century cathedral of Cloyne. Although set in a landscape that was very fertile and settled quite early in the Anglo-Norman period, this is a very modest cruciform building with a plain nave arcade.

this cathedral was, when the Anglo-Normans first saw it, probably the most sophisticated work of cathedral architecture in Ireland, as well as the least alien to them stylistically: although Hiberno-Scandinavian in 'authorship', it was actually an aisled Romanesque church with a crypt of possible German influence.[130] After 1181, the year that the first Anglo-Norman archbishop was appointed,[131] its east end was cleared away and rebuilt in a robust and slightly old-fashioned English Romanesque style.[132] The

2000); the now-lost buildings associated with the chapter (the clerical staff) of the cathedral are discussed in M. O'Neill, 'Christ Church Cathedral and its environs: medieval and beyond', *MD*, 11 (2011), 298–319. The restoration of its sister-cathedral, St Patrick's, is discussed in idem, 'Nineteenth-century architectural restorations' in Crawford and Gillespie (eds), *St Patrick's Cathedral*, pp 328–49.   **130** The evidence of its character is (a) the plan of the crypt, and (b) the record in the nineteenth century of *ex situ* Romanesque capitals. For the latter, see R. Moss, 'Tales from the crypt: the medieval stonework of Christ Church Cathedral', *MD*, 3 (2002), 95–114 at 111–12; for an attribution of the capitals to Archbishop Gréine, see S. Kinsella, 'Mapping Christ Church Cathedral, Dublin, *c*.1028–1608: an examination of the western cloister' in Bradley, Simms and Fletcher (eds), *Dublin in the medieval world*, pp 143–67. We should be careful not to exaggerate the quality of the Hiberno-Scandinavian cathedral church: had it been as elaborate as these few capitals suggest, might we expect a lot more of its carved stone to have survived?   **131** G. Hand, 'The rivalry of the cathedral chapters in medieval Dublin', *JRSAI*, 92 (1962), 193–206 at 194–5.   **132** A slightly different chronology is argued by Michael O'Neill, 'Christ Church Cathedral as a blueprint', pp 183–4.

remainder of the pre-Anglo-Norman cathedral must have been retained for some time because the Early English Gothic nave was only added in the early 1200s. It might have been started after 1216, although recent thinking puts its start-date in 1234.[133]

By the time the bishops of Ireland were being equipped with new churches in the second quarter of the thirteenth century, the repertoire of Gothic forms and motifs had already been in circulation for some years thanks to the Cistercians. Gothic designs clearly arrived in Dublin and Waterford cathedrals directly from England, but the builders of other cathedrals in Ireland must have acquired masons from pools that were already active on monastic, especially Cistercian, commissions. One thing is clear about the cathedral churches: while some were accomplished works of architecture, few were places of innovation; most of them followed trends rather than set them (fig. 67).

CLAUSTRAL MONASTERIES

As momentous a consequence of twelfth-century reform as the creation of the new diocesan structure was the introduction into Ireland of monastic orders following the rules of SS Benedict and Augustine. Pre-1100 monasticism in Ireland was not unregulated – by its nature monasticism requires regulation – but the new millennial pan-European monastic ideas and formats did not penetrate Ireland until Irish reformers had created the appropriate environment.

The monasteries of the assorted communities in Ireland that followed the two rules, as well as the cathedral-complexes in which the bishops were assisted by monastic chapters, adhered generally to the pan-European practice of claustral planning. This involved the placement of the key devotional and residential monastic buildings around a courtyard with covered walkways. Only very minor houses – cells attached to the Cistercians, and very small remote priories or cells of the Augustinians – deviated consistently from this norm; in some monastic houses where there is no evidence of a cloister it is possible that the claustral ranges were in timber (as at the Third Order Franciscan house of Bonamargy, founded *c*.1500). The constraining physical environment of monastic life, replicated spatially from one community to another, reinforced the behavioural boundaries that were created by monastic rules. However, that is not to deny individualism, either in architectural form or in the behaviour of monastic clergy. So long as the basic layout of monasteries adhered to the template, there was considerable scope for individual expression, even with foundations of the same order. One finds it not just in the architectural detailing, which is to be expected, but in the micro-planning and liturgical provisions, which is perhaps a little more surprising. The tension between over-arching rules and the

---

133 O'Neill, 'Design sources for St Patrick's Cathedral'. This date is accepted by Stalley, 'Cathedral-building in thirteenth-century Ireland', p. 29. However, the new interpretation is not entirely unproblematic. First, had work on the nave started as late as 1234, would the Romanesque transepts have escaped refurbishment if not replacement? Second, how can a gap of up to forty years between Romanesque choir and Gothic nave be explained without special pleading in a cathedral in a city of Dublin's rank?

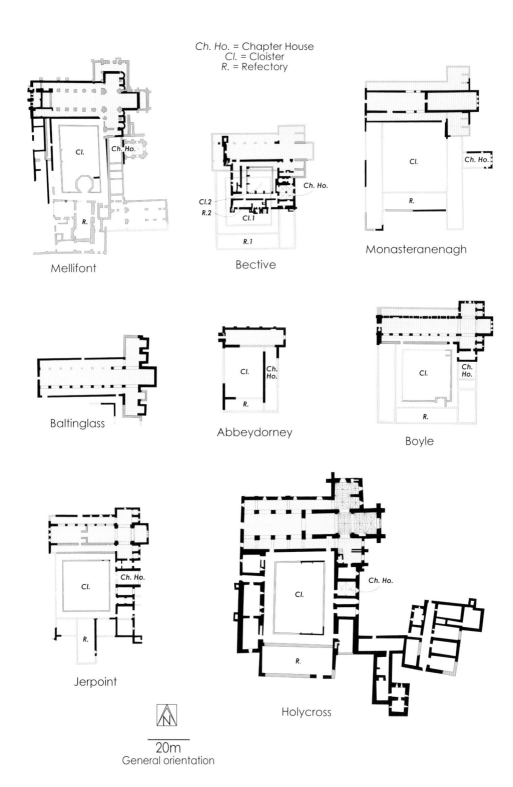

Ch. Ho. = Chapter House
Cl. = Cloister
R. = Refectory

Mellifont

Bective

Monasteranenagh

Baltinglass

Abbeydorney

Boyle

Jerpoint

Holycross

20m
General orientation

68 (*and opposite*) Cistercian monastery plans.

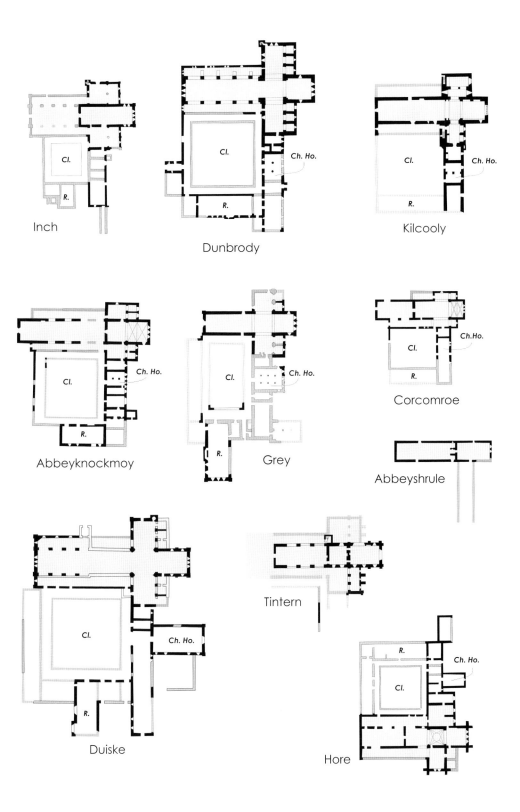

Inch

Dunbrody

Kilcooly

Abbeyknockmoy

Grey

Corcomroe

Abbeyshrule

Duiske

Tintern

Hore

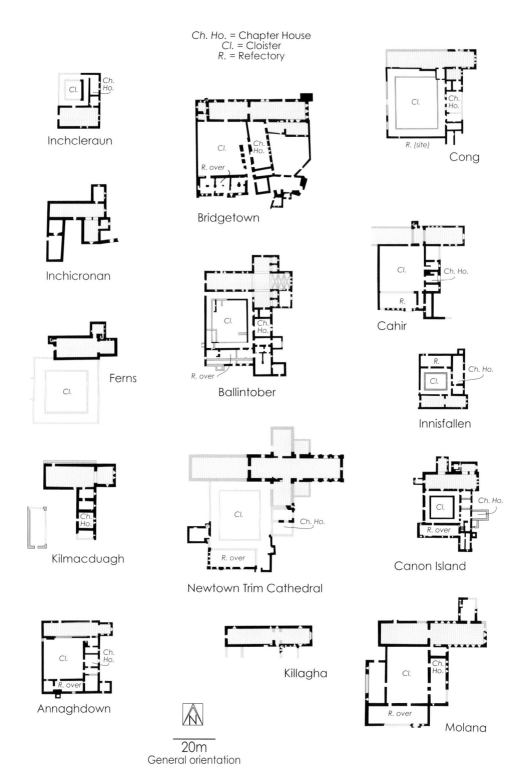

Ch. Ho. = Chapter House
Cl. = Cloister
R. = Refectory

Inchcleraun

Cong

Bridgetown

Inchicronan

Cahir

Ferns

Ballintober

Innisfallen

Kilmacduagh

Newtown Trim Cathedral

Canon Island

Annaghdown

Killagha

Molana

20m
General orientation

69 (*and opposite*) Augustinian canons' monastery plans.

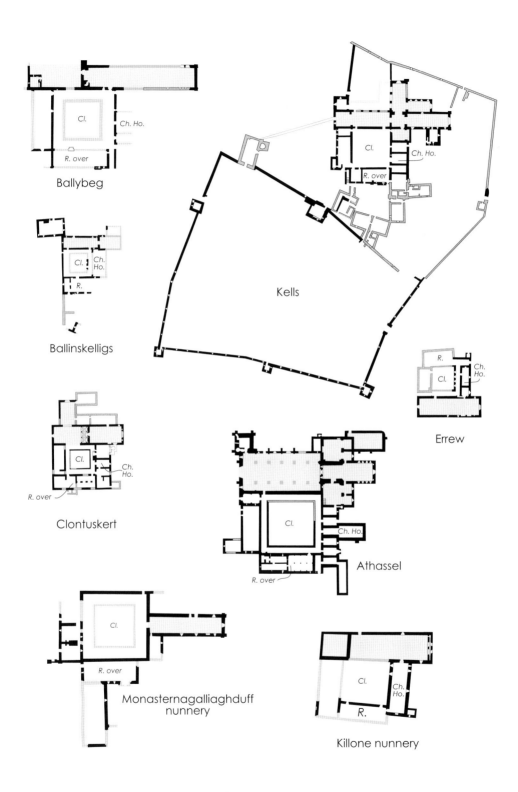

Ballybeg

Cl.
Ch. Ho.
R. over

Ballinskelligs

Cl.
Ch. Ho.
R.

Kells

Cl.
Ch. Ho.
R. over

Errew

R.
Cl.
Ch. Ho.

Clontuskert

Cl.
Ch. Ho.
R. over

Athassel

Cl.
Ch. Ho
R. over

Monasternagalliaghduff nunnery

Cl.
R. over

Killone nunnery

Cl.
Ch. Ho.
R.

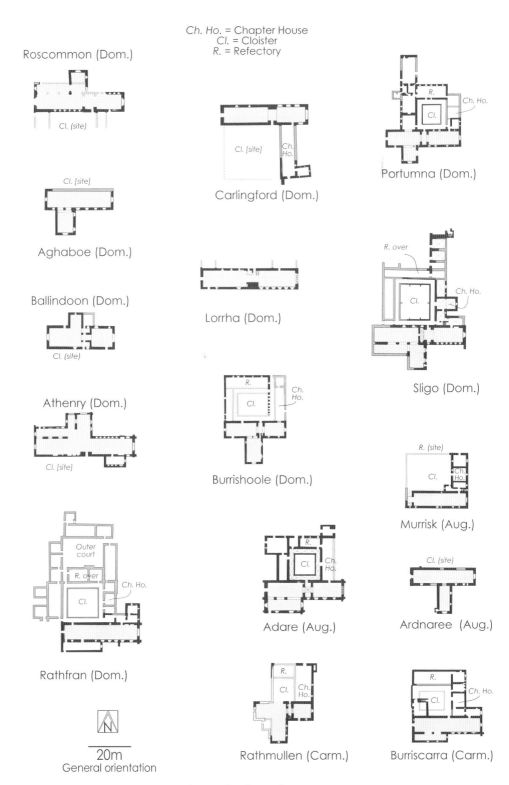

Ch. Ho. = Chapter House
Cl. = Cloister
R. = Refectory

Roscommon (Dom.)

Carlingford (Dom.)

Portumna (Dom.)

Aghaboe (Dom.)

Lorrha (Dom.)

Ballindoon (Dom.)

Sligo (Dom.)

Athenry (Dom.)

Burrishoole (Dom.)

Murrisk (Aug.)

Rathfran (Dom.)

Adare (Aug.)

Ardnaree (Aug.)

20m
General orientation

Rathmullen (Carm.)

Burriscarra (Carm.)

70 Dominican, Augustinian and Carmelite friary plans.

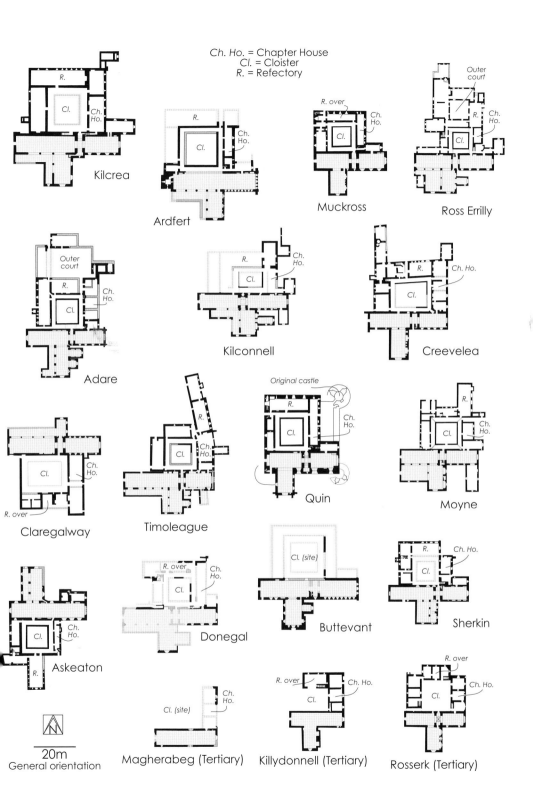

Ch. Ho. = Chapter House
Cl. = Cloister
R. = Refectory

Kilcrea

Ardfert

Muckross

Ross Errilly

Adare

Kilconnell

Creevelea

Claregalway

Timoleague

Quin

Moyne

Askeaton

Donegal

Buttevant

Sherkin

20m
General orientation

Magherabeg (Tertiary)

Killydonnell (Tertiary)

Rosserk (Tertiary)

71 Franciscan friary plans.

72 The belfry in Claregalway Friary church (Franciscan). In 1433 indulgences were granted by the pope to those who would visit the church on selected days and contribute materials or manual labour for its completion (*CPL*, 5, p. 266).

improvising strategies of monastic clergy – the circumvention of vows of silence by the use of sign language, for example[134] – is intrinsically interesting, and reminds us that monastic communities have an anthropology.[135]

A selection of claustrally planned monasteries of the four orders that were the most prolific builders is shown in figs 68–71. No attempt is made to distinguish between phases of construction in these small plans (with two Cistercian exceptions), and they are not presented in any particular sequence.

Before looking at the claustral elements in detail we will have a quick look at the churches. Cistercian monasteries have the most immediately identifiable monastic plans thanks to the architectural consistency of their churches. With very few exceptions, these were transeptal buildings, and their transepts had at their eastern sides between

134 Medieval brethren circumvented vows of silence by using sign language. The Augustinians of St Thomas' Abbey in Dublin were adept at this: see H.F. Berry, 'On the use of signs in the ancient monasteries with reference to a code used by the Victorine canons at St Thomas' Abbey, Dublin', *JRSAI*, 22 (1892), 108–23. For wider context, see S.G. Bruce, *Silence and sign language in medieval monasticism: the Cluniac tradition, c.900–1200* (Cambridge, 2007). 135 For an anthropological approach, see O'Keeffe, *The archaeology and architecture of monastic Ireland, 1100–1600*.

73 The late medieval tower in Cashel Friary church (Dominican). This tower barely cleared the roof of the church. Given its design, it is unlikely to have functioned primarily as a belfry.

74 The nave arcade in Claregalway Friary church was built when a new side-aisle was added in the late Middle Ages to the thirteenth-century building. It is very typical of the type of arcade erected (sometimes as parts of brand new foundations) in the 1400s in churches of all orders (mendicant and otherwise) and types (collegiate churches, for example): the arches are carried on circular capitals atop cylindrical piers, and are pointed (see fig. 52 for a contrast, and fig. 53 for a parallel). A small square hole on the pier on the right-hand side remains from a timber screen, reminding us that the interiors of churches were divided by screens.

one and three flat-ended chapels; Mellifont alone had round-ended chapels in its earliest (1140s) phase but they were replaced with the more conventional flat-ended type when the whole monastery was substantially rebuilt under Anglo-Norman patronage. In Cistercian churches both the choirs and the transeptal chapels were customarily vaulted, and even where the vaults have disappeared one can often see evidence that they once existed. The naves were normally aisled, though nave arcades did not always extend westwards for the full length. Towers, the need for which was debated within the Cistercian community in general, rose over the junctions of the naves, choirs and transepts, which is the space called 'the crossing'. The survival rate of Cistercian churches is relatively high, and all are quite well known. The only substantial ruin that could be described as relatively neglected – at least relative to its importance – by scholars is probably Monasteranenagh.

There is also some consistency in the plans of churches of the friars, though it is much less striking and does not allow us make easy distinctions based on formal architecture between Dominican, Franciscan, Carmelite and Augustinian mendicant establishments. The mendicant churches tend to be long, the choirs of which take up at least one-third of their lengths. Belfries mark the nave–choir junctions, forming elaborate canopies over passages (often described as 'walking places')[136] connecting the cloisters and the churches. The classic mendicant belfry is tall and narrow, with no obvious accommodation. Although most of the examples are late medieval (pl. VI, fig. 72), the type first appeared in the thirteenth century, as at Buttevant (where only the base survives of a tower that was inserted within a few of decades of the church's consecration; see fig. 44). Not all mendicant houses went for such elegant towers at the nave–choir junction (fig. 73). Thirteenth-century mendicant churches were generally unaisled, but aisles were sometimes added in the late Middle Ages, a process that involved the removal of one wall and its replacement with an arcade, normally carried on cylindrical drums (fig. 74).

Amid the consistency are some exceptional thirteenth-century monuments. Buttevant, for example, built by the Barry family to replace the nearby Augustinian priory of Ballybeg as their church of dynastic burial, was in the very centre of a new planned town rather than at its edge. Its choir was raised over a two-storeyed crypt; the only Franciscan crypt in Ireland, it may have been a conversion of an older building, possibly a castle.[137] If so, it was not unique: later mendicant friaries – Carrickbeg and Quin, both Franciscan, and Banada, Augustinian – were built on castle sites.[138] There is also a tradition that Maurice fitzGerald had originally intended to build a castle in Youghal on the site of its Franciscan friary, and that when his son abused the workmen rather than provide them with drink to celebrate an unnamed saint's feastday (St Francis'?), Maurice gave the site over to the Franciscans instead as an act of reparation.[139] The most puzzling of all the thirteenth-century mendicant churches must be that at Timoleague. The choir and the adjacent part of the nave are thirteenth century, and Anne-Julie Lafaye has suggested that they belonged to an earlier, probably monastic, foundation of uncertain affiliation that was later taken over by the Franciscans.[140] A distinguishing feature of the apparent pre-Franciscan church is its use of passages through its thick walls – a blocked window overlooking the choir from the upper passage is visible in the top left-hand corner of fig. 49 – and these are best contextualized in the English Gothic tradition which produced the Dublin cathedrals (see fig. 8) and Newtown Trim Cathedral. So-called 'thick wall' (or *mur épais*) construction involving mural passages is typical of Norman architecture and survived from the Romanesque into Gothic in England. The upper passage at Timoleague is interrupted by round (rather than pointed) arches and could not have been used without some bridge between the piers of the arches. If bridges were suspended across these arches, effectively dividing the arched spaces into two storeys, the arrangement constitutes what architectural historians describe as a 'giant order', a device of ancient

---

136 O'Sullivan, *In the company of the preachers*, passim.   **137** O'Keeffe, 'Buttevant Friary and its crypt'; idem, 'Buttevant friary church in the thirteenth century'. Only one Franciscan crypt is known in England (O'Sullivan, *In the company of the preachers*, p. 353).   **138** Ó Clabaigh, *The friars in Ireland*, p. 205; for Banada, see also C. Lynn, 'Castle-sites in the west of Ireland', *JGAHS*, 40 (1985/6), 90–113 at 95–6.   **139** M. Archdall, *Monasticon Hibernicum* (Dublin, 1786), p. 80. **140** Lafaye, *Medieval mendicant communities in east Munster*.

Classical origin that was sometimes adopted in European Romanesque and Gothic architecture. Parallels for Timoleague's crude but authentic 'giant order' would include the now-demolished Waterford Cathedral.[141] The feature points to a date for Timoleague early rather than late in the 1200s, which would support Lafaye's suggestion that it was not originally Franciscan.

New mendicant churches of the 1400s (and even into the early 1500s) were usually aisled on one side – the other side had the claustral ranges – from the outset, though there are exceptions (Muckross, Sherkin, Creevelea). The aisles were normally accompanied by new wings (often described for convenience, though inaccurately, as transepts) off which were small east-facing chapels. Funded by local patrons, these chapels were usually partitioned in wood originally and each normally comprised little more than an altar under a window. Franciscan churches are marginally the largest of the mendicant churches and their 'transepts' and 'transeptal chapels' are marginally more elaborate. That this reflects greater resources and larger member-intake is suggested by the larger claustral ranges attached to them.

The churches of Augustinian canons regular are the most variable of all. Some of those built by the Gaelic-Irish before the Anglo-Norman invasion (or built after that invasion but in lands that remained Irish) are of nave-and-chancel design, their short chancels suited to pre-1215 liturgy (as at Ferns, Annaghdown and Kilmacduagh). Some were of Cistercian character. Ballintober, for example, could easily be confused for Cistercian. Also leaning towards the Cistercian character was Athassel, though some of its elements – statue niches beside its east window, its buttressed west wall, its vaulted nave-aisles and so on – speak of other influences. Tristernagh Priory church, now lost apart from a fragment of its west end, might have been the most Cistercian of all the Anglo-Norman Augustinian houses, judging by the late eighteenth-century depictions that show its transepts and choir having storeyed elevations like those of Dunbrody and Duiske churches. In fact, its geographical proximity to the Cistercian abbeys of Abbeylara and Abbeyshrule suggests that they, now fragmentary themselves, were originally substantial structures, and that there was a rich local tradition of early Gothic architecture in the western part of the lordship of Meath. Some other Augustinian foundations, like Canon Island and Clontuskert, are mendicant-like. Some Augustinian churches had belfries, and these were customarily placed not at nave–choir junctions but at the west ends of the naves; some of the belfries are end-of-nave porch-towers but others, as at Athassel and Kells, for example, are on the north sides of the west ends of the naves and had habitable lower storeys. The towers are not of consistent design. The early thirteenth-century examples at Askeaton and Inistioge Augustinian priories share the unusual feature of a square lower part supporting an octagonal upper part.[142]

141 For Waterford, see Stalley, 'Three Irish buildings', pp 66–71.   **142** The west tower of the parish church of Knocktopher also had an octagonal top on a square-plan base. The south tower at Carlingford Castle and the town gate of Trim Castle have similar forms; the former is *c.*1200 and the latter is an early addition, probably also *c.*1200, to a structure of the 1170s. The Butter Gate in Drogheda, one of the gates on the medieval town wall, was originally of similar design. The depiction of the octagonal crossing tower at Tristernagh (now demolished) in Francis Grose's *Antiquities of Ireland* (London, 1794) suggests a late medieval insertion (it springs from

75 The west end of the nave of the church of the priory of the Holy Trinity at Ballyboggan. Note the survival of the steeply sloping sills of side-wall windows that one could neither look in nor look out. Even with a large window in its west wall, this was a dark interior.

If there is such a thing as a typical Augustinian priory church, at least of post-1169 vintage, it is surely represented by Newtown Trim, Kells, Bridgetown and Molana, churches with long, narrow choirs. Ballybeg has the longest church of all. Its choir alone was nearly 30m long. The original length of the nave is uncertain, but if it was as long as is suggested by the position of the cloister, as it must have been, it was by some distance the longest church ever built in Ireland, surpassing the churches of Duiske Abbey (Cistercian) and Newtown Trim Cathedral, and Ballyboggan Priory church (also Augustinian). What is striking about these early thirteenth-century Augustinian priory churches of Anglo-Norman foundation is the austerity of their architecture (fig. 75). It is tempting to attribute this pattern to relative poverty in the formative years of the lordship, but it is probably more correct to see their high and little-fenestrated walls as both expressions of colonial might and admissions of colonial insecurity. It might be worth noting how the de Barrys of north-central Cork first sponsored the long and (presumably) grim church of Ballybeg around 1230 before shifting their patronage twenty-odd years later to a new and slightly more opulent church of Franciscans in the new town of Buttevant. Viewed in this light, the priory of Athassel, built in the early thirteenth century, emerges as a work of great optimism.

pointed corbels, which are late medieval in type), but Tristernagh's location in the same lordship as Trim and Drogheda (Meath) might tempt us to date it to the early thirteenth century.

The cloister garth and cloister alleys

The essence of the claustral plan is a central and unroofed court or cloister – *claustrum* is Latin for 'enclosure' – with the church and other key buildings and rooms arranged around it in a series of ranges. By the time it first appeared in Ireland, probably with the Cistercians at Mellifont in the early 1140s, its spatial principles were firmly established.[143] Evidence that it was in Ireland before Mellifont is weak. According to a late medieval source, Sitriuc, Dublin's late tenth- and early eleventh-century king, 'gave gold and silver sufficient to build a church with all its court', and Dúnán, the first bishop, built the chapel of St Nicholas 'on the north side, with other buildings according to the wish of the founder.'[144] The suggestion here is of a pre-Mellifont monastic claustral plan attached to the city's cathedral. However, we should reject it on the grounds that the introduction of regular canons to the cathedral is first recorded in 1162.[145]

Analysis of proportional systems using the methods set out above (pp 90–3) suggests often that the cloisters were the first parts of monasteries to be laid out. However, the structures around the cloisters were not all built at the one time, and in many cases were possibly not even built as intended. The very valuable Register of Athenry tells us, for example, that different parts and features of Athenry's Dominican priory were built under different patrons, Anglo-Norman and Gaelic-Irish, men as well as women.[146] Bective Abbey is unusual in having had its cloister rebuilt. Its original claustral area was quite large, and its chapter house remains, but the present cloister is a small though attractive late medieval example, more mendicant than Cistercian in design, and conventional thinking is that it represents a late contraction of the monastery.[147]

A cloister court itself had relatively few uses. It could be used for burial, as has been revealed by recent excavations of the Dominican house in Trim,[148] and future excavations may show that this was not uncommon. Many – most? – courts were probably kept as lawns, enjoyed for whatever flora or wildlife nature sent to visit them, but they were not 'gardened' in the sense that we understand today; there were no doors into them, and in any case they were not sufficiently well drained.[149] In abbeys

---

143 For its history, see W. Horn, 'On the origins of the medieval cloister', *Gesta*, 12:1/2 (1973), 13–52. The best general survey remains W. Braunfels, *Monasteries of western Europe: the architecture of the orders* (London, 1972). More thought-provoking are M. Cassidy-Welch, *Monastic spaces and their meanings* (Turnhout, 2001); and A. Müller, 'Presenting identity in the cloister: remarks on Benedictine and mendicant conceptions of space' in Müller and Stöber (eds), *Self-representation of medieval religious communities*, pp 167–89.   **144** A. Gwynn, 'The origins of the see of Dublin, pt 1', *Irish Ecclesiastical Record*, 57 (1941), 40–55 at 46–8.   **145** *CSMD*, ii, p. 266; see T. O'Keeffe, 'Architecture and regular life in Holy Trinity Cathedral, 1150–1350' in Kinsella (ed.), *Augustinians at Christ Church*, pp 23–40.   **146** *RA*.   **147** Given the unusual manner in which it intrudes on the original south aisle of the church, would it be too far-fetched to think that it was rebuilt in the late sixteenth century as part of a bigger programme of building work at the site when the abbey was transferred into private possession at the Dissolution?   **148** F. O'Carroll, 'Interim report: archaeological research excavations at the Black Friary, Trim, Co. Meath' (The Irish Archaeology Field School, 2014 [accessible via www.ifas.ie]), p. 58.   **149** S. Landsberg, *The medieval garden* (Toronto, 2003), pp 35–6; part-excavation of the court at Tintern

76 The eastern alley of the undershot cloister at Ardfert Friary (Franciscan). Vaulted alleys, such as this, are only found in undershot cloisters in Ireland (although cloister alleys with lean-to roofs were often vaulted outside Ireland).

and priories the church was normally on the north side of the cloister, which meant that it did not cast a shadow across the court; the positions were sometimes reversed, as at Augustinian Errew and Cistercian Hore, while at Monasternagalliaghduff, a house of Augustinian canonesses, the church projects from the east side of the cloister.[150] In mendicant friaries and in nunneries the cloister was normally north of the church; again, there are exceptions, such as Franciscan Askeaton and Carmelite Castlelyons, where the positions were reversed.

The cloister court or garden was ringed by covered walkways or 'alleys' that were separated from the court by a continuous wall penetrated by unglazed windows (as at Athassel and Errew) or, far more frequently, by unglazed arches (hence we have so-called 'cloister arcades').[151] The alleys were accessible from outside the monastic complexes via passages or slypes, the number of which was not consistent from one monastic house to another. The alleys were normally covered by lean-to roofs but a novel and very satisfying alternative found in late medieval mendicant contexts (and not just in Ireland) was the so-called undershot cloister, in which the first-floor levels

yielded no evidence of garden use (Lynch, *Tintern Abbey*, pp 75–6).   **150** T.J. Westropp, 'The history and antiquities of St Catherine's, Old Abbey, Co. Limerick', *JRSAI*, 14 (1904), 53–64. **151** For a useful discussion of Early English style cloisters in Ireland, see also J. Montague, 'The cloister arcade' in Clyne, *Kells Priory, Co. Kilkenny*, pp 187–206.

77 The east range at Cong Abbey (*c*.1200) from the interior, showing the chapter house and, to the left, a processional slype (or passage) doorway. The lateral windows in the west wall of the chapter house would have allowed activities inside to be heard and even viewed from the adjacent cloister alley, especially Collation.

of the buildings around the court override the alleys, thus providing stone roofs that could then be vaulted (fig. 76).[152] The alleys themselves served several purposes. Their primary function was to provide covered access between different parts of the establishment, often for communities moving in procession. Thus, we commonly find that the alleys are lined up with doorways. Devotional images carved on the arcade supports in some cloisters – St Francis appears in several Franciscan friaries[153] – suggest a second function: contemplation and prayer. A possible third function was to provide space for occasional activities, copying books being an obvious one.[154] A possible fourth function, best known from Cistercian houses but not exclusive to them, was to accommodate Collation (or *Collatio*), an evening meeting of the community (see fig. 77).[155]

With the sole exception of Monasternagalliaghduff, the church always occupied the full length of one side of the cloister. While it was always accessible from the cloister

152 For a discussion of cloister variation in mendicant contexts, see A. O'Donohue, 'Mendicant cloisters in Munster', *BAACT*, 34 (2010), 111–31.   **153** C. Ó Clabaigh, 'The cult of St Francis in late medieval Ireland' in Moss, Ó Clabaigh and Ryan (eds), *Art and devotion in late medieval Ireland*, pp 142–62.   **154** There is evidence of this in England: D.N. Bell, 'Libraries and scriptoria' in M.B. Bruun, *The Cambridge companion to the Cistercian order* (Cambridge, 2012), pp 140–50 at p. 142.   **155** T. Webber, *Reading in the refectory: monastic practice in England, c.1000–1300*

circuit, the nature of the access varied. To our eyes, the access simply depended on the exact position of the cloister relative to the church, but in the Middle Ages the relative positions of cloister alleys and churches were determined by liturgical and processional needs. Thus, at Athassel two of the cloister alleys – the west and east – lined up with doors into the nave of the great church to facilitate the processions of canons into the church at the west end of the nave and out of the church at the east end. Processional doorways were arranged similarly in Cistercian houses. In some Augustinian priories, such as Canon Island and Inisfallen, one of the two doorways led directly into the choir.

The norm in mendicant foundations, where the church was usually south of the cloister, was for a door somewhere along the south alley to give access to the space under the tower – the 'walking place' – at the junction of the nave and chancel. Because the doorway did not normally line up with the east or west alley – Muckross and Quin are among the exceptions – the passage from the cloister to the church was generally less dramatic than in the Augustinian and Cistercian houses. But the significance in terms of ritual and liturgy of the friars entering under the church tower cannot be overstated: the tower was effectively converted into a small (and often elaborately vaulted) ante-chamber or porch serving the choir. The oddest arrangement of doorways from a cloister alley to a mendicant church is at Askeaton, where one doorway leads into the centre of the nave and the other leads, via an angled passage, into the choir.

The east side of the cloister was always reserved for two main spaces, the chapter house or chapter room, which was more or less in the centre of the east range at ground-floor level and was flanked by other rooms and slypes, and the dormitory, which occupied the full length of the range at first-floor level. The chapter house was second in importance to the church within a monastery. It was the space in which the community, sitting on benches against the wall, was daily re-read the necrology (the list of saints to be venerated and of deceased benefactors requiring prayer) and re-instructed in the monastic rule through the reading of one of its chapters. It was where the community's business affairs were discussed. It was where brethren confessed their sins before the community. And, based on English evidence, it was even a place where monastic superiors might find themselves buried.[156] Although chapter houses were not chapels, they were treated architecturally with the same level of reverence: their entrance doorways off the cloisters were normally elaborate – a fact now disguised to us by the post-Dissolution removal of so many examples – and were sometimes flanked by windows (fig. 77). Chapter houses were normally as wide as the ranges in which they were positioned, but occasionally, particularly in Cistercian houses (as at Mellifont), they projected further to the east.

Identifying the uses of the rooms alongside chapter houses in the lower storeys of the east ranges of monasteries is marginally more challenging. If the room between the chapter house and the church had a door directly into the church choir, it is safe to assume that it served as a sacristy. The room on the other side of the chapter house might sometimes have been the 'warming room' or *calefactory*, a room with a fireplace.[157] More often than not, though, this space was occupied by the inner parlour. Derived from the same root-word as the modern French *parler*, to speak, the parlour was the one room where community members would be allowed to speak at certain times. In the Benedictine tradition guests could be received and given spiritual guidance in the inner parlour.[158] However, occasionally permitted conversations with the laity, including family, were generally restricted to the outer parlour, usually located in the west range and close to the church (as at Athassel).

The community's dormitory (or dorter) always occupied the upper level of the east range; the west range offered the same facility (above cellarage) to lay brethren in Cistercian houses, or to the overflow of clerics in very populous monastic houses of all the congregations. Beds were turned perpendicularly to the wall, each bed-head being positioned under its own window. Heads of community slept in the east ranges also, initially among the brethren but increasingly, if monastic houses grew especially big, in their own quarters. At Athassel is a well-appointed room off the dormitory and above the chapter house, and it is best interpreted as the prior's own lodging.

The principle governing the position of the dormitory was ease-of-access, perhaps even speed-of-access, between the bed and the choir stall. The first instalment of the daily round of prayer or Divine Office was Matins, timed for shortly after midnight.[159] A stair called 'the night-stair' was provided to allow the brethren move briskly to the east end of the church. Where the church of a claustral monastery had transepts, the night-stair descended into the west side of the transept; good examples survive at Athassel and Holycross. In churches without transepts the evidence can be more fugitive, and it is often not at all apparent how the community went from the dormitory to the church. Sometimes, though, the stair simply descended directly into the choir, as at Fore, but in other cases, as at Kilcrea, Muckross and Quin, the brethren descended into a cloister alley and walked from there into the church. The fifteenth-century redesign of the south transept at Kilcooly included moving the position of the night-stair so that the community had to enter the church through the easternmost bay of the nave.

Corresponding to the night-stair was a day-stair, providing access to the dormitory from the cloister. This was necessary to prevent the community traipsing into the choir to access their beds at night. The preferred position for the day-stair was at the opposite end of the east range from the church, close to the refectory (see below).

Visits to the church were scheduled. Visits to the toilet were not. Monastic residents answering the call of nature at night headed away from the church towards the toilet block (the reredorter or *necessarium*) at the end of the dormitory. The long wooden benches on which they sat, apparently with no partitions between them, had vertical slots below, and bodily waste cascaded into a drain in which it was carried to a river.

---

157 Such rooms may have been used for drying laundry: P. Fergusson and S. Harrison, *Rievaulx Abbey: community, architecture, memory* (New Haven and London, 1999), p. 140.   158 J. Kerr, *Monastic hospitality: the Benedictines in England, c.1070–c.1250* (Woodbridge, 2007).   159 Harper,

78 The ground-floor refectory and first-floor dorter at Askeaton Friary (Franciscan).

The day-stair brought monastic brethen to the toilet during the day, and its position at the end of the east range gave them access to the dorter without necessitating a walk through the dormitory.

The monastic refectory always occupied part or all of the claustral range opposite the church.[160] It was the space in which the community ate. Evidence outside Ireland suggests that it was also a place of potential penance: community members found guilty of disobedience could be instructed to eat separately from their fellow monastics in the refectory, or even on its floor, their physical dislocation symbolizing their enforced spiritual dislocation from the community.[161] The refectory customarily

Forms and orders of western liturgy, ch. 6.   **160** The only exception is Monastenagalliaghduff, where the refectory is in the 'right' position (in the south range) but the church is in an unconventional position.   **161** L.V. Hicks, *Religious life in Normandy, 1050–1300: space, gender and*

occupied a single-storey block in Cistercian architecture but it occupied the upstairs or first-floor space in a two-storeyed block in other monastic contexts; the explanation may be that Christ's Last Supper was in an upper room.[162] The Cistercians had a predilection for building their refectories at right-angles to the adjacent cloister walks. The scheme had two advantages: the refectories could be as long as they needed to be because they did not need to follow the dimensions of the cloisters, and the kitchens could be accommodated in the south ranges because there was room for them. Among the few non-Cistercian houses to feature a perpendicular refectory is the Franciscan friary of Askeaton. Here, it was at ground-floor level and, unusually, had a dorter above it (fig. 78). Askeaton's refectory is one of many to preserve its *pulpitum*, the place, usually recessed into the wall, from which a *lector* (or reader) read passages of sacred or exegetical texts aloud to the silent community during mealtime.[163]

Prior to entering the refectory the community washed its hands at the lavabo or *lavatorium*, and repeated the ritual after eating. The *lavatorium* was generally an arched recess in the outside (cloister-side) wall of the refectory. Ideally supplied with water through a lead pipe from a catchment at roof level, in many smaller monastic houses the likelihood is that water was carried in a vessel when the ritual of washing was taking place. The entrances to refectories were generally west-end, with the *lavatorium* recesses immediately to the east. Free-standing lavabos with central receptacles supplied by water-pipes – Cistercian Mellifont has Ireland's only extant example[164] – were sometimes built by communities following the Rule of St Benedict. The members of these communities ritually washed their feet every week (on a Saturday) and on Maundy Thursday, in remembrance of Christ washing the feet of his disciples.[165]

Outside a cloister but still within its precinct were other structures. One was the infirmary, for ill and aged members of a community. Stephen Lexington noted that Cistercian monasteries could also have infirmaries for lay brothers and the poor.[166] Separated from the main body of a monastery for obvious reasons, the infirmary often had its own cloister and usually had its own garden, presumably for the growing of plants and herbs of medicinal value. The most complete plan of an infirmary is at Cistercian Holycross, where a passage separates a series of care-rooms close to the river from rooms that may have been restricted to the carers. The precincts themselves were walled, spectacularly so in the case of Kells Priory (Augustinian), and the entrances had gate buildings, good thirteenth- and fifteenth-century examples of which remain at Athassel and Mellifont respectively.

social pressure (Woodbridge, 2007), p. 41.   **162** Painted images of the Last Supper decorate a good number of late medieval continental refectories, whatever their storey-level; there is even a carving of the Last Supper over the twelfth-century doorway into the refectory of St-Bénigne in Dijon.   **163** Although it deals with Germany, refectory reading is covered at length in D.H. Green, *Medieval listening and reading: the primary reception of German literature, 800–1300* (Cambridge, 1994).   **164** R. Stalley, 'Decorating the lavabo: late Romanesque sculpture from Mellifont Abbey', *PRIA*, 96C (1996), 237–64.   **165** B. Harvey, *Living and dying in England, 1100–1540: the monastic experience* (Oxford, 1993), p. 129.   **166** Stalley, *Cistercian monasteries of Ireland*, p. 173.

79 Rincrew 'preceptory' viewed from the courtyard. The building in the centre of the photograph had an upper storey, underpinned by an inserted late medieval vault; the building on the right, oriented at 90° to the latter, was single storey and its large and regular windows suggest a hall. If not a Templar property, might it have been a grange associated with the nearby Augustinian house of Molana?

HOSPITALLER AND TEMPLAR PRECEPTORIES AND CAMERAS

The two military orders came to Ireland in the aftermath of the 1169 invasion and participated in the protection of the lordship. The Templars arrived in the 1170s and are understood to have founded six preceptories, which were basically fortified monasteries (although the term preceptory also extended to describe the attached estate), and ten 'cameras', which were out-farms to which residences – *camera* means chamber in Latin – were attached.[167] As befitting the stated military purpose of their occupants, a significant number of the sites occupied elevated ground strategically overlooking bodies of water. Nothing survives of the main Templar house at Clontarf, and the above-ground remains elsewhere of the preceptories and cameras are fairly negligible. The most extensive remains are at Templehouse, a north-western outlier of the main south-eastern Irish distribution of sites. The partially surviving rectangular area here is probably thirteenth-century in origin, albeit with later alterations. On its west side stands a two-storeyed residential tower,[168] possibly the 'house' (*camera*) from

---

167 The enumeration is based on Gwynn and Hadcock, *Medieval religious houses*, pp 327–31, but its accuracy is questionable.   **168** Lynn, 'Castle-sites in the west of Ireland', 105–9.

80 The interior of Hospital Church looking eastwards from the first floor of the tower that was inserted in the late Middle Ages. A mid-thirteenth-century effigy against the east wall is presumed to represent the preceptory's founder, Geoffrey de Marisco; he died in France (in 1245), so the identification is problematic. The off-centre round window high in the east wall is unusual; there are five similar windows in the surviving gable of St Mary's parish church in Dungarvan, also early thirteenth-century.

which the place-name derives. If there was a hall on the site it must have been of timber. There is no above-ground evidence of a church. The medieval buildings that survive in fragmentary condition on three sides of a small courtyard at Rincrew are popularly (though, it must be said, without substantiation) regarded as Templar, with Raymond le Gros identified as the founder. There is nothing specifically religious in the complex, although one cannot rule out that the very fragmentary structure under vegetation on the north side of the courtyard was a church. The two extant structures, originally thirteenth century, are best interpreted as a ground-floor hall and a first-floor chamber (fig. 79). Earthworks of other preceptories survive at Clonoulty and Crooke, with a thirteenth-century parish church (pl. V) and part of a later medieval tower at the latter. The fifteenth-century Hospitaller tower-house at Kilcloggan stands inside what was probably a rectangular farm-courtyard belonging to the church of Templetown. The character of what survives at these sites is so heterogeneous that one can only conclude that the Templars did not use the claustral plan in Ireland.

The Hospitallers arrived in Ireland in 1172, and had their land-grants confirmed by the pope in 1212. Their estates in the thirteenth century were managed from fourteen preceptories, with some former Templar properties added to their portfolio in the early 1300s. The priory at Kilmainham, founded for them in the mid-1170s by Strongbow, held ultimate authority over all Hospitaller possessions. The buildings that stood at Kilmainham (in the grassy area between the Royal Hospital and 'Bully's Acre') are known to us only from various sources.[169] Second in importance to Kilmainham was the preceptory of St John the Baptist, Ainy, of which the long church in the village of Hospital is all that survives (fig. 80). There is structural evidence of a former cloister, added in the late Middle Ages. An even longer Hospitaller church survives within a large pentagonal enclosure at Mourne, but there is no evidence of a cloister.[170] Extensive earthworks, scattered fragments of apparently thirteenth-century masonry, and a tower-house (of uncertain relationship to the preceptory) survive at Kilteel; the Hospitallers appear to have incorporated the pre-Norman church of Kilteel in the complex of courts and other enclosures attached to the preceptory, but they must also have built a new church, now lost. Again, there is no evidence of a cloister, suggesting that, as with the Templars and notwithstanding the evidence at Hospital, the claustral form was not a core feature of their foundations.

CHAPELS

The churches encountered to this point were either the main places of worship for monastic communities or the principal sanctuaries at the centres of territorial jurisdictions (parishes or dioceses), or both. Churches that were neither were generally described as chapels. Somewhat confusingly, the same term describes the smaller sanctified spaces that were within or attached to larger churches. Chapels of both types are the most understudied buildings or spaces of an ecclesiastical nature surviving from the Middle Ages in Ireland.

Chantry chapels

Medieval elites, mindful of purgatory, could ensure a posthumous supply of prayers for their salvation through the establishment of perpetual chantries. These were remembrance or intercessory masses that were celebrated – or sung, *chantry* being a derivation from the Latin *cantaria*, to sing – in perpetuity by endowed celebrants. Chantry was not a physical 'thing' but a service provided by a priest (whose 'living' or salary was independent of the parish priest's), and it was customarily accommodated within a specially built chapel.[171] Irish chantry foundations have yet to be studied in detail, despite a wealth of historical evidence, but there is no doubt that the number of such foundations in Ireland was proportionally much less than on the larger neighbouring island, and it is probable that the proportion of chantries attached to urban churches was greater in Ireland.

169 C. McNeill, 'The Hospitallers at Kilmainham and their guests', *JRSAI*, 54 (1924), 15–30; G. Lennox Barrow, 'The Knights Hospitaller of St John of Jerusalem at Kilmainham', *Dublin Historical Record*, 38:3 (1985), 108–12; C. Kenny, *Kilmainham: the history of a settlement older than Dublin* (Dublin, 1995); L. Simpson, 'Dublin's famous "Bully's Acre": site of the monastery of Kilmainham?', *MD*, 9 (2009), 38–83; T. O'Keeffe and P. Grogan, 'Building a frontier? The architecture of the military orders in medieval Ireland' in Brown and Ó Clabaigh (eds), *Soldiers of Christ*. **170** Eamonn Cotter, pers. comm. **171** Although neither deals with Ireland, of

The endowments to the priests were financial, but when they included land, as they increasingly did during the thirteenth century, it meant that the land in question was 'alienated' or taken away from the landed family and locked up permanently in the possession of the chantry. Some regulation of this process was felt necessary when the number of new chantry foundations was noticeably increasing during the 1200s, so in 1279 it was ordained by statute that a royal licence would be required to endow a chantry with land. Thus, for example, we have a record from 1305 of the king, Edward I, asking his justiciar, John Wogan, to assess whether

> it would be to the K[ing]'s damage to give licence to Richard de Burgh, Earl of Ulster, to grant to 24 chaplains 40 librates of lands and rents in Loghre [Loughrea, Galway] and Typerbryde [Ballintober, Roscommon], … the chaplains to offer, in a chapel at Loghre and Typerbryde to be newly built, divine service daily for the soul of the earl and the souls of his ancestors; to hold to the chaplains and their successors forever.[172]

While the need for royal licences suggests a golden age of chantry foundation in the 1200s, the greatest age of such foundation in Britain and Ireland was actually the late Middle Ages, a flowering that might be linked to the inability of monastic houses to cater for the increasing number of requests for intercessory masses.[173] A valuable insight into the process of chantry foundation in this later medieval period is offered by the record of the foundation and sustaining of a chantry in Christ Church Cathedral, Dublin. In 1488 Gerald fitzGerald, eighth earl of Kildare, and Sir Roland fitzEustace undertook to oversee the collecting of yearly rents from lands that had been used to finance a new chantry endowment by one John Estrete. Kildare, fitzEustace and John Estrete together recommended that one of their canons would celebrate Mass in the chapel daily, and that the entire convent and choir should sing a Mass of the Holy Ghost every Thursday – with a bell to be rung in advance – for John Estrete, and for his benefactors (among whom were Kildare and fitzEustace themselves). It was further intended that the benefactors were to be regarded as co-founders and accordingly were to be remembered in prayer by the congregation.[174]

The chapels of chantry themselves were created either by cordoning off parts of existing churches or by building extensions; Simon Roffey calls these 'adaptive' and 'constructive' types respectively.[175] Whichever form they took, the chantry founders needed to negotiate with clergy of the churches in question, as did Mayor James Rice of Waterford who in 1482 persuaded the dean of the town's cathedral to remove a wall of the venerable building and give up some church land for a chantry chapel.[176]

interest are K.L. Wood-Leigh, *Perpetual chantries in Britain* (Cambridge, 1965) and J. McNeill, 'A prehistory of the chantry', *JBAA*, 164 (2011), 1–38.   **172** *CDI, 1302–7*, no. 436; a librate was customarily a portion of land valued at £1. For royal licences (albeit especially in England and France), see S. Raban, *Mortmain legislation and the English church, 1279–1500* (Cambridge, 1982).   **173** H. Colvin, 'The origin of chantries', *Journal of Medieval History*, 26 (2000), 163–73.   **174** Lyons, 'Sidelights on the Kildare ascendancy', pp 82–3. See also A.J. Fletcher, 'Liturgy in the late medieval cathedral priory' in Milne (ed.), *Christ Church Cathedral*, pp 129–41 at pp 138–9.   **175** S. Roffey, *The medieval chantry chapel: an archaeology* (Woodbridge, 2007), p. 90.   **176** E. McEneaney, 'Politics

Whatever its actual form, a chantry chapel normally possessed the same features for liturgy as the presbytery of the church in which it was incorporated – an altar, a *piscina* and a seat for the priest – but it also had a prominent tomb or at least a prominently displayed memorial.

Although a 'private' space in one sense, a chantry was not fully sealed off to members of the wider parish community. On the contrary, its interior was visible at very least through a partitioning screen, so as to encourage parishioners' prayers for the salvation of the souls of the founding family. Indeed, parishioners who were members of lay fraternities (collectives of the laity with very full devotion to religious life) either had chantries of their own[177] or had access to, and aided in the maintenance of, the perpetual chantries founded in their local parish churches by local noble families.[178] Although they had their own altars served by their own priests, lines of visibility between chantry chapels and the chancels of their host churches were sought after by the endowers. The positions available for chantries often militated against such intervisibility, but a squint window, angled through the church wall to provide a view of a high altar, was sometimes an option.

Distinguishing between perpetual chantries and other forms of in-church chapel can be difficult.[179] It is easy to assume that chapels other than Lady chapels (see below) were places of chantry, especially if they contain memorials. The historical identification of a chapel with a saint rather than a family might be an indicator of a non-chantry origin, but not of non-chantry use: put another way, chantries could be established within chapels that had already been founded and dedicated to saints.[180] In any case, given the fact that chapels within churches had their own priests or chaplains, and that those from whom such liturgists received their stipend doubtless expected prayers for their salvation, all such chapels were to some degree places of chantry.

Two of the most interesting examples in Ireland of buildings with 'constructive' chapels are Limerick Cathedral – a reminder that not only parish churches played host – and St Audoen's Church in Dublin (fig. 81). In the former, the side walls of the twelfth-century church were perforated to accommodate a suite of chapels, at least

and the art of devotion in late fifteenth-century Waterford' in Moss, Ó Clabaigh and Ryan (eds), *Art and devotion in late medieval Ireland*, pp 33–50 at p. 37.   **177** Stamullen Church, south chapel, for example, was a perpetual-chantry of the local fraternity; famous for its effigial and cadaver tomb sculpture, it was founded in 1458 for two chaplains, a clerk and four boys (*SRPI, Hen. VI*, p. 513). The fraternity itself was founded by Sir Robert Preston of Gormanston Castle. **178** C. Lennon, 'The confraternities and cultural duality in Ireland, 1450–1550' in C.F. Black and P. Gravestock (eds), *Early modern confraternities in Europe and the Americas: international and interdisciplinary perspectives* (Aldershot, 2006), pp 35–52; idem, 'The parish fraternities of County Meath'. The activities of fraternities were not confined to parish churches: in 1347 the Friars Minor of Kilkenny founded a fraternity for the purpose of raising funds to erect a new bell-tower (*campanile*) and repair the church (*The Annals of Ireland by Friar John Clyn and Thady Dowling*, ed. R. Butler (Dublin, 1849), p. 34).   **179** For the use of existing altars as place of chantry in parish churches – something which research may show to may have happened in Ireland – see C. Burgess, 'Chantries in the parish, or "through the looking-glass"', *JBAA*, 164 (2011), 100–29.   **180** For example, in 1444 a chantry was founded in the chapel of St Catherine in St Michael's parish church in Dublin (Ronan, 'Royal visitation of Dublin, 1615', p. 11 n. 35).

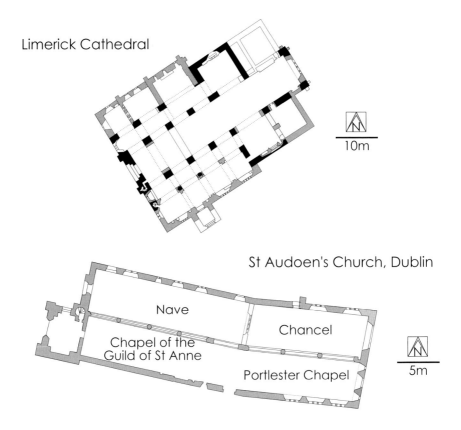

81 Plans of Limerick Cathedral and St Audoen's Church, Dublin. Note that the plan of Limerick is a composite based on several published plans, all of which differ in detail.

some of which were of perpetual chantry.[181] The alteration to St Audoen's was even more dramatic.[182] An early Anglo-Norman parish church, its nave-and-chancel plan had already seen some significant alterations before its north wall was removed *c*.1300 and replaced with an arcade opening into a new north aisle. The original nave was then transformed by royal licence in 1430 into a chantry chapel of the Guild of St Anne, Dublin's largest religious guild, with six priests appointed to serve altars to the Blessed Virgin Mary and SS Anne, Catherine, Nicholas, Thomas and Clare. In 1482 a new chantry chapel – the Portlester Chapel – was built to the east of the guild's chantry and to the south of the church's chancel. Its patron, Roland fitzEustace, first baron of Portlester, established it for his deceased wife Margaret and dedicated it to the Blessed Virgin Mary. Interestingly, a number of naves in the English Pale – Balrothery, Clondalkin, Howth and Lusk in Dublin, and Duleek and Dunshaughlin in Meath –

181 T.J. Westropp, 'St Mary's Cathedral, Limerick: its plan and growth' *JRSAI*, 5th ser. 8:1 (1898), 35–48, 112–25; R.F. Hewson, 'St Mary's Cathedral, Limerick: its development and growth', *NMAJ*, 4 (1944), 55–67. **182** M. McMahon, *St Audoen's Church, Cornmarket,*

also had single aisles added to the north sides of what had previously been plain naves, and we might presume that the changes to these churches, all of them known to have had confraternities, were to accommodate chantries.

Royal chapels

Chapels had patrons, and those with royal patrons are described very simply as 'royal chapels'. But we need to make a distinction between two concepts of royal chapel.

One was the royal chapel as an institution. Originating in the early medieval Holy Roman Empire, this was effectively a college of priests charged with certain liturgical duties particular to the royal household and operating free from episcopal juris-diction.[183] The extent to which the model was adopted in Ireland is unclear, but early twelfth-century links between Cashel and imperial Germany[184] lead one to think that Cormac's Chapel was one such chapel. Aspects of the design of Cormac's Chapel were copied almost immediately in Diarmait Mac Murchada's royal chapel at Ferns.[185] Were the rituals also copied?

The other type of royal chapel was simply a place of private prayer for a king, akin to the domestic (or castle) chapel that is discussed below (pp 173–8). This type was more common. We know that chapels were attached to post-1200 royal castles, but there is nothing in the documentation to suggest that these were served by colleges of priests. We also know virtually nothing of the architecture of these particular royal chapels, but we do have some information on their furnishings and contents. Thus, for example, in 1242 there was a mandate to the treasurer of Ireland to have glass windows made for the chapel in Dublin Castle.[186] Also, an inventory of items in the chapel of Athlone Castle from 1288 tells us that it contained

> 1 principal vestment, 1 chasuble with a cross of pearls, 2 mitres and a crozier, 1 chalice of silver-gilt, embroidered copes, a vestment for holy days, 1 silk frontal for the altar, 1 silk cope, 4 *tuallie*, 1 missal, 1 noted breviary, 1 noted gradual, 1 book of the dedication of churches, and another book of blessings, 1 small bible, 1 silver censor, 1 silver vase to put myrrh in, 1 silver vase to put holy water in, with a silver sprinkler, 2 silver ewers, 1 portable altar, 6 choir copes of *Baudekin*, and 3 of silk, 3 tunicles with a red chasuble, and 3 surplices.[187]

This must be adjudged a surprisingly well-stocked chapel for a single priest. It was certainly an improvement on the provision in the same chapel in *c.*1224 of a single chasuble, a consecrated altar, and a 'figured cloth to put before the altar'.[188] The

Dublin: archaeology and architecture (Bray, 2006).   **183** J.H. Denton, *English royal free chapels, 1100–1300: a constitutional study* (Manchester, 1970); J.W. Bernhardt, *Itinerant kingship and royal monasteries in early medieval Germany, c.936–1075* (Cambridge, 2002).   **184** Ó Riain-Raedel, 'Cashel and Germany'.   **185** O'Keeffe, 'Diarmait Mac Murchada and Romanesque Leinster'. **186** *CDI, 1171–1251*, no. 2581; for this chapel's history, see H.J. Lawlor and M.S. Dudley Westropp, 'The chapel of Dublin Castle', *JRSAI*, 13 (1923), 34–73; H.T. Lawlor, 'The chapel of Dublin castle', ibid., 18 (1928), 45–53.   **187** *CDI, 1285–92*, no. 406.   **188** *CDI, 1171–1251*, no. 1227.

inclusion of two mitres and a crozier in 1288 suggests readiness for a visiting bishop, which reinforces the argument that this was not a 'free' royal chapel.

Meriting inclusion in this discussion of royal chapels are the round towers, the first documented example of which is mid-tenth century (Slane) and the last recorded example of which was built in Connacht in the second quarter of the thirteenth century (Annaghdown) just after the Anglo-Normans had crossed into the province. Popularly regarded as places of protection for monks against marauding Vikings, a palpable nonsense that one still hears repeated by tour guides, references to these towers in native Irish sources make clear their roles as bell-towers and as places where relics were kept. As has been argued at length elsewhere, there is evidence that they had even more sophisticated ritual functions.[189] First, their doorways, all but one (Scattery) elevated above ground level, are often more elaborate than those of the churches built contemporaneously with them, which weakens the argument that they were only bell-towers, important though bell-ringing was. Second, the documented containment of relics within them suggests that their interiors were consecrated, or at least that they contained a consecrated space at the top, and the fact that in many towers the windows generally ascend clockwise, which is the direction of procession, suggests that such relics were perceived as being ritually carried clockwise from doorway to summit (when, in reality, they were carried vertically on series of ladders). Third, records of fatalities of ordinary (non-clerical) people in towers when church-sites were attacked (invariably by Irish armies) suggest that the towers were regarded as places where, thanks to consecration, sanctuary might be sought. So, why are the round towers included in this discussion of royal chapels?

The likelihood is that they were built under royal patronage, with those towers built by regional kings at major church-sites inspiring lesser powers to follow suit on church-sites under their authority. In 1120, for example, the round tower ('great belfry') in the great monastery of Clonmacnoise was 'finished by Gillachrist Ua Maoileóin, and by Toirdhealbhach Ua Conchobhair', the latter as king of Connacht,[190] while the round tower on the Rock of Cashel was almost certainly built by Muirchertach Ua Briain, king of Munster, nearly two decades earlier, probably after the 1101 reforming synod at which possession of the rock was granted to the church in perpetuity. Brian Bóruma probably built the round tower on Iniscealtra a century earlier. The association with kings was not confined to their patronage. Rather, there are two items of compelling if circumstantial evidence that at least some of the rituals enacted in and around them had royal participants. First, a newly inaugurated king of Tara was ambushed in the round tower of Kells (Meath) in 1076.[191] Second, a scion of a royal dynasty was brought into the round tower of Devenish by his kinsfolk and

---

189 O'Keeffe, *Ireland's round towers.*   **190** *Chron. Scot.* 1120; see also C. Manning, 'Some early masonry churches and the round tower at Clonmacnoise' in King (ed.), *Clonmacnoise studies*, 2, pp 63–95.   **191** 'Murchad, son of Flann Ua Maeleachlainn, at the expiration of three days and three nights after his having assumed the supremacy of Teamhair [Tara], was treacherously killed in the Cloicteach [round tower] of Ceannus [Kells], by the lord of Gailenga, Amhlaeibh, the grandson of Maelan; and the latter was himself immediately slain in revenge, through the miracles of God and Colum-Cille, by Maelseachlainn, son of Conchobhar' (*AU*, 1076; the event is recorded in six other annals).

killed in 1176.[192] If round towers did not have functions beyond the ringing of bells would a king have ventured into the tower in Kells, would his assassin have known to wait there for him, and would the contemporary chronicler of the killing have bothered to tell us where the killing happened? And why, of all places, would the round tower at Devenish be selected as a site of assassination by the people of Fermanagh? The base of a destroyed round tower sits at the foot of the present round tower at Devenish, the architectural sculpture of which fits a post-1176 construction. There is one obvious conclusion: the tower in which the killing took place was immediately demolished and a new tower built in its place, presumably under the patronage of a successor king.

Domestic/castle chapels

Medieval lords built small churches or chapels within their manorial or encastellated residences and employed priests as chaplains to their households. Farms owned by monastic houses (granges) also had chapels.[193] The number of such chapels known in Ireland is modest, but this is surely a consequence of poor documentation and the loss of those structures that were built of perishable material.[194] Drawing on the extensive and thoroughly researched English evidence,[195] we can speculate confidently that Mass was celebrated daily (and under episcopal licence) in elite households in medieval Ireland, that clerical staff additional to the chaplain was not unusual, and that prayers for deceased family members were normal in these environments. These elite households were, through their personal access to God and through the incorporation of devotional practices in their domestic lives, quasi-religious communities. There remains a question of the degree to which such domestic religiosity was actually institutionalized; was it, in other words, bound by canonical rules as were the religious practices in monasteries and chantries?

There are many documentary references to these domestic/seigneurial-castle chapels, especially in the period of Anglo-Norman lordship. Some provide no detail, such as the reference of 1240 to the chapels of 'the castle of Polsculi' (Portnascully) and 'the new castle of Clone' (Dunkitt).[196] Other references tell us more. A chapel in the 'little hall' in the manorial enclosure of Old Ross is mentioned in 1307.[197] In terms of

---

192 'Domhnall son of Amhlaoibh Ó Maoil Ruanaidh, king of Fir Mhanach, was burned by his own kinsmen in the round tower of Daimhinis' (*MIA*, 1176.3).   **193** See, for example, Hogan, *Llanthony Prima and Secunda*, pp 347–8.   **194** The 1298 extent (or survey) of the manor of Inch (Kerry), for example, records that the lordly residence was surrounded by a stone wall within which was, among other buildings, 'a chapel of worn-out pales covered with straw', while another manor of the same name (in Tipperary) had an 'old wooden chapel' within its castle-enclosure in 1303 (*CDI, 1293–1301*, no. 551; *RBO*, p. 52).   **195** See, for example, R.G.K.A. Mertes, *The English noble household, 1250–1600* (Oxford, 1988), pp 139–60; A.D. Brown, *Popular piety in late medieval England: the diocese of Salisbury, 1250–1550* (Oxford, 1995); W. Gibson, *A social history of the domestic chaplain, 1530–1840* (London, 1997); D. Webb, 'Domestic space and devotion in the Middle Ages' in A. Spicer and S. Hamilton (eds), *Defining the holy: sacred space in medieval and early modern Europe* (Aldershot, 2005), pp 27–47. It might be noted that castles of very high status in England and Wales had more than one chapel, but there is no evidence that it was the same in any Irish castle.   **196** *CDI, 1171–1251*, no. 2485.   **197** *CDI, 1302–7*, no. 617; this is also mentioned in *CIPM*, 4, pp 306–7 and *CJRI, 1305–7*, p. 347.

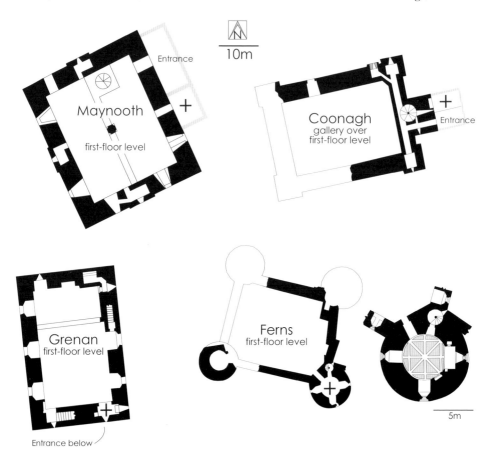

82 A selection of castle chapel plans.

architecture, some of the chapels were buildings in their own right, either free-standing or attached as very discrete blocks to other structures, and were protected within the enclosures of the residences, while others were dedicated east–west-oriented spaces within large buildings like donjons, gate towers and tower-houses (fig. 82).

Surviving examples of free-standing chapels are not easily identified. The so-called Desmond Hall in Newcastle West may originally have been one, but it would have needed deconsecration to be converted in the fifteenth century into the secular building that we see today. The best extant example of the free-standing type is at Dunsoghly, under the shadow of the great fifteenth-century tower-house. Chapel-spaces within other structures are more easily identified. The favoured position right through the Middle Ages was close to a main entrance, either above it (and directly so, if the design of the building permitted) or beside it. The entrance was thus protected by God's watchful eye. Trim's late twelfth-century chapel occupied the east-facing second-floor room directly above the donjon's original entrance lobby. Although it

83 The chapel in Barryscourt Castle. The sill of the window acted as the altar and there is a *piscina* on the right. Typically, it is located in the tower adjacent to the entrance.

was in the more 'public' side of the donjon's interior, access to it from the main floor was circuitous, reminding us of its essentially private nature. The near-contemporary chapel in Maynooth was in that donjon's fore-building, beside the main entrance. Also late twelfth century, perhaps, is the supposed chapel in Carrickfergus Castle's gate building.[198] The donjon of Coonagh Castle, built in the early 1220s, also had a chapel in its now-destroyed fore-building, but was timber-built rather than stone-built (see fig. 35).[199] Of roughly the same date is the tiny chapel or oratory in the donjon of Grenan Castle. It too was above the entrance, occupying a mural cavity in the corner of the large, private, first-floor room. Finally among our examples here, the most remarkable Anglo-Norman castle chapel in Ireland is the rib-vaulted circular example in Ferns Castle, built in the mid-thirteenth century.[200] Its spatial relationship to the donjon's original entrance is not known. Castle chapels appear to have been less common in later medieval Ireland. Large and prosperous households might have retained the services of chaplains, judging by the evidence from two of our grandest later medieval castles – Barryscourt (fig. 83) and Bunratty – but the owners of smaller tower-houses lived without personal clergy. The only conventionally sized tower-house with a certain chapel is Ballyhack, a possession of the Cistercians.[201]

Other chapels, other contexts

A Lady chapel was a sanctuary within which was an altar dedicated to the Blessed Virgin Mary and in which a cycle of prayer and a Mass (the so-called 'Lady Mass') was celebrated in her honour at least weekly (on a Saturday) if not daily.[202] Although not a chantry chapel, a Lady chapel could be so endowed.[203] Chapels attached to the choirs of churches are often assumed to have been Lady chapels, and in the absence of evidence to the contrary it is a reasonable assumption,[204] but there was actually no consistency in the positioning of Lady chapels, in Ireland no more than in England. Thus, in the two cathedrals of medieval Dublin, for example, the Lady chapels (both rebuilt in the 1800s) were effectively what are described as retro-choirs, positioned

198 For recent thinking on the date of the gate-building, see T. McNeill, 'Carrickfergus Castle, Co. Antrim', *CSGJ*, 28 (2014), 10–24 at 21–5. The twin-light window that illuminates the room in question is Romanesque but has Gothic-style banded shafts, so a date of *c.*1200 is likely. **199** O'Keeffe, 'The donjon of Coonagh Castle'; the castle of *Corcomohide* (now known as Castletown Conyers) had a donjon built to an almost identical plan, and it too had a chapel (*CIPM*, 6, pp 160–2). **200** T. O'Keeffe and M. Coughlan, 'The chronology and formal affinities of the Ferns donjon, Co. Wexford' in J.R. Kenyon and K. O'Conor (eds), *The medieval castle in Ireland and Wales* (Dublin, 2003), pp 133–48. **201** Colfer, *Wexford castles*, p. 247. **202** Harper, *Forms and orders of western liturgy*, pp 131–6. For a different aspect of devotion to the Blessed Virgin Mary, see C. Tait, 'Art and the cult of the Virgin Mary in Ireland, *c.*1500–1660' in Moss et al. (eds), *Art and devotion in late medieval Ireland*, pp 163–83. The 1453 synod of Limerick ordained that 'every church [in the province of Cashel] should have at least a statue of the Blessed Virgin Mary' (Begley, *Diocese of Limerick*, p. 290), but issued no instructions as to associated altars or chapels. When the famous juvenile imposter-king Lambert Simnel was annointed in Christ Church Cathedral in 1487 a crown was borrowed from the statue of the Blessed Virgin Mary in St Mary's church near 'Dame Gate' on Cork Hill (Lyons, 'Sidelights on the Kildare Ascendancy', p. 81). **203** The Guild of Tailors in Dublin, for example, had, by a charter of 1418, such a chantry in the Lady Chapel of Christ Church Cathedral (Ronan, 'Royal visitation of Dublin, 1615', p. 11 n. 36). **204** The cult of the Virgin was privileged in the liturgical rites that were associated with Sarum/Salisbury Cathedral in England and were followed widely in these islands (see N. Morgan, 'The introduction of the Sarum Calendar into the dioceses of England in the thirteenth century', *Thirteenth-Century England*, 7 (2000), 179–206), so Lady

directly beyond the conventional choirs (which was the most popular position for Lady chapels across the south of England), while the equivalent chapels were attached to north and south transepts at, respectively, Kells and Athassel Augustinian priories, and Kilkenny Cathedral.[205]

Rural chapels, lower in status than parish churches, were a common feature of the medieval countryside. Although founded by pious laymen of the parish rather than by the parish per se, they presumably served as de facto chapels-of-ease, sanctuaries to which parishioners had easy access, especially in large parishes. Evidence that they were not permitted to function outside the parish system comes from the 1453 synod of Limerick at which the bishops of the province of Cashel agreed that 'all emoluments arising from the erection of a new chapel, erected in a parish by pious laymen, belong to the parochial church'.[206] The numerical proportion of privately founded chapels to parish churches has never been calculated, but even a cursory review of the documentary evidence would suggest that such chapels greatly outnumbered churches. Thus, to give two random examples from the thirteenth century, the parish of Dungarvan had chapels that were 'members' of its church, while the church at Bunratty in 1288 had '10 adjacent chapels'.[207] It seems that in Ireland, as in England, many parishioners practised their religion in sanctuaries away from parish churches.[208]

Hospitals for the sick (who were sometimes described as lepers, though usually inaccurately so), elderly and disabled were invariably run by the monastic orders[209] for whom healing necessitated the provision of spiritual as well as physical care, and therefore they too had chapels. The period of hospital foundation in Ireland began well before the 1169 invasion and continued into the late Middle Ages, but with a peak in the colonial period. Alas, hospitals are better known from the documentary record than from the archaeological evidence. Thus, for example, the leper hospital of St Stephen in Dublin – on the site of the former Mercer's Hospital in Dublin, and close to modern-day St Stephen's Green, which was part of its land – was among the largest, and was founded around 1200. Its church was referred to at the Dissolution of the monasteries in 1540.[210] There is no trace of it. The best surviving hospital is that dedicated to St John the Baptist at Newtown Trim, across the river from the great cathedral with which it shared a founder, Bishop Simon de Rochfort. Run by *fratres cruciferi*, it was an enclosed site, bounded by high walls on three sides and by the river on the fourth. On the south side of the multi-period complex is the hospital's church, a long aisleless building of the early 1200s, originally divided by screens, of which one was apparently a rood screen.

After the Dissolution of the monasteries and the discontinuation of care provided by ecclesiastical communities, some wealthy families took a lead in providing care for

Chapels were probably very frequent indeed in Ireland.   **205** The altar in the Lady Chapel in St Patrick's was dedicated in 1235, and was used for the burials of some archbishops later in the century (*CAAR*, pp 78, 132).   **206** Begley, *Diocese of Limerick*, p. 291.   **207** *CDI, 1171–1251*, no. 2165; *CDI, 1285–92*, no. 459.   **208** N. Orme, 'Church and Chapel in Medieval England', *Transactions of the Royal Historical Society*, 6th ser., 6 (1996), 75–102.   **209** I. Metzler, *A social history of disability in the Middle Ages: cultural considerations of physical impairment* (London, 2013), includes references to Ireland and should inspire more detailed research on this often-forgotten population group.   **210** Ronan, 'Royal visitation of Dublin, 1615', pp 15–16, n47.

the sick and impoverished through the patronage of urban almshouses. A number of examples survive, such as the Shee Alms House in Kilkenny, properly named the Hospital of Jesus of Kilkenny, established by Sir Richard Shee and his wife in 1582 for six male and six female paupers.[211] Although they did not have chapels themselves, almshouses were located close to churches and were sometimes founded at points that penitents would have passed on their way to church, as is the case in Fethard and Youghal, where the examples were built in the early 1600s.[212] The siting was deliberate: patrons wanted their charitable benevolence to be seen by church-goers. The Youghal houses, founded by the earl of Cork at the junction of the town's main street and the narrow lane leading to the parish church, form an L-plan terrace, and their lower-than-normal doorways suggest that the entry required stooping. Was this intended as an act of public supplication?

NON-MONASTIC ECCLESIASTICAL RESIDENCES

Claustral living was normal for monastics. Other clergy made other types of arrangement. We are blessed with some good information from 1326 on the residences and associated service and agricultural buildings of the archbishops of Dublin.[213] For Swords we have the following description:

> there is a hall, a chamber for the archbishop annexed to it, of which the walls are stone and crenellated like a castle and roofed with shingles; and there are a kitchen there with a larder, whose walls are stone and roof of shingle, a chapel with stone walls and shingle roof; there was a chamber there for friars with a cloister now thrown down; near the gate is a chamber for the constable and four chambers for knights and squires, roofed with shingles; under these a stable and a bake-house; there was a house for a *deieria* and *carpentria*, now thrown down. In the haggard a grange of poles thatched, a timber granary roofed with bo[a]rds, a byre for housing nags and kine …

Extensive fabric survives at Swords.[214] Although it is hard to match this description with the standing remains, the Swords complex was not unusual, judging by St David's episcopal palace in south-west Wales (fig. 84). Other sites described in 1326 had similar buildings in similar states of disrepair, but we are left to speculate about their spatial arrangements. St Sepulchre in Dublin had a stone hall, 'a chamber annexed', a kitchen and a chapel.[215] *Colonia* (Cullenswood?), attached to the manor of St Sepulchre, had a

211 C. Ó Cochláin, *Shee Alms House Kilkenny, 1582: the story of a restoration* (Kilkenny, 1986). **212** O'Keeffe, 'Townscape as text', p. 15; Kelly and O'Keeffe, *Youghal*. **213** *CAAR*, pp 170–96. **214** T. Fanning, 'An Irish medieval tile pavement: recent excavations at Swords Castle, Co. Dublin', *JRSAI*, 105 (1975), 47–82; R. Stalley, 'The archbishop's residence at Swords: castle or country retreat?', *MD*, 7 (2006), 152–76. **215** The architecture on the site today is discussed by D. O'Donovan, 'English patron, English building? The importance of St Sepulchre archiepiscopal palace, Dublin', *MD*, 4 (2003), 253–78.

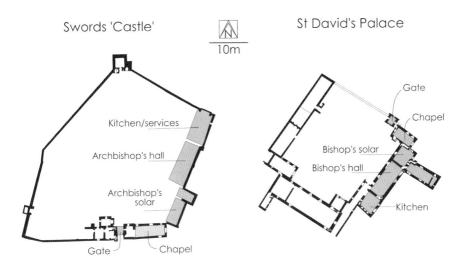

84 Comparative plans of Swords Castle and St David's Bishop's Palace. Drawing of St David's after J.W. Evans and R. Turner, *St David's, Bishop's Palace* (Cardiff, 1999).

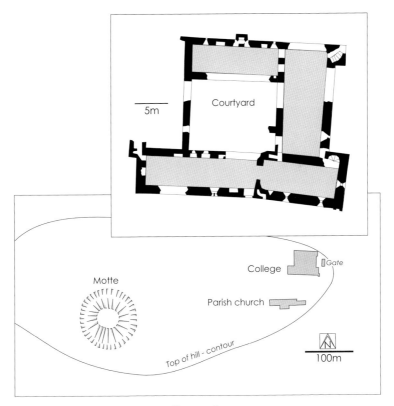

85 Plan of the early sixteenth-century college at Slane.

86 Ardcroney Church. The tower was inserted in the late Middle Ages into the west end of an earlier church. The first floor was a living space into which one can envisage the welcoming of guests, but the two upper rooms were certainly private.

stone hall, 'a chamber for the archbishop with chapel adjoining', a kitchen, a grange, a stable and a granary. Tallaght had no buildings left in 1326 apart from a chamber and 'other small cellars', and one small chamber for clerks. Clondalkin had a chamber ('the archbishop's house') and a chapel, a stone stable, and two small houses. Ballymore Eustace, where an archiepiscopal castle was first recorded as early as the 1180s,[216] had a hall, 'a chamber for the archbishop', a chapel, a 'small chamber for clerks', a kitchen, a stable, a grange, a 'chamber for the constable' and a granary. A hall-and-chamber block at Kilmacduagh (see fig. 45) is likely to have been the possession of that see's bishop.

There was no hard and fast template by which collegiate priests lived, but their residences – called colleges – needed at very least a communal hall, a kitchen and sleeping rooms. The small building associated with the college founded by the St Lawrence family at Howth before 1500[217] was as simple as possible: it had a communal hall with a service area at one end and, set perpendicularly to it, rooms for the priests at the opposite end. This is a plan-type that was commonly used for English domestic architecture in general, so we might speculate that it was the work of an English-born builder. More complex was the college at Slane, founded in 1512 at the behest of Sir Christopher Fleming and his wife for four priests, four lay brothers and four choristers. Here, a claustral plan was used, with a central court (not a cloister, strictly speaking) surrounded by domestic structures on all sides (fig. 85). The head of a college was presumably given better accommodation than his fellow priests, as was a prior and abbot in a monastic complex, and it is conceivable that the small tower that survives on the site of Ardee's college was one such residence; after all, it does not tally with the description made at its foundation in 1487 that 'certain chaplains employed in the Church of St Mary's may be compelled to reside there in common – in a hall and rooms fittingly laid out and constructed – and support themselves on the fruits and emoluments of their services'.[218]

Parish curates, finally, had a number of domestic options, and these have been reviewed in a valuable essay by Helen Bermingham.[219] Their accommodation was sometimes incorporated in the body of the parish church, usually as an upper-floor loft at the west end of the nave or, less frequently, above the chancel. Houses of tower form were sometimes attached to the churches in the later Middle Ages, usually at the west end; these are quite similar to tower-houses in form (see ch. 5). Found all over Ireland (fig. 86), they are especially common in the English Pale and on its fringes (see Taghmon, for example), where priests were as jittery about personal safety as non-clerical landowners. Free-standing priests' houses, lastly, are the least frequently identified. Rural priests may well have had non-stone houses beside their churches; urban priests may well have lived in houses on streets besides their churches.

216 *CAAR*, p. 18. **217** Leask, *Irish churches and monastic buildings*, II, pp 29–30. **218** J. Bradley, 'The Chantry College, Ardee', *CLAHJ*, 22:1 (1989), 16–19 at 18. There were six such chaplains. **219** 'Priests' residences in later medieval Ireland' in FitzPatrick and Gillespie (eds), *The parish in medieval and early modern Ireland*, pp 168–85.

CHAPTER 4

Castles: from the Anglo-Norman invasion to the Black Death

Visitors to castles are persuaded by popular books, cinematic representations (*Braveheart*, most obviously, filmed at Trim and Dunsoghly) and tour-guides to visualize those castles principally as places of war, with soldiers firing crossbows through arrow-slits or pouring boiling oil from parapets on besieging armies. Such images are generally exaggerations (and, in the case of the boiling oil, largely fictitious), and they do a disservice to the buildings themselves as well as to the medieval societies in which castles were created and used. If we are to understand and appreciate our castles properly, we need to separate the realities of war (and peace) in the medieval world from the Disneyesque fantasies that have been attached to the buildings. We especially need to understand how castles worked as the domestic and ceremonial spaces of well-to-do, sometimes certifiably aristocratic, households.

The two most recent works of synthesis on Irish castles – the books by Tom McNeill and David Sweetman – provide the newcomer to architectural history with a more-than-adequate overview of the development of the castle as a physical structure in the periods covered by this chapter and the next.[1] I will cover that ground here, but I also want to present an overview that is illuminated from a slightly different angle. My main concern here is with explaining how castles worked *on the inside*. Given that relatively few of them were put to work in situations of 'war' (especially in the later Middle Ages), and given the lack of incontrovertible evidence of an overriding concern for defensibility should they be dragged into conflict (again, especially in the later Middle Ages), the emphasis here is on their accommodation of the rituals of domestic life.

MEDIEVAL TERMINOLOGY

Many definitions of 'castle' are to be found in the scholarly literature, both Irish and international. That offered by Sweetman is fairly representative: 'what makes a *true* castle is its defences ... [A] castle is essentially feudal and is the fortified residence of a lord in a society dominated by the military'.[2] This is one among many rephrasings of a definition that has been in circulation since the nineteenth century, not just in these islands but across western Europe. But does it actually tally with the medieval

---

1 McNeill, *Castles in Ireland*; Sweetman, *Medieval castles of Ireland*.   **2** Sweetman, *Medieval castles of Ireland*, p. 41, emphasis added.

understanding of 'castle'? This is a very important question, and to answer it without recourse to cliché we need to return to first principles, and that requires us to look outside Ireland before we begin to look at evidence from Ireland itself.

The etymological roots of 'castle', first of all, are the Latin *castrum* (and its diminutive form, *castellum*), and the Norman-French *castel* (which was derived from *castrum*). It is apparent that *castel*, the most obvious root of the modern word 'castle', was 'borrowed' into the English language twice, first from the original Latin *castellum* as early as the ninth century, and then from the Norman-French *castel* around the time of the mid-eleventh-century Norman invasion of England.[3] In its earlier borrowing, as *castellum*, it seems to have connoted a defended settlement of village- or town-scale. We encounter the later borrowing of *castel* in the Anglo-Saxon Chronicle, where it was used to refer to places fortified by the small number of Normans who settled in England in 1051–2. This later borrowing is the more significant in the sense that *castel* really entered the English language at that mid-eleventh-century point in time, with *castrum* (not *castellum*) as its preferred Latin translation. This brings us to a key point. Scholars in England – we will discuss Ireland presently – believed for many years that the words *castellum* and *castel/castrum* must have connoted very different things from the eleventh century on, and they decided that the latter pair of words, representing 'castle' as we know it today, referred specifically to a new phenomenon associated with feudalism, namely the 'private' fortress of a feudal lord. Forty years ago, R. Allan Brown, one of the most influential of all castle scholars, expressed it thus:

> If one enquires what it is that distinguishes the castle from other types of fortification both earlier and later, and wherein lies its uniqueness and feudality, the answer lies in its definition: for the castle is a fortified residence, uniquely combining the dual role, and moreover it is the private, as opposed to public, and the residential fortress of a lord, who may or may not be the King or Prince.[4]

This is probably as close as one gets to a classic expression of the definition of a medieval castle, and it is an enduring definition, not least in Ireland. But in recent years some scholars have challenged its cast-iron certainty, and on very good grounds.

First, detailed interrogation of the documentary sources in the lands ruled by the kings of England and France from the eleventh century on has completely undermined the view that places called 'castle' in the Middle Ages had *no* public or communal function.[5] This denial of the type of 'private' ownership of castles discussed by Allan Brown is not tantamount to suggesting that locals could just traipse in and out of their local castles. Rather, it is to acknowledge that castle lords had, by medieval custom, a range of community responsibilities, from legislation and its enforcement, to community protection, the provision of infrastructure, patronage to the church, and so on, and that castles were vested in the lords for the prosecution of many of these responsibilities. So, when we stand in front of a castle today, in Ireland as elsewhere,

3 A. Cameron et al. (eds), *Dictionary of Old English: A to G* (Toronto, 2007); see also 'castle, n.', OED.
4 *Origins of English feudalism* (London, 1973), p. 30.   5 Coulson, *Castles in medieval society*, p. 37.

we should resist the temptation to see it as a hostile or hostility-inducing intrusion in the landscape, its inhabitants always alert to danger, its parapet lined with rocks for dropping on enemies. A castle was no less at the heart of peaceful medieval community life and identity than a parish church.

The second challenge relates specifically to the world of earth-and-timber castles. Careful study of the linguistic evidence pertaining to castles before the great age of stone-castle construction, combined with a critique of the concept of 'feudalism' and with archaeological work on the earth-and-timber fortifications of the eleventh century,[6] suggests that the distinction between the medieval 'feudal castle' (starting in the mid-eleventh century in England and in the early twelfth century in Ireland) and earlier forms of protected/fortified residence was not as cut-and-dried as Brown intimated. It is apparent now, for example, that the word *castel* was not imported into the Old English language to signify a new type of site or architecture fulfilling a new function (as Brown presumed). Rather, it was simply the word that the Normans had grown accustomed to using to describe the residences and settlements founded under their elite authority in Normandy, a word that they then brought with them to England.[7] In other words, there was continuity in the forms and, especially, functions of earth-and-timber defensive architecture from Anglo-Saxon to early Norman times in England, but not in the language used. I make this point here, in a book on Ireland, because if the appearance in England of the word 'castle' does not necessarily represent a change in the form and function of fortification from before 1066 to after 1066, the same might be said of Ireland before and after 1169. Just as *castel* (re-)entered Old English in 1050, it entered Middle Irish too, as *caistél*, possibly in the second decade of the twelfth century, forty years before the Anglo-Norman invasion of Ireland. Rendered *caistél* or *caislén*, it was first used by Gaelic-Irish annalists to describe a small number of 'castles' erected mainly in Connacht in the 1120s and 1130s.[8] It then continued in general use in the language as *caislén*, the Irish equivalent of the English 'castle'; *caistél* seems to have been the word of choice, with *caislén* (the origin of the modern Irish *caisleán*) as a possible diminutive. The fact that these native Irish 'castles' are mainly found in western Ireland might indicate that 'castle' was a local terminological preference, chosen, as McNeill put it, by men 'attracted to new, fashionable and boastful words'.[9]

---

6 See, for example, S. Reynolds, *Fiefs and vassals: the medieval evidence reinterpreted* (Oxford, 1994) for feudalism; and B. English, 'Towns, mottes and ringworks of the Conquest' in A. Ayton and J.L. Price (eds), *The medieval military revolution* (London, 1995), pp 45–61, for the archaeological evidence.   **7** A. Wheatley, *The idea of the castle*, p. 25; see also Coulson, *Castles in medieval society*, esp. pp 32–40.   **8** In 1124 the term *caistél* appears with respect to foundations of Toirdelbach Ua Conchobhair at Galway, Collooney and Ballinasloe. Athlone had a *caistél* in 1129, while Ardnakillen Lough (*Loch Cairrgin*) and Tuam each had a *caislén* in 1136 and 1164 respectively. For the annalistic references to these castles and a discussion of their forms and contexts, see B.J. Graham, 'Medieval timber and earthwork fortifications in western Ireland', *MA*, 32 (1988), 110–29; T. O'Keeffe, 'The fortifications of western Ireland, AD1100–1300, and their interpretation', *JGAHS*, 50 (1998), 184–200; other words used sometimes in the early twelfth century for these 'castles' include *dún, dúnad, daingean* and *longphort*: see O'Conor, *The archaeology of medieval rural settlement*, pp 82–7; T. O'Keeffe, *The Gaelic peoples and their archaeological identities, AD1000–1650* (Cambridge, 2004), pp 9–12.   **9** *Castles in Ireland*, p. 10; T. O'Keeffe,

The third challenge to the classic definition relates to the term *castellany*, derived from the medieval Latin *castellania*, which commonly described the area – a rural estate or even a town – that was controlled from a building described as a castle. It usually had the same name as the building itself.[10] It is not always clear if an historical reference to a 'castle' is specific to a building or to a territory. An early example in Ireland of the word 'castle' being used to connote territory comes from 1170–1 when there is a reference to a burgage (a town plot, basically comprising a house and long rear garden) in the 'castle' of Dublin.[11] There was no castle in the conventional sense in Dublin for another thirty-plus years, so here is an example of 'castle' being used to refer to a jurisdiction – a town, in this case – rather than a building. Similarly, the record that 'the castle of Bun-finne [Buninna] was burned and despoiled, both corn-reeks and houses' in 1306, implies that 'castle' connotes here something more than simply a fortified residence.[12] Rather than be frustrated by such apparent ambiguity, we might regard it as a window into how the medieval mind worked: the distinction between a site and a territory, between a 'castle' as a physical object rooted to the landscape (as in Brown's definition) and that landscape itself, might not have been made in the Middle Ages in the way that we make it now.

This has been quite a long discussion of medieval words, but it has an important purpose. Tracing the etymology of 'castle' and scrutinizing some of the contexts of the word's use in the Middle Ages show the extent to which the definition of 'castle' has narrowed considerably since the Middle Ages. A complex concept, it was (at least in the period covered by this chapter) an expression of territory and territorial authority as well as a signifier of an actual physical structure. From the very outset in Europe (the tenth century, if not further back), there was no consistency of size, plan or even material in the structures that it described (when, that is, it was used specifically to describe a structure): the word 'castle' was shared in medieval Ireland, as it was elsewhere, by structures that ranged from small earthen mounds (mottes) in remote hilly landscapes, to vast stone-built complexes at the centres of large estates, to small tower-houses surrounded by hedges. The buildings of the most politically significant castles accommodated the administrative, judicial, defensive/protective, performative/ symbolic and domestic functions and responsibilities of the medieval elite, but in no consistent or recurring order. Castles of lesser political standing had a shorter and slighter roster of functions and yet they too claimed the same 'castle' identity.

CASTLE BUILDING IN IRELAND, 1169–*c*.1350: POLITICS AND PATTERNS

Prior to the fourteenth century, castles – and here we are discussing structures rather than territories – were instrumental in the creation and maintenance of the network of social and service relationships that are often described by historians as 'feudal'. This

---

'The pre-Norman "castle" in Connacht: a note on terminology', *JGAHS*, 66 (2014), 26–32. **10** Coulson, *Castles in medieval society*, gives this word as *castellary*; see also 'castellany, n.' OED online. The term *castellaria* is used in Ireland (see *RAST*, no. 3, for a reference to the *castellaria de Dundalc*, of Dundalk).   **11** *CAAR*, p. 2.   **12** *AU*, 1306.6.

network connected the king at one end of the medieval power spectrum to the lowly tenant at the other. Property and privilege were divested to barons by the king, and then from the barons to lesser lords in their turn. This hierarchic aristocracy, between the king at one end and the lesser lord at the other, was a castle-owning aristocracy. All aristocrats below the king in this hierarchy were obliged to provide military service to the rank above, either by serving as knights themselves or, more commonly, by providing knights to serve on their behalf. Such service might be on the battlefield, or in the garrison of a superior's castle, and it was always of fixed duration (usually forty days). Lords who owed military service to the king could 'buy out' by paying a tax called scutage, which they increasingly did during the thirteenth century in Ireland.[13] At the lower level of this great social hierarchy, below the lordly class, was the great mass of tenantry, comprising those who were given their own small parcels of lands to rent and who provided *labour* services (rather than *military* services) in return for lesser privileges. Castle-ownership trickled down to quite minor lords in this complex hierarchy, but not to the tenantry.

We see evidence of this social-political hierarchy in Ireland in the decades in which Anglo-Norman lordship was established. Henry II and his son John granted large territories to barons like Richard de Clare (Strongbow) and Hugh de Lacy,[14] and they in turn granted (in the process that we call 'subinfeudation') subdivisions of their lands to lesser lords, who in turn made grants of parts of their lands to lesser individuals, and so on. By the time Henry III came to the throne in 1216 large parts of eastern Ireland – eastern Ulster, almost all of modern Leinster, and eastern Munster – had been subinfeudated. For several decades the Gaelic-Irish of Connacht resisted various Anglo-Norman attempts at annexation of their province, but its fertile lowlands were eventually subinfeudated after 1235.[15]

Among all the medieval English kings to claim sovereignty over Ireland, John, monarch from 1199 to 1216 (and the last to visit Ireland until Richard II in the later 1300s), was by far the most active builder of castles on the island, but only two of his castles, Dublin and Limerick, were of the monumental scale befitting royalty. The castles built by the senior baronage – the next level down in the feudal hierarchy – were relatively few, reflecting that class's relatively small membership, but they were sometimes very big (Hugh de Lacy's Trim, most strikingly) and were sometimes in the vanguard of contemporary north-western European architectural developments (William Marshal's castles of Kilkenny and Carlow, for example). Middle-ranking lords in the hierarchy were more numerous, and so castles of middle rank are more numerous too. Rarely, though, were these castles substantial in size or particularly innovative in design.

---

13 A.J. Otway-Ruthven, 'Knight service in Ireland', *JRSAI*, 89 (1959), 1–15; S.G. Ellis, 'Taxation and defence in late medieval Ireland', *JRSAI*, 107 (1977), 5–28.   **14** John's older brother, Richard, who preceded him as king, spent almost all of his regal career on the Continent and in the Mediterranean, so he is a relatively minor figure in Irish history, but he left one significant legacy: William Marshal, later lord of Leinster and a great castle-builder, ascended to his position of power under Richard's direct patronage.   **15** H. Perros, 'Crossing the Shannon frontier: Connacht and the Anglo-Normans, 1170–1224' in T.B. Barry, R.F. Frame and K. Simms (eds), *Colony and frontier in medieval Ireland: essays presented to J.F. Lydon* (London,

During the subinfeudation of southern Leinster and eastern Munster in the late 1100s and early 1200s it was only the more senior and better-endowed lords who built castles.[16] However, ownership of castles appears to have trickled quite low down the social hierarchy in other parts of Ireland under Anglo-Norman control: in the earldom of Ulster (modern Cos Antrim and Down) and the lordship of Meath (modern Cos Meath, Westmeath and Longford) there are many castles of modest earth-and-timber type (see below, pp 194–9), their lordly owners of such low nobility that it is often difficult to identify them by name. It was not that lesser lords in south Leinster and east Munster were specifically barred by anybody from building castles, or that they lacked the requisite resources. The best way to understand the different levels of encastellation from one part of Anglo-Norman Ireland to another is simply to think of it as a quilt made up of different political regions, each with its own settlement dynamics, and its own preferences in respect of the culture of castle construction and ownership. Indeed, even in those places – Ulster and Meath, mainly – where lesser lords did build castles, they were rarely able to afford to build *stone* castles and had to make do instead with earth-and-timber castles. Connacht is the one exception: many of the lesser Anglo-Norman lords who settled there after 1235, all of them migrants from other parts of Ireland, built their castles in stone.

The processes of choosing sites, organizing labour, obtaining materials and paying people for their labour or expertise often went unrecorded in the Middle Ages, and records from Ireland are particularly poor. We can make some general comments, though, based on what we know of the situation elsewhere in Europe. Sites for castles, first of all, were chosen according to factors such as territorial centrality, access and visibility. Patrons – kings and lords, in other words – were probably involved very often in choosing the designs of their castles. Most would have worked in some consultation with professionals who were skilled in the arts of building. Those professionals, whom we tend to describe collectively as master masons,[17] usually worked to individual commissions (secular/military as well as ecclesiastical) rather than as full-time employees of particular patrons. Unfortunately, we know little about master masons and other professionals in Ireland, with the exception of William of Prene, a carpenter involved in the programme of royal-castle construction in the 1280s.[18] Master masons were hugely respected for their skills and were very well reimbursed: English records, probably the best in Europe for identifying such masons and their commissions, reveal how the most highly regarded among them (such as Master James of St George, perhaps the most famous castle-designing master mason in medieval Europe) were sometimes paid much more than the household knights of their patrons. There is a famous legend that Roesia de Verdun killed (or arranged the killing of) her master mason at Castleroche to prevent him replicating its design (pl. VII) for another patron.[19]

1995), pp 117–38.   **16** T.E. McNeill, 'Early castles in Leinster', *JIA*, 5 (1989/90), 57–64.   **17** We should not describe them as architects; in the medieval mind only God was the architect (N. Coldstream, *Masons and sculptors* (London, 1991), p. 5).   **18** R.A. Stalley, 'William of Prene and the royal works in Ireland', *JBAA*, 131 (1978), 30–49.   **19** Barry, 'The study of medieval Irish castles', pp 131–2. The legend, already unconvincing, is undermined by the lack of

Acquiring suitable stone must have delayed building-projects in the early years of Anglo-Norman lordship. One imagines that, depending on location, few stone buildings of the native Irish avoided cannibalizing by the new castle builders. In 1213, for example, 'all the cemeteries and buildings of the town [of Coleraine] were thrown down excepting only the church to supply materials for erecting [a] castle', while in 1245 'stones and lime of the spital house of the Trinity' were used to build Sligo Castle.[20]

We know little about the recruitment of labour on the building projects. A mid-thirteenth-century account of the building in 1186 of the motte-castle at Durrow by Hugh de Lacy gives us interesting information on one of the ways in which labour was organized. It was reported in 1243 that two Irish men of uncertain social rank had asked Hugh 'to measure their [allotted] portion of the castle moat, telling him to measure it himself, so that they might not be cheated', which he proceeded to do, accompanied by one Gilla cin Inathar Ó Miadaig, another member of the labour force. When Hugh stooped to take the measurement, Ó Miadaig struck him with a wood-axe and killed him.[21] This singularly detailed and graphic account of a twelfth-century homicide suggests that individuals working as unskilled labour on building projects were apportioned certain quantities of work. While this particular example is from Anglo-Norman Ireland, such practices were not restricted to colonial castle builders: it is known that in 1297, for example, the building of ramparts was among the services that Irish kings exacted from their subjects.[22]

Financial liquidity, even more than labour supply, impacted powerfully on the process and progress of building. Where did money come from? The most powerful lords had vast lands, and wealth was generated by them through their control of markets, their collection of rents and fines from their manorial courts, and so on. Mortgages were often still required, however, and foreign bankers, mainly Italian, provided them.[23] The best records we have of the cost of building castles in Anglo-Norman Ireland are royal records of the 1200s, although they are far from comprehensive. The pipe roll of 1211–12 provides some useful information on expenditure.[24] The £733 16s. 41d. that was spent on Limerick Castle at that time was relatively substantial, and one can be fairly certain that it paid for the gate building and the north-east corner tower, if not also the side of the castle overlooking the river.[25] Similarly, whatever work was done at Athlone at the same time was probably completed with the £129 12s. spent there. By contrast with these stone castles, the earth-and-timber royal castle at Clones cost, according to the same pipe roll, about £15, with another £36 spent on supplies and carriage. We have no information on the cost of contemporary baronial castles, but we might note that the early thirteenth-

evidence for Roesia ever having set foot in Ireland. Its origin might actually be the story that the wife of the count of Bayeux had her master mason Lanfred beheaded after he built the tower of Ivry-la-Bataille (M. Chibnall, *The ecclesiastical history of Orderic Vitalis* (Oxford, 1968–80), iv, p. 290; O'Keeffe, 'Castleroche'). **20** *AFM*, 1213.5; *AC*, 1245.3. **21** *AC*, 1243.4. **22** *SRPI, John–Hen. V*, p. 203. **23** M.D. O'Sullivan, *Italian merchant bankers in Ireland in the thirteenth century* (Dublin, 1962). **24** *IPR, 1211–12*. **25** For a new and comprehensively argued view on the castle's phasing, see D. Tietzsch-Tyler, 'King John's Castle: staged development, imperfect

century donjon of Adare Castle is exactly the same size as the donjon of Peveril Castle in England's Peak District, and that was built about thirty years earlier at a cost of a little under £200.[26] The availability of money at Limerick contrasts with the situation at Dublin Castle in 1204 when King John mandated his justiciar to collect debts to help get the great royal castle underway, or in 1236 when Henry III insisted that he could not built new castles in Connacht 'unless the necessary money be collected from the magnates as an aid'.[27] Substantial money – about £3,500 – was made available for the re-building of Roscommon Castle between 1275 and 1285, and it is significant that there is no record of additional money going to the project until 1305 when we get a fascinating record of payments to the castle's 'keeper': back-wages at a rate of 2*d*. per day to be given to 'an artilleryman formerly assigned to the castle to make and repair warlike engines and quarrels with their furniture' for Roscommon and other Connacht castles; 13*s*. 4*d*. 'for apparel of the same artilleryman for one year according to the agreement made with him for his service'; 40*s*. 'for repair of the well of the castle, and strengthening it with stone of the thickness of three feet, so that the well may remain of the breadth of 5 feet, and depth of 32 feet, and that it be competently covered with wood'; 100*s*. 'for repairing and perfecting three drawbridges of the castle, and the portcullises of two gates of the castle, and two outward bridges with two gates added to the bridges'; 40*s*. 'to close the postern of the castle with stone and chalk, of the thickness of 7 feet, to repair the steps of the entry of the hall, and to cover the oriel of the castle'; 6 marks 'for vaulting the tower near the hall, towards the south, with two arches' and an unspecified amount 'to make a conduit for the water of St Bridget's Well, to carry it off into the lake under the castle'.[28] By contrast, at Newcastle McKynegan, another royal castle, a mere £26 19*s*. 2½*d*. was made available to build the new castle in 1279–80, although £74 6*s*. 9*d*. was provided for building a tower there in 1280–2.[29] In 1299 £113 1*s*. 2*d*. was made available for a new hall at Rindown Castle, with the sheriff of Roscommon granted an additional 20*s*. to supervise its construction.[30] These examples show that the crown invested relatively little in castle building in Ireland, and that the castles that it did fund were intended to add to the protection of the lordship rather than provide accommodation for a royal visit. Later in the Middle Ages, as we will see in the next chapter, subsidies were offered by parliament to castle builders in the Dublin region who were loyal to the crown, provided they built to specified dimensions. Those subsidies were usually only £10, though they sometimes rose to £40. The amounts were probably insufficient for those landowners who could not afford to build in the first instance, while it is difficult to imagine any landowner who could afford to build a castle changing his design to avail of so meagre a grant.

What do we know of the role of the Anglo-Norman castles in warfare? In general, warfare across medieval Europe was dominated by attacks on castles: although the most

realization', *NMAJ*, 52 (2013), 135–71.   **26** B. Morley, *Peveril Castle* (London, 1990), p. 19. **27** T. O'Keeffe, 'Dublin Castle's donjon in context' in Bradley, Simms and Fletcher (eds), *Dublin in the medieval world*, pp 277–94; *CDI, 1171–1251*, no. 2366.   **28** *CDI, 1302–7*, no. 306. **29** McNeill, *Castles in Ireland*, p. 96; G.H. Orpen, '*Novum Castrum McKynegan*, Newcastle, County Wicklow', *JRSAI*, 38 (1908), 126–40.   **30** *38 RDKPRI*, p. 54.

famous battles of the Middle Ages took place on open ground – Hastings in 1066, and Bosworth in 1485, for example – medieval armies generally did not head out 'into the field' to engage each other in open combat but concentrated their efforts on attacking or defending castles. Part of the explanation may be that, with so many of the participating soldiers fulfilling military-service contracts of fixed duration (often of forty days), combat needed very careful organization and timing, and a castle provided a fixed focus in the landscape around which a campaign could be planned with some exactness. Only in exceptional circumstances were castles attacked for the purpose of complete destruction; castles on the 'wrong side' in the English civil war of the twelfth century, for example, were destroyed. Normally castles were attacked to be possessed, because to gain possession of a castle was to gain possession of the land attached to it. We have many references to the destruction by the Gaelic-Irish of Anglo-Norman castles in Ireland, but also many examples of the Anglo-Normans restoring power very quickly by rebuilding, with Trim Castle in the 1170s being a case in point.[31] Sites destroyed by the Irish sometimes stayed that way, and if the Irish did reuse those sites for their own castles, it was rarely if ever an immediate reuse. The evidence from Clare is instructive. The first castle (earth-and-timber?) at Bunratty was built by Robert de Muscegros in 1251–2, and was apparently replaced by Thomas de Clare with a new stone castle in 1277. Vulnerable thanks to its location, new locks for the castle gate and a new wooden tower outside that gate were among changes and additions felt necessary in 1289. Successful defence against two sieges shortly afterwards – a truncated siege of sixteen days in 1298, and a siege of full, forty-day, duration in 1299 – cost a total of more than £300.[32] The Anglo-Normans lost control of the castle to the Irish shortly afterwards, however, but there is no evidence that the new owners of the site rebuilt the castle until the fifteenth century. Thomas de Clare's other castle at Quin was probably still under construction when it was attacked and destroyed by Cumea More Mac Conmara in the mid-1280s. A fourteenth-century source, *Caithréim Thoirdhealbhaigh*, describes how

> its ditch was crossed, earthworks carried, great gate battered in and hewn down; its strong walls were breached, its English stammerers captured; the place was cleaned out of horses and warlike stores, and in the actual great castle a huge pile of stuff was given to the flames that ran riot till the whole became a black-vaulted hideous cavern.

There is no evidence that the site was reoccupied until a century later when a magnificent Franciscan friary was shoe-horned into the ruin.[33]

31 See S. Duffy, 'The "Key of the Pale": a history of Trim Castle' in Hayden, *Trim Castle*, pp 6–28. For Gaelic-Irish lordly sites in Connacht seized by the Anglo-Normans after 1235, see J. Malcolm, 'Castles and landscapes in Uí Fhiachrach Muaidhe, c.1235–c.1400' in L. Doran and J. Lyttleton (eds), *Lordship in medieval Ireland: image and reality* (Dublin, 2007), pp 193–216 at pp 197–205.   32 G.U. MacNamara, 'Bunratty Castle', *NMAJ*, 3 (1913–15), 220–313. See also Sherlock, 'Bunratty Castle'.   33 B. Hodkinson, 'Was Quin Castle completed?', *NMAJ*, 44 (2004), 53–8.

I Fethard has the best preserved medieval town wall in Ireland. This section, viewed from across the small river on the south side of the town, bounds the churchyard. The (restored) battlements are thirteenth century in type, and the wall here is probably of that date (as indeed might be most of the wall on the south side of the town). The church is thirteenth-century but its tower is late medieval. The (restored) tower on the far left is a substantial mural tower of the late Middle Ages. The small castle on the far right, 'Edmond's Castle', is also late medieval and is clearly an insertion into older walling. It is likely to have been a priest's residence because there was direct access from it to the churchyard.

II Grenan Castle, built in the 1220s, had imported Dundry stone used for its quoins and window-surrounds. Although much of the dressed stonework of this very fine building has been robbed, the light-coloured quoins survive.

IV The south side of the nave of Kilcrea Friary church (Franciscan) is original and opens into a wide aisle and an aisled transept.

V The interior east end of Crooke Church, with its typical thirteenth-century arrangement of graded lancets. The churches associated with preceptories of the military orders served as parish churches, and nothing about their architecture, except perhaps in the case of the church of Mourne Abbey, suggests that they were used by monastic communities.

III (*opposite*) A fireplace inserted in the late sixteenth century into a former window embrasure in the upper room of Kilcrea tower-house. Window embrasures were appropriated for such insertions because the walls were already thin and could therefore be converted easily into flues. The survival of the original twin-light window in this example, albeit re-set, suggests that the builders were concerned to maintain for outside viewers the illusion of functioning fenestration.

VI Although historical sources suggest a foundation date in the fourteenth century, the Franciscan friary of Kilconnell is substantially of fifteenth-century date. Its belfry, typically mendicant in its elegance, was built as part of a mid-century expansion. Note how the builders, concerned that rainwater would seep into the spaces between the walls of the belfry and the roofs abutting it, inserted flat stones into the belfry to deflect rain onto the roofs and towards the gutters.

VII The gate house and (to the left) great hall of Castleroche, *c.*1235, viewed from the site of the small town that once occupied the flat ground in front of the castle. Medieval women rarely built castles, although they came into the possession of castles when their husbands died. Roesia de Verdun, who built Roche, is the stand-out exception from Anglo-Norman Ireland.

VIII Liscarroll Castle. The tower in the foreground has a well-preserved base-batter. A wall-batter is an ascending incline; basically, buildings with batters narrow quite visibly as they rise. The *base*-batter, which is rarely encountered in non-thirteenth-century contexts in Ireland, is distinguished by two things: its angle at ground-level is between 40° and 60°, and there is a very sharp, linear break between it and the wall above it. Military explanations of different levels of plausibility have been offered for the development of the base-batter: attackers were kept back from a wall-face and were therefore in view from battlements, mining was more difficult because of the enhanced wall-thickness, and missiles dropped from above were deflected outwards. The base-batter had an aesthetic value: like a widening tree-trunk, it 'rooted' the building to the ground, enhancing its appearance of sturdiness.

IX Buttevant Castle. The tower on the left is thirteenth century, and that on the right appears to be nineteenth century in its entirety.

X One of the rooms (mir the wooden partitions on either side, of course) in t wing opposite the entranc to Ballymoon Castle. Indicative of a later thirteenth-century date is the loop with oillets, the pointed-segmental rear ar of the loop, the hooded fireplace (see also fig. 109) and the shouldered arch (sometimes called a 'Caernarfon arch' because is common in the late thirteenth-century Welsh castle of that name) of the toilet doorway.

XI Ballycarbery Castle, one of the most picturesq of Irish castles, was probably built in the early sixteenth century. There are some remains of a (surprisingly) small bawn.

XII Loughmoe Castle. The tower on the right remains from the medieval castle. The new wing on its left is not dated precisely. The earliest parallel for its extensive use of string-courses – the horizontal bands of masonry that mark for outside viewers the floor levels – is Rathfarnham Castle of the 1580s. Curved battlements, fragments of which are still visible, are not known in Ireland before their use in Portumna in the 1610s, though one cannot rule out their use at Rathfarnham, where the original parapet no longer survives.

XIII The upper room of the tower-house at Loughmoe. The door to the left of centre in the photograph opens from the main spiral stairs. A second stairs, accessible via the door in the side of the window on the far left of the photograph, leads to the parapet.

XIV Monea Castle, built in 1616 by Revd Malcolm Hamilton, the rector of Devenish, is probably the most attractive of the Ulster-Scottish castles, and is certainly one of the most Scottish. The manner in which the shapes of the towers metamorphose from round to square before terminating in stepped gables is typical of Scottish architecture from *c.*1570 into the seventeenth century.

Such was the success of the Gaelic-Irish at destroying the castles of Anglo-Norman settlers that we must presume that the defending garrisons were really quite small. Even a castle of the size of Carrickfergus had a modest garrison: in 1211–12 it was protected by between six and ten knights, between fifteen and sixteen soldiers below knights in rank, and between three and five crossbowmen.[34] We do not know how well equipped were these castles. An inventory of *c.*1224 of the contents of the stores of the royal castles of Athlone, Limerick and Dublin tells us the equipment that was available for their defence, and it was a modest assemblage indeed: Athlone had four coats of chain mail, two of them with head pieces, nine iron hats, one helmet, two mangonels (large, wheeled catapults) with 120 strings and slings, one cable, one crossbow with a wheel, and two thousand bolts; Dublin had two mangonels, one crossbow with a wheel and one with a stirrup, and 4,500 bolts; Limerick had nothing at all.[35] After Castleroche was completed in the middle or late 1230s and war was raging with the Irish,[36] the free tenants of the de Verdun lands were required to do service at the castle,[37] indicating that it was not only trained soldiers who could be called on to man the battlements of castles.

CASTLES OF EARTH AND TIMBER

This book is concerned with stone buildings, but no account of stone-castle architecture should omit some consideration of earth-and-timber castles, or of the timberwork that was once very common in stone castles too. The importance of the latter is self-evident: timber buildings stood side-by-side with stone buildings on many castle sites, while the ghosts of timber features – scaffolds, partitions, hoardings and so on – sometimes survive in the stonework or in the mortar-plaster on that stonework. Earth-and-timber castles survive today as mounds and ditches in the landscape, so it is easy to assume that, in the absence of their timber buildings, they have no architecture any more. But the opposite is the case: the earthworks were 'built' to recurring designs, their shapes planned in advance and their layers of sods, soil and gravel built up with full cognizance of the stability of those materials. They have, then, an intrinsic architectural interest. We need to know about these earthworks in a book on stone architecture for two more specific reasons. First, the great towers or donjons of the 1100s and 1200s evolved from the same culture that produced mottes, and they share a concern – an obsession, even – with the principle of elevation over the countryside. Second, stone castles were sometimes built on the sites of earth-and-timber castles, and in most such cases the masonry was put where timberwork had been. Indeed, at some sites, as has been argued convincingly for Clonmacnoise Castle, timberwork was retained alongside new stonework.[38]

---

34 *IPR, 1211–12*, p. 61. **35** *CDI, 1171–1251*, no. 1227. **36** *CR, Hen. III, 1234–7*, p. 364; *CDI, 1171–1251*, no. 2334; the later thirteenth-century date assigned to the castle in V.M. Buckley and P.D. Sweetman, *Archaeological survey of County Louth* (Dublin, 1991), p. 333, is not correct. **37** B. Smith, *Colonisation and conquest in medieval Ireland: the English in Louth, 1170–1330* (Cambridge, 1999), p. 35. **38** K. O'Conor and C. Manning, 'Clonmacnoise Castle' in King

87 Knockgraffon motte. This huge earthwork, the flat summit of which is characteristic of mottes, dominates the site of a now-lost medieval settlement, the ruined parish church of which still survives. Overgrown fragments of a tower – apparently late medieval – stand on the small bailey attached to this motte. The sites of abandoned medieval settlements can often be identified where mottes and churches are found together, as is the case here and at Buolick, for example.

Mottes and ringworks

Two basic castle-earthwork types are identified by archaeologists in these islands, and in Ireland both are conventionally dated to the later 1100s and early 1200s, the years during which Anglo-Norman lordship was being established. A motte (or motte-castle) is primarily a flat-topped mound surrounded by a rampart (fig. 87). A 'ringwork' (or 'ringwork castle') is primarily a ramparted enclosure, the interior of which is not quite as elevated, if at all (fig. 88). The first provided elevation and was itself highly visible on the landscape, even before any timber structure was built; the second depended more on its timberwork for its elevation.[39]

The motte has been the subject of scholarly research in Ireland since the late 1800s.[40] A castle-type capable of quick construction in hostile territories, it is associated with the spread across eastern Ireland of land-hungry Anglo-Norman settlers in the late

(ed.), *Clonmacnoise studies*, 2, pp 137–65.   **39** A variation on the ringwork is the promontory fortification (and its close morphological relative, the 'partial ringwork'). Baginbun is the best-known example of the former (K. O'Conor, 'A reinterpretation of the earthworks at Baginbun' in Kenyon and O'Conor (eds), *The medieval castle in Ireland and Wales*, pp 17–31), and examples of the latter are at Ferrycarrig (I. Bennett, 'Preliminary archaeological excavations at Ferrycarrig ringwork, Newtown td, Co. Wexford', *JWHS*, 10 (1984–5), 25–43) and probably Glanworth (Manning, *Glanworth Castle*, p. 136).   **40** See, for example, G.H. Orpen, 'Motes and Norman

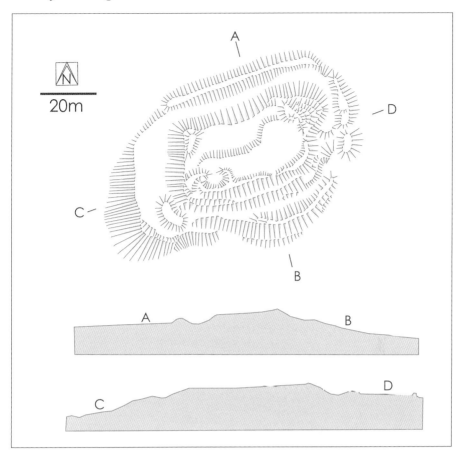

88 Castlerahan 'ringwork' castle. This near-rectangular earthwork in the frontier zone between Anglo-Norman Meath and Gaelic-Irish central Ulster is likely to have been built (or even refashioned from an older earthwork) by the Anglo-Normans. Lower in elevation than a motte, and with a bank around part of its summit, it can reasonably be identified as a 'ringwork' castle (P. O'Donovan and C. Parker, 'The castle at Castlerahan, Co. Cavan' in Manning (ed.), *From ringforts to fortified houses*, pp 53–64).

1100s and early 1200s. Its demonstrable role in effecting the westward advance of the Anglo-Norman frontier should not disguise the fact that mottes were also built after land had been secured and the immediate threat of Irish attack had diminished.[41] A prophecy in a late fourteenth-century Gaelic-Irish poem that 'the high green strongholds [of every foreign castle] will be broken in pieces by shots' suggests that

castles in Ireland', *JRSAI*, 37 (1907), 123–52; B.J. Graham, 'The mottes of the Norman liberty of Meath' in Murtagh (ed.), *Irish midland studies*, pp 39–56; T. O'Keeffe, 'The archaeology of Norman castles in Ireland: pt 1: mottes and ringworks', *AI*, 4:3 (1990), 15–17; K. O'Conor, 'Motte castles in Ireland: permanent fortresses, residences and manorial centres', *CG*, 20 (2002), 173–82; T.E. McNeill, 'Mountains or molehills? Different uses for mottes in the lordships of eastern Ireland', *AJ*, 168 (2011), 227–71; B. Colfer, *Wexford castles*, pp 37–51. **41** K. O'Conor, 'The later

89 A LiDAR image of the east side of Ferns village showing earthworks that are barely discernible at ground level (image courtesy of Steve Davis, UCD School of Archaeology; data courtesy of the National Roads Authority). Left of centre is a low circular mound, beside which (to its top left) is the ruin of the Augustinian abbey founded by Diarmait Mac Murchada. He had a 'stone house' and 'camp' at Ferns in 1166. The Anglo-Normans then built their first castle at Ferns *c.*1180 according to Gerald of Wales (*AT*, 1166.13; A.B. Scott and F.X. Martin (eds), *Expugnatio Hibernica by Giraldus Cambrensis* (Dublin, 1978), p. 171). This low mound could be the remains of the latter castle, but it is more likely to be the fortress of Diarmait, with the abbey right beside it.

mottes were still used, or at least perceived, as castles of oppression almost two centuries on from their earliest constructions.[42]

Few would now dispute that Gaelic-Irish lords beyond the boundaries of the Anglo-Norman jurisdiction also built mottes, and there is circumstantial but convincing evidence that some Gaelic-Irish castles of the pre-Norman period were of motte-form too.[43] The likelihood is that large mottes located in places known to have been significant in pre-Norman times, such as Knockgraffon (fig. 87) and Rathmore (Kildare), are actually Anglo-Norman adaptations of earlier mound-form monuments, some of which were prehistoric burial mounds and most of which functioned as seats of pre-Anglo-Norman lordly power (fig. 89). These qualifications notwithstanding, the distribution of identified sites – a suggested total of 422 in the Republic alone in 2012[44] – generally reflects the geographical 'shape' of Anglo-Norman lordship up to

construction and use of motte and bailey castles in Ireland: new evidence from Leinster', *JKAS*, 17 (1987–91), 13–29; T. O'Keeffe, 'The frontier in medieval Ireland: an archaeological perspective', *Group for the Study of Irish Historic Settlement Newsletter* (1995), 16–18. **42** Leerssen, *Mere Irish and fíor-Ghael*, p. 161. **43** Graham, 'Medieval timber and earthwork fortifications'; O'Keeffe, 'Fortifications of western Ireland'; T.B. Barry, 'The origins of Irish castles: a contribution to the debate' in Manning (ed.), *From ringforts to fortified houses*, pp 33–40. **44** ASI

90 Croom Castle. The curve of masonry is best explained as a skin attached to an early earthwork mound. There is nothing particularly thirteenth century about the style of the masonry, but the tower on the left, which is later medieval, is certainly an addition.

the end of King John's reign. About 35 per cent of these mottes have adjoining embanked enclosures called baileys, which provided enclosed space for buildings that could not be accommodated on the tops of the mounds. Rarely were stone buildings erected on top of mottes, presumably because of the danger of subsidence on freshly piled earthen mounds; at Athlone, famously, a newly erected stone tower fell, killing nine.[45] There are some exceptions to the rule, as at Clough, Donaghmoyne (where the masonry is fragmentary) and Shanid. A rare example in Ireland of a motte later encased in stone is Croom (fig. 90), and the earthwork in question may have been raised before the Anglo-Norman arrival in the district.[46] Uniquely in an Irish context, the (no longer extant) motte at Meelick contained, quite literally, a building: in 1203 it was piled on top of a church, with the top part of the church apparently converted into a 'blockhouse'.[47]

(www.archaeology.ie); I think this total is too large by at least seventy or eighty sites.   **45** G.H. Orpen, 'Athlone Castle: its early history, with notes on some neighbouring castles', *JRSAI*, 37 (1907), 257–76.   **46** According to *An Leabhar Muimhneach*, 'Domhnall Mór… built… [the] Castle of Croom by the Maigue' (C. Devane, '"The Black Castle of Adare": a history of Adare Castle' in L. Dunne and J. Kiely, 'Archaeological excavation report. Adare Castle, Co. Limerick', *Eachtra Journal*, 16 (2013), 1–28 at 7). The encasement of mottes in stone is known in England, as at Farnham in Surrey, Berkeley in Gloucestershire, and Whittington in Shropshire.   **47** 'William [de Burgh] went on a great hosting to Connachta and laid it waste. He entered

The ringwork, by contrast, is a more recent arrival in scholarly literature in Ireland. A substantial paper in 1969 by David Cathcart King and Leslie Alcock on such earthwork-enclosure castles in England and Wales opened the door for the identification of comparable monuments here.[48] Dermot Twohig in 1978 was the first Irish scholar to walk through that door, but Derek Renn had actually pointed to examples in Ireland back in 1970.[49] Seminal writings by Terry Barry in 1983 and 1987 brought the subject of ringwork castles in Ireland to wider attention.[50] He and David Sweetman are the most senior of the many archaeologists who now believe that castles deserving of the 'ringwork' label survive in significant numbers in Ireland. Tom McNeill and I are the only prominent archaeologists who have queried the number of examples,[51] but to little effect: in 1987 the number of suggested ('possible') identifications on the entire island was forty-five, but the number in the Republic alone is now, more than twenty-five years later, more than twice this.[52]

One reason that there has been some dissent, even if it has only been articulated by two castle specialists, is that ringworks are virtually impossible to identify in the field, certainly without excavation. Unlike mottes, which are very distinctive in the landscape when well preserved, many of the sites described by some archaeologists as Anglo-Norman ringworks are quite indistinguishable from those sites that other archaeologists (and indeed some of the same archaeologists!) describe as Gaelic-Irish ringforts of the pre-Anglo-Norman period. The great majority of identified ringworks are actually monuments that had been identified previously and unproblematically as earlier medieval ringforts; included among them may even be some monuments that should perhaps be reclassified as potential prehistoric ritual monuments.[53] It is difficult, frankly, to identify an objective reasoning by which many of the re-identifications have been suggested: I would regard 83 per cent of the ringwork-castle identifications by the Archaeological Survey of Ireland as excessively speculative by any objective reading of the site-descriptions. The frantic rush to identify ringworks has been an ill-advised turn in the study of earth-and-timber castles in Ireland: instead of pausing to explore (by reference, for example, to other parts of Europe where both are found) why low-elevation enclosures were used in some instances in preference to mottes, or to explore the cultural implications of Anglo-Normans sometimes deploying an earthwork form identical to the older indigenous earthwork form that we describe as 'ringfort', some archaeologists have been engaged in a trolley dash across Ireland, scooping into the

Mílec, built a castle around the church, made a blockhouse of the church, and remained therein eating meat during Lent' (*AIn.*, 1203.2).   **48** D.J.C. King and L. Alcock, 'Ringworks of England and Wales', *CG*, 3 (1969), 90–127.   **49** D.C. Twohig, 'Norman ringwork castles', *Bulletin group for the study of Irish historic settlement*, 5 (1978), 7–9; D. Renn, *Norman castles of Britain* (London, 1968).   **50** T.B. Barry, 'Anglo-Norman ringwork castles: some evidence' in T. Reeves-Smith and F. Hamond (eds), *Landscape archaeology in Ireland* (Oxford, 1983), 295–314; idem, *The archaeology of medieval Ireland* (London, 1987), pp 46–55.   **51** McNeill, 'Early castles in Leinster', p. 58; O'Keeffe, 'Mottes and ringworks'; idem, 'Afterword' in J. Lyttleton and T. O'Keeffe (eds), *The manor in medieval and early modern Ireland* (Dublin, 2005), 188–98.   **52** The ASI (www.archaeology.ie) locates 117 examples in the Republic (2012), but this is certainly fewer than the number reported anecdotally around the country.   **53** The low-lying and broad-ditched Dungar, for example, identified as a ringwork castle in Sweetman, *Medieval castles*

'ringwork' category any enclosures that might not be classic ringforts, and more than a few that are. Leaving aside the stone castles, if we accept without query the current combined head-counts of mottes and ringworks in Ireland – a grand total of over 500 in the Republic alone, and still counting – we would have to conclude that Anglo-Norman Ireland was the most rapidly and densely encastellated region in the history of medieval Europe. It is a nice boast, but were there that many Anglo-Normans in Ireland immediately after 1170, and did they really have the resources and power, and indeed the need, to build on that extraordinary scale?

Etymology

The motte takes its name from an actual medieval word, whereas 'ringwork' is a modern, descriptive term. From the ninth to the eleventh centuries *motte* (*mota, motta*) was used on the Continent to refer to a piece of turf or sod.[54] There was no military connotation; banks of such sods were used to control water movement around mills, for example. The word was first used consistently to signify the mound of a castle, formed literally of layers of sods, in eleventh-century France and England. Its use for that purpose was largely restricted to those two countries (and to a lesser degree to Ireland) in the high Middle Ages. We should note, though, that the terminology was not always used unambiguously or without interchange with other words. In its French 'heartland', for example, *mota* was sometimes replaced with *dunjo* (or donjon) but with no apparent change in basic meaning.[55]

Although Ireland has several hundred mounds identified today as mottes, the term was used relatively little in medieval written sources to describe any of these, the reason being perhaps that a motte/mound was but one of the elements of a castle and generally did not require separate mentioning. Most of the references are actually from the early fourteenth century, a whole century after the peak of motte construction.[56] It is somewhat ironic that the oldest and best historically documented motte in Ireland, the motte (*la mot*) of Trim Castle that the Irish 'threw completely down/And levelled … even with the ground' in 1172,[57] is not regarded as a motte at all by modern castle scholars but as a 'ringwork'.[58] The same is true of Newcastle McKynegan, where the earthwork now classified by the Archaeological Survey of Ireland as another ringwork castle is obviously the *mota* around which a wall was built in 1298.[59]

---

of Ireland, p. 13, might be a prehistoric henge or ringbarrow.   **54** Anon., 'Les fortifications de terre en Europe occidentale du Xe au XIIe siècles', *Archéologie Médiévale*, 11 (1981), 18–19; see also R. Higham and P. Barker, *Timber castles* (London, 1992), p. 361.   **55** In the famous accounts of the French castles of Ardres in 1117 and Guines in 1181 the *domus* (or house) was built on, respectively, a *super dunjonem* and *dunjo* (G. Fournier, *Le château dans la France médiévale* (Paris, 1978), p. 286).   **56** See, for example, the references to 'motes' in *RBO*, pp 27–8, 52, 62.   **57** *The deeds of the Normans in Ireland: la geste des Engleis en yrlande*, ed. and trans., E. Mullally (Dublin, 2002), ii, lines 3300–1.   **58** Hayden, *Trim Castle*, passim. For a contrary view of the relationship of the supposed 'ringwork' to the stone castle at Trim, see T. O'Keeffe, 'Trim Castle uncovered: some thoughts', *Ríocht na Midhe*, 24 (2013), 160–8.   **59** *38 RDKPRI*, p. 47; the earthwork's construction predates 1210 when the *Novum Castellum* is first mentioned (Orpen, 'Novum Castrum McKynegan', p. 129).

Timber buildings

The timber architecture on earthwork castles has long disappeared. The few excavations in Ireland have yielded little, and they suggest a timber architecture of little sophistication. There was, for example, a small tower on four thick wooden uprights (trimmed logs, basically) and an adjacent wooden 'house' of flimsy construction on the motte at Lismahon.[60] One can visualize here a band of Anglo-Normans scouring the Lismahon countryside for timber, dragging their found material back to the motte, and converting it quickly into a couple of buildings with few trimmings. But there is documentary evidence that the timber buildings on mottes were sometimes prefabricated and then assembled on site: accounts were rendered in 1170–1 for two or three wooden towers (*castella lignea*) and seven hundred planks that had been sent to Ireland.[61] While it is not stated that these structures were specifically for mottes, it is useful to note that prefabricated timberwork carried by the Norman invaders to England in 1066 was erected on their motte at Hastings.[62] As late 1276–7, though, long after the motte-building phase was over, wooden towers were being made for use on the perimeter of Rindown Castle.[63] In the mid-thirteenth century there was even some traffic in prefabricated timberwork *out* of Ireland; in 1244–5 the justiciar was instructed by the king to organize the construction of eight *bretachiae* or brattices for export, while ten years later two thousand timber boards were to be exported to Gascony for conversion into wooden towers.[64] The value of the prefabrication attested to in these records was presumably not confined to the speed of assembly: timber structures could be dismantled and moved to other places if needed, as can be seen from the record of 1302 of the timber 'of a certain house' in Ayr in Scotland being brought 'at great cost and under armed guard' to a ship bound for Dublin.[65]

A brattice, the Latin spelling of which in medieval Ireland is derived from the Norman-French *breteske* or Old French *bretesche*, was a timber structure, either a tower on a motte or a building at the entrance to an enclosure.[66] The former was its meaning in the reference to the construction of a *mote et britagium* at Roscrea in 1213.[67] The *bretage* 'beyond the gate' of the manorial enclosure at Dunfert (Danesfort) in 1307 is presumably an example of the latter meaning: it was apparently some sort of barbican.[68] The contexts of the usage of 'brattice' in medieval England suggest that it sometimes also applied to the timber galleries that were attached (though not necessarily permanently) to the tops of stone walls, as originally found at Castleroche and Coonagh (fig. 91); the *britagium* mentioned at Caherconlish in 1288 might well have been for use on the little-known later thirteenth-century castle nearby that is now known as Brittas (see below, p. 245).[69]

60 D. Waterman, 'Excavations at Lismahon, Co. Down', *MA*, 3 (1959), 139–76.   **61** *CDI, 1171–1251*, no. 27.   **62** Higham and Barker, *Timber castles*, p. 155.   **63** *36 RDKPRI*, p. 35. There is also a reference to 'a wooden castle' more than three centuries later Derrymullin (*SP, Hen. VIII*, 2, p. 452).   **64** *CDI, 1171–1251*, nos 2735, 2736, 2775; *CDI, 1252–84*, no. 346.   **65** *CJRI, 1295–1303*, p. 375.   **66** Higham and Barker, *Timber castles*, p. 362.   **67** *CDI, 1171–1251*, no. 2760. Goddard Orpen suggested that Brittas placenames in Ireland preserve memories of the former presence of brattices ('Mote and bretesche building in Ireland', *EHR*, 21:83 (1906), 417–44).   **68** *CDI, 1302–7*, no. 667.   **69** *Pipe roll 17 Edward I*, 20. Orpen thought, surely incorrectly, that

91 Coonagh Castle. The large sockets at two-thirds of the height of this donjon belong to a hoarding that was originally just below the battlements. The tower was heightened by a few metres in the fifteenth century when the castle, originally a baronial fortress that was owned by the crown for several decades, was in Gaelic-Irish ownership.

ANGLO-NORMAN STONE CASTLES: AN INTRODUCTION

There were three main phases of castle building in stone in Ireland: (a) the late twelfth, thirteenth and early fourteenth centuries, up to an entirely notional date of 1350; (b) the later Middle Ages, continuous with the latter phase but with a perceptible increase in activity from the later 1300s and continuing into the later 1500s; and, continuous

this *britagium* referred to an earthwork castle ('Brittas Castle, County Limerick, with the original "bretesche"', *JRSAI*, 18 (1908), 183–4).

with the latter phase but falling mainly outside the scope of this book, (c) the
seventeenth century. The gap between the first two phases, insofar as there was one,
can be attributed to a combination of two factors. One was a general economic decline,
driven in part by climatic deterioration. The other was increasing lawlessness within
the lordship, and more specifically the tendency of the English of early 1300s to
respond by funnelling money into armed forces rather than encastellated buildings.
The gap between the second two phases was not so much chronological as cultural:
new stylistic ideas of Renaissance origin from England and Europe infiltrated post-
Reformation Ireland, precipitating a change in how castles functioned and were
perceived. The stone castles of the first phase, the subject of this chapter, are clustered
chronologically in the thirteenth century, with a low peak in the second quarter of the
century. The numbers built in the late 1100s and early 1300s are small. The castles of
this entire phase are mainly Anglo-Norman; there are few surviving Irish-built castles.

   In much of the literature on castles of this first phase there is a heavy emphasis on
their military capabilities. One sees this in Sweetman's book in particular. This is
largely an inheritance of Leask, who was influenced in turn by English castle scholars
of the early twentieth century, particularly the brilliant Sydney Toy, whom he knew
in person and whose pan-European survey, *Castles: a short history of fortifications from 1600
to AD1600* (London, 1939), is a classic work.[70] The emphasis is not misplaced: there is no
doubt that defence always mattered hugely to castle-owning communities across
Europe and that the general development of the castle as an architectural 'thing' was,
as Toy recognized, driven by considerations of the efficacy, physical and symbolic, of
certain defensible types of structure and of certain spatial arrangements of particular
elements like wall-towers. However, few scholars now believe, as scholars everywhere
once did, that the builders of castles searched quite so assiduously for architectural
designs that optimized defensibility while accommodating domestic needs; few now
believe that the castles of every generation 'improved' militarily – and were so regarded
by contemporaries – on those of the previous one. Information did not travel so fast
or so widely that castle builders everywhere shared a common view of the architectural
design that constituted the vanguard at any one moment. With certain spectacular
exceptions (such as Château Gaillard in Normandy, and the northern Welsh castles
built by Edward I), innovations in design, insofar as they registered in any common
consciousness, were measured by local or regional standards rather than by national or
international standards. In a land like Ireland, where a sizeable garrison behind stoutly
built stone walls would suffice to repel most attacks, castle-owning lords who adopted
sophisticated ideas must have been as preoccupied with making architectural fashion-
statements to their neighbours as they were with keeping their households safe. Far-
reaching innovation in castle design really only occurred when agents of great wealth,
like royal houses, started new buildings for which they had very specific military
functions or which they intended to be showcases. Design ideas would trickle down
from these exalted levels to the builders of other castles, but not immediately (if at all),
and certainly not without some dilution. It is worth noting that the designs of two

---

70 Reprinted as *Castles: their construction and history* (London, 1985).

92 Some thirteenth-century windows for bowmen: (a) classic long (or 'plunging') loops for longbowmen in the curtain wall at Trim Castle, *c*.1220; (b) a balistraria, or crossbow-loop, with a distinctively splayed top at Carlow Castle, pre-1220; (c) arrow-loops with round terminals and oillets (circular viewing holes for the bowman, from the Anglo-Norman *oillet*, meaning 'little eye') at Tullowmacjames, post-1250; (d) a loop, possibly a balistraria, with ornamentally splayed terminals and oillets at Brittas Castle, *c*.1280.

royal castles (Dublin and Limerick) and one baronial castle (Kilkenny) in Ireland were up-to-date by the standards of their time (the early thirteenth century) but were not copied directly in the few decades that followed. Had the lordship been wealthier, there might have been greater emulation of such contemporary 'vanguard' designs in Ireland, or greater experimentation with new designs.

Identifying and naming thirteenth-century castle buildings

It is relatively easy to identify thirteenth-century castles. There are characteristic types of enclosure-plan (discussed below), as well as *fairly* characteristic forms of arrow-loop and balistraria (fig. 92),[71] but the key to identification is often in the fabric itself. This means that even the most ruined or vegetation-strangled buildings of the period can reveal their dates to the careful observer. First, thirteenth-century castle walls tend to be very thick, rarely falling below 2m (whereas later medieval walls rarely exceed 1.5m). Second, they have base-batters, distinctive and sometimes quite dramatic aprons of stone attached to the lower parts of walls (pl. VIII). Many base batters have been stripped of stone over the years, but scars remain and are easily identified. Third, as was noted earlier (p. 80), mortar that survives on the underside of arched surfaces preserves the impressions of the timber slats used to stabilize those surfaces during construction.

Keeps, donjons, great towers and 'hall-houses'

Some words are needed here on the identification of those thirteenth-century focal buildings of castles – the central or most prominent buildings – that are popularly called 'keeps' but are also (and sometimes interchangeably) described as donjons, great towers and 'hall-houses'. The term 'keep' reflects the popular view that such a building was intended to *keep* the household safe when a castle was attacked, and especially if its outer enclosure was breached. The term was only recorded for the first time in the later fourteenth century in France, and it was not used widely until after the Middle Ages. It is no longer popular among scholars.[72] One cannot say the same, unfortunately in my view, about the term 'hall-house', a made-up term of fairly recent vintage that has achieved in only two decades an extraordinary currency in Ireland. I have argued at length elsewhere (and reiterate part of the argument below (pp 223–4)) that it should be dropped immediately from our vocabulary.

The two other terms are more acceptable. 'Great tower', first, is derived from the Latin, *magna turris*, which was sometimes used in contemporary sources in north-western Europe.[73] Although 'tower' connotes to us today a building of some height, the buildings described as 'great towers' were not always especially tall. It seems, then,

---

71 'Loop' is possibly derived from the high medieval Dutch *lûpen*, 'to lie in wait, watch, peer' (*cf* 'Loop', 'Oillet', 'Balistraria', OED online). I say 'fairly' because late medieval gun-loops sometimes imitate thirteenth-century arrow and crossbow loops (as does one at Athclare Castle, for example).   72 J.R. Kenyon and M. Thompson, 'The origin of the word "keep"', *MA*, 38 (1994), 175–6; see also P. Dixon, 'The myth of the keep' in G. Meirion-Jones, E. Impey and M. Jones (eds), *The seigneurial residence in western Europe, c.AD800–1600* (Oxford, 2002), pp 9–14.   73 Thompson, *Rise of the castle*, p. 181.

that the adjective 'great' was intended to signal that the building to which it was attached served a greater or more central role in the functioning of a castle than any of its other towers. The physical, spatial and functional distinctions between halls and chambers will be discussed at length presently, but it is important at this juncture to make the observation that in most cases these 'great towers' contained private chambers, if not also rooms that could be used for reception, and that they did not, certainly from *c.*1200, contain what medieval people themselves understood as halls. It would not be unacceptable to describe them as 'chamber towers' rather than 'great towers'. The other acceptable term is donjon, derived from the Latin *dominion*, meaning 'lordship'. This is now preferred to 'keep' by castle scholars in England. Although little used originally in medieval Ireland – it was used in the later 1300s to describe the original de Clare castle of Bunratty[74] – its great advantage as modern nomenclature is that it signals a building that, regardless of the use to which its interior was put, symbolized lordly power to the outside world.[75] I use donjon and 'chamber tower' somewhat interchangeably in this book – the former seems rather more poetic when describing a focal building that must have impressed contemporaries by virtue of its mass or embellishment – without compromising the integrity of the analysis of the functions of the interiors of these structures.

One of the basic skills needed to study castles in Ireland is to be able to distinguish in the field between these thirteenth-century focal buildings and the later tower-houses. First, the Anglo-Norman buildings have, almost without exception, no original vaulting. The main rooms were pinned between timber floors and timber ceilings/roofs. Vaults were often inserted later in the Middle Ages. There is a useful rule of thumb: if vaults are demonstrably original, the building is almost certainly of late medieval date.[76] Second, the Anglo-Norman buildings were normally entered at first-floor level.[77] Some tower-houses had first-floor entrances, but never (to my knowledge) without a ground-floor entrance as well. Third, the Anglo-Norman structures sometimes had windowless walls below the roof level. In other words, their roofs were often 'sunk down' (or 'countersunk') inside the buildings, disguised from external view by very high parapets (fig. 93).[78] Fourth, Anglo-Norman battlements, if they survive at all, have plainly rectangular (rather than stepped) merlons and are flush with the walls below (see pl. I, fig. 94, top).[79] Finally, Anglo-Norman latrines were often machicolated (overhanging), often on timber brackets in western Ireland (fig. 94, bottom), meaning that the human waste literally fell from the toilet seat to the base of the wall; in some instances the latrines were in small, roofed turrets that were very

74 *Caithr. Thoirdh.*, p. 8.   **75** P. Marshall, 'The great tower as residence' in Meirion-Jones et al. (eds), *The seigneurial residence in western Europe*, pp 27–44.   **76** An exception may be the roof-vault in Ballisnahyny, a thirteenth-century rectangular chamber-tower, which is regarded as an original feature by McNeill (*Castles in Ireland*, pp 149–50); the evidence that it is original is not unequivocal, however. The collapsed roof-vault in Fartamore, also thirteenth century, was a groin-vault and it does seem to be original.   **77** Exceptions to this are rare: Grenan, for example, had a ground-floor entrance while Coonagh had an entrance at a level equivalent to a second floor.   **78** C. Manning, 'Low-level roofs in Irish great towers', *CG*, 20 (2002), 137–40.   **79** The *merlon* is the part of the battlement that rises as a block of solid masonry, and the *crenel* (which gives its name to 'crenellation') is the gap between the merlons.

93 Maynooth donjon. There were only ever two floors inside this huge late twelfth-century building, the upper floor being open to a roof – actually a double-roof, both parts hipped – hidden from exterior view.

similar in size and construction to the machicolated variety but extended down to ground level (fig. 95). Latrine chutes, which are vertical wall cavities carrying human and other waste from toilets to external pits and run-offs, are not unknown in thirteenth-century castles but were more common in the late Middle Ages.

THE CASTLE HOUSEHOLD AND THE USE OF SPACE, 1170–1350

Life inside a medieval castle was dominated not by fear of attack but by the rituals of lordly life, many of them quite mundane. The heart of the castle household was the married couple, the lord and lady, whose union was forged by political convenience rather than love. Couples of the castle-owning classes married young, sometimes *very* young, and those who survived the high spousal mortality rate – higher among men, whose outdoor activities exposed them to greater dangers – married often.[80] Matilda de Prendergast, to choose an extreme example, was betrothed by the age of seven but her fiancé died, and she was married, widowed and remarried in her teens.[81] If children – we would regard them today as such, although there is a debate about the meaning

---

80 See D. Youngs, *The life-cycle in western Europe, c.1300–1500* (Manchester, 2006), ch. 6.
81 G.H. Orpen, *Ireland under the Normans* (Oxford, 1911–20), iii, p. 199.

94 The mid-thirteenth-century chamber tower of Kinlough: (*top*) the outline of the tower's original battlemented parapet is visible immediately below the gable, along with three of the small holes through which drained the rainwater that collected in the original roof-gully; (*bottom*) halfway up the building is the site of the large machicolated latrine (blocked when the building was re-edified as a tower-house in the sixteenth century), which was supported by two massive timber beams.

95 The mid-thirteenth-century turriform latrine in the chamber tower of Castlemagarret survived the later medieval rebuilding of the corner of the tower adjacent to it.

of that term in a medieval context[82] – were not married off at young ages they were dispatched as servants or sent to train for careers. This has interesting implications for how we imagine the households: few if any of the adolescents to be found in elite medieval households were the scions of those who owned the residences in question.

The spaces of castles – not just of donjons but of castles in their entireties – were to a large extent organized around the needs of the married couples, and those needs were not really individual needs based on personality and personal preference but were created by medieval culture itself. Part of that culture was what we might describe as lordly peregrination: couples who possessed several castles moved around their properties, bringing key members of their households with them. As Douglas Simpson put it half a century ago, a medieval castle

> was not normally armed to the teeth or stuffed with a garrison of professional soldiers, each at his action station. In times of peace it would contain simply the lord's *familia* or household. During his frequent absences, no more than a caretaker and a few servants would be at hand.[83]

82 See Gilchrist, *Medieval life*, p. 145.   83 W.D. Simpson, *Castles in England and Wales* (London, 1969), pp 13–14. In royal castles the 'caretakers' (or 'keepers', as they were described) were usually

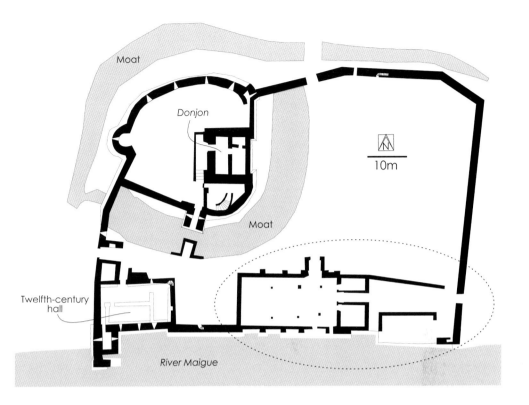

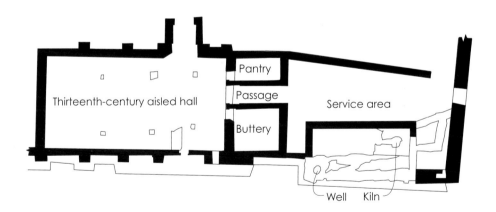

96 Adare Castle plan.

men of some substance. Niall O'Brien has usefully collected the names of those charged with the responsibility at the royal castles of Rindown and Cashel ('The keepers of Rindown Castle', *RHASJ*, 11 (2009), 28–33; 'Royal constables of Cashel Castle, Co. Tipperary', *THJ* (2013), 58–64).

When a lord and his wife were resident, a medieval castle housed a cohort of people – running to hundreds in the case of the royal court[84] – performing duties around them, some attending directly to their needs and others involved more peripherally. The make-up of that cohort varied from one castle to another depending on wealth and status. It would also have varied over time, and it almost certainly varied according to custom between castles of the Anglo-Norman and Gaelic-Irish polities. Based on what we know of England, the key household posts in major castles of English origin in Ireland, especially in the thirteenth century, were probably held by people who were of some noble background themselves, and these posts may even have been held by particular families by hereditary right. The posts in question include that of steward (responsible for the household's domestic affairs), chamberlain (responsible for the upkeep of the living space), master of the wardrobe (responsible for clothing) and marshal (responsible for the horses and stables). Of particular interest in Ireland is the office of butler, since the *paterfamilias* of the great Butler family, Theobald, held the office of chief butler of Ireland and took the patronym from there. A butler in a medieval castle was not a man-servant *à la* P.G. Woodhouse's Jeeves but had responsibility, symbolic as much as practical, for the buttery (in which wine was stored) and the pantry (in which bread was stored), the two service rooms that were normally positioned beside a hall (fig. 96).[85] Servants without rank, of which there must have been many, are rather more mysterious to us, since their lowly status kept them out of the contemporary documentation. It seems likely that thirteenth-century servants in Anglo-Norman castles were drawn from the labour force or *famuli* that the lords used to farm those lands (called demesne lands) that they did not let out to tenants but kept for their own use.[86] However they were sourced and paid, servants needed accommodation, but records of that are also lacking.

INTRODUCING HALLS AND CHAMBERS

Within the castles, lords and ladies had both 'public' and 'private' lives. There were times when their duties within the castle brought them in front of and into interaction with the full cohort of household officers, with their peers within the nobility, and even with their tenants. There were other times, though, when they could retreat to more intimate quarters. Some of the spaces to which they retreated were shared between them – the bedroom, for example – but other spaces were exclusive to one or other. Thus we have, for instance, references to chambers or rooms belonging exclusively to women.[87]

Identifying the spaces that could be described as 'public' and 'private' in the lives of castle lords and their wives is clearly as important to understanding castles as analysing

84 C.M. Woolgar, *The great household in late medieval England* (New Haven and London, 1999). **85** See M. Gardiner, 'Buttery and pantry, and their antecedents: idea and architecture in the English medieval house' in M. Kowaleski and P.J.P. Goldberg (eds), *Medieval domesticity: home, housing and household in medieval England* (Cambridge, 2008), pp 37–65. **86** R.H. Hilton, *The English peasantry in the later Middle Ages* (Oxford, 1975), p. 103; B. Hanawalt, *The ties that bound: peasant families in medieval England* (Oxford, 1986), p. 137. **87** *CDI, 1252–84*, no. 2010; *CDI*,

the military capacities of their architectural designs. Most castle specialists today are rightfully mindful of the danger of transposing modern ideas of public and private into the medieval past, but most would agree nonetheless that two rooms or spaces so regarded defined the boundaries of castle life not just in Ireland but across medieval western Europe. One was the hall (*aula* in Latin), the place of 'public' encounter, and the other was the chamber (*camera* in Latin), the place of 'private' retreat. Indeed, these two spaces – or, rather, concepts of space – defined not just castle life but virtually all medieval domestic life right down to the typical townhouse and peasant farmstead. A colourful example to demonstrate that point comes from Youghal in 1307. Basilia Don (Dunne?) of Youghal was engaged in an extra-marital affair with one Stephen le Clerk. One night, thinking her husband was away, she went to a tavern in the town for a rendezvous with Stephen. He bought the silence of the taverner with 5*s.*, and she bribed her maid with the gift of a cow. Her husband John, who suspected an affair and was actually hiding in the town, was alerted to the assignation and turned up at the tavern with a posse of friends. Stephen heard them enter the building and 'flying from the chamber [*camera*], came through the midst of the hall [*aula*], and met John Don and the others and a skirmish ensued, they threw him to the ground [and *absciderunt ejus testiculos*'].[88]

The distinction between *aula* and *camera* seems clear-cut and might suggest that it is easy to 'read' the key spaces of castles, but that is not the case. Making that distinction when standing inside a castle can be complicated by some interconnected factors.

First, 'public' and 'private' spaces – I will drop the inverted commas hereafter but readers should assume them to be always present – often share the same lexicon of features, such as windows with seats and fireplaces, so identifications of room-function are not automatic. The common assumption that halls are significantly more elongated (at length:breadth ratios of 2:1 and more) than chambers is not unreasonable but sometimes chambers had hall-like dimensions.[89] The sharing of features warns us not to regard public and private as fully separate realms in the Middle Ages. As Dominic Barthélemy expressed it, 'there was little to distinguish "chamber" from "hall" other than the fact that the former could accommodate fewer guests. The difference was in the degree of privacy, not in its nature'.[90]

The second factor is the simple matter of building survival. When a single structure remains of a castle, as is normally the case in Ireland, one is faced with an instant dilemma. Were the *aula* and *camera*, or spaces equivalent to them, within that one structure originally, or were those functions or concepts of space divided between structures of which only one survives? In domestic contexts lower down the social scale than 'castle' a single habitable building may have constituted the domestic component of the 'home', so both *aula* and *camera* functions would have been under the one roof, perhaps sometimes with nothing more than a curtain or drape between them. The Youghal tavern was probably of that design, with the hall wedged between the tavern (facing the street) and the chamber (facing the yard or garden to the rear). I

1293–1301, no. 551.   **88** *CJRI, 1305–7*, pp 376–7.   **89** Goodrich Castle in Herefordshire and Aydon Castle in Northumbria, for example.   **90** 'Civilizing the fortress: eleventh to thirteenth century' in G. Duby (ed.), *A history of private life, ii: revelations of the medieval world* (Cambridge,

will argue below, in this chapter and the next, that in castles the functions/spaces were actually divided between different structures, and that the division was linked to status, with hall/*aula* serving a very particular symbolic role.

Third, as we know from large and well-preserved castles on the other side of the Irish Sea, there was sometimes more than one hall and there was often more than one room answering the description of chamber.[91] In these cases one can be challenged sometimes to distinguish between rooms, clusters of rooms, and particularly between principal chambers and 'lodgings'.

Finally, unlike with the claustral monasteries discussed in the last chapter, there is no repeating pattern to the arrangements of castle rooms relative to each other, so there is no easy means of identifying a room's function based on relative position in sites where the distinction can be made. One would expect kitchens, for example, to have been close always to the domestic buildings where food was consumed, as at Castleroche (where the mysterious square building in the courtyard is likely to have been a kitchen), but they were sometimes separated from each other by courtyards.[92] (Equally, one might not think of a room over a main gateway being a castle chapel if one had evidence that the drawbridge and portcullis windlass was positioned in that space, and yet there are examples of such machinery in chapels over gates.)[93]

The challenge of interpreting the meaning of *aula* and *camera* is made all the greater by other words used in medieval and early modern culture to describe domestic space, especially *sal/salle* and *sol[l]ar*.[94] The context of use of the latter in England suggests a sun-lit upper-floor 'private' space of restricted access that was connected functionally if not also physically to a hall; in late medieval examples of its use known to us in Ireland it seems to refer to an upper storey and there is no reference to a hall.[95] The distinctions that scholars in England have made between solars and chambers have not been consistent, suggesting a problem of nomenclature and interpretation that has not been acknowledged much less addressed. Based on a reading of the English literature, we can proceed on the assumption that the distinction between solar and chamber was not so significant that the former could not be described reasonably as a form of chamber or as the sun-lit space where chamber functions might be located. Thus, the solar does not detain us here. The other word, *sal/salle*, is used frequently in medieval and early modern sources outside Ireland. Given that it was not used in Ireland, however, it might seem to be unworthy of discussion here, but establishing its boundaries of meaning is useful. Apparently of early medieval Germanic origin and

---

MA, 1988), pp 397–423 at p. 421.   **91** In *c*.1224, for example, an 'alms hall' (additional to the great hall) and three chambers, one identified as the sheriff's, were among the rooms in Dublin Castle (*CDI, 1171–1251*, no. 1227).   **92** Sherborne in Dorset, and White Castle and Skenfrith in south Wales, for example.   **93** Caernarfon and Harlech castles in Wales, and Etal Castle in Northumbria, for example.   **94** The spelling 'sollar' is favoured by the Oxford English Dictionary ('Sollar, n.', OED online) but 'solar' is the generally preferred spelling.   **95** For the etymology in England, see M. Thompson, *The medieval hall: the basis of secular domestic life, AD600–1600* (Aldershot, 1995), pp 8–10. For Irish examples of 'solar', see below, pp 270–1. The northern European terminology outlined here is derived from H. Ronnes, 'An archaeology of the noble house: the spatial organisation of fifteenth- and sixteenth-century castles and country houses in the Low Countries and the privacy debate', *Medieval and Modern Matters*, 3 (2012), 135–63.

etymologically unrelated to *aula*, it was generally not used in post-Anglo-Saxon England but it was used in medieval contexts in France (*salle*) and Germany (*Saal*) to describe spaces not unlike those described as halls in a medieval English context. With respect to France, the word *salle* was used in the Middle Ages (and is used in modern French castellological literature) with different qualifying adjectives to refer to different types of domestic space, but apparently always in contradistinction to the high-status 'private' accommodation offered by the *grande chambre*. Thus, for example, one finds the *salle haute* ('upper *salle*') signifying a communal space for members of the nobility, with the *grande chambre* beyond it, and the *sale basse* ('lower *salle*', often physically underneath the *salle haute*) signifying the communal space of lower ranks. *Salle* is the root of *sallette*, a small room that developed late in the Middle Ages and attached to the *salle haute*, and functioned as a private dining space for the lord and lady. It was the forerunner of the seventeenth-century *salon*. If it is tempting to translate *salle* as 'hall' in the Angevin sense, the evidence in Germany rings a warning bell. There, or at least in some parts of it, a *Saal* was a first-floor room that was perched on a ground-floor *Hofstube*, but, unlike in France where the upper or *haute* space was of higher social rank and was the space from which the inner household retreated to the *sallette*, the *Hofstube* was the better-lit, better-heated and better-serviced space. It was the space from which the late medieval inner household retreated to the *Tafelstube*, the equivalent of the *sallette*. We will return in the next chapter to the phenomenon of lordly households 'retreating' to increasingly private spaces within their residences.

Returning to the *aula/camera* distinction, we can in general (and notwithstanding the issues discussed above) regard the hall as the central venue of both family and estate life, whether it was simply a form of family room attached to a chamber, as would have been the case in non-aristocratic residences (as in the residence attached to the Youghal tavern), or a large, self-contained and somewhat theatrically designed building in its own right, as was the case in a castle. In the twelfth and thirteenth centuries halls were the places where households ate and entertained, and where in residences of high rank the activities pertaining to the legal and administrative affairs of an estate were carried out. Although public to the extent that they accommodated communal gatherings within appropriately theatrical and brightly lit settings, they were certainly not public-utility spaces: membership of the cohort of people who could enter a hall was restricted. Chambers, by contrast, were the spaces wherein members of households carried out activities – sleeping, washing, robing – that they regarded as inappropriate to the hall. There seems to have been a distinction in high-rank residences between what was sometimes described specifically as the 'great chamber' and what we might describe in contradistinction as the 'inner-chamber'. The former was the space to which a lord and lady retreated having been in the hall but it did not offer them full isolation, whereas the latter was the more private retreat.

Despite their importance in castle culture, and the fact that they are referred to repeatedly in medieval sources, relatively little has been written specifically about halls and chambers in medieval Ireland. The end-result is a scholarly literature in which the identifications of halls and chambers, and discussions of their roles relative to each other, is casual, demonstrably ambiguous and even at times contradictory. The core

97 Athenry Castle. The first-floor room in this rectangular tower is universally regarded as a hall, but its upper-floor position (in an age when halls were *generally* ground-floor) and its dimly lit interior (discernible from the outside by simply observing its fenestration) make it highly improbable that the room functioned as a hall in the sense that was understood in the Middle Ages. Its fine sculptured details might tempt one to be less dogmatic, but there are many other contemporary castle buildings in Ireland that are of the same basic form and lack any sculptural decoration. More decisively, this particular building looks down on an actual ground-floor hall (see also fig. 99).

problem, I think, is that 'hall' is used indiscriminately by castle scholars in Ireland and with little apparent cognizance of how the term was used in the Middle Ages: a rectangular room may be hall-like in its proportions, but that does not mean it had hall functions (fig. 97).

The documentary evidence for halls and chambers, 1170–1350

Contemporary written references to halls and chambers are few relative to the number of buildings that survive. Halls are mentioned right through the Middle Ages but somewhat sporadically, while references to halls and chambers together, in the same castle- or residence-context, are mainly clustered in the late 1200s and early 1300s, and again in the later decades of the Middle Ages. We are concerned here with references up to *c.*1350, but it is very useful to bear in mind while reading the following discussion that the references of the later Middle Ages (see ch. 5) convey the very same impression about the physical character and use of halls and chambers as those references of the thirteenth and fourteenth centuries. This is worth noting here because the patterns of which we have hints up to *c.*1350 are confirmed by the later evidence as *real* patterns.

In a small number of cases we have a reference to a hall but no accompanying reference to a chamber. A typical example is the hall described in the early fourteenth century as 'opposite the castle' (i.e. the donjon) in Carlow. It was the place where 'the pleas of the county and assizes' – court cases, essentially – were held.[96] This same hall may have been for dining, but Carlow Castle was probably a big enough castle for two halls, one for administration, which is the one we know about, and one that was needed for communal eating because it was not thirteenth-century custom to eat one's meal in the chamber.

Dublin Castle, the great royal castle that was begun in 1204, certainly had more than one hall by the middle of the thirteenth century. There had been a timber hall close to the castle site in late 1171, built by the city's Hiberno-Scandinavian inhabitants in their own fashion or style in order to accommodate Henry II on his visit to Ireland.[97] The earlier of the two post-1204 halls in the castle occupied the site now occupied by St Patrick's Hall. It was of stone, and probably provided space for the conventional administrative and dining needs of the castle until 1243. In that year, under instruction from Henry III who was intending to visit Ireland (which he did not actually do), a new hall was built to provide a more opulent stage for the administration of the city and, symbolically, the entire Irish lordship. That new hall was to be '120 feet in length and 80 feet in breadth, with glazed windows, after the manner of the hall of Canterbury'. It was to have 'beyond the dais' both a round window ('30 feet in diameter') in the gable, and, either on the gable wall or on a wooden panel behind the high table, a painting of 'the king and queen sitting with their baronage'. The entrance was to be provided with 'a great portal'. Water was diverted to the hall by a pipe connected to the city's water conduit. Presumably this water was destined for a *lavatorium*, a place where hands could be washed before and after eating.[98]

References to halls and chambers *together* in the one settlement complex generally date from the late 1200s and early 1300s.[99] The lateness of the chronology is not a sign of a change in pattern but merely reflects the chronology of the surviving document-ation, as well as the fact that most manorial surveys (which provide us with much

96 *CJRI, 1305–7*, p. 345; *CDI, 1302–7*, no. 617.   **97** *The annals of Roger de Hoveden*, trans. H.T. Riley (London, 1853), pp 352–3.   **98** *CDI, 1171–1251*, nos 2612, 2793. In early 1244 building work was suspended and the treasurer was ordered to make sure that the site was 'well covered in, so that it might not be damaged by intemperence of the weather'; the king was keeping money for a campaign in Scotland (*CR, Hen. III, 1242–47*, p. 152) but a few months later he instructed that work recommence and be completed according to the original specifications (*CPR, 1232–47*, p. 428).   **99** An early exception is from 1224 when reference is made to a 'hall, houses and chambers' in the castle at Trim (*CDI, 1171–1251*, nos 1176, 1180).

information) were not made until late in the thirteenth century anyway. It is a little
unfortunate that the references do not specify whether or not the halls and chambers
were in separate (either detached or semi-detached) buildings, although there is a strong
case for thinking that they were separate: a distinction would probably not have been
made between them were they not separate, and the architectural evidence from all
over western Europe would support that interpretation. These later references of *c.*1300
are split between castles of the major landowners and manorial residences of the non-
castle-owning higher tenantry. Indicative of that documentary evidence are the
following five examples.

- 1282:   payments for locks for 'the *hall*, chapel, *chamber* and prison' are recorded in
            Drogheda Castle
- 1298–9:   a *hall* 'of pales [timber planks or beams] with an earthen wall and thatched'
            and a *chamber* 'with a cellar built of stone and thatched' are recorded at the
            manor of Inch (Kerry)
- 1307:   'a *hall* constructed of wood covered with wooden shingles, a stone *chamber*,
            a kitchen and other wooden chambers' are recorded in the castle at Callan
- 1321:   'the *hall* [and] the lord's *chamber*' of *Corcomohide* Castle are recorded as 'badly
            roofed' and had neither doors nor locks
- 1333:   'an old castle surrounded by a stone wall … [in which are] ruinous buildings,
            a *hall*, a *chamber*, a kitchen and other houses' is recorded at Ballintober.[100]

We should not presume that the functions of the halls in castles such as Drogheda,
Callan, *Corcomohide* and Ballintober, all major centres of power, differed significantly
from those of castles and settlements of lower rank (such as Inch). Halls for communal
gatherings, especially of a prandial nature, were needed in all residences, regardless of
rank. Moreover, even minor estates needed administration, and therefore needed places
where business could be transacted with some public transparency. A fascinating story
from the manor of Culmullin in 1288 casts a bright light on how even low-level
political power – the power simply to administer an estate – was invested symbolically
in the physical presence of a hall: Thomas Leon, on the verge of death, had himself
carried (from his chamber?) to the door of his manorial hall, where 'he took [hold of]
the ring of the door' and announced publically his grant to Geoffrey, his son, of the
manor appurtenances.[101] Here, the hall – indeed, the hall's door handle – stood as a
proxy for the entire estate.

There is a common pattern in the references to co-existent halls and chambers in
the late 1200s and early 1300s: there is a single main chamber and a single hall, and the
latter is always mentioned first. This pattern obviously reflects the hall's greater
importance in the public role of a settlement, whether or not that settlement was

---

100 *CDI, 1293–1301*, no. 551 (Inch); *CDI, 1302–7*, no. 659 (Callan); *CIPM*, 6, pp 160–2
(*Corcomohide*; this can be identified as the unnamed castle in Castletown Conyers townland in
Limerick); H.T. Knox, 'Occupation of Connaught by the Anglo-Normans after AD1237
(continued)', *JRSAI*, 33 (1903), 58–74 at 59 (Ballintober); *36 RDKPRI*, p. 66 (Drogheda).
101 *CDI, 1285–92*, no. 453.

encastellated. It might even reflect the fact that by the end of the thirteenth century the hall was often the more recent and therefore perhaps the more stylistically 'modern' building: there is archaeological evidence (as at Adare and Trim) and historical evidence (as at Rindown and Newcastle McKynegan)[102] of new halls being built (presumably to replace older halls) in castles in the second half of the thirteenth century. Where a material is specified in references such as those given above, the chamber was always of stone whereas the hall could be of timber or stone. Status may have been a determinant of material: the halls of major castles such as Carlow, Dublin and Rindown were certainly stone-built. In many of the documented cases above, and others not listed here, the chamber was probably the upper room in a stone tower; that at Inch, revealingly, had a vaulted room ('a cellar built of stone') under its upper storey, signifying a chamber above a basement. No distinctions are ever made in the documentary references between great chambers, the spaces to which lords and ladies retired with their inner circles having been in the halls, and inner-chambers, spaces of greater personal isolation.

There are references in which mention is made only of the hall or the chamber. At Forth (Castlemore), for example, a stone chamber was documented in the manorial settlement in 1307,[103] but there is no reference to the hall that must surely have accompanied it. By contrast, in the enclosure of the manor of *Fermail*, also in 1307, there was a 'hall constructed with a stone wall and covered with wooden shingles',[104] but no record of an accompanying chamber. There are also cases in which neither the hall nor the chamber is mentioned specifically but other words are used instead: in the manorial enclosure at Ballysax in 1306–7, for example, there was a tower (*turra*) 'in bad condition and ruinous, and a small wooden grange covered with straw ... '.[105] It is tempting to interpret *turra* (or *turris*, more properly) as the chamber, and to presume that the hall, of timber, was at very least too decayed to be mentioned.

DESIGN OPTIONS FOR HALLS AND CHAMBERS

Now we can turn to the physical evidence. It is possible to identify three major options available to thirteenth-century castle builders for the containment of halls and chambers. They are presented in the following sections. In presenting these options, I must stress that this is not a watertight reconstruction of how the builders perceived 'public' and 'private' spaces and gave them fixed architectural expression: the buildings grouped here under one option heading are not necessarily related to each other but simply cohere conceptually to some degree, reflecting an idea that circulated in castle-building society. Also, the functional/structural boundaries between halls and chambers within each of the three options, and indeed the boundaries between the

102 For Rindown, see *CDI, 1293–1301*, no. 456 and S. Harbison, 'Rindown Castle: a royal fortress in Co. Roscommon', *JGAHS*, 47 (1995), 138–48; for Newcastle, see *36 RDKPRI*, p. 53; *38 RDKPRI*, p. 47. 103 *CJRI, 1305–7*, p. 346 ('a stone chamber covered with shingles and boards'); *CDI, 1302–7*, no. 617 ('a chamber of stones and lathes roofed with planks'). 104 *CDI, 1302–7*, no. 670. 105 Ibid., no. 617.

options themselves, were fluid rather than fixed. This is a critical point. Architectural distinctions between spaces in which public performances were rendered somewhat private by restrictions on entry, and ones intended to be private but not intimately so, are not always obvious to us, and might not have been made obvious by the castle builders themselves. Architectural space is, after all, not in itself intrinsically public or private but is made public or private by the ways in which it is used, and uses can change. So, who can say that legal pleas were never intended to be heard in rooms that functioned most of the time as great chambers, or that doors into the halls that were designed primarily to serve castles' administrative and dining needs were never intended to be sealed off for the exclusive use of the lord and lady? Indeed, in the thirteenth-century recension of the Arthurian legend, *The Death of King Arthur*, the chamber was used for a banquet presided over by Guinevere while the king hosted a banquet in the hall.[106] The point I am making is that we cannot be too dogmatic in interpreting the architecture.

Option 1: the hall-and-chamber donjon

Two buildings in Ireland, the donjons of Trim and Maynooth castles, contained halls and chambers side-by-side at the same floor level. Both were built in the 1170s.[107] The reason we have only two examples is simply that the format went out of fashion: it had been popular for Norman (pre-1154) and early Angevin (1154–c.1180) 'keeps' or donjons in England and France, but was very much on its last legs when the Anglo-Norman invasion of Ireland took place.

The essence of Trim's original design of 1174–80 was a rectangular block with two storeys inside screen walls that rose high above roof level; the donjon that we see today is a product of later heightening. The first-floor level, which was the level of entry, was divided by a screen (later replaced with a wall) into two parts of unequal size (fig. 98). Based on what we know of English castles, the larger one, located immediately inside the entrance, was the hall, while the one further back was the chamber. The latter was really a great chamber in the sense that it offered immediate retreat from the hall, and was warmed by a wall-hearth (the flue of which is typical of its period in being a circular), but it was not a place of great privacy; more intimate space was provided in the donjon's small projecting towers, accessible by spiral stairs.

Maynooth's donjon was also designed as a two-storeyed block, taller externally than it needed to be internally. Its vast first-floor room, entered from outside via a stone fore-building (rather than timber stairs, as at Trim) would have been partitioned longitudinally from the outset; today, the base of a single central pier is the only stonework surviving from a partition, but is unlikely to be original. As at Trim, the rectangular area nearest the entrance can be adjudged the hall, with the great chamber

106 Barthélemy, 'Civilizing the fortress', p. 420.   **107** R. Stalley, 'The Anglo-Norman keep at Trim', *AI*, 6:4 (1992), 16–19; T.E. McNeill, 'Trim Castle: the first three generations', *Archaeological Journal*, 47 (1990), 99–117; Condit, 'Rings of truth at Trim Castle'; K. O'Brien and J. Fenlon, *Trim Castle, Co. Meath* (Dublin, 2002); Hayden, *Trim Castle*; O'Keeffe, 'Trim Castle uncovered'. For Maynooth, see T. O'Keeffe, 'Trim's first cousin: the twelfth-century donjon of Maynooth Castle', *AI*, 27:2 (2013), 26–31.

98 The interior of the donjon of Trim Castle today, looking down into the original hall (where the small models of the original castle are displayed) and at part of the later stone partition that separated it from the original chamber. In the donjon's original late 1170s configuration the outer walls were higher than the roof, as was the case at contemporary Maynooth as well (fig. 93): on the upper part of the wall on the far left a later window embrasure cuts through the inverted-V scar from the original roof of the hall; similar scarring survives from the roof of the chamber.

located behind the partition. Impressive though it was, the Maynooth donjon was not very practical. There were no toilets. There was no provision in the building for accommodation more private than the partitioned-off chamber.

Option 2: the physically detached hall and chamber

The archaeological evidence indicates that most castle builders of the thirteenth century in Ireland preferred, like their contemporaries in England, to detach the hall from the chamber. Because they are detached, we can discuss them separately.

Halls

Although the documentary record suggests that halls were very common originally, even to the extent of being a feature of every castle site, extant examples are relatively few. This presumably reflects the fact that a lot of them were timber-built and perhaps also that those that were actually stone-built were quite thin-walled and therefore susceptible to destruction.

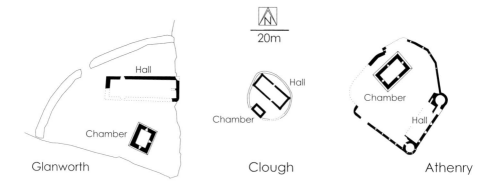

99 Glanworth (*c.*1200 phase), Clough and Athenry castle plans.

The halls were generally single-storey buildings, following the fashion in contemporary Angevin England.[108] Early Anglo-Norman examples standing close to but detached from chamber-towers include the relatively small late twelfth-century example at Carrickfergus, represented now by windows only, the even more fragmentary example suggested at Glanworth and dated by Con Manning to *c.*1200, and the excavated example at Clough, dating from the early thirteenth century.[109] The building flanked by round towers along the side of the enclosure at Athenry Castle has been identified as a great chamber by Tom McNeill, but there is no doubt that it was the castle's (typically ground-floor) hall (fig. 99).[110]

The earliest surviving castle-hall in Ireland must be the western hall at Adare (see fig. 96). Usually dated to *c.*1200, Caitríona Devane's recent translation of the appropriate passage of *An Leabhar Muimhneach* (The Book of Munster) makes clear not only that it was erected before 1194 but that the Anglo-Norman chamber-tower or donjon to its north occupies a site that was also encastellated by a native king.[111] The importance of the Adare evidence cannot be overstated: the physically detached hall and 'castle'/chamber format that we see at this site apparently predates the Anglo-Norman arrival in the district. Did Domnall Mór ua Briain know of the format from his interaction with Anglo-Normans or was it already known in Gaelic-Irish culture?

The greatest of all Irish castle-halls was the 1243 hall of Dublin Castle, already mentioned. Sufficient survives of its model, the archbishop's hall in Canterbury,[112] for

---

108 One possible exception – a first-floor hall – may be the main building of Clonmacnoise Castle. It might even have been built between 1215 and 1221 under Geoffrey de Marisco's guidance as justiciar (*CDI, 1171–1251*, nos 600, 1015). It is dated *c.*1213–16 in K. O'Conor and C. Manning, 'Clonmacnoise Castle', p. 163. **109** McNeill, *Carrickfergus Castle*, pp 53–4; Manning, *Glanworth Castle*, pp 62–4; T.E. McNeill, 'Clough Castle reconsidered' in Manning (ed.), *From ringforts to fortified houses*, pp 41–51. **110** McNeill, *Castles in Ireland*, p. 89. A hall was positioned Athenry-style between two towers, possibly in the third quarter of the thirteenth century, at Dunstaffnage Castle in western Scotland. **111** 'Domnall Mór [ua Briain]… built the Black Castle of Adare and the great hall to the south of the Castle' (Devane, 'The Black Castle of Adare', p. 7). **112** See T. Tatton-Brown, 'The great hall of the Archbishop's Palace'

100 Mid-thirteenth-century Trim Castle hall, viewed from the top of the late twelfth-century donjon.

us to reconstruct in our imagination how it appeared. It would have been three-aisled, with marble piers carrying the arcades.[113] Its 'glazed windows' were probably side-wall windows, set between buttresses. They were probably twin-light windows, and possibly had quatrefoils or cinquefoils above them, as had Canterbury's; examples of such windows can be seen today at Gowran and Bridgetown, and one cannot rule out the possibility that the design diffused in Ireland from the hall in Dublin. The 'great portal' may have been protected by a projecting porch.

Detached castle-halls at Adare and Trim may reflect the influence of the Dublin Castle hall. The former – the eastern hall of that castle (fig. 96) – was aisled, buttressed externally, and entered through a projecting square porch. The hall at Trim was inserted into the corner of the curtain wall (fig. 100) as a replacement for the original Hugh de Lacy hall inside the donjon. A reference of 1224 suggests there may have been an early phase of construction under the patronage of Walter de Lacy,[114] but the structure we see today must be attributed almost in its entirety to Geoffrey de

in N. Coldstream and P. Draper (eds), *Medieval art and architecture at Canterbury before 1200* (Leeds, 1982), pp 112–19.   **113** Late in the thirteenth century the justiciar allegedly made off with 'marble pillars' – presumably the aisle piers, and probably of Purbeck marble – from the great hall of Dublin Castle for use in Dunbrody Abbey (*CDI, 1285–92*, p. 13). The evidence for a basement is a description of 1678 in which it is noted that the hall was 'raised upon severall stately pillars in thye lower part whereof was kepy his Maiesties store' (J.B. Maguire, 'Seventeenth-century plans of Dublin Castle', *JRSAI*, 104 (1974), 5–14 at 10).   **114** *CDI, 1171–1251*, nos 1176, 1180.

Geneville who inherited Trim through marriage in 1254. It had neither external buttresses nor a projecting porch, but it was triple-aisled, which makes it rare in Ireland. Rather than dating to the end of the century, as is the conventional view, it is more likely to be mid-century, if only because de Geneville was active in building activity around that time (founding a Dominican friary in Trim in 1263).[115] He had a close relationship with Henry III, so it is very likely that this hall, internally about 80 by 40 (medieval) feet, was modelled on the longer but similarly aisled hall of Dublin Castle, 120 by 80 (medieval) feet.[116] The so-called Magdalene Tower at the north-west corner of the Trim hall presumably provided accommodation for household officials; de Geneville himself would have availed of the more spacious accommodation within the donjon.[117]

1. Rectangular chamber-towers

Chambers were accommodated within buildings of different shapes but the most common were rectangular. Almost all the surviving examples were two-storeyed originally with the chamber over a basement, and almost all were entered at first-floor level. Readers familiar with the scholarly literature will know that most of the buildings of this design, Ballylusky among them (fig. 101), are now classified as 'hall-houses'. This term is now so deeply embedded in the Irish literature that it requires a brief detour here. Sweetman defined 'hall-houses' as

> two-storey, rectangular-shaped buildings with a first-floor entrance ... They have a defensive ground floor having only slit-opes, while the timbered first floor contained the hall and more open windows ... Because of their lack of defensive features it is possible that they should not be classified as castles. However, since most of them date to the early thirteenth century and are virtually indistin-guishable from hall-keeps they are [acceptable as castles].[118]

The on-line Archaeological Survey of Ireland defines a hall-house as

> a building, usually two storeys high with a first-floor entrance, which leads to *a single undivided chamber/hall* open to the roof and extending the length of the building.[119]

---

115 For the late-century date, see Hayden, *Trim Castle*, p. 2. A mid-century date would also align it with the hall of the late 1230s in Castleroche, so wide that it must have been triple-aisled too.   **116** The discovery of Purbeck marble in the excavation of the Dominican friary founded by de Geneville in Trim (O'Carroll, 'Black Friary, Trim', p. 59) probably underscores his link with the royal house.   **117** To this list of halls can be added the thirteenth-century example excavated on Courthouse Lane in Galway, which had opposed entrances at the low end and secondary external buttresses (D. Delany, 'Courthouse Lane (97E82): excavation' in FitzPatrick, *Archaeological investigations in Galway city*, pp 164–78).   **118** Sweetman, *Medieval castles of Ireland*, p. 80. See also idem, 'The hall-house in Ireland' in Kenyon and O'Conor (eds), *The medieval castle in Ireland and Wales*, pp 121–32.   **119** www.archaeology.ie; italics added. It might be noted that more than half a century ago P.A. Faulkner had used the terms 'upper hall house' and 'end hall house' ('Domestic planning from the twelfth to the fourteenth centuries', *AJ*, 115 (1958),

101 Ballylusky Castle, a typical mid-thirteenth-century two-storeyed chamber-tower. The doorway visible in this photograph at ground level is a later insertion; the original doorway is above and to its far left, close to the corner.

I do not subscribe to the consensus that 'hall-house' is a meaningful category and that its 'discovery' represents a great leap forward for Irish castle studies, and I have spelled out elsewhere problems with its basic conception as well as instances where its attachment to surviving buildings is startlingly misguided.[120] In brief, at best the term confuses, and at worst fundamentally misrepresents, those functional/spatial relation-ships between halls and chambers in the 1200s that we know from written sources in Ireland and from comparative evidence outside Ireland. Alas, it seems that almost no rectangular thirteenth-century focal building can now escape rebranding. Those few that have been spared it are described as 'hall-keeps', with the distinction between a 'hall-house' and 'hall-keep' based on the presence (in the case of the latter) or absence (in the case of the former) of *visible* significant outer defences. This is a very poorly thought-out distinction. As I have pointed out elsewhere, the peak of absurdity is the classification (in the official narrative of Irish castle studies) of the focal building at Athenry (see figs 97, 99) as a 'hall-keep' while the focal buildings of the similarly ranked

150–83), but not to describe buildings like those in Ireland.   **120** T. O'Keeffe, 'Halls, "hall-houses" and tower-houses in medieval Ireland: disentangling the needlessly entangled', *CSGJ*, 27 (2013/14), 300–9; idem, '*Aula* and *camera*: the architecture of public and private lives in medieval Irish castles', *Virtus: Jaarboek Voor Adelsgeschiedenis*, 21 (2014), 11–36.

castles of Dunmore and Moylough in the same county, which are virtually identical to and contemporary with Athenry, are classified as 'hall-houses' because neither has surviving outer defences. Scotland is the only other part of these islands where 'hall-house' is part of the castle studies vocabulary, but Geoffrey Stell has now raised objections to the 'hall-house' identifications there as well, and suggests that the concept's longevity in both places, despite its self-evident problems, can be explained quite simply by scholars on either side of the Irish Sea trusting in mutual delusion each other's certainty that the concept is valid.[121] I expect that attempts will be made to refine the definition of 'hall-house' to deal with criticisms, but what is really needed, and I am hopeful that the next generation of scholars will do it, is the abandonment of the term altogether.

To return to the evidence, the earliest building in this group of chamber-buildings is the donjon of Carrickfergus, built by John de Courcy several years after his arrival in Ulster in 1177 and his installation as its earl.[122] It is a classic example of what used to be called a 'tower keep': it is a tower with four floors, the two upper floors (above the entry-level reception floor) being the private chambers; that at the top – evidently de Courcy's chamber – had a mural gallery (a wall passage) running around it just below roof level. The basement was divided longitudinally in stone from the outset, but the floors higher up may have been divided only by wooden arcades (later replaced by the walls we see today), simply because the structure was too wide for wooden floor-timbers to run from wall to wall. Carrickfergus is in the tradition of the turriform multi-chamber donjons built in England through the middle and later decades of the 1100s; by the time it was built, the format was no longer fashionable for new buildings in England (notwithstanding some late stragglers, including some on the opposite side of the Irish Sea in Cumbria),[123] so its archaic design may have been deliberately intended by de Courcy to give his *caput* at Carrickfergus a whiff of history, of authority more ancient than it was.[124] The audience for such a gesture would have been English or Anglo-Norman: the nuances of architectural design, at least in the late 1100s, were intended to speak to settler-peers rather than to the Gaelic-Irish.

Multi-storeyed rectangular structures like Carrickfergus were not common at all in Anglo-Norman Ireland. Grenan, almost certainly built by 1226 (see pl. II),[125] is perhaps the outstanding example of three-storeyed rectangular chamber-tower or chamber-donjon (or, as we might prefer to call it because of its elongated shape and the likelihood that other structures stood on either side of it, chamber-block). Its ground-floor entrance, facing onto a courtyard originally, leads to a mural stairs that ascends

121 G. Stell, 'Scottish "hall-houses": the origins and development of a castellological concept', *CSGJ*, 28 (2014/15), 134–9. I am very grateful to Dr Stell for sending me a copy of his paper in advance of publication. 122 McNeill, *Carrickfergus Castle*; C. Donnelly, J. Ó Néill, J. McNeill and P. McCooey, 'De Courcy's castle: the first phase of Anglo-Norman building activity at Carrickfergus Castle, County Antrim', *MA*, 49 (2005), 311–17. 123 H. Summerson, *Brougham and Brough castles* (London, 1999); for de Courcy's Cumbrian connections, see S. Duffy, 'The first Ulster plantation: John de Courcy and the men of Cumbria' in Barry, Frame and Simms (eds), *Colony and frontier in medieval Ireland*, pp 1–28. 124 O'Keeffe, 'Angevin lordship and colonial Romanesque in Ireland'. 125 D.M. Waterman, 'Rectangular keeps of the thirteenth century at Grenan (Kilkenny) and Glanworth (Cork)', *JRSAI*, 98 (1968), 67–73.

102 The roll-moulded arch of one of two very large windows in Ballyderown Castle, one of the earliest stone castles of the Anglo-Norman settlement of Munster. Strategically sited in a small block of land between the rivers Funcheon and Araglin (hence the place-name, *Baile idir dhá abhainn*, the place between two rivers) and their confluence with the Blackwater, neither the outworks of the castle nor the settlement that would have accompanied it survives today.

to a big room at first-floor level, itself partitioned into a large space (the great chamber?) and a smaller room (the inner chamber?), with stairs leading off the latter to the now-missing top floor (the bed chamber?). The first-floor room at Grenan has been described as a hall by various writers, and it is certainly more hall-like than the rooms in the same relative position in other rectangular towers, but this cannot have been its function: the access to it (an internal rather than an external stairs) and the presence of a habitable storey above it would be inconsistent with a hall identification in a thirteenth-century Angevin context, and the presence within it of a private chapel (see above, p. 178) rules out that interpretation anyway.

The norm in Ireland up to the end of the thirteenth century if not into the fourteenth (see Kindlestown, discussed below (pp 263–4)) seems to have been what Pamela Marshall describes as the single-chamber donjon, composed of one room over a basement,[126] although some of the Irish examples – those without obvious countersunk roofs – may have had small attic rooms as well. There are two early examples in north Cork. Ballyderown, attributable to Robert de Caunteton who was granted an extensive district in east Cork in the 1180s,[127] is the more ambiguous building of the two, in that its architecture has a grandeur that one rarely finds outside halls. The

126 'The great tower as residence', p. 31. **127** O'Keeffe, 'An early Anglo-Norman castle at Ballyderown'; P. MacCotter, 'The sub-infeudation and descent of the Fitzstephen/Carew moiety of Desmond, pt II', *JCHAS*, 102 (1997), 89–106 at 90.

103 Tomdeely Castle. This exceptional building stands beside a ruined thirteenth-century church within a small settlement complex now comprised of earthen banks and ditches.

building's early dating is secured by the two very large round-arched window frames at first-floor level in one of its three surviving walls. These were roll-moulded externally (fig. 102), a treatment that allows us describe them as Romanesque; we do not know what form the window-openings took because there is no parallel in Ireland (nor any obvious exact parallel outside Ireland), but the likelihood is that there were deeply recessed round-arched twin-lights, possibly with a tympanum above each.[128] Smaller and much plainer, and more typical than Ballyderown of the chamber-donjons that appeared during the 1200s, is the example at Glanworth, dated by Manning to *c*.1200.[129] It had a habitable room (with an outside entrance) above a poorly lit basement. Even with its small attic room, it is a classic example of what has been described as the 'seigneurial minimum'.[130]

Two-storeyed chamber-donjons like Glanworth are found in those parts of Munster that were settled during King John's reign, as at Adare and Mullinahone, and are especially common in Connacht, settled after 1235 by castle-building Anglo-Norman

128 McNeill's implied criticism of the early date assigned to Ballyderown (*Castles in Ireland*, p. 238) is, frankly, perverse: Ballyderown is one of the few Anglo-Norman castles in Ireland with architectural details that are capable of fairly exact dating.   **129** Manning, *Glanworth Castle*, p. 140. **130** G. Meirion-Jones and J.R. Pilcher, 'The seigneurial domestic buildings of Brittany, 1000–1700' in Meirion-Jones and Jones (eds), *Manorial domestic buildings*, pp 158–91 at p. 176.

lords who were already domiciled elsewhere on the island, almost exclusively in Munster and Leinster.[131] In some Connacht examples such as Athenry and Dunmore, both built between 1235 and 1240, the outer walls rose high above the inner roofs, disguising the fact that these were, like the donjons of Trim and Maynooth before them, actually low buildings internally. The towers located on the east side of the Lough Corrib and clustered in south Mayo lack this characteristic. General similarities between them and their close proximity to each other suggests a common team of masons working in the area.

Much more work needs to be done on specific family links that may explain similarities between the Connacht towers and those elsewhere in Ireland. For example, widely chamfered external corners are unique to one Limerick castle, Tomdeely (fig. 103), located on episcopal land and presumably therefore an episcopal castle,[132] one Tipperary castle, Clohaskin,[133] and three Mayo castles, Shrule, built by 1244, possibly by Matthew fitzGriffin,[134] and Ballycurrin and Castlemagarret (both undocumented to my knowledge, but contemporary with Shrule). There must be a connection.[135] Moreover, evidence of internal partitioning at first-floor level at both Tomdeely and Castlemagarret (presumably between a great chamber and inner chamber in each case), reinforces the sense of a connection. Future research should aim to explain such connections.

2. Cylindrical chamber-donjons

The great tower of cylindrical design became moderately popular in Angevin culture around 1200, ironically at the very time that the chamber-tower in general was going out of fashion in England. A novel design of the 1100s in France, right at the end of that century it caught the imagination of the French king, Philip Augustus, and it was his adoption of it, exemplified by the donjon at the heart of the Louvre in Paris, that inspired the Angevin towers. Ironically again, the type's transmission to the Angevin world was at precisely the time that Normandy was being lost by the Angevin king, John, to Philip. Among the various donjon shapes with which French builders up to and including Philip Augustus were experimenting in the twelfth century, the plain cylinder was perhaps the least equipped for comfortable living, but there is an argument that part of its attraction was an iconographic link with the architecture of the Holy Land from which the first cohort of crusaders had returned at the end of the eleventh century.[136] In any case, it looked new and dramatic, and it was presumably this drama rather than any iconography that made it so appealing to the Angevins.

---

131 H. Perros, 'Anglo-Norman settlement in Connacht in the thirteenth century', *Group for the Study of Irish Historic Settlement Newsletter*, 7 (1996/7), 1–6. There is one pre-1235 example: Castlekirke (*Caislen-na-Circe*) was built with Anglo-Norman know-how by Áed, son of Ruaidrí Ua Conchobhair, to whom Richard de Burgh restored the kingship of Connacht in 1232 (*AC*, 1232.4; the name Castlekirke was used in 1225 (*AC*, 1225.17) suggesting an older fortress on the site). **132** J. McCaffrey (ed.), *The Black Book of Limerick* (Dublin, 1907), passim. **133** C. O'Brien, 'A 13th-century hall house at Clohaskin, Co. Tipperary', *NMAJ*, 35 (1993), 104–6. **134** Perros, 'Anglo-Norman settlement in Connacht', p. 5 n. 4. **135** The form is very rare outside Ireland: the only non-Irish parallel I know for chamfers of this width is in a square tower in Dirleton Castle in Scotland, dating to the 1220s. **136** Discussed in O'Keeffe, 'Dublin

104 The donjon of Mocollop. The thirteenth-century parts of the castle, including the gate tower in the foreground, were built in sandstone, and the later work, mainly confined to the upper half of the donjon, was built in limestone (T. O'Keeffe and D. Whelan, 'A little-known Anglo-Norman castle of the first rank: Mocollop, Co. Waterford' in B. Murtagh (ed.), *Castles and defences in Ireland and abroad: essays in honour of David Newman Johnson* (Dublin, forthcoming)).

Outside France, the cylindrical donjon is found most frequently in Ireland and south Wales, two regions in these islands where new castles were being built around 1200. The first example of a cylindrical donjon to have been built in Ireland was probably in Dublin Castle. The mandate of 1204, discussed earlier (p. 191), almost certainly relates to one of the corner towers of the castle; the remainder of the enclosure and the other towers were added in the subsequent couple of decades. Although Manning identifies the Bermingham Tower as the likely donjon, I think that the Record Tower, for which he has produced a definitive account,[137] is a far better candidate: its position relative to the other towers of the castle and to Dublin's town wall strongly suggests that it is primary, and its size and internal lay-out resemble other such donjons outside Ireland.[138]

Calculating the number of examples of cylindrical donjons in Ireland is somewhat problematic. The undisputed examples apart from Dublin are Cloughoughter, Dundrum (Down), Dunmore, Inchiquin, Kilkenny, Mocollop (fig. 104), Nenagh and Waterford,[139] all of which are simple cylinders, and Ardfinnan and Dungarvan (both

Castle's donjon in context', p. 294.   **137** C. Manning, 'The Record Tower, Dublin Castle' in Kenyon and O'Conor (eds), *The medieval castle in Ireland and Wales*, pp 72–95.   **138** O'Keeffe, 'Dublin Castle's donjon in context'.   **139** 'Reginald's Tower' is the donjon of the royal castle

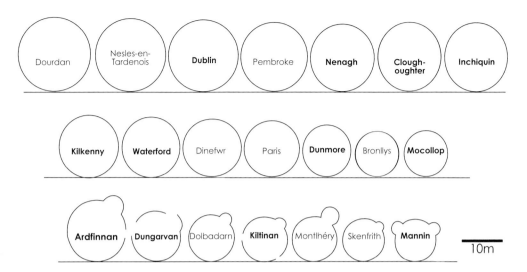

105 Outline plans of some Irish cylindrical donjons and some Welsh and French parallels.

royal), Kiltinan and Mannin Lough, all of which have, in common with some French and Anglo-Welsh examples, small projecting turrets (fig. 105). If Dublin is the earliest (followed within a decade by Kilkenny and Nenagh), the latest is probably Mannin Lough, the only known example in Connacht; now very fragmentary, this Munster-style castle was almost certainly built around 1140 by a Munster-born Geraldine, John fitzThomas.[140] Some other towers, like Parkavonear, associated with the important ecclesiastical site of Aghadoe nearby, are regarded as thirteenth-century not because of the architectural features that they possess but because they lack the features that would signal a later medieval date. Some, like Derrinlaur and Low's Castle, are possible (maybe probable in the case of the former) examples, substantially altered (if not built entirely) in the late Middle Ages. And some are so fragmentary, such as Latteragh, that excavation is needed to establish their girth, not to mention their date.

Especially problematic in terms of identification are those thirteenth-century cylindrical towers that are attached to curtain walls and are a little too big or elaborate to be mere corner towers but are not distinctively big enough to be automatic choices as examples of donjons. Two, Buttevant and Arklow, illustrate this particular problem. There is one surviving thirteenth-century circular tower at Buttevant, disguised by later alteration (pl. IX).[141] Was it a mere corner tower (albeit a large one) of a large enclosure, or did it serve as a donjon? The likelihood is the latter, but without excavation of the site one could not rule out the possibility that it was one of two towers (the other one replaced by a nineteenth-century imitation) in a castle enclosure

of Waterford mentioned in 1215 (*CDI, 1171–1251*, no. 584).   **140** For the history, see Orpen, *Ireland under the Normans*, iii, pp 202–3. The fragmentary remains at Mannin include a small hall, represented only by a grassy foundation.   **141** E. Cotter, 'The archaeology of medieval

106 Arklow Castle as illustrated in Francis Grose, *Antiquities of Ireland* (London, 1786).

of the same design as, say, Brittas or Clonamicklon (see below, pp 245–6).[142] Ruined and overgrown, the tower at Arklow is very difficult to interpret today. Its small diameter strongly suggests that it was simply a corner tower, and that is the best judgment of it, but some doubt is raised by antiquarian drawings (fig. 106) that show a high base batter, two habitable upper square-plan floors above it, and the base of a machicolated latrine of a type that we see at Nenagh (which was, like Arklow, a Butler castle). These are features that suggest that it was a donjon.[143]

3. Polygonal chamber-donjons

Polygonal or multi-sided donjons were much less common than cylindrical donjons in these islands. There are only three certain examples in Ireland: Castleknock, Athlone and Shanid. There is no direct historical link between them. All three are cousins of the late twelfth-century donjons of similar plan in France and England. Castleknock is late twelfth century and can be attributed to Hugh Tyrel who was granted the district by charters issued by both Hugh de Lacy and Henry II in the 1170s. Less than one-third of its donjon survives at one end of an oval walled enclosure on the summit of an enormous earthwork, identified convincingly as the late prehistoric *Cnucha*,

Buttevant' in Cotter, *Buttevant*, pp 1–18 at pp 8–9.   **142** The same questions might be asked of the surviving thirteenth-century cylindrical tower at Leixlip.   **143** The problem of distinguishing between big corner towers and donjons is not unique to Ireland: see R. Avent, *Laugharne Castle* (Cardiff, 1995), pp 34–6.

107 Athlone Castle donjon. Only the lower part of this building is original.

mentioned in the *Dindshenachas* poems.[144] The date of Athlone – a royal donjon (fig. 107) – is uncertain. It can be no earlier than 1210, the year in which the building of a castle *in stone* is recorded,[145] and probably post-dates by a few years the documented collapse in 1211 of a stone tower (mentioned above, p. 197), possibly an original donjon. Unfortunately, most of this important structure was rebuilt in the nineteenth century. The third example, Shanid, was probably built by Thomas fitzMaurice between 1204 and 1213.[146] It sits spectacularly on a motte but is (or, rather, was) itself a very modest building, a mere two storeys in height. Finally, mention should be made of one other possible and slightly unusual thirteenth-century polygonal donjon in Limerick: Glenogra. The larger of the two surviving polygonal towers of this major fitzGerald castle, long presumed to be fifteenth century but actually thirteenth century, is large enough to have operated as a donjon.[147]

144 Michael Herity was the first to identify the earthwork as late prehistoric ('Motes and mounds at royal sites in Ireland', *JRSAI*, 123 (1993), 127–51 at 143–4).   **145** *ALC*, 1210. **146** K. Nicholls and P. MacCotter attribute Shanid to his son John fitzThomas and indicate a date around the 1220s ('Feudal warlords: the knights of Glencorbry' in T. Donovan (ed.), *The knights of Glin: seven centuries of change* (Glin, 2009), pp 48–79 at p. 51) but this might be a bit late for its design. See also G.H. Orpen, 'Notes on some County Limerick castles', *JRSAI*, 39 (1909), 30–41 at 34–9.   **147** It is discussed and illustrated in T. O'Keeffe, 'Further thoughts on Richard de Burgh's castle at Sligo' in M.A. Timoney (ed.), *Dedicated to Sligo: thirty-four essays on Sligo's past*

108 Carlow Castle as illustrated in Francis Grose, *Antiquities of Ireland* (London, 1786) a few decades before half of the structure was blown up.

4. Corner-towered donjons

There is one final group of thirteenth-century buildings to consider: the so-called 'towered keeps', first described by Leask in his *Irish castles*. These are rectangular blocks with cylindrical corner towers. Leask placed four standing buildings in this group, Carlow (fig. 108), Lea, Ferns and Terryglass, but identified also one lost example, Wexford.[148] He also suggested that the design was a uniquely Irish invention, noting that towers of similar design elsewhere were later, but he was not aware of late twelfth-century French donjons of comparable design.[149] Moreover, the group is not as homogenous as he suggested; indeed, one might suggest that the castles do not constitute a coherent group at all: Carlow and Lea are of similar plan-type, but Ferns has a larger and more irregular central block, while Terryglass is distinguished by corner towers of different sizes.[150]

(Sligo, 2013), pp 103–6 at p. 106.   **148** For the possibility that Tullow Castle was another, see T. O'Keeffe, 'The castle of Tullow, Co. Kildare', *JKAS*, 16:5 (1985), 528–9. The towers in Delvin and Enniscorthy are similar in plan but late medieval in date.   **149** Idem, 'The archaeology of Norman castles in Ireland: pt 1'.   **150** K. O'Conor, 'The origins of Carlow Castle', *AI*, 11:3 (1997), 13–16; idem, 'Anglo-Norman castles in County Laois' in P.G. Lane and W. Nolan (eds), *Laois: history and society* (Dublin, 1999), pp 183–212; O'Keeffe and Coughlan, 'The chronology and formal affinities of the Ferns donjon'; H.G. Leask, 'Terryglass Castle, Co. Tipperary', *JRSAI*, 73 (1943), 141–4.

109 The interior of Ferns donjon. The trefoil-headed windows and the loops with oillets are typically post-1250. The 'hooded' fireplace – a type characterized by a canopy over a lintel that is supported by corbels or pillars – is also a common later thirteenth-century type although there is an earlier example in Coonagh Castle (*c*.1225).

Carlow is, as Leask suggested, the earliest donjon with corner towers in Ireland. There is no documented date of construction but it is probably the work of William Marshal in the second decade of the 1200s, and, like his other major castle in Leinster, Kilkenny, reflected his familiarity with castle building in France. It had two storeys over its basement, with entry at first-floor level and a straight inter-mural stairs connecting the two upper levels. The positions of its machicolated latrines and of the stairs linking the two floors suggest that the interior was fairly private. Lea, probably of mid-thirteenth-century date, has a donjon of similar plan, but it rose a storey higher and had a better illuminated interior. Its first-floor room may have been for reception; its two upper-floor rooms provided accommodation. Ferns was probably built just after the mid-century point by William de Valence, the half-brother of Henry III. It had two storeys over its basement (fig. 109). Its irregular shape raises the possibility that it was not a single roofed-over space but had rooms arranged around a central light-well. It is not inconceivable that its principal first-floor room was actually a proper hall; it is, after all, a building that does not follow the rules of other donjons. Terryglass, a Butler castle, is too featureless for precise dating. Its original entrance was in the same relative position as the entrances into the donjons of Carlow and Lea. The contrasting sizes of the corner towers suggest some functional distinction between the north and south ends of the donjon; the north end may have had a reception room at first-floor level, with the chamber beyond it to the south.

Option 3: the hall-and-chamber block

The essence of this design-option is the placement of the chamber and hall side-to-end, with the *side* of the chamber behind or beyond the dais at one *end* of the hall. This, like option 1 above, was well established in Norman and Angevin England, but, unlike it, was still very popular after 1200. Such 'hall-and-chamber blocks' form a very heterogeneous group in Anglo-Norman Ireland. Some examples are shown in fig. 110. All are regarded as 'castles' (or parts of 'castles') but the format was by no means exclusive to such high-status contexts. The physical attachment of the chamber to the hall might be an indicator that the halls in these contexts were rather less public than those that were detached from chambers.

The earliest example, Dunamase, is the only one in which the hall and chamber are contained side-to-end in a building deserving to be described as a donjon. Probably built by Geoffrey de Constantin or Meyler fitzHenry in the 1170s or 1180s, this large building seems to have been divided into a lower-floor hall (perhaps above a low or demi-basement) and a two-storeyed chamber.[151] There appears to have been no other significant accommodation in the castle, so the lower storey of the chamber was probably the great chamber and the upper storey the solar or inner chamber. Dunamase was a free-standing structure; in other words, there was no other building attached to it. Such free-standing hall-and-chamber blocks are not that common in Ireland. Greencastle (Down), constructed between 1226 and 1242,[152] should possibly be included as an example, but it is by no means an unambiguous building. Here, one end of the first-floor room was clearly partitioned off, apparently to create a hall with, at one end, a small space of private lordly retreat, complete with a corner latrine. The

151 B. Hodkinson, 'A summary of recent work at the Rock of Dunamase, Co. Laois' in Kenyon and O'Conor (eds), *The medieval castle in Ireland and Wales*, pp 32–49; see also K. O'Conor, 'Dunamase Castle', *JIA*, 7 (1996), 97–115.   **152** McNeill, *Castles in Ireland*, p. 88.

closest parallel for Greencastle is Grosmont in Wales, dated to the first decade of the thirteenth century and described in the literature as a 'hall block'.[153] A chamber appears to have been provided (within a couple of decades?) in the curtain wall at Greencastle, thus enlarging the private space available to the lord. A very fine hall-and-chamber block stands in the outer ward of Askeaton Castle. Its two-storeyed chamber tower (now much-reduced) did not provide the sole accommodation in the castle: rather, it seems certain that a more private place of retreat, an inner chamber, was provided in a tower on the rocky outcrop in the centre of the small island on which the castle stands. The hall in Askeaton was on the ground floor but refurbishment gave it a first-floor hall in the fifteenth century, leaving insufficient thirteenth-century fabric for us to date with any accuracy. But a pre-1250 date is likely. There seems to have been a similar structure in Carrigogunnel Castle, a native Irish castle in the same region, but identification and dating are rendered difficult by the poor condition of the remains. Another hall-and-chamber block of similar size to Askeaton, but with a more elevated hall originally, was built against the curtain wall of the royal castle in Limerick, possibly in 1230.[154] Other possible free-standing examples of hall-and-chamber blocks containing (possible) first-floor halls are Kilfinny Castle (pre-1250?) and Kilmacduagh's supposed episcopal residence (post-1250?). Perhaps the most interesting pre-1250 hall-and-chamber block in Ireland is at Castleroche. The chamber was in the gate building, which was the first major stone structure to have been built on the site. The first-floor hall, above a low but fenestrated basement, seems to have been built a little later, but only by a few years, and in an apparent after-thought was connected to the gate building by a passage. The end result, achieved before 1240 in all probability, was a hall-and-chamber block of unusual plan.[155]

There are some very interesting hall-and-chamber blocks surviving from the end of the thirteenth century in south-east Ireland. Rathumney, possibly built between 1280 and 1300, had a central (and relatively short) ground-floor hall flanked by a two-storey chamber with a latrine turret at one end and, separated originally by a cross-passage, a service tower at the other end (fig. 111).[156] The design has closer parallels in English manorial architecture below the level of the castle than it has in castle architecture in either of the two islands,[157] so it seems best to regard it as a rare survival of a high-status freehold residence. Clonmore's block, which was of higher social rank, is trickier to make sense of, largely because the block is part of a large castle that was

---

153 J. Knight, *The three castles* (Cardiff, 1991), pp 16–19.   **154** The pipe roll for Henry III records that 'a *chamber* was constructed in Limerick Castle' in 1230 (see G.H. Orpen, 'Motes and Norman castles in Ireland (cont.)', *EHR*, 22:87 (1907), 440–67 at 447 n. 189).   **155** O'Keeffe, 'Roesia de Verdun and the building of Castleroche'.   **156** For an accurate plan and interpretation of its use of space, see O'Callaghan, 'Fortified houses, south Wexford', pp 3–5.   **157** Anthony Emery has recorded many examples in his invaluable three-volume *Greater medieval houses of England and Wales, 1300–1500* (Cambridge, 1996–2006). In East Anglia, for example, Weeting has a late twelfth-century ground-floor hall with a two-storeyed service tower at one end and a three-storeyed residential tower with a projecting garderobe turret at the other end, and this template, which is the template for Rathumney, survived to the start of the sixteenth century (see idem, II: *East Anglia, central England and Wales*, pp 22, 103).

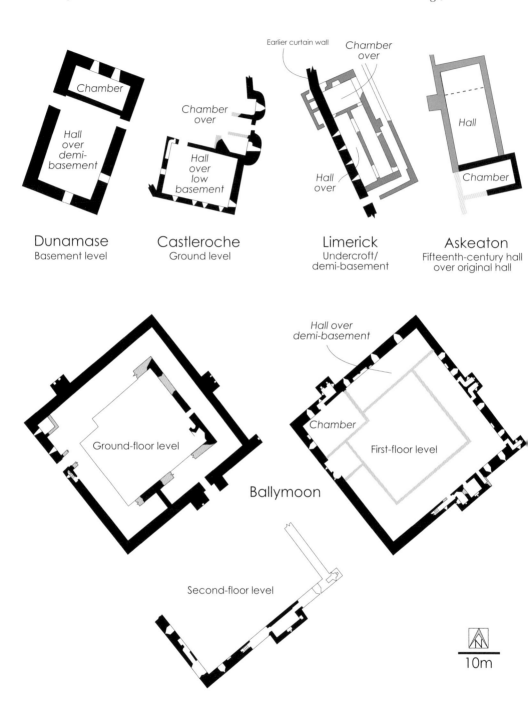

110 Some Irish hall-and-chamber blocks.

111 The interior of Rathumney. The partition walls between the ground-floor hall and the towers at either end of this long building are now missing, but the sites of the towers can be determined from the corbels that supported their first-floor levels.

built in a series of phases with short intervals between them. There is some uncertainty concerning its sequence and function, but (contrary even to some of the hints in the stonework itself) the whole castle could have started life as a single pre-1280 hall-and-chamber block, the hall being (unusually) at first-floor level, with a larger courtyard and other buildings added to it in the succeeding decades to create the large castle that we see today. In the same county, finally, is Ballymoon, one of most remarkable of all the buildings in Ireland. One of the must-see buildings in this book, it is worth a more extensive discussion here.[158]

Ballymoon's overall design (see fig. 110) is utterly unique in Ireland, and it has moderately close but no exact contemporary parallels outside Ireland. It is a near-square enclosure castle with all the rooms arranged suite-like around a courtyard. The continuous outer wall survives intact, but the inner wall is represented by isolated chunks of masonry. There are traces of a few stone partitions between the inner and outer walls, and clearance of the castle's interior by archaeological excavation would tell us if there were more or if many of the partitions were of timber (pl. X). Most of

---

158 The most recent discussions are O'Keeffe, 'Ballyloughan, Ballymoon and Clonmore' and idem, 'Discovering Versailles in the smallness of my own experience' in J. Fenwick (ed.), *Lost and found* (Bray, 2003), pp 213–24.

the rooms appear to have been made the same width in order to conform to the overall plan, and to that extent Ballymoon anticipates what we see in the tower-houses of the 1400s. There are some irregularly positioned towers projecting from the exterior and they provide a modicum of flanking defence, but systematically planned defensibility was not a priority for this castle. Among the many remarkable things about Ballymoon is that it was obviously left unfinished; nearly all the walls terminate about the same height, which is not only inconsistent with an act of destruction but is consistent with how large enclosure walls appear to have been built (as one can see at Liscarroll, for example, where the horizontal lines in the masonry represent phases of construction). We can tell from what survives, particularly truncated toilet chutes, that it is actually missing another floor level.

There have been attempts to reconstruct the room-use in this castle. The hall has always been obvious, the principal chamber not. The probability, supported by an analysis of the other sites listed here, is that Ballymoon had a conjoined hall-and-chamber block occupying the full west side of the courtyard (fig. 112). The former was an exceptionally long and narrow room, heated by a massive (and unique in Ireland) double fireplace at the south end, and lit by two high windows along its length. It had a demi-basement. The well-heated south end of the hall was the so-called 'high end', where the dais was positioned. In the corner of the building behind (south of) the hall was the chamber block: a stack of rooms, now two storeys but originally three, including a projecting tower with two side-by-side latrines at first-floor level. Its basement was subdivided in the manner of donjons of many decades earlier (Adare, for example) but it was never vaulted. At first-floor level it served as the great chamber, the space into which the lord and lady retreated after leaving the hall. The more secluded inner chamber may have been in the missing storey above, or it might actually have been on the other side of the gate passage. The location of the kitchen in Ballymoon is more problematic. It should ideally have been planned for the low end of the hall, but the large room nearest to the hall at that end probably provided lodgings for a senior officer of the household.[159] The likelihood is that the kitchen was at the south end of the range opposite the hall. This is not an ideal reconstruction – food would have needed carting across the courtyard to the hall – but it is difficult to see an alternative, and there are, as was noted earlier, parallels across the Irish Sea for kitchens across courtyards from halls.

This extraordinary castle can be dated by its architectural features (pl. X) to the end of the 1200s. Who built (or started to build) it? I have suggested elsewhere that it was planned as an Irish residence for Roger Bigod, the earl of Norfolk who held land in Carlow in the late thirteenth and early fourteenth centuries.[160] Marc Morris, in a detailed study of the Bigod accounts, has noted the record of the building of the castle on the earl's estate at Fennagh, a few miles north-east of Ballymoon, under the direction of one Ralph Gugon, a London master mason who came to Ireland with

---

159 The identification of lodgings on the adjacent and opposite sides of the courtyard is supported by near-contemporary (*c*.1300) evidence in England as at Goodrich and Oakhampton: see D. Renn, *Goodrich Castle* (London, 1993); A. Endacott, *Oakhampton Castle* (London, 2003). **160** O'Keeffe, 'Discovering Versailles'.

112 The chamber (*left*) and hall (*right*) at Ballymoon. The length of the chamber can be judged by the length of the horizontal recess for a floor timber. The position of the wall that closed-off the high end of the hall is marked by some toothing (on the left side of a window and the double-fireplace). There seems to have been a gap between the chamber and hall, suggesting a cross-passage. The hall was above a demi-basement. Oddly, the floor of the hall could hardly have been supported on timbers of the size suggested by the small joist-sockets that survive, which makes one wonder if the floor was held up by (stone?) supports in that demi-basement. Excavation would resolve this and many other problems at Ballymoon.

Roger in 1280–1. In that year the treasurer in Carlow recorded £84 'for the construction of the castle' of Fennagh. Morris suggests that this expenditure relates to Ballymoon.[161] There are three caveats to be entered. First, that amount of money could not have financed the work that we see at Ballymoon: it would have cost much more to bring the castle to even its incomplete state. Indeed, in the field to the north-west of the castle and visible from it is a moated site, which may be the site of an intended hunting lodge attached to a deer park, and that too would have incurred greater expense than is accounted for. Second, there is the antiquarian account in the late 1700s of a big castle in the village of Fennagh itself – 'at Fenagh Church are the ruins of an old castle, which appears to have been well fortified by strong ramparts and a double ditch'[162] – the site of which was almost certainly in the field (now partly built-on) opposite the modern church in the centre of the village. Was this the castle designed

161 M. Morris, *The Bigod earls of Norfolk in the thirteenth century* (Woodbridge, 2005), p. 122.
162 W.W. Seward, 1797, Topographia Hibernica, *or the topography of Ireland, ancient and modern:*

by Gugon? Third, there is another castle of the late 1200s at Ballyloughan, several miles south of Ballymoon and south-west of Fennagh, and probably built by some of the same workforce.[163] If Gugon's castle was not in Fennagh it might have been in Ballyloughan. Whatever the case, we are left to wonder what impact Ballymoon would have had on Irish architectural history had it been completed as planned. Would it have inspired imitators, or would it have remained a spectacular cul-de-sac? It is one of Irish architectural history's greatest 'what ifs'.

ASYMMETRICAL AND SYMMETRICAL CASTLE ENCLOSURES

All of the buildings mentioned above were originally within enclosures, either of stone or of timber. The survival rate of the stone-built enclosures is proportionately rather poor; being relatively thinly walled, their stone has been robbed. But there is also a small number of castles for which all that survives above ground is the enclosure. We will discuss the big later thirteenth-century examples below. McNeill has published a number of sites, Gaelic-Irish and Anglo-Norman, in which the enclosures are small and polygonal and crown earthworks of one type or another. He has suggested that the examples that belonged to the Anglo-Norman community were simple campaign castles, intended for garrisons rather than resident households:[164] Seafin, dated 1252, is the only one in Ireland with structures on its circuit, and it resembles Coity Castle (and possibly also Loughor) in south Wales (fig. 113). Given that they surmount earthworks, it is likely that, as with their comparanda across the Irish Sea, their outlines in stone either reflect the outlines of earlier timber defences or were built *ab initio* as stone translations of familiar timber defence-types. One cannot rule out the possibility that in some cases in Ireland the underlying shapes reflect earlier, pre-Norman monuments, the enclosing elements of which were in timber. After all, Anglo-Norman mottes were sometimes built inside earlier ringforts.[165] Small circular Irish-built cashels (stone forts) on lake-islands in Connacht – Castle Hag is the best-known example – are morphologically similar to the sites recorded by McNeill, but were certainly not campaign castles and were probably not places of last refuge, but were instead places of safe residence. These too can also be paralleled across the Irish Sea: there is a famous cluster of examples dating from the twelfth to the fourteenth centuries in south-west England (Launceston, Restormel and Totnes) but Rothesay Castle, a western Scottish

giving a complete view of the civil and ecclesiastical state of that kingdom ..., n.p.   **163** Indeed, Ballyloughan may also have had a hall-and-chamber block: there is no archaeological evidence, but there is room for a hall about 16 x 8m, possibly of timber, between its gate-building and its south-west corner tower, the latter possessed of a first-floor chamber. In this reconstruction, the hall would be on the left of the entrance, which is the common pattern.   **164** 'Castles and the changing pattern of border conflict in Ireland', *CG*, 17 (2002), 127–33.   **165** The near-circular enclosure around the donjon of Adare Castle also seems to have traced the outline of a ringfort (L. Dunne, 'Adare Castle: raising bridges and raising questions' in Manning (ed.), *From ringforts to fortified houses*, pp 155–70 at p. 169); another Limerick example of the same phenomenon may be the remarkable castle in Lotteragh Upper.

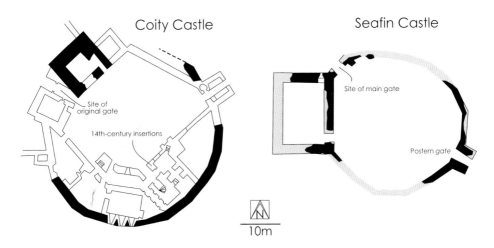

113 Coity and Seafin castles (D.M. Waterman, 'Excavations at Seafin Castle and Ballyroney motte and bailey: the identification of the castle of Magh Cobha in the light of recent research', *UJA*, 18 (1955), 83–104; C.A. Ralegh Radford, *Coity Castle* (Edinburgh, 1976)).

parallel dating from *c.*1200, might be more pertinent in making sense of these Irish enclosures.

Rectangular castle enclosures with squared (or square-towered) corners dating from the thirteenth century are very rare. The earliest *rectilinear* curtain wall design in Ireland must be the west curtain at Trim (through which one enters the castle today). Originally a long screen wall with square towers at the corners and a central gate tower of square plan, it can be assigned to Hugh de Lacy's patronage, probably on his arrival back from military service with the king in 1174.[166] It is a classic late twelfth-century enclosure wall. Not unrelated though a little later is the wall at 'King John's Castle' in Carlingford, not a royal castle at all but another de Lacy castle. Two other examples of different character but no less interest are almost within earshot of each other in Galway: Rathgorgin and Tooloobaunbeg.[167] Located on the demesne land of Richard de Burgh, these *c.*1240(?) enclosures, entered through small square gate towers, were of higher rank than mere curtilages (see above, p. 62) but give us a hint of what such curtilages might have looked like.[168] We might note here also that there is a small group of relatively regular, rectilinear-plan, enclosure-castles crowning prominent rock outcrops in Cork, notably at Kilmaclenine (with no surviving donjon or hall inside), Mogeeley (which has remains of a probable thirteenth-century donjon in one corner)

166 O'Keeffe, 'Trim Castle uncovered'.   **167** G.H. Orpen, 'The mote of Oldcastle and the castle of Rathgorgin', *JGAHS*, 9 (1915–16), 33–44; H.T. Knox, 'Tooloobaun Castle', *JGAHS*, 9 (1915–16), 126–8.   **168** Another possible example is Ballingarry (Tipperary), a big, empty courtyard, with a small two-storeyed gate-house; Caimin O'Brien has recently suggested that it is an early fourteenth-century, Irish-built castle ('The castle in Ballingarry, County Tipperary: a fourteenth-century Gaelic castle?' in Manning (ed.), *From ringforts to fortified Houses*, pp 171–86).

and Ballincollig (presumed to be fifteenth century, like its central tower, but with possible earlier fabric in its enclosure wall).

Castle enclosures with round or U-shaped bastions first appeared in Ireland in the early 1200s, which is about the time that they were being developed overseas. Without question, these enclosures were designed originally to meet military needs. The templates were developed in the later twelfth century outside Ireland, and when the designs were executed by the Anglo-Normans in Ireland it was probably not because they were actually needed in the Irish context but because they represented the fashionable language of fortification. On the whole, the examples in Ireland divide into three groups: a small number of early thirteenth-century examples of high rank, a moderately sized group of mixed-rank examples, mainly from the 1270s to the early 1300s, and a final Connacht-Ulster group, again small in number but of high rank, dating from the 1270s to the first or second decade of the 1300s (fig. 114). These castles were labelled 'keepless' by Leask, but that term has thankfully gone out of fashion: quite aside from the possibility that towers in some of them, especially the earlier ones, were regarded as great towers or donjons in the Middle Ages, it was always absurd that these castles were described according to features that they are believed to have lacked!

The first group has just four examples, three of which – Dublin, Limerick and Kilkenny – were laid out, though not actually finished, between 1204 and 1212. Dublin was the largest. It was the first to see building work (on a donjon – it was not, *pace* Leask, 'keepless') but was not finished until the 1230s.[169] It is difficult to get too excited about this one-time royal castle today, such has been the scale of replacement of medieval walls through the ages, but in the early thirteenth century it was in the vanguard of castle development in north-western Europe; it is worth a visit for that alone. Work must have been well advanced in Dublin by 1211–12 for the crown to have authorized significant expenditure – £733 16s. 11d. on a second royal castle, that of Limerick. Unlike Dublin, this seems not to have had a donjon: the north-eastern tower is the oldest (even if only by a short interval) of the castle's corner towers and is marginally the largest, but its design is not consistent with a donjon identification. No English castle of comparable design (other than Helmsley in Yorkshire, which we can surely rule out) is early enough to have provided the model for either Dublin or Limerick, which makes one wonder if the designer – assuming it to have been the one individual – had worked in France in the last two decades of the twelfth century. One tell-tale sign of French influence is the smallness of the gate towers relative to other towers in both castles. Limerick has two other signifiers of probable French influence: the backs of its two gate towers were built flush with the inside of the curtain walls, and its north-eastern corner tower is set in an angled stretch of curtain wall.[170] Though anonymous, the designer of Dublin and Limerick may well have played a key role in bringing to English attention new French ideas about castle design. These two works, which are his only obvious commissions, are of international interest. The third castle in this group, William Marshal's Kilkenny, was built after 1207 and, like Dublin, had

---

169 The towers were still being built in 1228–9 (*35 RDKPRI*, p. 30).   **170** Respective French parallels include Mez le Maréchal and Goulancourt.

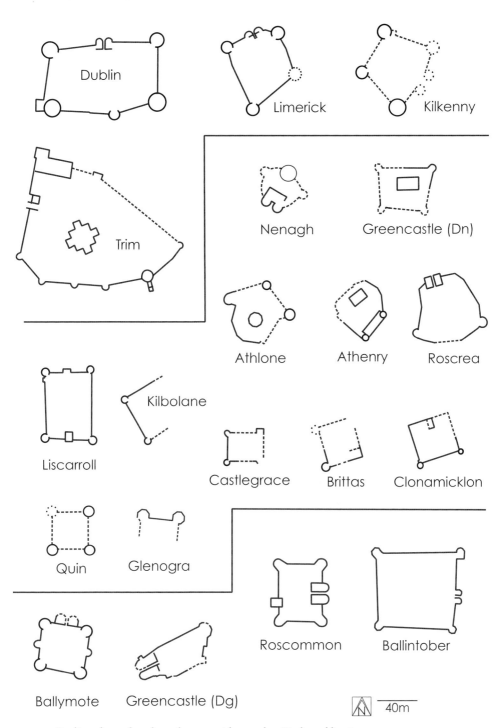

114 Outline plans of castle enclosures with round or U-shaped bastions.

115 The only surviving tower of Brittas Castle.

a corner donjon of cylindrical plan. The castle's overall plan can also be paralleled in France.[171] Geophysical work around the site of the present gate into the castle suggests a gate building of twin-towered type.[172] The final example, the great curving curtain wall added to Trim Castle, probably in the second quarter of the thirteenth century, differs from the others both in its asymmetry and in the uninhabitability of its towers.

171 Saumur, for example.   **172** D. Tietzsch-Tyler, 'Kilkenny Castle', *Castle Studies Group Bulletin*, 13 (2011), 4.

116 One of the two surviving towers of Kilbolane Castle.

Oddly, the completed curtain wall (1174–*c.*1225) did not fully enclose the donjon but merely swung from one end of the riverbank to another, leaving the river to provide the protection in between.

The second group of enclosures is independent of that first group, and represents a new tradition, carried from England. The enclosure at Greencastle (Down) is dated to the mid-1200s by McNeill, which would make it the earliest of the group.[173] Some of the examples are irregular in plan. Athlone Castle had two round towers and a curtain wall built around the perimeter of the late twelfth-century motte by Geoffrey de Geneville in 1273–4.[174] Similarly irregular and only slightly later is the plan of Roscrea.[175] The east side of the enclosure at Athenry, where the hall stretched between two towers, is so similar in scale to Athlone that a similar date might be suggested. There are at least six castles that, if not quite symmetrically planned in each case, do at least have walls meeting at 90° angles. Castlegrace is not dated; it could have been built at any stage in the period 1250–1300. The much-neglected Brittas (fig. 115) is similarly undated, but the provision of a *britagium* for Caherconlish in 1288, if it does indeed refer to this castle (see above, p. 200), suggests that it had recently been completed. Building work started at Quin Castle in 1279 or 1280, and it was probably still in the process of construction when burned down around 1285.[176] The two Cork

173 *Castles in Ireland*, pp 88–91.   **174** *36 RDKPRI*, p. 40.   **175** Manning, *Roscrea Castle*, p. 167. **176** Hodkinson, 'Was Quin Castle completed?'.

117 The entrance front of Clonamicklon Castle. This very important castle has three major phases. The latest phase is late sixteenth century and is represented by the tower-house with its surviving gable and chimney, and by most of the fabric of the corner tower on the right. The middle phase, from the early 1300s, is represented by most of the castle's enclosing wall and by the large tower on the left, to which a domestic wing, possibly a hall-block, was attached. The first phase is represented by the thirteenth-century chamber tower, the thick walls of which are visible to the right of the tower-house that was attached to it.

castles of Kilbolane (fig. 116) and Liscarroll (see pl. VIII) are more or less contemporary with each other – they are the same width and Liscarroll is simply twice the length of Kilbolane – and there are historical pointers to their construction between the later 1260s and mid-1270s.[177] The little-known Clonamicklon, finally, has an enclosure of probable early fourteenth-century date, making it the latest work in this group (fig. 117).[178] The original castle of Dunluce, of which two drum towers survive, is excluded from this list as it appears to have been built *c*.1500.[179]

The third group comprises one major royal castle, Roscommon, and a small number of important baronial castles associated with Richard de Burgh, earl of Ulster. To deal with the latter sites first, Ballymote was built after 1299, Greencastle (Northburgh) was built around 1305, and Ballintober was presumably built around 1300.[180] These are very

177 T. O'Keeffe, 'Liscarroll Castle: a note on its context, function and chronology' in Cotter (ed.), *Buttevant*, pp 51–66.   **178** This castle was associated from the seventeenth century with the Butler viscounts Ikerrin, descended directly from Edmund Butler (*c*.1268–1321), 'chief butler of Ireland' from 1299 (R. Mackay, 'Butler (le Botiller), Edmund', *Dictionary of national biography*). It is probable that he, or his son, John 'of Clonamelchon' (?1306–30), built the enclosure. **179** Breen, *Dunluce Castle*.   **180** D. Sweetman, 'Archaeological excavations at Ballymote Castle, Co. Sligo', *JGAHS*, 40 (1985/6), 114–24; D.M. Waterman, 'Greencastle, Co. Donegal', *UJA*, 21

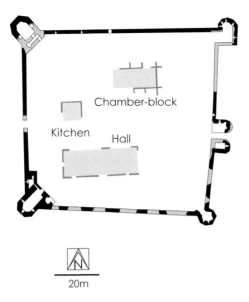

Chamber-block

Kitchen

Hall

20m

118 Ballintober Castle: walled enclosure and internal structures as revealed by geophysical survey. The identifications are conjectural. The identification of the large building as the hall is based mainly on its size but also on its position: it is actually quite common to find medieval halls located, as this building was, on the left side of an enclosure relative to the entrance. The identification of the kitchen is based on its position relative to the supposed hall but also on its shape: kitchens in medieval castles in England are often square. There is no reference to a chapel in 1333, which would tend to rule out that interpretation for the apparently buttressed building. Perhaps marginally too big originally to be a free-standing chamber, it may have been part of a chamber-block (with a great and inner chamber, and perhaps some extra rooms). The buttresses might have been to support an upper floor, but their irregularity leads one to question if they were actually buttresses at all. They may instead be the wall-butts of missing appended structures.

well-known buildings and there is little to add to McNeill's analysis, except in the case of Ballintober where geophysical work has produced very significant results (fig. 118).[181] Traces have been found of some of the buildings – 'a hall, a chamber, a kitchen and other houses' – mentioned in a 1333 inquisition (see p. 216). The manner in which these structures sit inside the curtain wall, not touching it at any point, suggests that they and the enclosure are not of the same date, and both the scale of the enclosure and the wording of the inquisition ('an old castle surrounded by a stone wall') would lead one to think that the stone walls that we see today belong to the later of the two phases. If this interpretation is correct, the claim that the castle was

(1958), 74–88; N. Brady, *Ballintober Castle, County Roscommon*, Roscommon Heritage Poster Series 7 (Roscommon, 2012); McNeill, *Castles in Ireland*, pp 101–3. Richard's now-lost castle in Sligo is discussed in K. O'Conor, 'Sligo Castle' in M. Timoney (ed.), *A celebration of Sligo* (Carrick-on-Shannon, 2002), pp 183–92 and O'Keeffe, 'Further thoughts on Richard de Burgh's castle at Sligo'.   **181** Brady, *Ballintober Castle*.

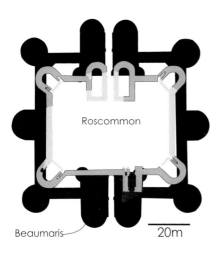

119 Roscommon and Beaumaris plans superimposed. Note how the plan of the former fits almost exactly into the plan of the latter.

specifically 'built to impose [an Anglo-Norman] presence on the O'Conor lands of north Roscommon'[182] must be queried. On the contrary, it seems as if the enclosure walls were intended, rather like a late medieval bawn (see below, p. 265), to protect a settlement already existing, rather than to project power outwards.

Roscommon is the major castle of the group.[183] Built with about £3,500 granted between 1275 and 1285, most of it accounted for in 1277–8, it replaced a recently destroyed royal castle of unknown type which had been erected in 1269–70 at a cost of £98.[184] The symmetry of the castle's design links it to a number of Edward I's world-famous northern Welsh castles, while the plan of its gate building is paralleled fairly closely at Aberystwyth, from Edward's first Welsh building-campaign of 1277, and at Harlech and Beaumaris, from his second campaign, after 1283. Roscommon's closest cousin is the last-named of these, and the metrologies of the two plans suggest they were built according to a common template (fig. 119). The significance of this observation is considerable. Master James of St George, a master mason from south-east France, is celebrated widely as the genius behind the famous second-campaign castles in Wales. But he did not arrive in north Wales until spring or, more likely, early summer 1278,[185] by which time the plan of Roscommon had been laid out. Chronologically, Roscommon stands alongside Rhuddlan (from 1277) as an early expression of Edward's interest in symmetrical castles. Its particular significance resides in the fact that it was the first of his castles to possess a symmetrically quadrangular courtyard with a gate building along one of the curtain walls. The basic design was not new – we saw its use in Dublin fifty-odd years earlier – but earlier versions were not properly symmetrical. The proportions of Roscommon are so close to those of

182 Ibid.   **183** M. Murphy, 'Roscommon Castle: underestimated in terms of location?', *JGAHS*, 55 (2003), 38–49; M. Murphy and K.D. O'Conor, *Roscommon Castle: a visitor's guide* (Boyle, 2008).   **184** McNeill, *Castles in Ireland*, p. 96; *CDI, 1252–84*, no. 891.   **185** N. Coldstream, 'James of St George' in D.M. Williams and J.R. Kenyon (eds), *The impact of the Edwardian castles in Wales* (Oxford, 2010), pp 37–45.

Beaumaris that one must conclude that the classic symmetrical design of Edwardian vintage was first worked out in western Ireland.[186] This is no great surprise – Edward was fighting in Ireland as well as in Wales – but it elevates Roscommon Castle to the status of a building of genuine international importance.

Gate towers and gate buildings, 1170–1300

Points of entry into castle enclosures were always defended, and much attention was paid by medieval master masons to how they should appear visually and work practically. Ireland has an interesting selection of types.

The simplest format is the rectangular tower with a through-passage (fig. 120). Trim Castle's town gate (called Trim Gate) can be attributed to the 1170s.[187] The small tower attached to its north side seems to have contained a prison. Much smaller but not dissimilar is the gate tower of *c*.1220 at Clonmacnoise. Dunamase was provided with a simple rectangular gate tower in the late 1100s, and it was unusual in that, first, its long axis was shared with the line of the curtain wall to which it was attached, and second, its entrance passage was off-centre. In the early 1200s it was replaced by a second tower of the same shape but on a rotated orientation, and this time the entrance passage was flanked by narrow chambers to facilitate bowmen.[188] Roughly contemporary, if not actually late twelfth century, is the scheme at Carlingford.[189] Here two separate square-ended towers, again equipped for bowmen, flanked the passage; it is not clear if this was actually a single building with a central passage, or a proper twin-towered design. The same basic arrangement, albeit executed less boldly, is found in the original early thirteenth-century gate houses of Glanworth (with two prisons in one of the towers) and Cahir, as well as in the late thirteenth-century gate house of Rathnageeragh.[190] The largest and, for its date, the most unusual of the rectangular gate towers is at Roscrea. The lower part, which includes the passage (and has a prison on one side), is possibly of the 1240s, and the upper part is of *c*.1280.[191] Like the first gate tower in Dunamase, its axis is shared with that of the curtain wall attached to it. Simple rectangular towers with through-passages that are not flanked by side-chambers are not so easily dated. The gate tower at Mocollop is probably post-1250.[192] But the two examples at Adare, of which the outer (or main gate) is clearly the product of later alteration, cannot be assigned to any particular stage of the thirteenth century. The

---

186 T. O'Keeffe, 'Landscapes, castles and towns of Edward I in Wales and Ireland: some comparisons and connections', *Landscapes*, 11:1 (2011), 60–72. 187 O'Keeffe, 'Trim Castle uncovered'. Trim's other gate-tower, the famous barbican tower, possibly dates from the 1240s and was modelled on an English design, such as St John's Tower at Dover (J. Goodall, *The English castle* (New Haven and London, 2011), p. 172). 188 Hodkinson, 'Recent work at the Rock of Dunamase'. Dunamase's third gate-tower, a small round-fronted tower into the triangular ward is discussed in T.E. McNeill, 'The outer gate house at Dunamase Castle, Co. Laois', *MA*, 37 (1993), 236–8. 189 The castle is recorded in 1211–12: *IPR, 1211–12*. 190 Manning, *Glanworth Castle*, p. 140; P. Holland, 'The thirteenth-century remains at Cahir Castle', *NMAJ*, 35 (1993–4), 62–71. The date given to Rathnageeragh in T. O'Keeffe, 'Rathnageeragh and Ballyloo: a study of stone castles of probable 14th to early 15th century date in County Carlow', *JRSAI*, 117 (1987), 28–49, is too late. 191 Manning, *Roscrea Castle*, pp 167–8. 192 O'Keeffe and Whelan, 'Mocollop, Co. Waterford'.

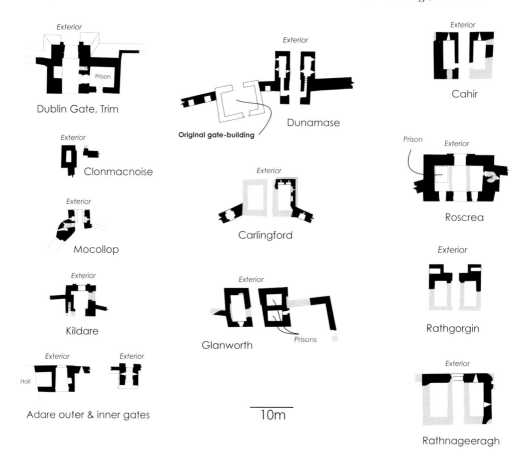

120 Rectangular gate towers and gate buildings, 1170–1300.

gate tower of Kildare Castle, converted into a standard tower-house in the sixteenth century, has two shallow external pilasters on either side of the (now-blocked) passage, and these can be paralleled at Trim (1170s) and Roscrea (1240s). One reason for thinking Kildare is closer in date to Trim than Roscrea is that it was attached by a curtain wall to a motte (now removed), and so was built when the motte still provided the castle's focal point.

The classic gate-building design of the thirteenth century has two near-circular or D-shaped towers flanking a gateway (fig. 121). McNeill suggests that the gate building at Carrickfergus was erected before 1200, which would make it the oldest in Ireland.[193] Not entirely dissimilar, and probably not much younger, are the gate towers at Nenagh.[194] As at Carrickfergus, the towers were near-circular on the outside, and the adjoining curtain walls ran back rather than sideways; the building behind the towers

193 McNeill, 'Carrickfergus Castle', pp 21–5. **194** B. Hodkinson, 'Excavations in the gatehouse of Nenagh Castle', *THJ* (1999), 162–82.

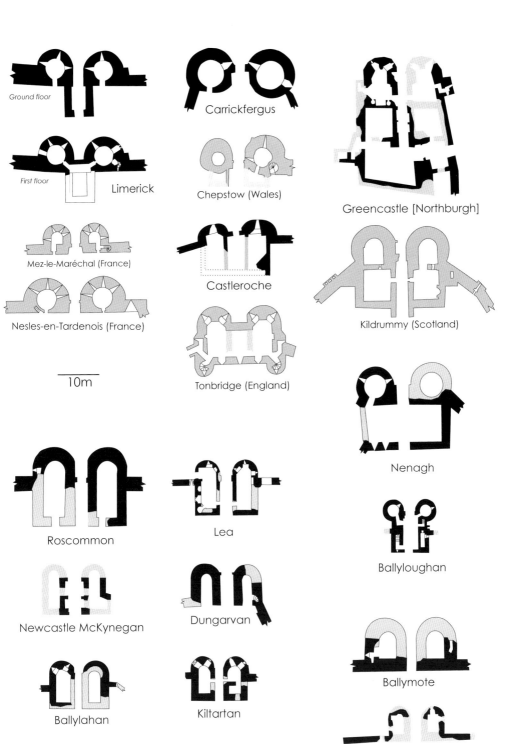

Ground floor

First floor

Limerick

Carrickfergus

Chepstow (Wales)

Greencastle [Northburgh]

Mez-le-Maréchal (France)

Nesles-en-Tardenois (France)

10m

Castleroche

Tonbridge (England)

Kildrummy (Scotland)

Nenagh

Roscommon

Lea

Ballyloughan

Newcastle McKynegan

Dungarvan

Ballylahan

Kiltartan

Ballymote

Ballintober

121 Twin-towered gate buildings.

and sitting over the gate passage seems to be an addition, possibly mid-century (judging by the fragmentary moulded stonework). In the early thirteenth-century gate buildings at Dublin and Limerick (and possibly also the now-missing example in Kilkenny Castle) the rear-walls of the gate towers were flush with the inside of the curtain walls, a feature identified above (p. 242) as indicating influence from France; the scheme was repeated independently at Ballintober and Ballymote at the end of the thirteenth century. Next in sequence chronologically is the gate house of Castleroche, a structure of immense significance.[195] This was under construction in the mid-1230s. That date is interesting. It predates by a few years Henry III's building campaign at the Tower of London, one element of which was the designing of a great twin-towered gate house. That structure does not survive, but it is understood to have inspired a series of other gate houses, of which that at Tonbridge in Kent (from the 1250s) is believed itself to have inspired additional copies.[196] In both the Castleroche and Tonbridge gate houses the towers projecting to the front do not contain separate rooms – they are not *really* towers, in other words – while the first- and second-floor spaces above the passages in both structures provided high-status accommodation. Now, this scheme became very common after the 1250s, and the Irish gate buildings of that date (Ballintober, Ballylahan, Dungarvan, Kiltartan, Lea, Newcastle McKynegan and Roscommon) conform to it, but it was an unusual scheme in the second quarter of the thirteenth century. Earlier than Tonbridge and earlier even than Henry's work at London, Castleroche emerges as a very significant pit-stop in the development of twin-towered gate buildings in these islands. Interestingly (and suggestively), its builder, Roesia de Verdun, was known personally to Henry III, and it was to him that she reported her success in completing Roche's construction in 1236. The latest-dated twin-towered gate building in Ireland, finally, is probably at Greencastle (Northburgh), for which the (now very fragmentary) gate building of the 1280s at Kildrummy in Scotland, probably the work of Master James of St George, may be the closest parallel.[197]

Drawbridges

The gateway was potentially a point of weakness in the defence of a castle or walled town, and one option for additional protection was the installation of a drawbridge, literally a bridge that could be withdrawn to expose a gap, a deep pit or section of

---

195 O'Keeffe, 'Roesia de Verdun and the building of Castleroche'. Recognition of Castleroche's originality as a work of architecture has been compromised, I think, by McNeill's assertion that its design 'must be based on that of Beeston' (*Castles in Ireland*, p. 87), the famous mountain-top castle in Cheshire. Connections between the builders of Roche and Beeston are not disputed, and both castles were even known as *castellum de Rupe* (M.S. Hagger, *The fortunes of a Norman family: the de Verduns in England, Ireland and Wales, 1066–1316* (Dublin, 2001), p. 81) but architecturally they have almost nothing in common.   **196** Goodall, *The English castle*, p. 191. **197** C. Tabraham, *Kildrummy Castle and Glenbuchat Castle* (Edinburgh, 1995), p. 7. Andrew Tierney suggests that the tower-house of Ballyadams began life as a twin-towered gate-building with fourteenth-century Welsh parallels ('Ballyadams, Co. Laois: a remnant of an Anglo-Norman castle in disguise?', *Laois Heritage Society Journal*, 3 (2008), 169–80). Harry Avery's Castle has a twin-towered façade rather like a gate-building but incapable of functioning as one, and is probably late fourteenth century (McNeill, *Castles in Ireland*, pp 163–5).

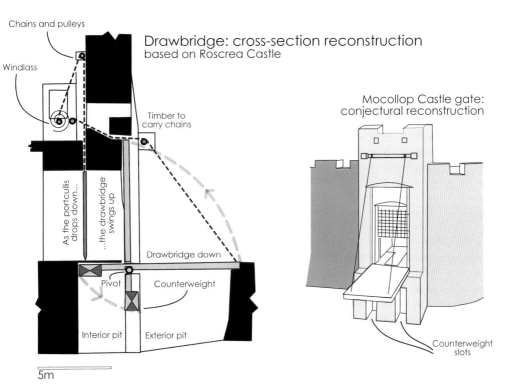

122 Reconstruction of a counterweighted drawbridge.

fosse, in front of the gate. There were two basic ways in which this was effected in the Middle Ages, one involving horizontal forces and the other vertical forces. In the first, the bridge was wheeled back in on rollers (or even sometimes rotated on a horizontal plane). This option appears not to have been taken up very often in Ireland (Lea was a rare exception). In the second, which is attested to more frequently in Ireland, the bridge rotated vertically on a pivot or hinge and was pulled up by chains; as it came up it simultaneously exposed the pit in front of the gate and sealed up the entrance. The chains that pulled up the bridge from high inside the gate tower were usually also connected to the portcullis, an iron-clad wooden grill set in vertical side-wall slots or grooves. As the bridge rose in front of the gateway, the portcullis dropped down behind it to provide a second protective screen. The force needed to pull up the bridge was considerable, so counterweighted beams were attached on the other side of the pivot, so that as the bridge was pulled up by the chains, the counterweights fell under force of gravity into a pit inside the gate; a counterweighted drawbridge thus had two pits, one on the outside, which was protective, and one on the inside solely to accommodate the counterweights. The value of the counterweights was not simply that they allowed the bridge be elevated less effortlessly. The weights of the beams allowed the pulled-up drawbridge achieve proper verticality, which would not have been possible with the chains alone. Slots for the counterweights were normally in the wall underneath the pivot to allow them fall the full 90° (fig. 122).

The best place in Ireland to see how a counterweighted drawbridge of the type described worked is probably Roscrea Castle, where one was installed in the middle or later thirteenth century; there were similar drawbridges at other sites, such as Mocollop, Adare (where there was an inside pit but no slots underneath the pivot) and Dundrum (Dublin).[198] The number of identified medieval drawbridge sites in Ireland is relatively small, but archaeological excavation would certainly increase the number significantly. The Irish examples are mainly thirteenth century, but the evidence of a simple, pulley-operated drawbridge at Bunratty shows that important later medieval castles may have had them as well. It might be noted that while a drawbridge without a portcullis was rare, a portcullis without a drawbridge was not: the survival of portcullis grooves in a medieval gate, in other words, does not necessarily mean that there was also originally a drawbridge. Most castles would have had just the one drawbridge and portcullis, but large fortresses often had several; it is documented that Roscommon Castle had three drawbridges and two portcullises in 1304.[199]

---

198 O'Keeffe and Whelan, 'Mocollop, Co. Waterford'; Dunne, 'Adare Castle'; E. O'Brien, 'Excavations at Dundrum Castle', *AI*, 3:4 (1989), 136–7. Around 1224 there was in Dublin Castle a great chain for 'the bridge turniz' (*CDI, 1171–1251*, no. 1227).   **199** *CDI, 1302–7*, no. 306.

CHAPTER 5

Castles: from the Black Death to the plantations

The preceding chapter paid more attention to identifying the use of space in high medieval castles than it did to the military aspects of their architectural designs. In this chapter we will follow the same theme through the castles of the late Middle Ages, mainly the fifteenth and sixteenth centuries, the period in which tower-houses proliferated. Continuity is the key concept: castles of the 1200s and 1400s – the Black Death (1346–53) is a useful median point, though it has no particular significance in itself – are outwardly very different from each other, but once we strip away the many dissimilarities we can recognize the survival into the late Middle Ages of those templates of architectural design that were created in the thirteenth century.

However, two things did change in castle culture between the end of the 1200s and the early 1400s. First, the right to own a castle (or, more accurately perhaps, the capacity to own a building that would be recognized by contemporaries as a castle) trickled lower down the social hierarchy in English parts of Ireland than it had previously: people whom we do not 'see' in the archaeological record prior to the fifteenth century announce themselves to us through their possession of castles, mainly tower-houses, in the late Middle Ages.[1] Second, the castle, both as a concept of lordly authority and as a physical entity, was as central to elite Gaelic-Irish culture of the late Middle Ages as it was to contemporary 'English' culture; this was even true among those native septs that engaged in periodic redistributions of land, a practice that might seem, on paper anyway, to have militated against serious investment in stone buildings.[2] The Gaelic-Irish castle builders of the late medieval period included brehon lawyers, chroniclers and highly skilled craftsmen, as well as different ranks of lord.[3]

Our understanding of the dynamics of these two changes is handicapped somewhat by an incomplete knowledge of the process of social and cultural change in general during the fourteenth century. This might seem a very surprising statement given how much we know about the fast contraction under Gaelic resurgence (and other

---

1 Money generated in the economic boom of the later 1200s and by enterprising, moat-building, arable farmers during the Edwardian wars may help to explain in part the rise of a new castle-owning gentry in the later 1300s and 1400s. See O'Keeffe, 'Aristocrats, immigrants and entrepreneurs'; idem, 'Landscapes, castles and towns of Edward I'. **2** See H.S. Pawlisch, *Sir John Davies and the conquest of Ireland* (Cambridge, 1985), pp 60–1. The process is discussed in O'Conor, *Medieval rural settlement*. Important case studies feature in A. Tierney, 'Pedigrees in stone? Castles, colonialism and Gaelic-Irish identity from the Middle Ages to the Celtic revival' (PhD, UCD, 2005). **3** The only systematic review of Gaelic-Irish castle-builders is R. Loeber, 'An architectural history of Gaelic castles and settlements, 1370–1600' in P.J. Duffy, D. Edwards and E. FitzPatrick (eds), *Gaelic Ireland: land, lordship and settlement, c.1250–c.1650* (Dublin, 2001),

123 Was the builder of the small tower-house in Carlingford known as 'The Mint' announcing his – it probably was a man – ethnic identity through the use of small 'Irish' motifs, such as interlace, in the decoration of its windows?

processes) of the area of colonial lordship at the end of the 1200s, about the wars between old colonial and old Gaelic-Irish families in the 1300s, and about the attempt by the crown to stop the acculturation of English families via the Statutes of Kilkenny (1366). But what is less clear is how certain cultural practices of the fifteenth century actually emerged from the fourteenth-century crises. It is hardly surprising that those people of Anglo-Norman descent who built new castles in the late Middle Ages were armed with an inherited knowledge of the physical forms that castles could take and of the ways in which castle spaces were used, but it is somewhat more surprising that the new castles of the Gaelic-Irish of the late Middle Ages also reveal for the most part an Anglo-Norman pedigree, not just in their architectural forms but also, even more importantly, in their patterns of usage, their domestic rituals. If, as the old mantra holds, 'the (Anglo-)Normans became more Irish than the Irish themselves', the fact of the adoption of the tower-house in parts of Ireland that remained outside the English lordship suggests that the obverse also holds. This observation should only surprise those who perceive the late Middle Ages as a period of seemingly endless inter-ethnic hostility (fig. 123).

CASTLE BUILDING IN THE LATER MIDDLE AGES

Contrary to what was once believed to be the case, thanks mainly to Leask's book on castles, the fourteenth century in Ireland did not see a cessation of all building activity. However, the rate of construction does seem to have decreased during that period, and most of the building activity was concentrated on churches rather than castles.[4]

pp 271–314.   **4** See T.E. McNeill, 'Church-building in 14th-century Ireland and the "Gaelic Revival"', *JIA*, 3 (1985–6), 61–4.

The building stock that the castle builders of the thirteenth century in Ireland bequeathed to the nobility of the fourteenth century was substantial. Political and societal changes through the 1300s determined how that nobility dealt with this inheritance in the late Middle Ages. The descendants of the old Anglo-Norman families were often content to occupy but make few improvements to the castles they inherited. The donjon of Trim, for example, survived the entire duration of the late Middle Ages more or less the way it was left around 1200, other than a few alterations made at its upper levels around 1300. New vaults over basements (as at Castle Carra, for example), new windows and chimneys (as at Kinlough, for example), new latrine turrets (as at Ballyderown, for example) and new parapets (as at Shrule, for example) were often as far as major structural alteration went in the cases of thirteenth-century focal buildings. It is a moot point whether we should think of buildings so altered as tower-houses (or, more precisely, that we should think that they were 're-imagined' as tower-houses by their late medieval owners). Some Anglo-Norman gate structures were certainly converted physically into tower-houses by the decommissioning of their entrance passages: at Ballyloughan, for example, the relatively small twin-towered gate building had its passage blocked at both ends and it was functionally 'turned around' so that what had been the back in the thirteenth century was the front in the fifteenth.

There may also have been some abandonment of castellated properties during the 1300s by those who had owned several in the 1200s, the motivation being a simple desire to economise. We know that kings, barons, bishops and even minor lords started off-loading properties at the start of the fourteenth century in England, which was a less troubled place than Ireland. Patterns of off-loading of castellated properties in Ireland have yet to be identified, but it is apparent from even a cursory examination of the historical sources that Ireland's stock of castles built by or owned by the crown in the thirteenth century was whittled down in number.[5] The fate of Coonagh is instructive: in 1251, following an unresolved nine-year legal tussle between two parties, the crown took possession of what had been a baronial castle and maintained it as a royal castle, but by the start of the fourteenth century it had been off-loaded to another baron (who off-loaded it as fast as he could). It eventually ended up in Irish hands.[6]

It was not until the fifteenth century, long after the 'feudal age' had passed, that the castle-building industry in Ireland was as buoyant as it had been in the thirteenth century. A small cluster of documentary references to new buildings at the end of the 1300s and the start of the 1400s possibly marks the start of that period of renewed buoyancy (although it must be noted that there are also references around the same time to other castles being attacked and destroyed, which may be evidence that there were far more 'new' castles in the 1300s than we are aware of). Brian Hodkinson has documented an early, pre-1402, urban tower-house in Limerick, demolished in 1696 but known from early maps.[7] Mountgarret, a substantial part of which fell down in 2010, started life as a 'castle of stone crenulated' in 1409.[8] Kilclief (fig. 124) is early

5 An exception is the lost castle in Cashel, established as late as the 1330s (O'Brien, 'Royal constables of Cashel Castle'). 6 O'Keeffe, 'The donjon of Coonagh Castle'. 7 'Thom Cor Castle; a 14th-century tower house in Limerick city?', *JRSAI*, 135 (2005), 119–29. 8 W.H. Grattan Flood, *History of the diocese of Ferns* (Waterford, 1916), p. 85; some 'early' fabric survived

fifteenth century, possibly of the 1410s; several other castles near Kilclief are of near-identical plan, such as Jordan's Castle (Ardglass) and Audley's Castle, and are presumably of similar date.[9] Kilclief is a very important castle because it shows that the architectural forms associated with tower-houses in Ireland were sufficiently standardized by the second or third decade of the fifteenth century to make an appearance in north-east Ireland, distant from the main distribution area of tower-houses. The features in question include (a) the rise and fall of the projection of the parapet at the corner turrets, (b) the stepped battlement with angled top-stones, and (c) the externally machicolated chimney.

Of particular interest are those castles built in this *c*.1400 period by the Gaelic families of Clare, the midlands and the north-west. Most of the examples in the latter two regions are gone,[10] but fragmentary remains at two near-contemporary sites give us a glimpse of the design options available to their castle builders of *c*.1400: the much-reduced tower at Emper, built 1405,[11] seems to have been a bulky structure in the lineage of the thirteenth-century chamber blocks discussed in the previous chapter, while Tulsk, built the next year, seems to have been a more conventional tower of a type that was widely built in the 1400s.[12] More interesting still, though more problematic, are the Clare castles. Sadly neglected Dangan Iviggin (Daingean Uí Bhigín) has a rectangular chamber-tower with two high internal vaults. A major Gaelic-Irish castle of the Shannon Estuary region, later supplanted in regional significance by Bunratty, it is known to have been built by one Cumheadha MacNamara. Two people bear this name, one who died in 1306 and the other around 1370. The shape and character of the structure would support the pre-1306 date, but the vaults, which are original and can be paralleled in tower-houses, point to the later fourteenth-century date.[13] The second castle, Rossroe, given a pre-1402 date by

its substantial sixteenth-century remodelling. The fact that crenellation is mentioned at all might be significant: aristocratic houses in later medieval England were crenellated under licence, and because the capacity to obtain a licence in the first instance was a measure of social standing, the crenellation was de facto a signifier of class: C. Coulson, 'Structural symbolism in medieval castle architecture', *JBAA*, 132 (1979), 73–90. Licences were not needed in Ireland, but that is not to say that crenellation had no similar symbolic role.   **9** M. Jope (ed.), *Archaeological survey of County Down*, p. 233 (Kilclief). White Castle, Athy, is commonly regarded as 1415–17, which would put it roughly contemporary with Kilclief, but the tower-house has now been dated to the sixteenth century by Ben Murtagh ('The dating of the White Castle, Athy, Co. Kildare: an outlying bastion of the Pale' in Potterton and Herron (eds), *Dublin and the Pale in the Renaissance*, pp 145–81).   **10** Finnea (*MIA*, 1397.16); Ballymahon and Stonestown (ibid., 1401.8,9); Granard (ibid., 1405.5); *Áth na Stuaidhe* and *Tír Leicín* (ibid., 1406.13, 14), and Ballindoon and Collooney (*AFM*,1408.19, 20). Earthworks and foundations of considerable archaeological potential survive at Barry (*MIA*, 1401.8, 1403.5 [demolished], 1405.6 [rebuilt]). An earlier 'outlier' of this group is Lissardowlan (*AFM*, 1377.6).   **11** *MIA*, 1405.7.   **12** Ibid., 1406.12; Tulsk's destruction is recorded a year later: *AFM*, 1407.6; I am supposing here (in the absence to date of the final excavation report) that the early fifteenth-century castle can be equated with the tower excavated in recent years by Niall Brady for the Discovery Programme (see the summary in Barry, 'The study of medieval Irish castles', pp 130–1).   **13** T.J. Westropp, 'Notes on the lesser castles or "peel towers" of the County Clare', *PRIA*, 5 (1898–1900), 348–65 at 351; R. Ua Cróinín and M. Breen, 'Daingean Ui Bhigin Castle, Quin, Co. Clare', *The Other Clare*, 10 (1986), 52–3; Ua Cróinín and Breen have published many very useful papers on Clare castles in this periodical.

124 Kilclief Castle. John Cely was bishop of Down from 1413 until he was removed from office in 1441 for living in this castle with his married mistress, one Lettice Thomas.

Thomas Westropp, is a classic tower-house of fifteenth-century type; a third castle, Newtown, assigned a late fourteenth-century date by Westropp, is now reduced to foundations but appears to have been another classic tower-house of a type that we would conventionally date well into the 1400s.[14]

14 Westropp, 'Notes on the lesser castles', p. 351.

125 Srah Castle. A small cross-shaped gun-loop and an even smaller key-hole gun-loop are among the openings for muskets in this late sixteenth-century tower-house.

The documentary and archaeological records concur to indicate to us that small castles, built in big numbers, were the new norm in later medieval Ireland. Most modern writers, Barry most prominent among them, see the scale of late medieval encastellation in Ireland as a product of (or, more particularly, a response to) endemic local warfare.[15] The castles themselves, though, were only modestly defensible, with gun-holes and gun-loops providing the main protection (fig. 125); at Ballynamona and Raheen each wall-face has a gun-loop on the underside of the point of a very wide triangular recess that blends into the wall as it widens and descends, but such elaborate

15 Barry, 'The archaeology of the tower house'; idem, 'The last frontier: defence and settlement in late medieval Ireland' in Barry, Frame and Simms (eds), *Colony and frontier in medieval Ireland*, pp 217–28; idem, 'Tower houses and terror: the archaeology of late medieval Munster' in H.B. Clarke, J. Prunty and M. Hennessy (eds), *Surveying Ireland's past* (Dublin, 2004), pp 119–28.

126 (*opposite*) Tombrickane Castle. Fire damage is easily identified: the shattered surfaces of the lower-storey stones testify to an inferno at some stage of this building's history. The fact that the stones at the higher floor level bear little sign of any fire suggests that the timber floor between the two levels caught fire and fell against, and burned, the lower walls.

schemes were very rare. The evidence suggests that such 'local warfare', if such a phrase is even warranted, was not particularly intense; the small prisons (oubliettes) found in some tower-houses, such as Kilcoe and Castle Cooke, are indicative of very local, possibly even estate-specific, law-and-order matters.[16] Anyway, the number of later medieval castle sites for which we have both historical and archaeological evidence of later medieval fighting – below ground as well as above[17] – is small relative to the number that survives; there is no reason to think that fire damage, where it occurs (fig. 126), is the result of an attack.

The proliferation of small castles after 1400 surely points to a fairly strong economy, with plenty of money available for building, and plenty of work for masons and other professional craftsmen. So, how much did a castle actually cost in the late Middle Ages? The answer depends on the size of the castle, of course: the big buildings at the centres of lordships can hardly be compared with the castle erected in Omagh in one week in the early sixteenth century.[18] In the early 1600s it was asserted by Matthew de Renzy, a German-born planter in Offaly, that £600 or £700 was needed to build the 'meanest' castle,[19] but this is surely an exaggeration upwards: it appears that castles with tower-houses in Co. Down cost between £300 and £400 to build only a quarter of a century earlier.[20] Also, the fact that a subsidy of less than 2 per cent of the amount named by de Renzy was considered a reasonable amount to give a castle builder in the Dublin region in the 1400s (see below, pp 298–9) suggests that one could build a fine castle for several hundred pounds. Affordability, then, is surely part of the explanation for the great number of later medieval castles in Ireland. It is likely that the cost of engaging builders was even offset somewhat by lords billeting them on tenants according to the ancient custom of coign.[21] It is not inconceivable that many later medieval lords would have been unable to build castles of any opulence but for this custom. Is the lack of obvious accommodation for even a few soldiers in castle complexes of the late Middle Ages to be explained by their billeting on tenants?

WORDS AND DESCRIPTIONS

The word fortalice (*fortalitium* or *fortalicium*), derived from the Latin *fortis* (meaning 'strong'), had been used as far back as the twelfth century.[22] It was sometimes used interchangeably with 'castle'.[23] Appearing in the sources with greater frequency from the fourteenth century on, there is no evidence to indicate that *fortalicium* was a

---

16 E. Cotter, 'Kilcoe Castle: excavation of a later medieval coastal stronghold in County Cork', *JCHAS*, 117 (2012), 1–23. **17** K. Wiggins, *Siege mines and underground warfare* (Princes Risborough, 2003), pp 28–9. **18** *AU*, 1512.4. **19** Loeber, 'Gaelic castles and settlements', p. 272. **20** HMSO, *Historic monuments of Northern Ireland: an introduction and guide* (Belfast, 1983), pp 44–5. **21** For examples, see C.A. Empey and K. Simms, 'The ordinances of the White Earl and the problem of coign in the later Middle Ages', *PRIA*, 75C (1975), 161–87 at 172, 182. **22** 'Fortalice, n.', OED online; K. O'Conor, 'The later construction and use of motte and bailey castles in Ireland: new evidence from Leinster', *JKAS*, 17 (1987–91), 13–29 at 14. **23** See *SRPI, John–Hen. V*, pp 61–2 for a late thirteenth-century instance, and *Inchiquin MSS*, nos 976, 1046 and 1051 for early seventeenth-century instances.

127 Kindlestown Castle. The ground floor, represented on the exterior by the putlog holes, has remains of an original (fourteenth-century?) vault. The first floor was clearly rebuilt. Although far more elongated than the tower-houses of the region, Kindlestown's combination of a vaulted basement and a latrine turret with chutes suggests a familial relationship with the classic tower-houses of the English Pale (see below, pp 298–301).

diminutive (as in *small* fort or *small* castle).[24] However, there is an indication in a reference of 1342 that fortalices (*fforceletz*) were, or at least could be, slightly lower in rank than *chasteux* (castles).[25] In the 1270s and again in the 1350s, *fortalicium* signified in the Dublin region a brand new stronghold or a re-edified older stronghold freshly garrisoned by central government in order to deal with the problem of Irish raids.[26] This process of building/re-edification, whenever or wherever it happened, was subsidized from the public purse.[27] Thus, for example, in 1300 the exchequer advanced £100 to John fitzThomas to build a fortalice in Rathangan, in 1305 it subsidized the building of a fortalice in Wexford with money levied from the local ploughlands, and in 1358 it generated £40 to fund the repair of one *castrum* and 100s. to repair two fortalices in Carlow.[28] Many, probably most, of these fortalices were stone-built, such as Kindlestown (fig. 127), but the fact that it was sometimes deemed necessary to

24 *Contra* D. Cathcart King, *Castellarium Anglicanum* (New York, 1983), p. xlix. **25** *SRPI, John–Hen.V*, p. 335. **26** R. Frame, 'The Dublin government and Gaelic Ireland, 1272–1361' (PhD, TCD, 1971). I am grateful to Prof. Frame for photocopying excerpts of his thesis for me many years ago. **27** It might be noted, however, that *fortalicium* did not connote a publically subsidised castle in other parts of Europe where it was used: see, for example, J. Zeune, *The last Scottish castles* (Buch am Erlbach, 1992), pp 96–8. **28** *CJRI, 1295–1303*, p. 362 (Rathangan); *1305–7*, p. 13 (Wexford); *RPH*, pp 66–70 (Carlow).

128 Rathcoffey Castle. There is no reason to doubt that the gate house is the building mentioned in 1417 and is fourteenth century; its round arches, which are very similar in execution to those in the Anglo-Norman donjon of Woodstock Castle, suggest a thirteenth-century date, but there is also an original twin-light cusped-ogee window that cannot be pre-1300 in an Irish context. The *torshous* no longer survives, but there is a sixteenth-century tower-house at the core of the ruined mansion.

describe fortalices as stone-built suggests that some were of earth-and-timber.[29] Subsidies for new castles in the Dublin region continued into the 1400s, as we will discuss below with reference to what is described by scholars as the '£10 castle act', but the word 'fortalice' was used less frequently by then. One exception is the grant of £10 for a 'castle or fortalice' (*chastell ou fforslet*) in 1459 in Bray (Cork Castle).[30]

Gaelic-Irish sources from the thirteenth and fourteenth centuries use the word *cúirt* (court) for 'castle', both native and foreign.[31] With the majority of late medieval focal buildings regardless of ethnicity being of tower form, we might expect a proliferation of references specifically to towers, but *tour* appears only sporadically. There is an early reference, dated 1417, to the *gathous* (fig. 128) and *torshous* (tower-house) at Rathcoffey.[32]

29 Kindlestown was described as a fortalice in 1377 (*RPH*, p. 66). It is incorrectly described and analysed as a 'hall-house' in L. Simpson, 'Dublin's southern frontier under siege: Kindlestown Castle, Delgany, County Wicklow', *MD*, 4 (2003), 279–368. William Douz's now-lost castle at Saggart was referred to specifically as a stone fortalice (*fortallitium lapidou*) in 1312 (*CFR, 1307–19*, p. 249). **30** *SRPI, Hen. VI*, p. 633. **31** For examples, see Leerssen, *Mere Irish and fíor-Ghael*, pp 162, 181. **32** *RPH*, p. 222; S. Quirke, 'A gatehouse to beyond the boundaries of the

'Castle' generally seems to have been the preferred term for 'tower', since a distinction was often made between the 'castle' and the hall. In one mid-fifteenth-century instance *tour* was interchanged with *pile* (peel).[33] In 1535 Robert Cowley referred to 'piles' in Ireland.[34] Half a century later, in 1584, Newcastle West had a 'lofty quadrilateral peel', while at Lough Gur part of the defence included 'a small castle or peel' with, unusually, a drawbridge (*pons abstrahend*').[35]

Before progressing to references to halls and towers together, and thus picking up where we left off with our discussion of thirteenth-century castle planning, it is useful to look briefly at some words used to refer to other spaces and structures. 'Bawn', which describes the walled enclosure associated with a later medieval castle, may be derived from *bódhún*, itself derived perhaps from *ba* (plural of *bó*) and *dún*. Sometimes rendered 'balne' in the Desmond Surveys of 1585–6,[36] its association with *bó*, cow, at least at the end of Elizabeth I's reign, is confirmed by Fynes Moryson who noted that the Irish, fearing raids or wolves, brought their cattle into their bawns at night, leaving them to 'stand or lie all night in a dirty yard without so much as a lock of hay'.[37] Richard Stanihurst, writing around the same time, did not use the word but was referring to the same type of structure or space when he described 'confined and protected compounds' into which the Irish put cattle to guard them from robbers.[38] But its use was probably not confined to enclosures for cattle to soil at night: for example, it was recorded in 1611 that the 'archbishop of Cashill hath begune a prittie castle at Termon Magragh w'ch he entends speedily to finish, haveing his materials ready at the place wher he meanes to buyld a bawne and finish the castle'.[39] In Gaelic-Irish castles the spaces enclosed by the bawn walls might sometimes be identified as the 'greens' to which reference was occasionally made, especially in the late Middle Ages.[40] The bardic poet Tadhg Dall Ó Huiginn (1550–91) described the castle at Lifford as 'the fortress of smooth-lawned Lifford'; he described 'the level green lawn about the sunny castle' of *Lios Gréine* as 'like plowed land, from the prancing of vigorous steeds: no one hath tilled the bright sod, but its state is caused by the exercising of young and spirited horses'; he also noted the castle green as a place where hostages might be 'proclaimed' after battle.[41] Another term, 'barbican', seems in the late Middle Ages to describe an enclosure (rather than an outwork associated with a fortified gate, which is its earlier connotation) and may even have been reserved for inner enclosures within bawns, as in the 1584 description of Mallow (see below, p. 267).

Pale: reflections on Rathcoffey, Co. Kildare' in Potterton and Herron (eds), *Dublin and the Pale in the Renaissance*, pp 104–24. **33** *SRPI, Hen. VI*, p. 26 (*tour*); *SRPI, Ed. IV*, p. 457 (*pile or tour*). **34** *CCM*, i, p. 70. **35** Desmond Survey [cf. www.ucc.ie/celt/], p. 159. **36** The castle enclosure at Ainy is so described (Desmond Survey [cf. www.ucc.ie/celt/], p. 151 and n. 678). **37** www.ucc.ie/celt/, p. 222. **38** Colm Lennon, *Richard Stanihurst the Dubliner, 1547–1618* (Dublin, 1981), p. 147. **39** R.J. Hunter, 'Carew's survey of Ulster, 1611: the voluntary works', *UJA*, 38 (1975), 81–2. **40** See *AU*, 1531.11, *AFM*, 1532.2, *ALC*, 1533.6 and *AU*, 1538.24. The earliest reference may be to the 'green' of Bunratty Castle in 1311 (*MIA*). **41** E. Knott (ed.), *The bardic poems of Tadhg Dall Ó hUiginn, 1550–1591* (London, 1920–6), pp 24, 26, 48. 'Greens' were not confined to castles, however, nor were castles the only contexts in which they were used for such public displays of power: see *AFM*, 1203.6 (Kilmacduagh monastery); 1356.15 (Dublin town); 1432.9 (Armagh town); 1442.12 (Kiltoghert church-site) and so on.

Documentary references to 'castles' and halls

We are fortunate to have a small corpus of references that reveals the relationships between towers and halls, and so allow us to pursue into the 1400s, 1500s and 1600s some of the patterns noted earlier. The references, both legalistic and anecdotal in nature, tend to cluster in the later sixteenth and seventeenth centuries. This is unfortunate but it does not create insurmountable problems of interpretation. The patterns observable at the end of the Middle Ages match so well those of the thirteenth century that we can assume similar patterns in the years in between.

Though it gives no information on room usage, pride of place among these references must go to the 1547 building account of the *castell* at *Bretasse* (probably Brittas, near Kilcash) in south Tipperary:

> the same castell to be of thre loftes besides the rofe, and the same substancially builded; the first loft to be with a vault and to be xiiii fote hy, and the other ii lofts to be every of them x fote hy; and the rofe to be substancially covered with slate and the gutters with gutterstone well embatelde; and to be furnisshed with a chymney in both of the ii over loftes and a substanciall persoum [?] with drawghtes accordinge; the same castell to have a goode substanciall berbikan of stone as is at Pollywherie [Poulakerry], and to the neither gate of the castell to have a goode grate of iron; and the said castell to be substancially buylded with goode lyme and stone, the walls to be vi fote thick undre the vault and iiii fote above, and furnisshed with dores and wyndowes and all other things necessarie to a castell, as shalbe thought goode by the iudgement of Mr Derby Ryan and the tresoror of Lismore, calling to them one mason and one carpenter.[42]

The actual castle no longer survives. It is not clear if it was planned as a three- or four-storey tower. Three 'lofts' suggest the former, which would be atypically low for a sixteenth-century Ormond tower. Alternatively, given that 'loft', a later medieval term, means the space under a roof,[43] there may have been two rooms under a lower vault (an arrangement that we find in standing buildings), the upper room of the two being the loft in the literal sense, with the two further rooms above described as lofts because they were sealed by the 'rofe … substancially covered with slate and the gutters with gutterstone well embatelde'. Significantly, no single room is highlighted as having special significance, either by use of a word other than 'loft' or by the specification of a fireplace or elaborate fenestration. There was no hall inside the tower, in other words.

But there may have been a hall *outside* the tower, as was demonstrably the arrangement in other castles. For example, in 1568 one Dermot O'Dea was allowed in arbitration to retain occupancy of two rooms in the tower-house of Dysert (O'Dea) Castle as well as occupancy of 'the hall adjoining the castle' that his father had built.[44] In 1584 Askeaton had 'a large hall' and 'a great chamber' in separate structures, Newcastle West had 'a great hall, large chamber [and other] very good rooms', also in separate buildings, and Desmond Castle, Castleisland, had a hall (the given measurements of

---

42 *COD, 1547–1584*, pp 22–3.   **43** 'Loft, n.', OED online.   **44** *Inchiquin MSS*, no. 890; the hall

which suggest a ground-floor hall) with an adjoining parlour over which were two chambers, as well as a 'great dining chamber', a chapel with a tower attached, vaults containing the buttery and pantry, and various other lodgings.[45] Also from 1584 is a description of the 'house and castle' at Mallow. Here, the hall and tower were also separate if physically connected structures, with a continuous suite of basement vaults shared between them:

> One castle containing in itself two small courts and one great barbican, namely, where the howse standeth, the entrance in is on the north side ffyrste into one of the said courts, and then turninge one the lefte hande ye enter by a doore, beinge in a highe wall, into the Balne or Barbican, which is reasonable and large, and then goinge a little way, turninge one to lefte hande, have ye an entrance by an other stone wale, wher as the castell or howse standeth, the lower rooms whereof ar sellors vaulted over. And in the wall one the lefte hande there be stayres of stone of XII. stepps in heyght that leadeth one the right hande into the Hall, which is about LX. foote longe and XXVI. foot wyde, within the howse, and is deepe, with a highe roofe, the Tymber whereof seemeth to be sounde, and is covered with thacke, somethinge decayed at the north ende; towards the west corner there is a square buylding vaulted as the other is but not so broade, and riseth somewhat higher than the roofe of the hall in which, over the sellor, ar fower strong rooms that may be made meete for lodgings; the uppermost, savinge one, is vaulted.[46]

Stanihurst also distinguished between the halls and towers of castles in 1584. The former, he noted, were

> reasonably big and spacious palaces made from white clay and mud. They are not roofed with quarried slabs or slates but with thatch. [There] they hold their banquets but they prefer to sleep in the castle [tower] rather than the palace because their enemies can easily apply torches to the roofs which catch fire rapidly if there is but the slightest breeze.[47]

William Camden (who, it should be noted, lacked the first-hand knowledge of Stanihurst) repeated the tenor of this description in 1610, noting that the castle of Strabane and

> some other castles of less note, which, like those in other parts of the island, are no more than towers, with narrow loop-holes rather than windows; to which adjoins a hall made of turf, and roofed overhead with thatch, and a large yard fenced quite round with a ditch and hedge.[48]

---

was described as 'the great hall' in 1584 and 1599 (nos 938, 944).   **45** Desmond Survey [cf. www.ucc.ie/celt/], pp 156, 159; J. Fenlon, 'Moving towards the formal house: room usage in early modern Ireland', *PRIA*, 111C (2010), 141–68 at 143–4.   **46** H. Berry, 'The manor and castle of Mallow in the days of the Tudors', *JCHAS*, 2 (1893), 21–5.   **47** J. Barry and H. Morgan (eds), *The* De rebus in Hibernia *of Richard Stanihurst* (Turnhout, 2013), p. 113.   **48** *Camden's Britannia*

In 1591, Ludolf von Münchhausen, a German visitor to Ireland, spent a night in a castle – 'the house of an Irish nobleman or squire' – and he too described a separate hall, though he did not use that term. He noted that the residences of that social class were usually 'in the form of a tower surrounded by a wall', and that they were not lived in but kept as fortresses. Obviously describing the particular castle where he overnighted, he noted that the actual 'house' or residence was 'nearby' to the tower, and was a badly built structure (by German standards, he stated explicitly) with a central hearth. At mealtime in this particular 'house', the nobleman and his wife sat at the top (the high end, as architectural historians would describe it), with servants arranged around them according to rank. The food suggests a household of modest means: 'some herring, bread, a handful of leeks and some salt' and a communal drinking mug. At the end of the meal, water was distributed for washing feet. Bales of straw overlain by blankets were used for floor-bedding, and the nobleman and his wife were the first to lie down.[49] Von Münchhausen's description suggests that they retired to sleep on the floor alongside everybody else in the 'house', not in the tower. In this regard his description contradicts Stanihurst's. It also contradicts what we know of the symbolic value of the bed as a physical object in medieval culture: 'the site of sexual consummation[,] it also served as the locale for birth and death, the pivotal transitions in the medieval extended life course'.[50] That aside, what he described was a hall with a detached chamber-tower – a tower-house, in our language – beside it.

Just as the servants were seated according to rank in the 'house' visited by Von Münchhausen, so too were visitors to aristocratic residences. Lughaidh Ó Cléirigh's biography of Red Hugh O'Donnell, written in 1616, contains a valuable description of an inauguration feast in the hall of Dungannon Castle, revealing to us how important were seating arrangements:

> The princes proceeded to feast, to toast one another and to make merry … The banquet-hall was arranged according to their dignity, O Domhnaill face to face with O Néill, and Conor Maguidhir next him, and the chief men in their due order also. The butlers proceed to attend and serve them afterwards. Meantime, when O Néill took the goblet with wine in his hand, he drank a draught to O Domhnaill. O Domhnaill takes the cup from the butler's hand, and looked around. He gave a quick glance of his keen eye through the hall all round and did not see Cúchonnacht Óg in the house; and as he did not see him he ordered him to be called to him immediately. This was done for him, and when he came he bade him sit by the side of his brother Rury in the central section of the palace in the midst of his people. When Cúchonnacht was seated, he then drank the cup and raised it in his hand for a space over him, and called him by the title of Muguidhir in the presence of the chief men of the province generally.[51]

abridg'd: with improvements, and continuations, to this present time, 1 (London, 1701), p. 81. **49** D. Ó Riain-Raedel, 'A German visitor to Monaincha in 1591', *THJ* (1998), 223–33. **50** Gilchrist, *Medieval life*, p. 128; for the significance of the bed in late medieval and early modern society, see R. Sarti, *Europe at home: family and material culture, 1500–1800* (New Haven and London, 2002), pp 119–23. **51** *Beatha Aodha Ruaidh Uí Dhomhnaill*, ed. P. Walsh (Dublin, 1948), p. 245.

References to towers/castles and associated halls/houses in castles continued into the early 1600s, when plantation provided a context for new descriptions. In 1601 McSwyne's Castle was described as McSwyne Bannagh's 'tower and his chief house'.[52] The adjective 'chief' might mean 'major' or 'principal', but it might equally connote the association of the house with the public and symbolic display of chiefly authority. Twenty-one years later, after plantation, the same castle was described as the

> ruinous Castle Rahan … with a bawn of lime and stone standing on a rock compassed 3 parts thereof with the sea … upon one side whereof there is an ancient building for lodgings of lime and stone, and a gatehouse newly built and some part of the bawn repaired, in which house, Herbert Maxwell with his wife and family dwell.[53]

The lodgings were in the tower and the house may be the same as that mentioned in 1601. In 1608 we have for Castlebrake 'the castle at the town [of Castle brake], the hall, the parlour at the end of the hall, the kitchen, the brewhouse, the bakehouse and the rest of the houses within the bawn …'.[54] As with McSwyne's Castle, in 1622 Moross was described as having a tower and a house: it was 'formerly an old Irish castle and the walls of a small house upon which Arthur Terry … hath set a roof of birch timber, thatched, the walls of the castle being in some parts repaired, having neither roof nor floor'.[55]

Despite their structural modesty, these halls or houses were, as places of communal feasting for visiting parties and especially neighbours, essential to the maintenance of social rank.[56] As late as 1682 Clonderlaw was described as 'a very ancient castle and a house of great hospitality'.[57] These halls or houses might also have continued to have the sort of symbolic value that Thomas Leon's hall had in 1288 (see above, p. 216). Significantly, an attorney who visited Castlepook in 1631 to witness a quitclaim entered the house in the bawn, not the tower; the nature of the house is not specified, but a modest house has been found in archaeological excavations beside the extant tower.[58]

Do we know from documentary sources what was inside the actual towers? The little information we have is extremely interesting. In 1584 the tower at Lough Gur had nine *cubicul'* (translated by modern editors as 'sleeping rooms') and two *loci easeament'* ('reception rooms'), Rathmore (Limerick) had 'divers other necessary places or *cubicul'* ('rooms') strongly built for defence', and an unnamed castle in Shanid manor, 'built in quadrilateral form, 50 feet in length without the walls and 30 feet in breadth',

---

52 *CSPI, 1600–1*, p. 278.   **53** V.W. Treadwell, 'The plantation of Donegal: a survey [pt 1]', *Donegal Annual* (1953–4), 511–17 at 514.   **54** K.W. Nicholls, *The O'Doyne (Ó Duinn) manuscript* (Dublin, 1985), p. 40.   **55** V.W. Treadwell, 'The plantation of Donegal: a survey [pt 2]', *Donegal Annual* (1954–5), 41–6 at 42.   **56** Von Münchhausen asserts this; see also K. Simms, 'Guesting and feasting in Gaelic Ireland', *JRSAI*, 108 (1978), 67–100. The same obligations of communal hosting fell on 'gaelicized' Anglo-Normans (see, for example, Leerssen, *Mere Irish and fíor-Ghael*, p. 173).   **57** B. Ó Dálaigh (ed.), *The stranger's gaze: travels in Clare, 1534–1950* (Ennis, 1998), p. 64.   **58** J. Ainsworth and E. MacLysaght, 'Survey of documents in private keeping, second series', *Analecta Hibernica*, 20 (1958), 3–361 at 6; my thanks to Eamonn Cotter, the site's excavator, for bringing this site to my attention.

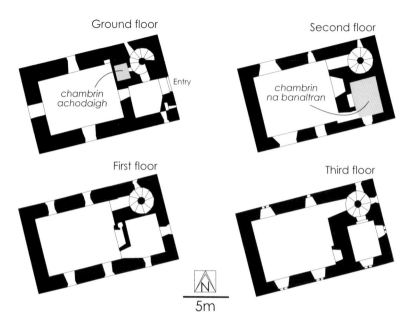

Ground floor

Entry

chambrin achodaigh

Second floor

chambrin na banaltran

First floor

Third floor

5m

129 Togher Castle plan.

contained 'five … places or *cubicul*' ('rooms') in two *solar* ('upper floors') or stor[ey]s'.[59] None of these had a room described as a hall. In the nineteenth century the traditional names of rooms in Togher, a major MacCarthy castle built between 1590 and 1602, were recorded for posterity: a tiny (?guard-) chamber off the stairs that was called *chambrin achodaigh*, translated as 'the tyrant's little chamber', and a small subsidiary chamber higher up that was called *chambrin na banaltran*, translated as 'the little chamber of the nurse' (fig. 129).[60] No room was described as a hall.

Evidence from Clare tells us that the rooms in towers could be owned independently by different members of a family, or leased out to others, thus making the castle the microcosm of the estate and its pattern of landownership. Thus, for example, in 1598 the owner of Carownegowle [Carrownagoul] Castle retained his chamber in the garret of the castle that he leased out, in 1603 Margaret Ny Brien was bequeathed in a will the 'upper half' of the castle of Shealy [Shallee], and in 1618 Donnogh Grana O'Brien had possession of three rooms in the castle of Magownegan [Magowna].[61] The most detailed such reference is from 1607, when Donough O'Brien had conveyed to him the 'lower half' of the castle of Castletowne', comprising

> the two sellers, the roome called the porters roome, the roomes aboue the sellers comonely called *Gystallagh*, the roome comonely called *seomra i vohowna* and the roome comonely called the house of office otherwise called a private house.[62]

59 Desmond Survey [cf. www.ucc.ie/celt/], pp 152 (Lough Gur), 153 (Rathmore), 157 (Shanid manor). **60** J. Lyons and H.W. Gillman, 'Togher Castle and district, County Cork', *JCHAS*, 1 (1895), 481–97. **61** *Inchiquin MSS*, nos 937, 956, 1007. **62** Ibid., no. 967. *Gystallagh*, the

That chambers could be identified so specifically is supported by a reference to a 'solar' and 'carpenters chambre' in the castle of Turlough.[63]

The practice of allowing different parties ownership of different spaces in castles was probably not confined to Clare. In 1584 the bawn of the castle of Ballycapple was shared among co-heirs of the Kennedy sept.[64] There may have been a similar though undocumented division of the interior of the large bawn at Pallas Castle. The area of the bawn is 2,000m² and divides spatially into four blocks of 500m² each. The early sixteenth-century tower-house looks at first to have been crammed into a corner of the bawn but actually sits in the middle of one of these quarter-divisions, as if one branch of the Burkes of Pallas developed *their* particular plot within the bawn. The two big residential towers (of later fifteenth- and early seventeenth-century dates) of which the major Pale castle of Liscartan is composed were described as separate castles in 1654–6, even though a wing connected them, and it is likely that each was owned separately by the only two landowners (Sir Robert Talbot[t] and Adam Missett) who had land there.[65]

The best-known description of the internal layout of a tower of the period is unquestionably that of Luke Gernon, written *c.*1620. It is a remarkable passage, worth citing in full:

> We are come to the castle already. The castles are built very strong, and with narow stayres, for security. The hall is the uppermost room, lett us go up, you shall not come downe agayne till tomorrow. Take no care of your horses, they shall be sessed among the tenants. The lady of the house meets you with her trayne. I have instructed you before how to accost them. Salutations paste, you shall be presented with all the drinkes in the house, first the ordinary beere, then aquavitae, then sacke, then olde-ale, the lady tastes it, you must not refuse it. The fyre is prepared in the middle of the hall, where you may sollace yourselfe till supper time, you shall not want sacke and tobacco. By this time the table is spread and plentifully furnished with variety of meates, but ill cooked, and with out sauce. Neyther shall there be wanting a pasty or two of redd deare (that is more common with us then the fallow). The dishe which I make choyce of is the swelld mutton, and it is prepared thus. They take a principall weather, and before they kill him, it is fitt that he be shorne, being killed they singe him in his woolly skynne like a bacon, and rost him by ioynts with the skynne on, and so serve it to the table. They say that it makes the flesh more firme, and preserves the fatt. I make choyce of it to avoyd uncleanely dressing. They feast together with great iollyty and healths around; towards the middle of supper, the harper beginns to

name by which it seems that the cellars (as distinct from the room above them) were known, is probably derived from the Irish *gustal*, meaning chattels, while *seomra i vohowna* refers in all probability to 'the room of Mahown [O'Loghlen]'. My thanks to my UCD colleagues Dr Caoimhín Breatnach and Prof. Máire Ní Annracháin for their advice on these translations. **63** Ibid., no. 1321.   **64** K.W. Nicholls, 'Gaelic landownership in Tipperary from surviving Irish deeds' in Nolan (ed.), *Tipperary: history and society*, pp 92–103 at pp 94–5. See also Tierney, 'Pedigrees in stone?', pp 178–80.   **65** *Civil Survey (Meath)*, p. 231.

tune and singeth Irish rymes of auncient making. If he be a good rymer, he will make one song to the present occasion. Supper being ended, it is at your liberty to sitt up, or to depart to your lodgeing, you shall have company in both kind. When you come to your chamber, do not expect canopy and curtaynes. It is very well if your bedd content you, and if the company be greate, you may happen to be bodkin in the middle. In the morning there will be brought unto you a cupp of aquavitae. The aquavitae or usquebath of Ireland is not such an extraction, as is made in England, but farre more qualifyed, and sweetened with licorissh. It is made potable, and is of the colour of Muscadine. It is a very wholsome drinke, and naturall to digest the crudityes of the Irish feeding. You may drink a knaggin without offence, that is the fourth parte of a pynte. Breakfast is but the repetitions of supper. When you are disposing of yourself to depart, they call for Dogh a dores, that is, to drink at the doore, there you are presented agayne with all the drinkes in the house, as at your first entrance. Smacke them over, and lett us departe.[66]

The passage seems to contradict other accounts of later medieval castle-halls in Ireland. Gernon seems to describe an upmarket version of the 'house' in which Von Münchhausen was entertained, and he specifically calls it 'the hall', but it is the topmost room in the tower. Rory Sherlock, author of an important paper on domestic planning and tower-houses, puts great faith in this passage. His view is that 'examples of tower-houses which had halls within them, in the style of Gernon's castle, and which had halls alongside them, in the style of that described by Stanihurst, existed side-by-side in late medieval Ireland', and he claims evidence that halls in tower-houses were sometimes the upper rooms, perched *above* the more private chambers, and at other times the middle-rooms *below* a chamber or two.[67] Large rooms inside tower-houses are so commonly described in modern literature (as distinct from medieval sources) as halls that his reading of the evidence can be regarded as a clear articulation of a fairly conventional, even consensus, understanding of the evidence.[68] But I would dispute the thesis that the locations of halls and chambers were ever interchangeable within stacks of rooms in medieval architecture, and would dispute especially the thesis that a hall, as that term was understood in the Middle Ages, could ever be placed above the chamber(s). There is an alternative reading of Gernon's remarkable testimony that brings its information into line with other bodies of evidence.[69]

---

66 The date of 1620 was assigned to it by C. Litton Falkiner, who first published Gernon's discourse *Illustrations of Irish history and topography, mainly of the seventeenth century* (London, 1904), pp 345–62: see www.ucc.ie/celt/published/E620001/. The lack of a reference to a man-of-the-house suggests that this was a dowager's residence.   **67** R. Sherlock, 'The evolution of the Irish tower-house as a domestic space', *PRIA*, 111C (2011), 115–40 at 117; idem, 'Changing perceptions: spatial analysis and the study of the Irish tower house', *CG*, 24 (2010), 239–50. **68** See, for example, T. Reeves-Smyth, 'Community to privacy: late Tudor and Jacobean manorial architecture in Ireland' in A. Horning, R. Ó Baoill, C. Donnelly and P. Logue (eds), *The post-medieval archaeology of Ireland, 1550–1850* (Bray, 2007), pp 289–326 at p. 292. **69** T. O'Keeffe, '*Aula* and *camera*'.

A hall as conventionally understood in the medieval tradition might *very occasionally* have been accommodated in the structure of an Irish tower-house. Bunratty seems to have had one, as we saw above (p. 86), but given that castle's exceptional size and prestige this hall might have been more than a simple in-tower version of what was conventionally an external structure. The main second-floor room in Barryscourt Castle, accessed by a straight stairs (see fig. 39), might have been a hall in the same vein as that in Bunratty; its identification as a hall is strengthened by the fact that there is a chamber tower (including a private chapel) behind what would have been its high end. However, the identification is difficult to square with the fact that it is at second-floor level, which is very high, and with the fact that there is a long hall attached to the bawn *outside* the tower-house.[70] It is worth noting here the parallels between Barryscourt and the so-called Desmond Tower in Askeaton Castle. The latter had, like Barryscourt, a fine hall-like room at first-floor level with a chamber-block rising higher over one end of it. But that room was not a hall. It was, as McNeill puts it, 'an outer great or presence chamber', with more intimate accommodation in the turret, and it surely equates with the 'great chamber' mentioned (along with the 'large hall' in the outer courtyard) in 1584.[71]

Regardless of the couple of possible exceptions, Gernon was not hosted in a hall, no matter what his choice of term might suggest, and he seems to be unique among contemporary commentators on Irish castles in describing a room at the top of a tower as a hall.[72] For us to adopt his use of the term would be very foolish, as it would blur the very distinction that the other sources from the 1200s on make for us about the use of space. The dining function traditionally suited to the hall had clearly been moved up to the top of the particular tower visited by Gernon, at least for the meal to which he was welcomed. It had been moved to the type of high-grade chamber that one frequently finds above other chambers in tower-houses (fig. 130) and is accessible only by ascending spiral stairs that pass the doors of those chambers. Are we engaged in special pleading to counteract Gernon's testimony? No. Jane Fenlon noted that in Ireland, as

> in England and other countries, halls had, by the end of the sixteenth century, been reduced in status within the hierarchy of rooms. No longer would they have been used by the lord for his meals, instead parlours would serve for informal meals and the great chamber for ceremonial dining.[73]

---

70 For the hall, see D. Pollock, 'The Barryscourt hall and the remains of some other timber buildings' in Manning (ed.), *From ringforts to fortified houses*, pp 261–72. 71 McNeill, 'The larger castles of later medieval Co. Limerick', *BAACT*, 34 (2010), 176–88 at 180. 72 Incidentally, the halls that have been identified – not necessarily correctly, of course – inside Scottish tower-houses (such as Craignethan Castle and Huntingtower) are never, to my knowledge, identified *above* chambers, as Gernon's 'hall' would have been. 73 Fenlon, 'Moving towards the formal house', p. 144. The northern European evidence is discussed in Ronnes, 'An archaeology of the noble house'.

130 The end-wall (opposite the stairs) of the upper room of Lackeen Castle, viewed from the turret that rises over it. Often described by modern commentators as halls or even 'great' halls, these rooms were in the tradition of the great chamber; unlike halls, they had chambers (and sometimes 'reception rooms') *beneath* them, and they were accessible by narrow spiral stairs rather than by straight stairs. The three arches above the main window – an arrangement that is especially common in the upper rooms of big tower-houses in the southern half of Ireland (see also pl. XIII) – was aesthetically pleasing but also had a structural purpose, allowing the wall above the window to be thickened so that space was available for the gable and the parapet, and sometimes even an actual wall-passage.

That change was actually underway as early as the mid-fourteenth century in England and, it seems, in Ireland too.[74] Moving dining rituals into the upper room of a tower, an act sometimes facilitated by having upstairs oven-fireplaces (as at Blarney, where it was inserted, and Togher, where it is original), certainly blurred the distinction between chamber and hall, and reminds us that architectural space is made 'public' or 'private' by how it is used, but it did *not* convert that upper room into a hall. The fact

74 In the poem *The vision of Piers Plowman* it is lamented that the lord and lady no longer liked to sit in the 'chief' hall that 'was made for meals' but prefered to eat by themselves 'in a privy parlour … or in a chamber with a chimney': J.M. Dent and E.P. Dutton (eds), *The vision of Piers Plowman [by] William Langland* (London and New York, 1978), passus 10, lines 96–101. My thanks to my UCD colleague, Prof. Alan Fletcher, for drawing my attention to this reference. A similar change in Ireland is suggested at Kilteel in 1335: 'if he [Robert Clifford, porter] should choose to diet in his chamber he should have the apartment beyond the gate of the castle'

is that external halls continued to be built in Ireland, indicating that, even though the inner households may have preferred to eat informally in their towers, even with guests, 'ceremonial dining' (feasting) remained within its traditional venue, the hall.

It seems clear, then, that Gernon was a guest in a tower no different from many others. His account testifies to the tendency of the later medieval elite households in Ireland to retreat (as comparable and contemporary European inner households did) both upwards and inwards, occasionally allowing into their private space a range of functions – receiving special guests, eating – that had previously been exclusively reserved to the hall. A lesser visitor might not have seen the inside of this Limerick tower but have eaten his meal and even spent the night on a blanket-and-straw bed in the 'house' or hall at its foot. If it was his status as a guest that ensured Gernon a ready supply of drink and the entertainment of a harpist, it was also what gained him access to the inner sanctum of the castle.[75]

The shifting relationship between the public and private realms attested in Gernon's testimony is captured very subtly in the phrasing of the later medieval references themselves. The (timber) hall always preceded the (stone) chamber in descriptions of the thirteenth and early fourteenth centuries, but the order of words was reversed from at least before the end of the fourteenth century. Thus, in 1344 the manor of Dunshaughlin had a messuage (dwelling house) and a hall while the nearby manor of Moyglare had a stone tower, a hall and a chamber, and in 1459 a property in 'Boyrebalistret' in Cashel had a 'castle, hall and place'.[76] The pattern continues into the seventeenth century. In 1607 an inquisition makes reference to 'building, repairing and keeping staunch … castles, halls and bawns'.[77] In 1618 an inquisition records that the settlement of Jago (now Gaganstown) contained 'one castle very ruinous and nearly prostrate and one ruined hall'.[78] And, to finish, there are Civil Survey references that maintain the word-order, sometimes with 'slate-house' replacing 'hall': for example, 'The Castle and Slate house of Castle John inhabitted' and 'Upon this land standeth a good castle, a slate house wanting repaire with a large bawne & severall cabbins'.[79] By this time, the mid-1600s, the references to slate-houses may of course be signalling to us that the towers were regarded as inadequate for occupation and that houses, although mentioned second, had assumed a new importance. I have no doubt that this was the case, but would argue that the 'shapes' of these records, with the castles/towers still meriting first mention, suggest some conceptual continuity with late medieval castle culture.

(Earl of Mayo, 'Kilteel Castle', *JKAS*, 1:1 (1891), 34–7 at 35). And from the late fourteenth century there is the suggestive record from the monastic grange of Duleek of a building with domestic space (including a 'knight's room') at first-floor level above a pantry and larder, with the 'ruined old' hall mentioned separately (Hogan, *Llanthony Prima and Secunda*, p. 348).   **75** For a different articulation of the same argument about the private nature of tower-houses and the absence of halls from their interiors, see Eadie, 'Detecting privacy and private space in the Irish tower house'; I am grateful to Dr Eadie for sending me copies of her forthcoming papers, each of which reinforces the argument.   **76** P. Dryburgh and B. Smith (eds), *Handbook and select calendar of sources for medieval Ireland in the national archives of the United Kingdom* (Dublin, 2005), p. 59 (Dunshaughlin, Moyglare); *COD, 1413–1509*, p. 429 (Cashel).   **77** K. Nicholls, *Gaelic and gaelicised Ireland in the Middle Ages* (Dublin, 1972), p. 33.   **78** *RPH*, p. 27.   **79** *Civil Survey*

Tower-houses, clearly to be equated with the 'castles' and 'towers' mentioned above and therefore to be interpreted as the containers of chambers, survive in significant numbers, usually as the only upstanding buildings on their sites. We will discuss their architecture in detail below. The survival rate of the halls/houses – both the 'soft' ones built of organic materials[80] and stone-built ones – is very much poorer. While halls of organic material could not survive in the Irish climate, many stone-built halls were denied greater longevity by virtue of their thin walls: for example, the castle of Downeen (formerly Downings), standing on a tiny windswept island near Rosscarbery, retains a substantial part of its chamber tower, but only foundations remain of its hall/house.[81] It is not inconceivable, of course, that in very minor castles, especially those very remote from centres of lordship, the hall was sometimes dispensed with as a separate structure or concept of space and its entire range of functions brought under the same roof as the sleeping quarters, but we can be confident that any medieval lord who built a turriform chamber, no matter how minor his status or how small the tower, had or desired to have a hall separate from that tower.

Towers and halls/houses

The chronological and spatial relationships between tower-houses and their associated halls/houses are complex. The structures can be contemporary or of different dates, and conjoined or detached. To add complication, the halls/houses were very often of timber originally and, in all probability, were not infrequently replaced in stone.

Examples of conjoined stone towers and timber halls of the same date are difficult to identify but were probably not uncommon. Conjoined stone towers and stone halls of the same date, akin to the hall-and-chamber blocks of the 1200s, are more easily identified but apparently were not common. One of the finest examples was at Granny. Here, as in many English examples, the hall was flanked by contemporary domestic structures at *both* ends; only one of the two towers – the lesser one, according to Place's drawing – still stands today (fig. 131).[82]

Granny's hall was an elaborate structure, well worthy of the term 'hall'. Less elaborate and less legible was the coeval arrangement of elements in the famous group of later sixteenth-century Wexford castles of which Coolhull is the classic site (fig. 132).[83] The 'halls' here were at first-floor level and were not entered directly from the outside, two aspects of their architecture that raise serious doubts about the legitimacy of their modern descriptions as 'halls'. Moreover, the adjoining towers at these sites were simply too small to provide particularly comfortable accommodation

(*Tipperary*, 1), pp 101, 106.   **80** The term 'soft' comes from C. Cairns, *Irish tower houses: a County Tipperary case study* (Athlone, 1987), p. 17. See also T.B. Barry, 'Harold Leask's "single towers": Irish tower-houses as part of larger settlement complexes', *CG*, 22 (2006), 27–34. **81** Incidentally, the island was accessed by a wooden drawbridge in the late sixteenth century (*Pacata Hibernia*, 2, ed. S. O'Grady (London, 1896), p. 209).   **82** The drawing is reproduced in J. Fenlon, *Ormond Castle: visitor's guide* (Dublin, 2008), p. 35.   **83** O'Callaghan, 'Fortified houses, south Wexford'; Colfer, *Wexford castles*, pp 187–98.

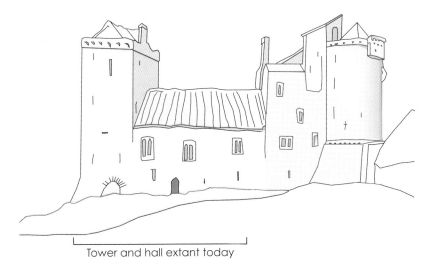

Tower and hall extant today

131 Granny Castle at the end of the 1600s, redrawn from the original by Francis Place; no attempt has been made here to 'straighten up' features of his drawing. The cylindrical tower with an attached square block on the right-hand side no longer stands.

(and in the case of Rathshillane, a related castle, there was no tower at all). While it would be wrong to deny some degree of 'public functionality' to the 'halls' of these castles, their spatial and architectural relationships with the towers suggest that they might be better interpreted as elongated great chambers, not unlike the first-floor room in the Desmond Tower of Askeaton Castle mentioned above. Kindlestown, which had a narrow tower at one end until its collapse in the early 1900s, is a fourteenth-century precursor. Perhaps the same interpretation can be made of Ballycarbery (pl. XI) as of Coolhull and its kin-group. Ballycarbery's upper room was divided into two parts of unequal length, the shorter one being 'private' while longer one straddled the same hall/great chamber divide that we observe at Coolhull. Of course, it would not damage my thesis about halls and chambers were any of these long rooms to be interpreted as halls: private chambers are neither above nor below them, so their labelling does not affect the core assertion, which is that tower-houses did not contain halls.

Coeval towers and halls/houses attached to each other, as at Granny, are the exception rather than the rule. Sometimes the towers are late medieval while the 'halls' predate them. Examples include Castle Barrett (where the Anglo-Norman 'hall' is at first-floor level and might therefore have been a chamber), Ileclash or Licklash (where the tower is an early edition to a now-lost thirteenth-century hall) and Ormond Castle in Carrick-on-Suir (where two towers – the ones that are seen rising over the gabled roof of its famous Elizabethan-era frontage – were added to a rectangular building of clear thirteenth-century date). At Drimnagh, the residential gate tower was also added to what was either a first-floor hall or an elongated chamber, but the gap in date between the two parts is not as long as in the examples just given. More frequently, the towers predate the lower-elevation buildings, whether those buildings were

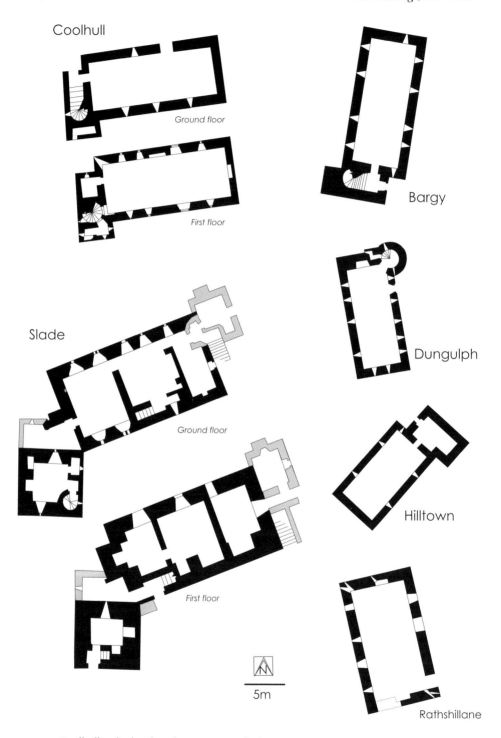

132 Coolhull and related castles in Co. Wexford.

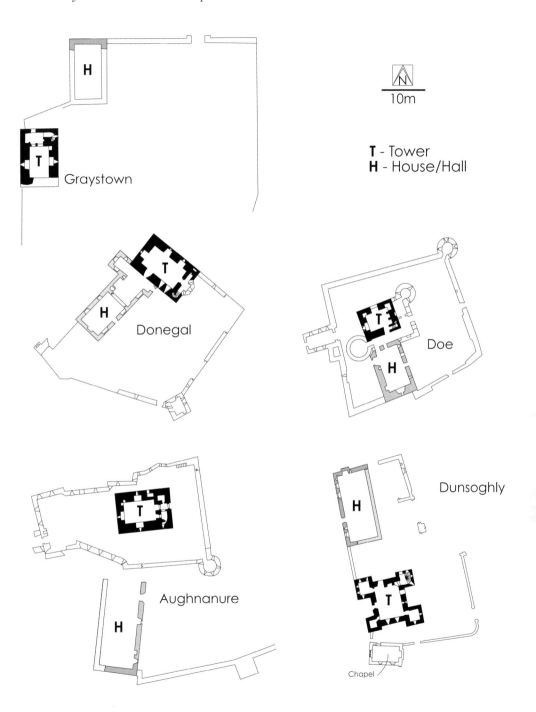

10m

T - Tower
H - House/Hall

Graystown

Donegal

Doe

Aughnanure

Dunsoghly

Chapel

133 A selection of tower-and-hall plans.

attached to them or stood separately from them. Those buildings took a variety of forms (fig. 133). Simple rectangular plans, though executed in different sizes, can be seen at, for example, Aughnanure, Graystown and Srah; in each of these cases, as in others like them, it is possible to argue that an older hall/house was replaced in stone.[84] Sites where the add-on 'halls'/'houses' are of more complex plan include Athlumney, Athcarne, Deel, Donegal and Rathcline.[85] These and other sites are a mixture of native, Old English and plantation castles.

Perhaps the most interesting site at which an older tower-house had a new structure attached to it is the Purcell-owned Loughmoe. The tower itself was built in the late fifteenth century, and is distinguished by externally rounded corners (in which regard it compares well with some important north Cork tower-houses such as Cloghleagh and Castle Cooke). A long rectangular wing was added in the early seventeenth century to the tower's entrance façade (pl. XII, fig. 134). The original room-functions within the wing are uncertain but all the elements present in contemporary Portumna were probably represented.[86] Loughmoe Castle as redesigned was entered from the east, but its symmetrical west-facing rear was actually intended to be seen as its façade. A cross-passage (but with only one end-of-passage door, not two) ran between the tower-house and the new wing, and this was represented on the outside of the façade by a small adjustment to the placement of windows. What is so fascinating about Loughmoe, then, is how, as the medieval period turned into the modern period and as Renaissance symmetry replaced medieval asymmetry, there was retained in the fenestration a subtle hint of the old, traditional, hall-and-chamber format. Loughmoe is a gem of a building; its continued decay is cause for concern.

TOWER-HOUSES

The survival rate of towers is higher than that of halls; examples are almost every-where in Ireland, and they pay no obvious respect to where the boundaries ran between the island's various medieval ethno-political populations. More than one thousand

---

84 O'Keeffe, 'Halls, "hall-houses" and tower-houses', pp 259–61 (Graystown and Srah).
85 Some of these have been published properly: T. McNeill and M.A. Wilkin, 'Donegal Castle', *UJA*, 58 (1999), 81–9; J. Lyttleton, 'Rathcline Castle: an archaeology of plantation in Co. Longford' in M. Morris and F. O'Ferrall (eds), *Longford: history and society* (Dublin, 2010), pp 135–59. At Deel, the least well-known of these, the house attached to the tower is an add-on, its original 'pie-crust' cornice and plain chimney putting it in the 1700s, but it has a corner machicolation that copies in design, but not detailing, the original on the tower.   86 The rooms in Portumna included a 'great hall' and various parlours (one 'large', one 'winter'), chambers (one 'great', two 'withdrawing', and two bedchambers) and closets: see J. Fenlon (ed.), *Clanricard's Castle: Portumna House, Co. Galway* (Dublin, 2012). See also O'Keeffe, '*Aula* and *camera*'.

---

134 (*opposite*) Loughmoe Castle interior, showing the original entrance façade of the tower-house, the original doorway, and the brackets of a machicolated parapet. The seventeenth-century wing was timber-floored throughout, as was normal for that era. Even from this angle one can see how many fireplaces were in the new wing.

examples survive in various states of repair. We simply do not know how many we have lost. Nineteenth-century Ordnance Survey maps of the north-eastern baronies of Kildare, to take a random geographical case study, mark just over two-dozen castle sites, which suggests a modest level of encastellation (not all of it later medieval) in a wedge of good land near the capital city, but 'missing' castles, enumerated from seventeenth-century sources (especially the Civil Survey), raise the number to 150 sites. It indicates a huge rate of destruction between the mid-1600s and the mid-1800s. Presuming most of these now-lost castles to have been tower-houses, one is struck by the number of townlands that had more than one, and especially by the concentrations in 'Newtown O More' (probably Newtownpark, near Blessington), which had four, and Rathmore (Kildare), with another four. The former was a rural townland, the latter a thirteenth-century settlement that had decayed by the 1400s.

The biggest concentration of towers is across the south of the country, from Wexford westwards onto the fertile lowland plains of south-west Leinster (Kilkenny) and eastern and central Munster (Waterford, Cork, Tipperary), and from there northwards into Limerick and across the Shannon into Clare and central Galway. Although there are other concentrations (particularly around the coast) and even some fairly large areas of emptiness on the map (such as central Ulster), the implications of the distribution are clear. First, the classic late medieval tower-house initially emerged as a coherent type of physical object – a 'landscape artifact' – not in Gaelic Ireland, nor in eastern Ulster where influence might have crept in from Scottish towers of the 1300s, but in the lands of former Anglo-Norman lordship in southern Ireland.[87] Second, its architecture was *understood*, as symbolic of status on the one hand and as an environment of domestic ritual on the other, by both 'English' and 'Irish' communities.

The tower-houses themselves exhibit considerable variability, but it is within a narrow spectrum, with patterns in that variability a matter of both specific location and geographical scale. Thus, for example, tower-houses of the fifteenth-century English Pale – incorporating virtually all of Cos Dublin and Louth, and the eastern sides of Cos Kildare and Meath – are demonstrably different in plan and detailing from those of, say, south Tipperary, though not sufficiently different for us to query the thesis that all tower-houses are manifestations of common architectural ideals. And just as the tower-houses of south Tipperary themselves exhibit variability, there is in the Pale an observable difference between tower-house design of the northern (Louth and Meath) and southern (Dublin and Kildare) ends.

These differences aside, we can generate a simple classification of tower-house architecture based on two variables. The first is what we might describe as 'outline-shape' at ground level, and the second is the internal plan. Regarding shape, the towers are often self-contained, simple square, rectangular or cylindrical blocks. Variability is

---

87 T. O'Keeffe, 'Rural settlement and cultural identity in Gaelic Ireland, 1000–1500', *Ruralia*, I (1996), 142–53. Scottish influence on northern Irish castles of the late Middle Ages requires some study, but it is really only apparent from *c*.1600 (see E.M. Jope, 'Scottish influences in the north of Ireland: castles with Scottish features, 1580–1640', *UJA*, 14 (1951), 31–47), which brings it beyond the scope of this book. Even the extent to which that early modern influence spread southwards out of Ulster (as at Robertstown Castle, for example) remains to be determined.

135 Court Castle. This is an odd-shaped tower-house: it is essentially square but one of its faces, visible in this photograph, is convex. Although outwardly suggestive of one half of a twin-towered gate building of the thirteenth century, it is entirely a structure of the fifteenth century. The castle in Clarecastle on the opposite side of the Shannon Estuary is a similar but more refined building.

introduced through the deployment of turrets at the corners of the main blocks. Towers with two or more turrets are most common in (though not exclusive to) the Pale, where they are arranged symmetrically (usually at opposite corners), or in a clockwise rhythm. There is also a small number of towers of unusual shape, such as the Limerick pair of Castletroy and Court Castle (fig. 135).[88] There is no particular chronological significance to outline shape, although towers with small cylindrical turrets at their corners, most common in the northern part of the Pale, do tend to be quite late in the sequence. The more interesting variable for classification is internal layout. Here, we might distinguish for convenience between towers with single *habitable* spaces at each floor level, and those that had chambers ancillary to the main rooms at each floor level (described hereafter as 'complex-plan' towers). Tower-houses of simpler layout were subdivided at each floor level, but the subdivision was between the main room and the narrow 'strip' that contained the stairs and maybe also a passage to a garderobe. We should not be too dogmatic about the distinction: Rockfleet, for example, the small tower-house to which Grace O'Malley retired in 1583 after the death of her second husband, straddles the divide between 'simple' and 'complex'.

88 See C.J. Donnelly, 'A typological study of the tower houses of County Limerick', *JRSAI*, 129 (1999), 19–39 at 28–9.

It goes without saying that the more complex the plan of a tower-house the greater its functional range: very complex plans could, for example, accommodate the 'reception rooms' and 'cubicles' mentioned in some sources, as well as provide ample toilet facilities. There was also greater drama moving through a complex-plan building: moving through a building is a process of discovery, as one space unfolds after another, and there were simply more spaces to be unfolded in complex-plan structures. The affect was heightened in those towers like Ballymarkahan, built around 1430.[89] Here, the five-storey main block had vaults over its second and fourth storeys, the latter vaults providing the stone floor of the large, elegant chamber below the roof, but there were five storeys below the upper chamber in the narrower part of the tower-house, four of them vaulted at angles perpendicular to the main vaults. Also, passages leading to latrines were carried on arches at the levels of the main-room vaults. More spaces also meant greater uncertainty, maybe a feeling of vulnerability, for even the most benign visitors: at almost every rotation of a spiral stairs in a complex-plan tower-house there was a doorway, and visitors might have found this somewhat disorienting, especially if the doors were closed.

The distinction between the two formats, simple- and complex-plan, can be understood in part as a consequence of vaulting or the lack of it. Thick walls were needed to support vaults, but those walls could be hollow-built to make inter-mural passages and chambers. Not all tower-builders made use of the thick walls that came with vaulting: in the Pale, for example, vaults were commonly deployed but complex-plans were achieved not by making small rooms and passages within the central blocks of the towers but by adding small turrets to those central blocks. In the later sixteenth century vaults generally went out of fashion everywhere in Ireland,[90] but this did not stop tower-builders from erecting complex-plan buildings.

Some features of tower-houses

Tower-houses have many features, some recurring frequently and some rarely. A full catalogue would require much more space than can be afforded here, so a brief summary should suffice.

Although they were rarely oriented with any concern for the cardinal points, it is very common to find that tower-houses were entered from the east. In most cases the main door is on the right-hand side of the façade as one faces it. The door surrounds often have small holes at the sides and at the top, and careful examination of these usually reveals considerable wear. These were holes through which were passed the chains that connected to 'yetts', grilles that were pulled up against the outsides of the doors – the door-surrounds are actually recessed for them – to provide an extra layer of protection (fig. 136). Inside the door of a tower-house itself was a small lobby,

89 Westropp, 'Notes on the lesser castles', p. 362.   90 Although dispensed with by tower-house builders, the use of a vault over a main space did not disappear completely from the architectural repertoire, as witness its use *c.*1620 in the plantation castle in Lisnaskea: see D.M. Waterman, 'Castle Balfour, Lisnaskea, Co. Fermanagh', *UJA*, 31 (1968), 71–6.

136 The doorway of the tower-house of Graystown Castle, showing evidence of a former 'yett' (a term probably derived from an older English word for 'gate').

directly in front of which was normally the door into the lower floor of the tower. In a small number of cases the door into that lower room is not directly in front of the main door but to the left side, and in its place is a wall with a small cross-window for musket-use.

Some towers have both ground-floor and first-floor entrances, and had no direct access between the two floor levels.[91] This 'dual-entrance' arrangement increased security for the upper rooms but it must be understood primarily in terms of the social use of space within the towers, specifically the separation of those upper rooms from the lower levels. It is difficult to avoid the conclusion that in possessing first-floor entrances the towers in question are reflecting the descent of the tower-house as a concept from the thirteenth-century chamber donjon or chamber-block, also entered at first-floor level.

The stairs usually rise to the left just inside the main doorway of a tower-house, often ascending as straight stairs to the corner (which is at first-floor level) before continuing as clockwise spiral stairs. In smaller towers the spiral stairs start almost immediately inside the doorway. Stairs that are on the right of the main doorway ascend as anti-clockwise spirals and are never, to my knowledge, preceded by long flights of straight stairs. The spiral stairs are continuous until they exit either at roof level (common in the Pale) or at top-floor level (common in southern Ireland). In examples of the latter, it is normal for another stairs, small and often hidden away in a window embrasure, to give access to the parapet (pl. XIII).

Most but not all tower-houses have fireplaces; in a small number of towers (probably all of early date within the sequence), heat was obviously provided by braziers with roof-louvres to carry the smoke away. When fireplaces do occur, they tend to be found at higher floor levels in both end-wall or side-wall positions. Most of the fireplace-surrounds have flat lintels, mainly formed of single stones but sometimes formed of many stones cut jigsaw-like (or 'joggled'). An arched effect is sometimes created by curvature where the lintel rests on the sides of the fireplace. Inserted fireplaces are not unusual. One should always be aware of the distinction (not always obvious) between an inserted fireplace, which is a radical structural alteration suggesting a change in how a room 'works', and an inserted fireplace-surround, which is a cosmetic alteration to a pre-existing opening.

Fireplaces necessitated chimneys. These generally rose on the parapets, sometimes separated from the battlemented wall (fig. 137) but more usually placed in such a way that they were a physical obstruction to anybody wanting to walk the full circuit of the parapet. As if in compensation for the inconvenience, they became display features in their own right, often rising to great heights not simply to carry smoke away but to show people from afar that the castles so provided were well-heated. There can be no doubt about the symbolic value of chimneys when one encounters in late sixteenth-

91 R. Sherlock, 'Cross-cultural occurrences of mutations in tower house architecture: evidence for cultural homogeneity in late medieval Ireland?', *JIA*, 15 (2006), 73–91.

137 Cullahill Castle. The large chimney stack on the left was inserted in the sixteenth century into this very large fifteenth-century tower-house. Care was taken in this case not to obstruct the parapet walkway, so it remained possible to walk between the chimney and the battlements. Tall stacks or blocks like this, either narrow and containing single flues, or wide and containing two or more flues (and with vertical grooves cut into the stonework to indicate the number of flues) were popular from the last quarter of the sixteenth century to the 1640s.

138 The diagonal chimneys of Terryland Castle are typical for the period around 1600. The first appearance of the form was probably in the later 1500s.

and early seventeenth-century contexts banks of chimneys in which one or two are actually flue-less (or dummy) chimneys (see above, p. 95). By that stage, parapets were no longer a frequent feature of castle architecture and the chimneys were increasingly incorporated in the gables, which, in the absence of the parapets, were themselves flush with the walls below. The chimneys themselves were simple monoliths until the late 1500s when, under Renaissance influence entering Ireland via the brick architecture of Elizabethan England, their stonework began to be embellished (figs 138, 139).

Toilets in Irish castles of all dates are commonly described in the scholarly literature as 'garderobes'. That term, derived from the Old French *garderobe*, a keep-robe, actually refers to the small room in which the toilet was placed rather than to the toilet itself.[92] The small rooms were normally at the ends of passages in both Anglo-Norman castles and tower-houses (and the passages were normally dog-legged in the former), thus maximizing the distance odour had to travel before it afflicted the senses; some tower-house garderobes even have small holes to provide extra ventilation (as at Coole and Dowth, where they are decorated). Insofar as there is a pattern, garderobes tend to be found on the north sides of tower-houses. The toilets themselves were simple planks or boards set into the side walls (the grooves often survive) and which had holes cut in

---

92 'Garderobe, n.', OED online. See also E. Fernie, 'Technical terms and the understanding of English medieval architecture', *Architectural History*, 44 (2001), 13–21 at 18.

139 The late sixteenth-century (?) chimneys at Carbury Castle are unusual in an Irish context in being star-shaped. Parallels include the brick chimneys at Grafton Manor, Worcestershire (1567–9).

them; some garderobes were so wide from side-wall to side-wall that the boards (or seats) may have had more than one hole to allow more than one person sit at the same time. The boards may have been covered with cloth when not in use,[93] to stop odours

93 John Russell's *Book of nurture*, a fifteenth-century etiquette guide for the young nobleman in

140 The toilet chute at Drumharsna Castle, typical in its size and in its position just above ground level.

rising back up into the garderobe and to keep flies out. The only significant difference between thirteenth-century and later medieval toilets is the system to carry away the waste: the late medieval norm, encountered rarely in earlier contexts (see Ballymoon Castle, for example), was for a chute within the thickness of the wall to carry the waste to a pit at the base of the wall (fig. 140). That waste could include broken pottery and other domestic items[94] as well as human excrement. Chute exits were quite high in some late medieval contexts (such as Blarney Castle and the gate tower of Liscarroll Castle), so excrement leaving such buildings would have been visible from afar, but the frequency with which such material was deposited more discretely at wall-bases in the late Middle Ages suggests an incipient modesty; of course, the longer the chute the less draughty the toilet seat, so that may have been a consideration too. 'Slop-stones', which are small drainage basins underneath windows, were probably used as urinals. They are often found on stairs. Urinating on stairs was apparently not unusual – the Brunswick Court Regulations of 1589 famously ordained that nobody 'whoever he may be, before, at, or after meals, early or late, foul the staircases, corridors with

the service of a great lord, recommended a green cloth; it also recommended some cotton or linen be left beside the toilet (as toilet paper, basically) as well as a basin, jug and towel for hand-washing afterwards (see F.J. Furnivall, *The babees book* (London, 1868), pp 179–80).   **94** T. Fanning, J.G. Hurst and J.M. Lewis, 'A mid-seventeenth-century pottery group and other objects from Ballyhack Castle, Co. Wexford', *PRIA*, 75C (1975), 103–18.

urine or other filth, but go to suitable, prescribed places for such relief'[95] – and the slop-stones, even if not intended as urinals, would not have discouraged the practice.

Tower-house defensibility

One often finds the tower-house defined in the literature as the fortified residence of a later medieval lord, and one often reads that tower-houses were necessitated by endemic small-scale warfare during the later Middle Ages. The enclosures around or attached to the towers should provide the first supporting evidence, and indeed some, like Glanworth and Granny, have cylindrical towers that appear at first glance to be thirteenth-century bastions but can be dated to the later Middle Ages by their gun-loops. But many bawns, like that at Knockkelly, for example, are too big to have been defended easily and their flankers, when they had them, were rarely designed to cover fields of fire.

Dating bawns relative to towers is difficult unless the two are physically connected (see fig. 133). Thus, for example, the bawn of Ballygrennan Castle is contemporary with that castle's exceptional late sixteenth-century tower-house, the bawn that abuts the early fifteenth-century tower-house at Ballycullen is an addition, whereas at Gragan the fifteenth-century tower-house was added to the bawn. Older earthworks were sometimes converted into bawns: Ballyshanny, Ballyganner and Caherdrinny castles, for example, occupy old *cathair* (stone fort) sites, the latter within a prehistoric hillfort. The 'bawn of sods' mentioned at Lisgannon in 1601 seems to have been a reused ringfort.[96] The enclosure of towers could involve more than simply building walls. Natural topography was often exploited. At Carrigarreely, for example, the rocky site was quarried, especially on two sides, to form an angled rectilinear shape, while at Rockstown the long rock outcrop had a ditch quarried through it right in front of the tower-house. Tower-houses sometimes occupied small islands, and it is possible that at least some of these were crannogs (such as Carrowena), even if partly natural (such as Rosclogher).

The towers themselves are rarely of a plan-type that suggests a heightened awareness of defensive needs, although there are some interesting exceptions in Cork (fig. 141). So, when we think of tower-house defence we tend to think of machicolations, bartizans and murder holes. A machicolation is usually a projecting stone structure or a projecting stone parapet that has a gapped floor through which 'things' could fall or be dropped vertically downwards.[97] The gapped or 'holed' floor is critical to the definition – the machicolation refers more correctly to the gap than to the structure above the gap – so, when we speak of features that are 'machicolated' we are signifying that these features are largely floorless. Most machicolated features in Irish castles are defensive in purpose, even if only symbolically in many cases, and indeed the term machicolation itself is alleged to originate in medieval Latin and Old French terms that

95 N. Elias, *The civilising process* (rev. ed. Oxford, 2000), pp 111–12. Portable urinals among the later medieval nobility are attested to by John Russell (Lurnivall, *Babees book*, p. 179). **96** O. Davies, 'The castles of Co. Cavan: pt II', *UJA*, 11 (1948), 118–19. **97** There is a mid-fifteenth-century record of a fatality caused by a stone dropped from the top of a castle (*AU*, 1451.1).

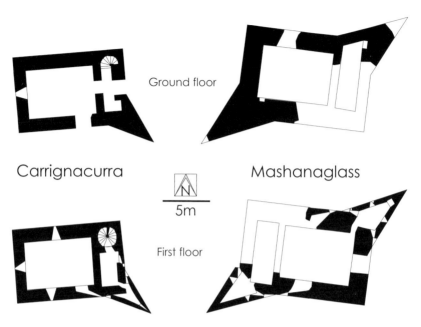

Ground floor

Carrignacurra   Mashanaglass

5m

First floor

141 Carrignacurra and Mashanaglass castle plans.

between them translate literally as 'neck-breaker' or 'neck-crusher'.[98] The oldest form of machicolation in Europe is probably the *slot machicolation*, literally a slot in the underside of an arch or behind an arch, less for dropping missiles through than for firing arrows through. There are no certain thirteenth-century examples surviving in Ireland,[99] but there are fifteenth-century examples in the Strangford area of Co. Down, at Kilclief Castle, Audley's Castle and Jordan's Castle. There is also an exceptionally interesting but little-known group of slot machicolations associated with tower-house doorways in Galway, as at Castle Taylor, Lydacan and Newtown.

The classic *murder-hole*, which is mainly found in tower-houses but also in gate buildings and gate passages, is actually a form of slot machicolation. It is simply a hole, square or slightly rectangular, in the floor of the room – which is directly over an entrance lobby or passageway. Unlike the other forms of machicolation discussed here, it is actually an *internal* feature: one has already passed through an outer doorway when one stands underneath a murder-hole. There is usually just the one, but sometimes there are more, as at Castlecaulfield, an early seventeenth-century plantation castle, where there are three in succession. The term 'murder-hole' suggests a violent function. There is no doubt that anybody standing underneath one, especially in a tower-house, was trapped by locked doors and was therefore vulnerable (to musket fire

98 J. Harris, 'Machicolation: history and significance', *CSGJ*, 23 (2009–10), 191–214.
99 Goddard Orpen suggested that the very ruined gateway of thirteenth-century Rathgorgin Castle had a slot machicolation ('The mote of Oldcastle and the castle of Rathgorgin').

rather than big rocks or boiling oil). A murder-hole would have added immeasurably, then, to a household's sense of security. Most of the time, however, the murder-hole allowed visitors to be 'inspected' from above before full entry was granted to them. Some pleasure may have been taken from the discomfort visitors must have felt waiting and knowing they were being watched from above! At Lackeen Castle there is even a small murder-hole 'protecting' the entrance to the upper room (fig. 130) from the stairs, and this should certainly be regarded as an inspection-of-visitors feature; after all, it was really too late for defence if an enemy had made it all the way up the stairs.

Next, a *machicolated parapet* is a parapet that, supported by corbels, projects from the plane of the wall below. In a machicolated parapet one cannot easily look out across the battlements because of the gapped floor. The most famous such parapet in Ireland – a classic example, in fact – is the parapet of Blarney Castle; kissers of its stone have to lean backwards *across* the machicolation, the gap, to achieve their gift of verbosity. Machicolated parapets of stone really only appeared in Ireland in the 1400s, remaining popular until the eve of the Cromwellian wars.

The simplest and most common form of machicolation (or 'machicolated' feature) is a *box machicolation*. This is a plain, floorless, rectangular box on corbels, normally projecting about 1m, and usually between 1m and 2m wide. It is really too small to contain what one might regard as a room: one does not *enter* a box machicolation so much as *lean* into it (or, when it is a latrine, sit into it). Most box machicolations of the later Middle Ages sit on the parapets of tower-houses and comparably dated buildings (including even some churches, such as Carron, where the example is original, and Ballycahill, where it is an addition), and they are normally directly over their doorways, although there are exceptions (fig. 142). The gaps are almost always lintelled; while one lintel looks much like another, there is an interesting little Wexford group – the castles of Killiane, Fethard-on-Sea and Slade, for example – in which the lintel is composed of a flat stone laid vertically. There are few exceptions to the trend of lintelling the box machicolation: one is in Peppard's Castle, Ardee, where there is a broad ogee-arch rather than a lintel, and another is in Ballinafad, where an arched effect was created by adding extra corbels underneath the lintel. The only real variations between box machicolations are actually in their corbels: these can be squared-off, rounded, double-rounded or tapered, but there is one case – Ardglass – where there are moulded corbels holding up a box; these may have been recycled from some other, probably ecclesiastical, building. There are some box machicolations that are *not* connected to parapets but which simply project from the flat walls lower down, though these are not as common: Ballinalacken and Ballagharahin have big examples, with gun-loops; Ballyhack and Tyntes Castle, Youghal, have unusual sloping 'roofs'; Knockane has a unique 'roof' that is nearly pyramidal; Shean More has an unusual pairing of examples (fig. 143). Small, sloping-roofed and machicolated box-like features that project from the mid-height corners or angles of many Irish tower-houses, such as Ballymalis and Aughnanure (fig. 144), are sometimes described in the Irish literature as bartizans.[100]

---

100 There is considerable confusion in the literature in these islands about what features could or should be described as 'bartizans'. The term is actually an invention of the eighteenth century.

142 Tourin Castle's box machicolation offers protection to a spot that seems not to have needed it!

143 Shean More Castle. Note the tiny gun-holes at the junctions of the machicolations and the castle's walls. This tower-house had entrances at ground-floor and first-floor levels, the latter (visible in this photograph) leading into a passage.

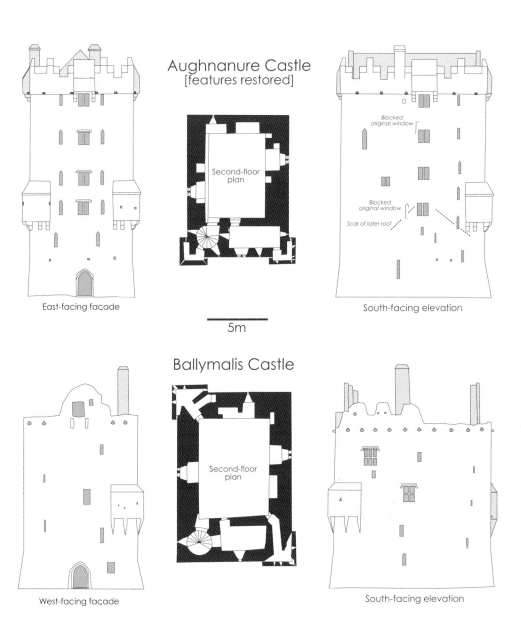

Aughnanure Castle
[features restored]

Second-floor
plan

East-facing façade

South-facing elevation

Blocked
original window

Blocked
original window

Scar of later roof

5m

Ballymalis Castle

Second-floor
plan

West-facing façade

South-facing elevation

144 Aughnanure and Ballymalis castle elevations. At Ballymalis the 'bartizans' are on opposite corners, which is the normal arrangement. At Aughnanure they are on the tower's façade, which contributes to its general symmetry.

These too normally have musket holes. As with the box machicolations, the types of corbels used in these machicolated bartizans vary considerably, sometimes even in the one building. At Danganbrack there are spiked and rounded corbels on the machicolations on opposite corners at parapet level.

On the whole, it is unlikely that any of these late medieval box machicolations were used for dropping missiles on unwelcome visitors, as such a scenario would have required permanent stockpiles of missile-like objects on the parapets. Rather, given the general absence of spy-holes associated with the main entrances into buildings, the box machicolation probably functioned as the murder-hole functioned: an inspection facility through which a musket could be fired in an emergency.

A sample tower-house tradition 1: 'sectionally constructed' tower-houses

There are many small, fairly localized, traditions of tower-house design in Ireland.[101] One such tradition is mainly confined to Cos Limerick, Clare and Galway.[102] It is the tradition of the 'sectionally constructed' tower-house; the name comes from Colm Donnelly's work.[103] These are literally two-sectioned tower-houses of two phases, the earlier phases being the narrow sections, containing the stairs and subsidiary chambers, and the later phases being the longer rectangular blocks containing the stacks of larger rooms (fig. 145). In other words, they follow the conventional complex plan-type discussed above, but with a discontinuity of construction between the two parts. Their phased construction is manifest externally in straight vertical joints, where the walls of the second-phase parts abut the quoined corners of the first-phase parts. Usually there are some 'through-stones' connecting both sections and helping to bond them together, and these seem in every instance to be original to the earlier parts, indicating that the narrow sections were built with the intention of having larger masonry structures added on. The vertical joints and 'through-stones' might not have been visible in the Middle Ages, of course, as tower walls were externally harled.

A number of the buildings retain both parts today: good examples are Lough Gur, Ballinalackin and Mannin. In these cases, the parts are nearly contemporary, and were there no vertical joints visible one would not immediately think of these as two-phase tower-houses.[104] At Rockstown, another tower-house with two near-contemporary sections, the vertical joint is visible on one side only, as if the builders proceeded to build the larger part of the tower-house having completed building on one-half of the narrow part. The most interesting 'sectionally constructed' tower-houses are those in which *only* the narrow, earlier, parts survive, as is spectacularly the case at Carrigaholt, where the second part was probably never finished. Other examples include Seefin and Tullovin. The fate of the larger (phase-two) parts of these tower-houses is intriguing.

101 Some are discussed in Sherlock, 'Cross-cultural occurrences of mutations in tower house architecture'.   **102** An outlier is the original tower-house in Parke's Castle (Foley and Donnelly, *Parke's Castle*, p. 41).   **103** C.J. Donnelly, 'Sectionally constructed tower houses: a review of the evidence from Limerick', *JRSAI*, 128 (1998), 26–34.   **104** Although it is a tower-house of quite different plan, the two parts (of different date) of Blarney tower-house also have straight joints in the manner of the sectionally constructed towers.

Some may have simply sheared away and collapsed, the bonding being insufficiently strong to hold them in place. Others may have been demolished, although this seems highly unlikely. The best explanation for these one-section-only examples is that they were never finished off, at least in stone. At Leamaneh, where the narrow (fifteenth-century) tower is abutted by a multi-storeyed house of *c*.1640, it is highly unlikely that the second section of the tower-house was ever finished in stone. The same could be argued of Ballinveala: no fewer than eighteen rows of 'through-stones' were incorporated into its narrow tower in readiness for the second phase of construction work, but there is no evidence that anything was ever built in the Middle Ages, and in fact the doorways that were opened to provide communication between the two sections were blocked off.

A sample tower-house tradition 2: the Pale

The Pale was the district around Dublin in the fifteenth century in which was the greatest concentration of landed families loyal to the English crown.[105] Composed more or less of Cos Dublin, Kildare, (east) Meath and Louth, its boundary was described in 1488 and again in 1492 (when an act of parliament ordained that it be enclosed with a rampart) as extending from Dalkey westwards along the foothills of the Dublin-Wicklow mountains to the Liffey valley, then northwards from Ballymore Eustace towards Kilcock, from which point it headed north-westwards and then north-eastwards across central Meath to northern Louth and an eventual termination at Dundalk (fig. 146).

Differences between the descriptions of the Pale border suggest great fluidity. It is safest to think of the Pale as ill defined geographically, with its outer edges, especially those most distant from Dublin, never regarded as sharp lines.[106] The tower-houses of the general Pale area are of special interest for two reasons: they are architecturally distinctive (and their distribution underscores the vague territoriality of the Pale margins),[107] and we have parliamentary acts that refer to a process of building towers within the region. Those acts, first of all, date from 1428 and 1430.[108] The first act ordained that the commons of Louth grant a £10 subsidy to any man who would, in the following five years, build a castle or tower twenty feet in length, sixteen in breadth and forty in height. The second act extended the condition to the other counties and extended the duration to ten years. There was a further provision in 1447 in parts of Meath for subsidies to be collected from ploughlands to help fund new castles of slightly smaller size (15 x 15 x 40 feet) in Meath but this was revoked by

105 Historical accounts of the Pale and its development are easily obtained. Highly recommended is M. Potterton and M. Murphy, *The Dublin region in the Middle Ages* (Dublin, 2010).   **106** T. O'Keeffe, 'Medieval frontiers and fortification: the Pale and its evolution' in F.H.A. Aalen and K. Whelan (eds), *Dublin city and county: prehistory to present* (Dublin, 1992), pp 55–77.   **107** This is not to say that every tower-house in the region is of the same tradition: Donadea, for example, is atypical for the region and would 'fit' better in Ormond.   **108** The date of the latter is normally given as 1429 but John Bradley and Ben Murtagh, in a useful discussion, have corrected this to 1430 ('Brady's Castle, Thomastown, Co. Kilkenny: a 14th-century fortified town house' in Kenyon and O'Conor (eds), *The medieval castle in Ireland and*

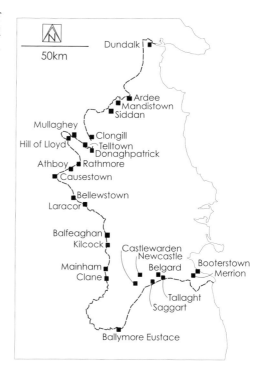

146 The boundary line of the English Pale at the end of the fifteenth century.

parliament in 1449, but a new act for four years was put in place for Kildare five years later.[109] The references to building of the towers often give us little information, but here is one of the better ones, from 1465, referring to a two-storeyed tower, not unlike perhaps the small thirteenth-century chamber tower in Inch, discussed above (p. 216):

> Also, at the prayers of Roger Penkeston of Ballynagappagh, gentleman in the county of Kildare. Whereas the said Roger has begun and made a tower of the height of one storey above the vault in Ballynagappagh aforesaid, in the frontiers in the march of the said county, which tower contains in length and breadth according to the form of the statute in that case ordained and provided and if it were finished it would be a signal refuge to all the inhabitants of the said county. Whereupon the premise considered: it is enacted, ordained and established, by authority of the said parliament, that the said Roger shall have ten pounds granted to him.[110]

Subsidies were not all set at £10. In 1467–8 a new castle was planned at Kilcullen for which £20 was levied. The people of the county were instructed 'with their carts, to carry stones for [its] building'.[111] One castle funded by a more substantial grant (in 1462) was Kinnafad, a rectangular tower-house with gun-loops, at the western extremity of the region:

Wales, p. 212 n. 1). **109** *SRPI, Hen. VI*, pp 17, 33–5, 107–9, 176, 299. **110** *SRPI, Ed. IV*, p. 397. **111** Ibid., pp 60–9.

£40 was granted to Sir Robert Preston lord of Gormanstown and Sir Thomas Plunket upon the county of Meath to raise the said castle … and also that the four baronies of Meath next adjoining to the said ford shall perform all manner of carriage of stones, lime, sand and trees, necessary to the said castle … to find meat and drink for all the masons, workmen of the said castle.[112]

Identifying examples of the early fifteenth-century '£10' castles, as Leask described them and as they continue to be known, is more difficult: places like Ballynagappagh no longer have standing remains, and surviving towers do not match precisely the measurements given. Some have suggestive proportions, such as Donore, identified as a likely example by Leask and designated a national monument in state care on that basis, but one cannot be certain. Leask believed these £10 castles to have been critical in the development of the tower-house in Ireland, going so far as to suggest that they were the progenitors of the national series; Sweetman has described the grant of 1429 [1430] as 'one inescapable historical fact about the origins of the tower house' and claims that it 'provided the impetus to build the typical tower house in the eastern part of Ireland'.[113] That these are relatively early tower-houses within the national corpus is not to be doubted, but their influence is very uncertain. My view is that it was negligible.

The Pale tower-houses, however they were funded (and we should presume that many of them were funded directly by their owners with little governmental help), have different plan-types, but almost all are distinguished by their simplicity, especially when compared with the complex designs used in Munster particularly: some are mere squares or rectangles (sometimes with rounded corners), others have stair-turrets alone, while others have stair- and subsidiary turrets; these turrets can be squared-off or rounded. Low-vaulted basements (without mezzanines, in other words) were normal, and finely crafted doors, windows and internal fittings are more rarely encountered than elsewhere. The majority of Pale tower-houses are smaller than the national average, and one in particular, Moygaddy, may be the smallest in Ireland: not much bigger internally than a snooker table and with a spiral stairs so cramped that one has to bend low to ascend to the room over the vault, it is a tiny chamber-tower with delusions of adequacy. Large tower-houses with four corner towers of mixed size are confined to the districts north of the capital. Dunsoghly is by far the best known of these, not least for its original timber roof. Half of a tower of similar size, now reduced to a single storey (with remains of a vault), sits in a garden in Kilsallaghan, a few miles to the north. Castletown, near Dundalk, is even bigger than Dunsoghly, but later alterations, ivy and encroachment by later buildings render it a less enjoyable building for the visitor. Also four-towered but slightly different in conception from those already mentioned are the two Meath castles of Killeen and Dunsany; the former had, and the latter seems to have had, an elongated main block, creating greater distance between the pairs of towers. The impression is of a hall-and-chamber block, with two towers, one containing the main chamber, attached to the corners of the upper-end of the hall, and two lesser towers at the lower end of the hall, their basements possibly

---

112 Ibid., p. 23.   **113** Sweetman, *Medieval castles of Ireland*, p. 137.

providing buttery and pantry facilities. The particular arrangement at Dunsany – now encased in later alterations but probably retrievable on close inspection – may have been the same as that at Baldongan, now demolished but known to us from very convincing late eighteenth-century depictions.[114] The earlier of two tower-houses at Liscartan, which has only three corner towers, also had an elongated main block, similar to Killeen, with a single chamber tower on the corner at one end, and two lesser towers (like Dunsany and Baldongan) at the other end.

Inscribing castles

Inscribed stones presenting the names or initials of their patrons, and providing dates of their construction (or less frequently of their repair, extension or rebuilding), appeared for the first time in Ireland in the sixteenth century, and are more common in castles than in other built contexts. Inscriptions on timber may have been common too but only one, at Bargy Castle, survives.[115] The practice of inscribing buildings with such information continued right through the seventeenth century and beyond, and indeed it even continues to this day, albeit mainly on public buildings.

Hanneke Ronnes' important study of Ireland's late medieval and early modern inscriptions – she enumerates fifty-four examples – shows a concentration of effort in the last quarter of the 1500s and the first half of the 1600s, with peaks between 1585 and 1594, and again between 1635 and 1644.[116] Indeed, after the 1640s the number of inscriptions falls away dramatically, reflecting perhaps a slow-down in the building industry itself during the Cromwellian period and into the Restoration. Before looking at the phenomenon in more detail, it might be noted that in relatively few instances were the inscriptions simply engraved into the stone surfaces; rather, the inscriptions were generally carved in false relief, with the letters and numbers (and sometimes armorial and other motifs) being created by a carving-away of the surfaces around them.

Several formulae were used. The simplest one involved the mere presentation of initials and a date; these are what Ronnes describes as date-and-initial stones. For example, a single patron was recorded at Graigue Upper Castle by the inscription O1594H, the date separating first- and last-name initials of a person's name. A husband-and-wife team was signified in an inscription by his initials on the left (the first to be read) and her initials on the right, accompanied by, and often flanking, the date. The dates on these stones may refer specifically to nuptials rather than to dates of house- or castle-construction, but since marriage was the circumstance in which such joint patronage was possible we can usually take the dates to refer de facto to the act of construction: thus, at Ballinacarriga Castle, for example, there is a stone of 1585

---

114 Almost identical, but with paired towers attached only to the low end of the hall, is Elcho Castle in Scotland, built *c.* 1560: see A. MacSween, *Elcho Castle* (Edinburgh, 2003), p. 9. **115** It reads 'I.H.S. 1591. R.R. M.S' (Colfer, *Wexford castles*, p. 191). For a general discussion of the I.H.S., see C.J. Donnelly, 'The I.H.S. monogram as a symbol of Catholic resistance in seventeenth-century Ireland', *International Journal of Historical Archaeology*, 9:1 (2005), 37–42. **116** H. Ronnes, 'Continental traces at Carrick-on-Suir and contemporary Irish castles: a preliminary study of date-and-initial stones' in Herron and Potterton (eds), *Ireland in the*

inscribed with 'RM' and 'CC' for Randal Murphy and Catherine Cullinane respectively, while at Grange Castle (Laois) the inscription of 1588 has 'RH' and 'gb', for Robert Hartpole and Grania O'Byrne respectively.[117] Where space was available on the surface selected for an inscription, and when a patron was so inclined, a fuller legend was proffered. Sometimes the inscriber communicated the same basic information as on a standard date-and-initial stone: at Clodah Castle, for example, the inscription on the fine fireplace reads 'Ano Dni, 1598, B.M.S.O.G. Decimo die Julii', with 'B.M.S.' being Brian MacSweeny and 'O.G.' being Orona fitzGerald. A popular alternative was to make the building speak for itself. The best known example comes from Derryhivenny Castle where the inscription is D:O'M ME:FIERI:FECIT 1643 (D[onal] O'M[adden] had me built [in] 1643); the 'me' here is usually presumed to refer to the tower-house but the inscription is actually in a flanker on the castle's bawn. Most impressive is the undated inscription above the doorway of the sixteenth-century castle in Milltown St John: retaining its original sharpness as few others do, it reads ROBERT' DE SCT'O IOH'E DN'S DE CVOLAGH LISMAINAN SCADANSTOWNE ET TOCIUS PLEBIS ILLIUS FECIT ME ('Robert St John, Lord of Cuolagh, Lismainan, Scadanstown and all of the people of that [district] made me').[118] Short or long, the inscriptions are usually in English or Latin. The latter was favoured for the shorter legends, but there are some long inscriptions in Latin, such as the thirty-two-word inscription on the long gallery fireplace in Ormond castle, Carrick-on-Suir. Far less common was the use of Irish: there is an invaluable inscription at second-floor level in Coole Castle – SEAGHA MACOCHL DO TINDSCAIN O SEO SUAS ★1575★ (John Mac Coghlan began from here up 1575) – and another from Park Castle, the site of the Mac Egan law school.[119]

Some inscribed stones carry heraldic arms as well as dates and the names/initials of their patrons. From Castle Eve, for example, an inscribed stone, now preserved in Rothe House, Kilkenny, is dated 1580 and bears the arms of John Sweetman. Many such examples indicate for us the dates of their host buildings, but there are exceptions: at Ballymaloe Castle, for example, a now *ex situ* plaque is dated 1602 and carries the initials and arms of John fitzEdmund fitzGibbon, and probably celebrates his knighthood (at Ballymaloe itself) by Lord Mountjoy rather than any specific act of construction.[120] Where heraldic arms alone survive, as at Castle Lishen, actually a fitzGerald castle, one needs to do some heraldic research for an identification.

Finally, the inscriptions are found in fairly prominent positions, which is not surprising as they were intended to be read by visitors. Some were positioned above (or, less frequently, high on one side of) the main external doorways of their host buildings, and were visible to all who had passed through the outer walls and had reached the point of entry into the main castle building; at Adamstown Castle an inscribed stone informing the visitor that one Nicholas Devereux had built the castle in 1556, was actually placed on the gateway of the bawn.[121] Entrance-area inscriptions

Renaissance, pp 255–73. **117** W.G. Strickman, 'Carved stone from Monksgrange, Queen's Co.', *JRSAI*, 52 (1922), 82–4. **118** Crotty, *Heraldic memorials in Fethard*, p. 67. **119** C. Manning, 'Revealing a private inscription', *AI*, 8:3 (1994), 24–6. **120** See R. Caulfield, 'Collection of several hundred original documents relating to the city and county of Cork, including the will of Sir John fitz Edmond Gerald, of Ballymaloe', *JRSAI* (1880), 268–73. **121** Colfer, *Wexford*

are normally on rectangular panels, recessed and stone-framed. Far fewer survive *in situ* than once existed. At Ballycowan Castle one can see a rare instance of a later panel – a heraldic panel with the arms of Sir Jasper Herbert, the motto 'By God of might, I hold my right' and a date of 1626 – inserted into a space in which there had been a smaller (non-heraldic?) panel originally. Perhaps the most impressive inscribed stone associated with an entrance is to be found at Dromore Castle, where a long, narrow, rectangular stone above the arched entrance carried an exceptionally long legend – the castle, it says, 'was built by Teigue second sonne to Connor third earle of Thomond and by Slany wife to said Teigue' – and bore a date of 15__, the latter part of the date now erased. While these inscriptions were fairly public, some inscriptions were for more exclusive readership. Fireplace lintels were one popular surface. The most spectacular example may be in the long gallery at Ormond Castle, Carrick-on-Suir, already noted, but other examples include Barryscourt and Ballinalacken castles, where inserted fireplaces are dated 1588 and 1644 respectively, and Carrigaholt and Knockgraffon castles with fireplaces dated 1603 in each case.

CODA: CASTLES AT THE END OF THE MIDDLE AGES

There was no moment in time at which castle building came to an end in Ireland, but, while 'castle' survived re-imagined as a medievalist concept in post-medieval aristocratic culture,[122] the building traditions just described clearly petered out in the later Elizabethan period. Indeed, the fact that the tower-house type survived at all into the late 1500s, little changed from how it was laid out in the 1400s, is testimony to the extent to which many of Ireland's landowning families remained generally detached from European Renaissance culture until relatively late. Although the date-and-initial stones are best explained by reference to such Renaissance culture, we cannot be certain that the tendency towards exterior symmetry that we see in tower-houses like Aughnanure (see fig. 144) reflects any contact with those post-medieval European building-cultures in which symmetrical composition was valued. Rathfarnham Castle, built in the 1580s, is probably the earliest surviving example of the new species of symmetrically composed residence favoured in the 1600s in Ireland. Equivalent in size and prestige to a substantial medieval castle but executed in Renaissance style, it is certainly the earliest surviving example in Ireland of the specific type that is distinguished by four corner towers.[123] Nearly contemporary is Mallow Castle, the earliest of a series of houses with corner towers flanking the façades but with single

castles, p. 172. **122** T. O'Keeffe, 'Lohort Castle'. **123** A. Gomme and A. Maguire, *Design and plan in the country house: from castle donjons to Palladian boxes* (New Haven, 2008), p. 39. For Portumna, the best-preserved example of the type, see Fenlon (ed.), *Clanricard's Castle*. It has been suggested that Mountfin House, very much smaller than Rathfarnham but similar in basic plan, was another late sixteenth-century house (R. Loeber and M. Stouthamer-Loeber, 'The lost architecture of the Wexford plantation' in K. Whelan (ed.), *Wexford: history and society* (Dublin, 1987), pp 173–200 at p. 183). Its owner, Samuel Molyneux, was not himself a planter but was clerk of the royal works in Ireland. The house was demolished as recently as *c.*1970.

147 Carstown House. Date-and-initial stones originally over the main entrance and from a mantelpiece place its construction in 1612.

towers projecting at the back. The common description of these houses in the literature as 'fortified houses' misses the point of their architecture completely. Yes, gun-loops tell us that their inhabitants still felt a need to protect themselves, and the manner in which the towers of some Rathfarnham-type examples are splayed indicates an awareness of contemporary artillery-equipped architecture, but 'fortified' is an entirely inappropriate adjective. Moreover, it implies somewhat deterministically that the designs of these houses represent *rapprochements* or compromises between the need for defence and the desire for comfort. By extension, it implies that they are products of an evolutionary process within Ireland itself, and that was not the case. Nowhere is that clearer than at Castlelyons, where the thirteenth-century castle of the Anglo-Norman Barry family was almost entirely rebuilt in the 1620s. Now in perilous condition, this one-time magnificent building, one of the first palatial residences in Ireland with timber rather than stone mullions and transoms used in its large windows, is almost as stylistically distant from the Middle Ages as a Georgian mansion.

What was the role of plantation in the transformation of Irish castle architecture? The answer is fairly obvious in Ulster, where new (Jacobean) planters meant new Scottish-style houses and castles (pl. XIV), but Ulster is slightly exceptional in that plantation was prosecuted more successfully there than elsewhere. The answer is a little more complex further south in Ireland. As in Ulster, new planter-castles were, of course, built in the areas that were planted, and James Lyttleton has usefully

148 Kanturk Castle is the earliest four-towered Renaissance house in Munster. Despite similarities, including the use of string-courses to mark the floor levels externally, Rathfarnham – probably the earliest in Ireland – is unlikely to have been its direct model, and we might speculate that some now-lost structure in Munster inspired it and other early seventeenth-century buildings of comparable design in the province. Kanturk was left unfinished so we can only speculate about its intended final appearance, but the survival of corbels to support a machicolated parapet tells us that, much as this great house looked to the future and anticipated the sense of order that characterized the Georgian mansion, it also looked back to an age when battlements connoted authority and warned away unwelcome visitors.

documented the important evidence from seventeenth-century Offaly.[124] But it is clear that new architectural forms for castles and other high-status residences first appeared independently of plantation (though not independently of the ideology in which plantation was conceived), as witnessed at Rathfarnham Castle. Second, the execution of those forms in the *period* of plantation cannot always be placed in the *context* of plantation; for example, one can hardly attribute the design chosen by the Plunkets of Carstown for their new house in the early seventeenth century (fig. 147) to ripples of plantation culture from Ulster or the midlands into Co. Louth.[125]

It is appropriate to finish this narrative at one castle in particular, Kanturk (fig. 148). When Donagh MacCarthy, the Gaelic-Irish lord of Duhallow, decided to build a new

124 J. Lyttleton, *The Jacobean plantations in seventeenth-century Offaly* (Dublin, 2013).   **125** M. Corcoran, 'Challenging narratives: an early modern house at Carstown' in Potterton and Herron (eds), *Dublin and the Pale in the Renaissance*, pp 125–44.

castle at Kanturk around 1609, he opted not to copy the design of nearby Mallow Castle, the newly built residence of the planter Sir Thomas Norreys, the lord president of Munster, but chose instead a version of the design first used in Rathfarnham.[126] Once patrons like MacCarthy embraced Renaissance design early in the seventeenth century, blurring in the landscape the distinction between residences of the Gaelic-Irish, the 'old English' (or Anglo-Irish) and the 'new English' (the planters), those few patrons who chose to build tower-houses risked seeming conservative, even old-fashioned. Of course, that might sometimes have been the intention: did Donal O'Madden of Derryhivenny, the (apparent) mid-seventeenth-century tower-house, engage in an act of conscious anachronism, using archaic forms to articulate the deep historical embeddedness of his family lineage?

---

126 For an imaginative analysis of Kanturk and its doorways, see J. Delle, '"A good and easy speculation": spatial conflict, collusion and resistance in late sixteenth-century Munster, Ireland', *International Journal of Historical Archaeology*, 3:1 (1999), 11–34 at 28–9.

Select bibliography of secondary sources

Barry, T.B., *The archaeology of medieval Ireland* (London, 1987).

Bracken, D. and D. Ó Riain-Raedel (eds), *Ireland and Europe in the twelfth century* (Dublin, 2006).

Bradley, J., A. Simms and A. Fletcher (eds), *Dublin in the medieval world: studies in honour of Howard B. Clarke* (Dublin, 2009).

Casey, C. and A. Rowan, *North Leinster* (New Haven and London, 1993).

Craig, M., *The architecture of Ireland from the earliest times to 1880* (London, 1982).

FitzPatrick, E. and R. Gillespie (eds), *The parish in medieval and early modern Ireland* (Dublin, 2006).

Hourihane, C., *Gothic art in Ireland, 1169–1550* (New Haven and London, 2003).

Kenyon, J.R. and K. O'Conor (eds), *The medieval castle in Ireland and Wales* (Dublin, 2003).

Kerrigan, P.M., *Castles and fortifications in Ireland, 1485–1945* (Cork, 1995).

Leask, H.G., *Irish castles and castellated houses* (2nd ed. Dundalk, 1951).

— *Irish churches and monastic buildings* (3 vols, Dundalk, 1955–60).

McNeill, T.E., *Anglo-Norman Ulster* (Edinburgh, 1980).

— *Castles in Ireland: feudal power in a Gaelic world* (London, 1997).

Murphy, M. and M. Potterton, *The Dublin region in the Middle Ages* (Dublin, 2010).

Ó Carragáin, T., *Churches in early medieval Ireland: architecture, ritual and memory* (New Haven and London, 2011).

Ó Clabaigh, C., *The friars in Ireland, 1224–1540* (Dublin, 2012).

O'Conor, K.D., *The archaeology of medieval rural settlement in Ireland* (Dublin, 1998).

O'Keeffe, T., *An Anglo-Norman monastery: Bridgetown Priory and the architecture of the Augustinian canons regular in Ireland* (Kinsale, 1999).

— *Medieval Ireland: an archaeology* (Stroud, 2000).

— *Romanesque Ireland: architecture and ideology in the twelfth century* (Dublin, 2003).

— *Ireland's round towers: buildings, rituals and landscapes of the early Irish church* (Stroud, 2004).

Potterton, M. and T. Herron (eds), *Dublin and the Pale in the Renaissance, c.1540–1660* (Dublin, 2011).

Salter, M., *The castles of Connacht* (Malvern, 2004).

— *The castles of Leinster* (Malvern, 2004).

— *The castles of north Munster* (Malvern, 2004).

— *The castles of south Munster* (Malvern, 2004).

— *The castles of Ulster* (Malvern, 2004).

— *Abbeys and friaries of Ireland* (Malvern, 2009).

— *Medieval churches of Ireland* (Malvern, 2009).

Stalley, R., *Architecture and sculpture in Ireland, 1150–1350* (Dublin, 1971).

— *The Cistercian monasteries of Ireland* (New Haven and London, 1987).

— (ed.), *Limerick and the south-west. British Archaeological Association Conference Transactions*, 34 (2010).

— (ed.), *Irish Gothic architecture: construction, decay and reinvention* (Dublin, 2012).

Sweetman, D., *Medieval castles of Ireland* (Cork, 1999).

Index